FARM JOURNAL'S Complete HOME BAKING BOOK

Other cookbooks by FARM JOURNAL

FARM JOURNAL'S COUNTRY COOKBOOK
FARM JOURNAL'S COMPLETE PIE COOKBOOK
LET'S START TO COOK
HOMEMADE BREAD
AMERICA'S BEST VEGETABLE RECIPES
HOMEMADE CANDY
HOMEMADE COOKIES
HOMEMADE ICE CREAM AND CAKE
COUNTRY FAIR COOKBOOK
GREAT HOME COOKING IN AMERICA
FARM JOURNAL'S HOMEMADE SNACKS
FARM JOURNAL'S BEST-EVER RECIPES
FARM JOURNAL'S GREAT DISHES FROM THE OVEN
FARM JOURNAL'S FREEZING AND CANNING COOKBOOK
FARM JOURNAL'S FRIENDLY FOOD GIFTS FROM YOUR KITCHEN
FARM JOURNAL'S CHOICE CHOCOLATE RECIPES
FARM JOURNAL'S COOK IT YOUR WAY

Farm Journal's Complete Home Baking Book

By ELISE W. MANNING
Farm Journal Food Editor

Recipes selected and edited
By PATRICIA A. WARD
Associate Food Editor

Book design supervised
By MICHAEL DURNING
Farm Journal Associate Art Director

FARM JOURNAL, INC.
Philadelphia, Pennsylvania

Distributed to the trade by
DOUBLEDAY & COMPANY, INC., Garden City, New York

Library of Congress Cataloging in Publication Data
Main entry under title:
Farm journal's complete home baking book.
Includes index.
1. Baking. I. Manning, Elise W. II. Ward,
Patricia Ann. III. Farm journal (Philadelphia,
1956-)
TX763.F33   641.7'1
ISBN 0-89795-005-4
Library of Congress Catalog Card Number 79-13383

Contents

Chapter 1: **Basics of Baking**   9

Chapter 2: **Great Country Yeast Breads** . . . 15

Chapter 3: **Best Country Quick Breads** 103

Chapter 4: **Beautiful Country Cakes** 137

Chapter 5: **Fun-To-Eat Country Cookies** . .215

Chapter 6: **Finest Country Pies** 281

Index 335

COLOR PHOTOGRAPHS

Fruit and Cream Tart   facing page 64
Medley of Baked Goods
Selection of Baked Goods
Cranberry-Raspberry Pie

Four Easter Breads   facing page 128
Soft Pretzels
Three Heirloom Recipes
A Trio of Batter Breads

Easy Cake Decorations   facing page 192
Peppermint Angel Food Cake
Strawberries and Cream Spectacular
Sourdough Bread and Golden Sourdough
Biscuits

Lemon Velvet Pie   facing page 256
Meatball-Vegetable Pie
Make-Ahead Freezer Breads
Three Choice Chocolate Treats

Color photographs by: William
Hazzard/Hazzard Studios, Fred
Carbone and Richard Tomlinson.
Line drawings by: Kevin Talbot

INTRODUCTION

For years, we have been collecting recipes for baked goods sent to us from farm and ranch women throughout the country. These recipes have been carefully filed in their proper categories—breads, cakes, pies and cookies—along with the warm, newsy letters from the women who sent them. Often, the writer told us, this was her best baking recipe and she wanted to share it with Farm Journal.

Since we had gathered such an outstanding collection of recipes and we knew that country women—and women everywhere—love to bake, we decided to compile a book just full of all these cherished home baked goods. Since so many country cooks had lovingly shared their treasures with us, we thought we would like to share them—just as lovingly—with you.

So for about a year, we have been baking intensively. Our Farm Journal Test Kitchens have been filled with the wonderful smells of breads, rolls, pies, cakes and cookies of every kind. We invited some of Farm Journal's other editors to be on our taste panel, and before we finished our book, they had gained a few pounds and had copied quite a few of the recipes to add to their own personal collections.

Baking, our farm and ranch women told us so many times in their letters, is a very important part of farm life...just as important as it was to their ancestors, who tucked their recipes carefully in their trunks before they immigrated to this country. Many of the recipes in this book are heirlooms; almost as many have won ribbons at fairs or great accolades at church suppers and community dinners. Farm women have been baking beauties to tote to the fair for generations. Some women have a complete wall full of shiny satin ribbons to show that they are outstanding in pie making or in turning out a pluperfect angel food cake, one that stands tall and regal and whose every crumb is as soft as velvet.

Farm women are known for their hospitality. In most farm homes, an invitation to "drop in for coffee" also means a homemade treat—such as an absolutely delicious coffee cake glistening with icing and studded with nuts. During such visits, recipes are often exchanged and carefully copied down by neighbors to be added to their files and to be passed on to other friends. These recipes make the rounds of the neighborhood and sometimes even the country. And eventually many of them reach us.

After we had tasted all kinds of pies, bread and rolls, after we had nibbled our way through hundreds of layer cakes and sturdy picnic-style cakes and every variety of cookie, we began to build our book.

We know there are many home bakers who have been turning out beautiful baked goods with nary a problem. They have been baking for a long time and they know exactly how to do it.

But over the years, we have also received questioning letters from many other women. They had each experienced a failure and didn't know why. Could we, they wondered, tell them what went wrong with their cake, pie, cookie, or bread?

So we decided to make this book a teaching tool as well as a recipe book. We have carefully plotted out step-by-step methods for making perfect baked goods. To each chapter, we have added a list of questions women ask most frequently when they have a less-than-successful baking result. We tell you why your lovely cake had no volume, why your pie crust was tough, why your bread had dark streaks, why your biscuit was lopsided or your cookie dry and crumbly.

With this knowledge, and with the "best of the best" country recipes that we share with you in this book, you can, we believe, please your family, your friends and yourself with perfect results every time.

Elise W. Manning
Farm Journal Food Editor

Chapter 1

The Basics of Baking

Do you have a friend or neighbor who you think was simply born with a talent for baking? Her pies are always perfect; her cakes, mile high, and her breads, beautifully shaped and golden brown?

You really do not need a "special gift" or a magic touch to be a fine baker. Baking skills are learned, they're not innate. It's possible to turn out a beautiful product each time if you practice and follow directions very carefully.

In this chapter, we give you general facts that apply to all baking. In subsequent chapters, we go into fine detail about how to handle each specific product so you can turn out a beauty every time.

Three basics important in every baking recipe are:
1. Measuring ingredients correctly and accurately,
2. Knowing that your oven is accurate, and
3. Using the right-sized pan—that is, the one called for in the recipe.

CHOOSE THE RIGHT PANS

The size, shape and material from which a pan is made all affect baking. Each recipe in this book specifies a pan size, and this is the size that should be used for best results from that recipe. If we have baked a recipe in a glass baking dish, we have said so in the recipe. Otherwise, all of our recipes have been baked in metal pans. If you do substitute a glass baking dish, then you should lower the temperature by 25°F. If you don't, your baked goods might burn or be overdone and dry.

To grease or not to grease a pan is very important. Our directions always specify whether to grease a pan. If the recipe does not call for greasing the pan, you need not do it. Also, you will note that some recipes call for a greased and waxed-paper lined pan. Some cakes that are very tender or that are very heavy with fruits and nuts are more difficult to remove from the pan; hence, the double treatment will help and your cake should come out in one piece instead of, perhaps, in pieces. Some rich cookies have so much butter in the batter that you don't need to grease the cookie sheet, while leaner ones will stick if the sheet is not well greased.

Many batters, such as those of muffins or cupcakes, are baked in muffin tins. You will notice that in most cases, we instruct you to pour the batter into greased muffin pans. However, in a few recipes, we suggest using the fluted paper cupcake liners. Those recipes were tested in liners because their products are tender and need the help of the liner to prevent sticking. Actually, we like to bake all of our muffins or cupcakes or little cakes in cupcake liners. They aren't too expensive, they do eliminate sticking and they ensure well-rounded, nicely shaped little cakes. But if you are watching your pennies, greasing the pans is sufficient unless liners are specified in the recipe.

YOUR OVEN

The major step in any baking takes place in the oven. And if your oven is not preheated or is not the correct temperature, you could ruin a beautiful cake or bread.

Always turn your oven on 10 or 15 minutes before you plan to use it. This allows time for it to heat to the temperature specified in the recipe.

It's a good idea to purchase an oven thermometer in a hardware or department store. It isn't expensive and could save you a lot of grief. Even though you have set your oven to the correct temperature, it's very possible that it could be off by 25° or more. Even if your oven is fairly new, it could be registering too high or too low.

To test the accuracy of your oven, place the thermometer inside when you turn on the oven. After 15 minutes or after the light for your oven has gone off, check the temperature. If the temperature registers lower or higher on the thermometer than you have set the oven for, simply adjust your oven dial to compensate. For example, if the correct recipe temperature is 375°F and the thermometer registers 400°F, set your oven dial back to 350°F.

If your oven is off register by 50°F or more, consult your local gas or electric utility company and ask to have the oven adjusted to the correct temperature.

BAKING INGREDIENTS

In the old days, measuring was a matter of judgement. Recipes often called for "butter the size of an egg," or a "heaping cup of sugar," or "enough flour to stiffen." The results of baking varied with each cook and each baking day. There were many disasters and poorly baked products.

In today's baking, there's no need for guesswork. Modern recipes are based upon exact standard measurements for perfect results. And all measurements must be level.

You need standard measuring cups made especially for liquids and another "nested" set designed especially for dry ingredients. You also need a set of standard measuring spoons.

Flour, the mainstay of all baked products, is sifted in all the recipes in our book. Flour has a tendency to pack down upon standing. Always sift the flour used in our recipes once before measuring.

To measure flour, lift the sifted flour lightly by spoonfuls into the dry measuring cup and level off by drawing the edge of a metal spatula across the top. Do not press the flour or shake it down into the cup. Whole grain flours are never sifted. They are simply stirred before measuring.

At the end of this chapter, we have included a chart we feel would be helpful. It tells you how to measure basic baking ingredients and what role each ingredient plays in a recipe.

TYPES OF WHEAT FLOURS

Wheat flour is the most important ingredient in home baking and is the framework for almost every baked product and pasta. Of the grains available for the production of flour, wheat is the most widely used in this country and most parts of the world. Some of our recipes call for rye, soy or other flours, but unless a special flour is indicated, a reference to "flour" is a reference to all-purpose wheat flour.

Wheat flours may be ground from the entire kernel or from the center portion, which is called the endosperm. White flours such as all-purpose and cake flour are ground from only the endosperm, while the whole wheat flours are ground from the entire wheat kernel (endosperm, germ and bran).

All-Purpose Flour. All-purpose flour is milled by grinding the endosperm of the wheat kernel after the bran and germ have been removed. All-purpose is a combination of soft and hard wheats from which the home baker can make a complete range of satisfactory products. This flour is enriched and may be bleached or unbleached.

Enriched all-purpose flour has iron and B vitamins added in amounts equal to or exceeding that of whole wheat flour. Enriched, bleached all-purpose flour is bleached chemically to whiten. Enriched, unbleached all-purpose flour is bleached by oxygen in the air and is off-white in color. Nutritionally, bleached and unbleached are equivalent.

Cake Flour. Cake flour is milled from soft wheat and contains much less gluten than all-purpose flour. It is soft and silky and is especially suitable for cakes, cookies, crackers and pastries.

Whole Wheat Flour. Whole wheat flour is a brown, coarse-textured flour ground from the entire wheat kernel. It contains the bran, germ and endosperm.

This flour has a smaller proportion of gluten, so baked products made from it tend to be heavier and more dense than those made from all-purpose flour. Whole wheat flour is rich in B-complex vitamins, vitamin E, fat, protein, and some minerals.

Stone Ground Whole Wheat Flour. Stone ground whole wheat flour is milled by coarsely crushing the kernel between heavy, slowly rotating stones. The nutritional value is the same as regular whole wheat flour.

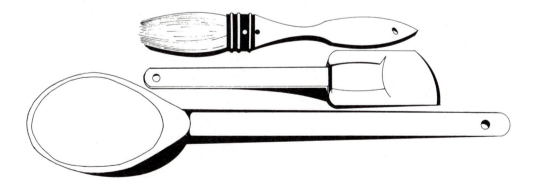

BASIC BAKING INGREDIENTS AND HOW TO MEASURE THEM

Ingredients	Contributions to Baked Products	Measuring Tools	How to Measure (always measure level)
Fat shortening lard butter margarine	Adds richness, tenderness and flakiness.	Nested cups or glass measuring cup for oil	*Solid fats*: Scoop from can to nested-type cup with rubber spatula. Press into cup firmly, level off top with metal spatula. *Cold, solid fats*: Let stand at room temperature until soft, then measure as above. *Oil*: Measure as for liquids (below).
Flour all-purpose enriched flour cake flour (for fine structure in cakes) whole grain flours	Creates framework or structure.	Nested cups	*All-purpose and cake flours*: Sift (even if it is presifted). Spoon into cup without shaking or packing down. Level off top with metal spatula. *Whole grain flours*: Do not sift, just stir. Spoon into cup. Level off top with metal spatula.
Sweetening white sugar brown sugar confectioners sugar (powdered) honey, syrups	Adds tenderness, flavor, crispness, brownness.	Nested cups or glass measuring cup for honey and syrups. Measuring spoons	*White sugar*: Spoon into cup, level off with metal spatula. *Brown sugar*: Pack firmly into cup with spoon, then level off with metal spatula. *Confectioners sugar*: Sift. Spoon lightly into cup. Level off top with metal spatula. *Honey and syrups*: Pour from jar or bottle into cup or spoon. Level off top with metal spatula.
Liquid milk (whole, evaporated and condensed) water juices	Helps ingredients react with each other; adds moistness; binds ingredients together.	Glass measuring cup	Set cup on a level surface. Lower head so measuring line is at eye level. Fill cup to desired mark.
Leavening Agent baking powder baking soda yeast	Makes framework rise, adds lightness and tenderness.	Measuring spoons	*Baking powder and soda*: Scoop with measuring spoon, level off with metal spatula. *Yeast*: Premeasured
Eggs	Provide flavor, golden color and moistness; bind ingredients together; whites help make structure in angel and sponge cakes.		
Flavoring salt vanilla lemon extract	Enhances existing flavor; adds new flavor.	Measuring spoons	*Salt*: Pour into measuring spoon, level off with metal spatula. *Liquid*: Pour into measuring spoon.

Great Country Yeast Breads

The earliest known bread was made by the Stone Age people more than 8,000 years ago. They combined flour and water into a dough and baked it on hot stones. They made their flour by grinding wheat between two stones.

The first leavened bread was invented in Egypt about 5,000 years ago. According to legend, an absent-minded baker mixed a dough from flour, sugar and water and forgot to bake it. By the time he remembered, the dough had soured. He tried to salvage the sour dough by adding some fresh dough to it. When the dough baked, it rose. The wild yeasts from the air had settled into the dough and started to ferment the sugar; little gas bubbles formed and caused the dough to puff up and rise. This was actually a leavened bread process but it wasn't explained scientifically until the 17th century.

Wheat was brought to the Western Hemisphere by early Spanish settlers. In what would become the United States, the first English colonists were preparing to plant wheat within two weeks after they had landed in 1607. Commercial bakeries appeared as early as 1640; however, most of the baking was done in the home until the 20th century.

When the settlers in the Eastern part of this country began to pack up and move westward, wheat was planted in profusion in the rich earth of the Midwest. White flour was milled and became available to everyone. As wheat technology improved, farmers were able to produce many more acres of wheat.

In the early days, our ancestors made yeast from hops, but this yeast was an unreliable product with varied results. The next step in yeast perfection was a dry cake of very slow-acting yeast that had to sit in a "sponge" of water and flour overnight to give it time to grow and multiply. Next, a cake of compressed yeast was developed, but it needed refrigeration and was very perishable.

It wasn't until World War II that researchers discovered a way to remove water from the yeast and produce an active dry yeast. With active dry yeast, the guesswork was taken out of bread making and it was possible to create a fine loaf of bread by following specific procedures.

The wonderful selection of breads in this book reflects our heritage very strongly. When the immigrants sailed across the Atlantic, they brought a touch of home with them—their recipes copied down on scraps of paper. There were sturdy rye breads from Germany and Scandinavia, dark pumpernickel from Russia, handsome coffee cakes full of nuts and fruits from Bohemia and currant- and raisin-studded breads from England.

Recipes were shared and also changed to fit the ingredients on hand in the new land. As the recipes were carefully and lovingly handed down through generations, new methods and techniques were added and perhaps an ingredient or two, but the basic breads—and wonderful flavors—of the Old World remained.

In addition to our "heirlooms," we have some truly American breads that have withstood generations and are still popular today. These include New England corn bread, steamed Boston brown bread and the yeast bread made with molasses and cornmeal known as anadama.

When farm and ranch women sent us the recipes included in this book, they often enclosed interesting letters telling us the history of their homemade favorite. Many of the breads in this chapter are several generations old; others are family favorites of the current generation. But they all have been family-tested and voted the very best.

For example, a contribution from a Nebraska woman, Braided German Sweet Bread, dates back to 1887. Today's family members enjoy it at least once a month, she told us in a letter. A Kansas farm woman sent us the recipe for Caraway Rye Loaves. She's already passed on this cherished recipe to her daughter. We have tested it in our kitchens at Farm Journal and have already passed the recipe on to several friends.

An Indiana homemaker sent us her pet recipe for frankfurter rolls. She never buys them in the supermarket any more because her family refuses to eat them—since they've tasted "Mom's" homemade rolls.

It would be difficult to choose our favorite recipe in this chapter. There are so many that are just delicious. We suggest you try them all from the basic whites, whole wheats and ryes to the egg-enriched rolls and beautifully glazed coffee breads that are just perfect for very special occasions and holidays.

In addition to a great selection of breads, rolls and coffee cakes for every occasion, you can choose from several different bread-making methods to suit your schedule or baking experience. For traditional bakers, we have conventional breads that rise twice and bake to perfection. For days that you're extra busy, we have the hurry-up batter breads as well as a choice of freezer breads especially developed to be mixed and kneaded now and baked later.

For the less experienced baker, we suggest that you start with a basic white or whole wheat bread. Once you have made a perfect loaf of bread, go on to the more complicated yeast rolls and braids.

BASIC YEAST BREAD INGREDIENTS

Every yeast bread contains flour, yeast, liquid, sugar, salt and shortening. The fancier breads are enriched with eggs and may contain dried fruits, nuts and spices.

Flour. Wheat flour or all-purpose flour contains two proteins called gliadin and glutenin in just the right proportions to form a substance called gluten when the liquid is added. The primary purpose of gluten in yeast dough is to form an elastic framework in which the tiny bubbles of carbon dioxide gas formed by the yeast are captured. When the dough is first mixed, the combining of the liquid and the flour develops the gluten. Kneading spreads the gluten through the mass of dough so that the first rising has a network of gluten which holds in the carbon dioxide gas bubbles. Punching down and shaping the dough after it has risen breaks up the larger bubbles into tiny ones and separates and distributes them evenly throughout the dough. Baking sets these tiny little cells of gas and produces a baked bread or roll with an even, tender texture. Only wheat flour or all-purpose flour has the correct proportion of gliadin and glutenin to make gluten. The whole wheat flours do not contain enough gluten, and rye and soy flours contain no gluten; that is why you will find them used in combination with all-purpose white flour in our bread recipes. All of our recipes have been tested with all-purpose flour.

Yeast. Yeast is the leavening for yeast breads. It makes bread rise and gives it a lovely light quality. Yeast is a living plant that feeds on the sugar in the dough to produce the gas that makes yeast dough rise. The yeast plant is so small that if 4,000 yeast cells were placed side by side, they would measure a mere inch!

Yeast is all around us in the air and in the ground. However, not all of the yeast that nature provides is suited for bread making. The yeast that is used in bread making is now scientifically grown in manufacturing plants. A single strain of yeast is carefully selected. This is planted and fed until the quality of yeast is perfected for consumer use.

For many years, yeast was sold in compressed cakes that needed to be refrigerated. But after extensive research, active dry yeast was developed. This yeast is dried and put into tiny packets. Each packet is dated with an expiration date, after which the yeast should not be used. It can be stored until its expiration date in a kitchen cupboard and is much handier to use than the compressed cake. All of our recipes were tested with the active dry yeast.

Liquid. Milk and water are the two liquids generally used in making yeast doughs. They can be used singly or in any proportions of the two, but water is generally used to soften the yeast. An all-water dough produces a bread or roll with a wheatier flavor and a crisper crust. All milk in the mixture results in a finished product with a more velvety grain and creamy white crumb; this bread keeps better and toasts better.

Sugar. Sugar is the customary sweetener in yeast doughs although honey, molasses or corn syrup are frequently used in dark, whole-grain breads and in some of the sweet buns and coffee cakes. Sugar is needed by the yeast to do thoroughly its job of raising the dough. The tiny gas bubbles on which the light, porous texture of yeast products depend are formed by yeast and sugar working together. Sugar also adds a subtle sweetness and encourages a golden crust color.

Salt. Without sufficient salt, your baked products will be flat-tasting because salt has the power of bringing out the flavors of other ingredients. It also helps to control the action of the yeast.

Shortening. Some kind of fatty ingredient—vegetable shortening, margarine, butter or lard—is included in all yeast doughs. It gives the dough elasticity so that the leavening gas can expand freely and easily. It also adds flavor to the finished product, helps develop a crisp crust with an attractive sheen and prolongs freshness.

Eggs. Eggs help to make the texture fine and delicate and give extra flavor, richness and color to rolls and buns. They also add nutrients to the product, and, like the sugar, encourage a golden brown crust.

STEPS FOR MAKING YEAST BREADS AND ROLLS

Here are the basic steps used in making all yeast breads:
- *Step 1—Dissolving the Yeast*. The dry yeast is poured into lukewarm water and stirred until it is dissolved. To test for lukewarm, drop a little bit of water on the inside of your wrist. If it feels neither hot nor cold, it's lukewarm. The temperature

should be 105-114°F. If the water is too hot, the yeast will be killed and the bread will not rise. If you are a beginner and feel a bit doubtful about the right temperature with the "wrist" method, you can use a bread thermometer. But chances are, you will not have that problem. Many bread makers are careless and simply use hot water from the tap without any test and then run into trouble. Their loaves of bread are either very low in volume or they don't rise at all.

Some of the recipes in this chapter omit the dissolving step. Instead, the yeast is combined with the dry ingredients. This is known commercially as the Rapidmix method. The liquids are heated until they are *very warm*, to a temperature of 120-130°F. The yeast is protected by the flour and so the lukewarm temperature is not as critical. The dough feels a bit springier when you knead it, and the rising is a bit faster because of the higher temperature of the liquids. However, we have discovered from the recipes sent to us that most farm women stick to the conventional method of dissolving the yeast first in lukewarm water.

• *Step 2—Mixing.* Combine the yeast mixture, liquid, shortening, sugar and some of the flour in a large bowl. We use an electric mixer to make all of our breads. Beat this mixture, with an electric mixer at medium speed, for about 2 minutes. However, if you don't have a mixer, a bowl, a wooden spoon and a strong arm for beating will work just as well. Beat mixture hard with a wooden spoon until smooth, about 300 strokes. Add the rest of the flour, mixing at low speed or stirring by hand. We add the flour using the mixer until it gets a little unwieldy and the beater begins to resist the flour, then we stir the rest in by hand until a dough is formed.

You will notice that the recipes will instruct you to add flour until a soft dough is formed, or a moderately stiff or stiff dough. All doughs react differently, and we give you the clue in the recipe. Raisin breads and sturdy whole-grain breads often form a stiff dough, while rolls and sweet rolls and coffee cakes form a soft dough. The softer the dough, the more tender and delicate the crumb and texture of the loaf. Whole wheats and rye breads are not noted for their velvety, tender crumb; they are coarser, sturdier breads with a compact texture. Once your dough has been stirred until the right consistency is formed, it will have a bumpy appearance and will be sticky to handle. Now the dough is ready to be kneaded.

• *Step 3—Kneading.* This will make the dough smooth and even-textured and all the stickiness will be gone. You will have a lovely ball of shiny, smooth, elastic dough.

Kneading is the most fun of all the steps in bread making. You really can feel the dough change under your fingertips. Kneading simply means working the ball of dough with your hands to blend all the ingredients. But the most important purpose of kneading is to work and stretch the gluten in the flour to form the elastic framework we have discussed earlier in this chapter. The framework ensnares the gas produced by the yeast. As you continue to knead, the dough becomes more delicate and tender. This procedure only takes about 8 to 10 minutes. If you knead too little, the bread will turn out soggy and heavy. If you knead too much, the bread will be coarse with an uneven texture.

How to Knead:

1. Place the ball of dough on a lightly floured breadboard or table top, or cover the surface with a floured pastry cloth. If you are a beginner, it might be wise to purchase a pastry cloth. Rub flour into the cloth before you start kneading. The less flour that is worked into the dough, the more tender the bread will be. Use as

little flour as possible when you knead. Beginners will use more flour until they get the knack of handling the dough.

2. Flatten the dough very slightly by pressing firmly down on the ball of dough.

3. Now, with the fingers of both hands, fold dough over on itself toward you.

4. Push the ball away from you with the heel of your hand.

5. Grasp the dough with both hands and turn one-quarter around the board.

6. Repeat steps 2 through 5 rhythmically, in a rocking motion, until the dough feels smooth and elastic. Sprinkle a little flour onto your hands and the board when the dough becomes sticky. Try to use as little flour as possible.

• *Step 4—Rising.* The kneaded, satiny ball of dough is put into a greased bowl and turned over once so that the top is greased. This will keep the dough moist and prevent the surface from becoming crusty. Cover the bowl with a clean kitchen towel and put it in a warm place to rise. Keep it away from drafts. If your spot for rising is too cool, the dough will not rise at all if the yeast is killed or very little if the yeast growth is retarded. If the dough is put in a draft, it will collapse.

The best temperature for rising is about 80-85°F. Unless you're baking on a hot summer day, it's not likely that your kitchen will be that warm. A good spot for proper rising is in an unlighted oven with a large pan of hot water placed on the shelf beneath the dough. Or set the bowl of dough in a deep pan of water just warm enough to feel comfortable to your hand. Do not put the bowl of dough on top of a radiator. Radiators are often too hot and the yeast will be killed. If you are baking in the wintertime and your kitchen is quite cool, it would be a good idea to rinse the bowl out with hot water and dry it before you put your dough into it.

The dough will rise and expand slowly and steadily until it is doubled in bulk. It will turn from a firm compact ball to a light, spongy ball. The yeast is at work and is producing carbon dioxide gas which is making the dough rise.

In all of our recipes, we tell you to let the dough rise until it is doubled in bulk. The time will vary with the temperature and the ingredients. If a dough is filled with raisins and nuts, it will take longer.

To test for double in bulk, press two fingers deep into the dough. Pull them out quickly. If the indentation remains, the dough is doubled and is ready for punching down. If not, cover and let rise some more.

• *Step 5—Punching down.* This procedure releases some of the gases in the dough, breaks up big gas pockets into smaller ones and helps the yeast cells to breathe by bringing in fresh oxygen.

To punch down, thrust your fist into the center of the dough. When the dough collapses, pull in the edges of the dough from the sides of the bowl, kneading them into the center.

Turn the dough onto a floured breadboard with the punched center of the dough underneath.

• *Step 6—Shaping.* The dough has changed drastically by this time. It is pleasantly warm and lovely and light to handle. It feels pliable and responsive under your hands. First, let the ball of light, springy dough rest on the board, which should be very lightly floured, for about 10 minutes. This will make it easier to handle and shape.

Shaping is a very important technique. It will affect how your final baked loaf looks. Your goal is a loaf of bread that is symmetrical, not lopsided. You want a smooth, uniform surface and a fine, even texture. In order to produce this perfect loaf of bread, the dough must be evenly distributed in the pan with no folds or creases on the top or sides of the loaf. Good shaping technique will accomplish this and will also keep you from overhandling the dough.

Be sure you have everything ready before you begin shaping—greased pans, if they are called for in the recipe, for example, and a sharp knife to cut the dough. At this point, it is very important not to have too much flour on the board, because the kneading step is over and the flour will not be worked into the dough. Excess flour will cause dark, unpleasant streaks in the baked loaf of bread—so watch that flour!

After the dough has rested for five minutes, cut it in half with the sharp knife. With your hands, press one piece of the cut dough into an oblong $9 \times 8 \times 1$ inches. Using both hands, fold each 8-inch end of the oblong to the center, pressing down firmly. Pinch together the center fold and the ends of the dough to seal. Place loaf, sealed side down, into a greased loaf pan. Repeat procedure with second half of dough. Cover with a towel and let rise in a warm, draft-free spot.

For rolls, follow procedures for shaping in each individual recipe.

• *Step 7—Second Rising.* This step is required in most of our recipes. However, you will notice that there are some recipes that call for only one rising. A bread or roll that has had two risings is superior, we feel. And, apparently, our farm and ranch women think so, too, since so many of their recipes call for two risings.

In the second rising, as in the first, the dough is allowed to double in bulk. To test for this, very gently press your finger tip into the bread or rolls. If there is a slight indentation, it's ready for the oven.

• *Step 8—Baking.* Now you are close to having a beautiful loaf of bread! Put your bread pans into a preheated oven at the temperature that is called for in the recipe. Place the two pans on the center shelf. Allow about two inches between the pans so that the air can circulate freely.

Just set your timer and relax. Soon the wonderful aroma of baked bread will begin to fill the kitchen. The last 10 minutes of baking time is soon enough to check your bread to see if it is done.

• *Step 9—Testing for Doneness.* This is perhaps the most rewarding step. Hopefully, you will see a beautifully browned, well-rounded loaf of bread—the rewards of your labor.

Using potholders, remove pan of bread from the oven and tip the loaf out gently in your hand. It should slide out easily and feel light in weight. Notice the color. It should be a lovely brown, but slightly darker on the top than on the sides.

Tap the bottom of the loaf with your knuckles. It should give a hollow sound. If the bread does not seem done, return it to the oven for a few minutes.

• *Step 10—Removing from Pans.* Bread should be removed from the pans as soon as it is taken from the oven. Again, slide the loaf into your hands (which are protected by potholders, of course, one on the pan and the second on the loaf of bread). Place the bread on a wire rack, leaving space between the loaves for air circulation. Set the loaves in a draft-free spot so that the crust does not crack. If your bread is allowed to sit in the pans for even five minutes, it will be less than perfect. The condensation of the steam from the pans will seep into the bread and you will have a bread with a tough crust and a soggy crumb.

• *Step 11—Cooling Completely.* This might prove to be the most difficult step of all, especially if you have a husband or youngsters who have built-in timers that signal them when a loaf of home-baked bread is fresh from the oven. It is desirable to cool the bread completely, right to its center core, for the best texture. But if your family insists, cut the warm-from-the-oven bread with a sharp serrated knife using a gentle sawing motion. Have some nicely softened butter to slather on the slices and sacrifice a little texture for lots of praise.

• *Step 12—Storing.* Storing is an important step. Wrap cooled breads in foil or clear plastic wrap before storing in a well-ventilated bread box. Do not refrigerate baked yeast breads or rolls. Refrigerator temperatures cause breads to stale.

However, you can freeze breads, if you wish. Wrap cooled bread in foil or plastic wrap. When freezing frosted breads or coffee cakes, freeze breads first, then wrap in foil or plastic wrap to prevent frosting from smearing. Seal and label and date all breads. They will keep up to nine months in the freezer, though we prefer to use them by six months or less for optimum flavor. Thaw frozen breads in their wrappers.

KERNEL OF WHEAT

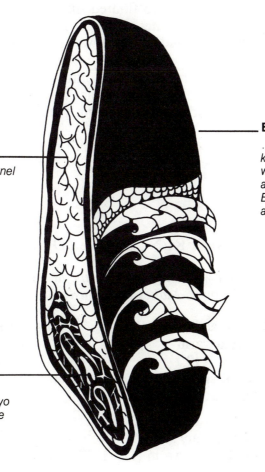

ENDOSPERM

. . .about 83% of the kernel and the source of white flour. Enriched flour products contain added quantities of riboflavin, niacin, thiamine and iron.

BRAN

. . .about 14% of the kernel. Bran is included in whole wheat flour and is also available separately. Bran is usually used as animal feed.

GERM

. . .about 2½% of the kernel. Germ is the embryo or sprouting section of the seed, usually separated because it contains fat which limits the keeping quality of flours. Wheat germ can be purchased separately and is included in whole wheat flour.

COUNTRY-STYLE WHITE BREAD

"My bread-making expertise may never match Grandma's, but this recipe makes fine bread for me anyway," an Ohio woman said.

2 c. milk	2 tblsp. sugar
2 tblsp. butter or	1 tblsp. salt
regular margarine	12½ c. sifted flour
2 pkgs. active dry yeast	
2 c. lukewarm	
water (110°)	

Scald milk in saucepan. Add butter and cool to lukewarm.

Sprinkle yeast over lukewarm water in large mixing bowl; stir to dissolve. Add sugar, salt, 6 c. of the flour and milk mixture to yeast mixture. Beat with electric mixer at medium speed until smooth, about 2 minutes.

Gradually stir in enough remaining flour to make a soft dough.

Turn dough out onto floured surface. Knead until smooth and satiny, 10 to 12 minutes. Place in greased bowl, turning once to grease top. Cover and let rise in warm place until doubled, about 1¼ hours.

Punch down dough. Divide into thirds. Let rest 10 minutes. Shape each third into a loaf. Place in 3 greased 9 × 5 × 3-inch loaf pans. Cover and let rise in warm place until doubled, about 1¼ hours.

Bake in 400° oven 25 minutes, or until loaves sound hollow when tapped. Remove from pans; cool on racks. Makes 3 loaves.

Overhang
Bread baked at too low a temperature will get too light before the cell walls harden. Then they stretch too far and collapse, leaving some of the dough hanging over on each side of the pan.

NO-KNEAD FRENCH BREAD

A Wisconsin woman got this recipe at a cooking class. Now many friends ask for it. Makes four crusty brown loaves.

2 pkgs. active dry yeast	2 tblsp. soft shortening
1 c. lukewarm	2 c. water
water (110°)	8 to 8½ c. sifted flour
2 tblsp. sugar	Cornmeal
3 tsp. salt	

Sprinkle yeast over 1 c. lukewarm water; stir to dissolve.

Combine sugar, salt and shortening in large mixing bowl. Heat 2 c. water to very warm (120-130°). Pour over sugar mixture. Cool to lukewarm.

Add yeast mixture; stir well. Gradually stir in enough flour to make a very soft dough. (No kneading is necessary.) Cover and let rise in warm place until doubled, about 50 minutes.

Punch down dough. Turn dough out onto floured surface. Divide dough into fourths. Let rest 10 minutes. Roll each fourth into 12 × 9-inch rectangle. Beginning at long side, roll up tightly like a jelly roll. Press edges to seal.

Sprinkle 2 large baking sheets with cornmeal. Place two loaves on each baking sheet. Score top of each loaf diagonally 6 times with sharp knife, about ¼-inch deep. Cover and let rise in warm place until doubled, 1 to 1¼ hours.

Bake in 400⁰ oven 25 to 30 minutes, or until loaves sound hollow when tapped. Remove from baking sheets; cool on racks. Makes 4 loaves.

BASIC WHITE BREAD

"My husband taught me to make this. I used to make a batch twice a week when my children were home," wrote a Michigan woman.

2 pkgs. active dry yeast	1 c. milk
½ c. sugar	2 tblsp. shortening
1½ c. lukewarm	1½ tsp. salt
water (110⁰)	7 to 7½ c. sifted flour

Sprinkle yeast and ¼ c. of the sugar over lukewarm water in small bowl; stir to dissolve. Let stand 10 minutes.

Scald milk. Pour over remaining ¼ c. sugar, shortening and salt in large mixing bowl. Cool to lukewarm.

Add yeast mixture and 4 c. of the flour to milk mixture. Beat with electric mixer at medium speed until smooth, about 2 minutes.

Gradually stir in enough remaining flour to make a soft dough.

Turn dough out onto floured surface. Knead dough until smooth and satiny, about 10 minutes. Place in greased bowl, turning over to grease top. Cover and let rise in warm place until doubled, about 1 hour.

Punch down dough. Divide in half. Let rest 10 minutes. Shape each half into a loaf. Place in 2 greased 9 × 5 × 3-inch loaf pans. Cover and let rise in warm place until doubled, 1 to 1¼ hours.

Bake in 375⁰ oven 25 minutes, or until loaves sound hollow when tapped. Remove from pans; cool on racks. Makes 2 loaves.

SOUTHERN WHITE BREAD

A Michigan family likes this bread. It was first made by a great-grandmother in Tennessee.

6 to 6½ c. sifted flour	1½ c. milk
1 c. yellow cornmeal	3 tblsp. butter or
⅓ c. sugar	regular margarine
1 tblsp. salt	1 c. water
2 pkgs. active dry yeast	

Combine 2 c. of the flour, cornmeal, sugar, salt and undissolved yeast in large mixing bowl.

Scald milk in saucepan. Add butter and water. Cool to very warm (120-130⁰).

Add liquid mixture to flour-yeast mixture. Beat with electric mixer at medium speed until smooth, about 2 minutes.

Gradually stir in enough remaining flour to make a soft dough.

Turn dough out onto floured surface. Knead until smooth and satiny, 8 to 10 minutes. Place dough in greased bowl, turning over to grease top. Cover and let rise in warm place until doubled, about 1¼ hours.

Punch down dough. Divide in half. Let rest 10 minutes. Shape each half into a loaf. Place in 2 greased 9 × 5 × 3-inch loaf pans. Cover and let rise in warm place until doubled, about 1 hour.

Bake in 350⁰ oven 35 minutes, or until loaves sound hollow when tapped. Remove from pans; cool on racks. Makes 2 loaves.

Toast Shells
Cut unsliced bread into 2-inch slices. Cut off crusts. Hollow out each slice with a sharp knife, leaving sides and bottom ⅜-inch thick. Brush all surfaces with melted butter. Place on greased baking sheet. Bake at 375° for about 15 minutes or until golden. Fill baked shell with creamed chicken or shrimp for a party luncheon.

Individual Toast Cups
Cut bread into ¼-inch slices. Remove crusts; brush both sides with melted butter. Press bread slices into each cup of 3-inch muffin pans. Bake at 375° for 12 minutes or until golden. Fill with scrambled eggs or creamed tuna fish.

ORANGE-CINNAMON SWIRL BREAD

"These plump loaves swirled with cinnamon have been popular at bake sales for years," wrote a Michigan homemaker.

1 c. milk, scalded	6 c. sifted flour
½ c. sugar	1 egg
¼ c. shortening	½ c. sugar
1½ tsp. salt	1 tblsp. ground cinnamon
1 tblsp. grated orange rind	Orange Icing (recipe
¾ c. fresh orange juice	follows)
2 pkgs. active dry yeast	
¼ c. lukewarm water (110⁰)	

Pour scalded milk over ½ c. sugar, shortening, salt, orange rind and orange juice in mixing bowl. Cool to lukewarm.

Sprinkle yeast over lukewarm water; stir to dissolve.

Add 2 c. of the flour, egg and yeast mixture to milk mixture. Beat with electric mixer at medium speed until smooth, about 2 minutes.

Gradually stir in enough remaining flour to make a soft dough.

Turn dough out onto floured surface. Knead until smooth, about 10 minutes. Place dough in greased bowl, turning once to grease top. Cover and let rise in warm place until doubled, about 1½ hours.

Combine ½ c. sugar and cinnamon; set aside.

Punch down dough. Divide dough in half. Let rest 10 minutes. Roll out each half to 15 × 7-inch rectangle. Brush surface with water. Sprinkle with one half of sugar-cinnamon mixture. Roll up like a jelly roll, starting at narrow end. Tuck under ends. Place in 2 greased 8½ × 4½ × 2½-inch loaf pans. Cover and let rise in warm place until almost doubled, 1 to 1¼ hours.

Bake in 375° oven 20 minutes. Cover with aluminum foil to prevent overbrowning. Bake 15 minutes more, or until loaves sound hollow when tapped. Remove from pans; cool on racks. When loaves are cooled, frost tops with Orange Icing. Makes 2 loaves.

Orange Icing: Combine 1 c. sifted confectioners sugar, 1 tsp. grated orange rind and 1 tblsp. fresh orange juice in bowl. Stir until smooth.

GOLDEN CINNAMON LOAVES

This recipe makes two tan-colored round loaves with a mild cinnamon flavor. Can be frosted if you like.

5¼ to 5¾ c. sifted flour	⅔ c. butter or regular
2 pkgs. active dry yeast	margarine
1½ tsp. salt	⅓ c. sugar
1 tblsp. ground cinnamon	2 eggs
1¼ c. milk	Cooking oil

Cinnamon Toast
Sprinkle 6 slices buttered white, whole wheat or raisin toast with cinnamon and sugar. Place on baking sheet. Bake at 350° for 5 minutes or until sugar melts.

Stir together 1¼ of the flour, undissolved yeast, salt and cinnamon in large mixing bowl.

Heat together milk, butter and sugar in saucepan over low heat until very warm (120-130°). Add liquid mixture all at once to flour-yeast mixture. Beat with electric mixer at high speed until smooth, about 3 minutes. Beat in eggs.

Gradually stir in enough remaining flour to make a moderately soft dough.

Turn dough out onto floured surface. Knead until smooth and satiny, about 10 minutes. Cover dough with bowl; let rest 30 minutes.

Punch down dough. Divide dough in half. Shape each half into a round loaf. Place rounds on greased large baking sheet. Brush with oil. Cover and let rise in warm place until doubled, about 1 hour.

Bake in 350° oven 45 minutes, or until loaves sound hollow when tapped. Remove from baking sheets immediately. Brush with cooking oil; cool on racks. Makes 2 loaves.

GLAZED CINNAMON BREAD

An attractive white bread with a pinwheel of cinnamon through the center of the loaf and drizzled with a thin confectioners sugar glaze.

1 c. milk, scalded	5 c. sifted flour
¼ c. butter or	2 eggs
regular margarine	⅓ c. sugar
¼ c. sugar	1 tblsp. ground cinnamon
1 tsp. salt	Melted butter or
1 pkg. active dry yeast	regular margarine
¼ c. lukewarm	Glaze (recipe follows)
water (110°)	

Pour scalded milk over ¼ c. butter, ¼ c. sugar and salt in mixing bowl. Cool to lukewarm.

Sprinkle yeast over lukewarm water; stir to dissolve.

Add 2 c. of the flour and yeast mixture to milk mixture. Beat with electric mixer at medium speed until smooth, about 2 minutes. Beat in eggs.

Gradually stir in enough remaining flour to make a soft dough.

Turn dough out onto floured surface. Knead until smooth, about 8 minutes. Place dough in greased bowl, turning over once to grease top. Cover and let rise in warm place until doubled, about 1 hour.

Combine ⅓ c. sugar and cinnamon; set aside.

Punch down dough. Divide dough in half. Let rest 10 minutes. Roll each half into 10 × 8-inch rectangle. Brush with melted butter. Sprinkle with one half of sugar-cinnamon mixture. Roll up like a jelly roll, starting at narrow end. Place seam side down in 2 greased 9 × 5 × 3-inch loaf pans. Let rise until doubled, about 1 hour.

Bake in 350° oven 30 minutes, or until loaves sound hollow when tapped. Remove from pans; cool on racks. When cooled, drizzle tops of loaves with Glaze. Makes 2 loaves.

Glaze: Combine 1 c. sifted confectioners sugar, 4 tsp. milk and ½ tsp. vanilla in bowl. Stir until smooth.

COUNTRY-STYLE WHOLE WHEAT BREAD

This 100 percent whole wheat loaf provides valuable nutrients and roughage in the diet. Has a nice hearty whole wheat flavor, too.

1 c. milk	2 pkgs. active dry yeast
⅓ c. dark brown sugar,	1 c. lukewarm
packed	water (110°)
3 tblsp. shortening	4½ c. stirred whole
4 tsp. salt	wheat flour

Scald milk. Pour over brown sugar, shortening and salt in large mixing bowl. Cool to lukewarm.

Sprinkle yeast over lukewarm water; stir to dissolve.

Add yeast mixture and 2¼ c. of the whole wheat flour to milk mixture. Beat with electric mixer at medium speed until smooth, about 2 minutes.

Gradually stir in enough remaining whole wheat flour to make a soft dough.

Turn dough out onto floured surface. Knead dough until smooth and satiny, about 10 minutes. Place dough in greased bowl; turn over to grease top. Cover and let rise in warm place until doubled, about 1½ hours.

Punch down dough. Divide in half. Let rest 10 minutes. Shape each half into a loaf. Place in 2 greased 8½ × 4½ × 2½-inch loaf pans. Cover and let rise in warm place until doubled, about 1½ hours.

Bake in 375° oven 1 hour, or until loaves sound hollow when tapped. Remove from pans; cool on racks. Makes 2 loaves.

Freezing Bread
To freeze baked bread and rolls, cool thoroughly. Wrap immediately with airtight seal. Freeze. If aluminum foil is used, reheat without unwrapping.

HEARTY PUMPERNICKEL LOAVES

A medium dark bread with nice full-bodied flavor; mashed potatoes added for moistness and chocolate for color.

2½ to 3 c. sifted flour	1 (1-oz.) square
1½ c. stirred rye flour	unsweetened chocolate,
¼ c. yellow cornmeal	cut up
2 pkgs. active dry yeast	1 c. prepared cold
1¼ c. water	mashed potatoes
2 tblsp. dark molasses	mashed potatoes
1 tblsp. cooking oil	1 tblsp. caraway seeds
2 tsp. salt	Cooking oil

Combine ½ c. of the flour, ½ c. of the rye flour, cornmeal and undissolved yeast in large mixing bowl.

Heat water, molasses, oil, salt and chocolate in saucepan over low heat until very warm (120-130°). Add liquid mixture to flour-yeast mixture. Beat with electric mixer at high speed until smooth, about 3 minutes. Add remaining 1 c. rye flour and potatoes. Beat 2 minutes more. Stir in caraway seeds and enough remaining flour to make a soft dough.

Turn dough out onto floured surface. Knead until smooth and satiny, about 5 minutes. (Dough will be sticky.) Cover dough with bowl. Let rest 20 minutes.

Divide dough in half. Let rest 10 minutes. Form each half into a large ball. Place on greased large baking sheet. Flatten loaf slightly with palm of hand. Brush with oil. Let rise in warm place until doubled, about 30 minutes.

Bake in 375° oven 30 to 35 minutes, or until loaves sound hollow when tapped. Remove from baking sheet; cool on racks. Makes 2 loaves.

RYE SANDWICH BREAD

"This recipe is from my mother. It's easy and makes the best rye bread I've ever had," wrote a Wisconsin farm woman recently.

2 pkgs. active dry yeast	2 tblsp. salt
4 c. lukewarm	2 tblsp. cooking oil
water (110°)	3 c. stirred rye flour
½ c. molasses	9 to 9½ c. sifted flour
½ c. sugar	

Sprinkle yeast over lukewarm water in large mixing bowl; stir to dissolve. Add molasses, sugar, salt, oil, rye flour and 3 c. of the flour. Beat with electric mixer at medium speed until smooth, about 2 minutes.

Gradually stir in enough remaining flour to make a soft dough.

(The dough is a little sticky compared to white bread dough.)

Turn dough out onto floured surface. Knead dough until smooth, about 8 minutes. Place in greased bowl, turning once to grease top. Cover and let rise in warm place until doubled, about 1½ hours.

Punch down dough. Divide into thirds. Let rest 10 minutes. Shape each third into a loaf. Place in 3 greased 9 × 5 × 3-inch loaf pans. Cover and let rise in warm place until doubled, about 1½ hours.

Bake in 375° oven 40 minutes, or until loaves sound hollow when tapped. Remove from pans; cool on racks. Makes 3 loaves.

CARAWAY LOAVES

This bread looks and tastes like rye, but its flavor is actually from buckwheat pancake mix and dry onion soup mix.

1 c. milk	1 c. lukewarm
3 tblsp. sugar	water (110°)
2 tsp. salt	2 c. buckwheat
2 tblsp. shortening	pancake mix
2 tblsp. dry onion	½ tsp. caraway seeds
soup mix	3 to 3¼ c. sifted flour
2 pkgs. active dry yeast	

Scald milk in saucepan. Pour over sugar, salt, shortening and soup mix in large mixing bowl. Cool to lukewarm.

Sprinkle yeast over lukewarm water; stir to dissolve.

Add yeast mixture, pancake mix and caraway seeds to milk mixture. Beat with electric mixer at medium speed until smooth, about 2 minutes.

Gradually stir in enough flour to make a soft dough.

Turn dough out onto floured surface. Knead dough until smooth and satiny, about 10 minutes. Place dough in greased bowl, turning over to grease top. Cover and let rise in warm place until doubled, about 1½ hours.

Punch down dough. Divide dough in half. Let rest 10 minutes. Shape each half into a loaf. Place in 2 greased 8½ × 4½ × 2½-inch loaf pans. Cover and let rise in warm place until doubled, about 1¼ hours.

Bake in 375° oven 20 minutes, or until loaves sound hollow when tapped. Remove from pans; cool on racks. Makes 2 loaves.

Light, Tender Breads
Soft doughs produce the lightest, tender-crumbed bread and rolls. To make the dough easier to handle, rub a little shortening on your fingers.

WHOLE WHEAT-POTATO BREAD

Nicely textured bread seasoned with tarragon leaves, garlic and onion. The mashed potatoes help to keep it moist.

1¾ c. sifted flour	1½ c. prepared seasoned
2 pkgs. active dry yeast	instant mashed potatoes
1 c. milk	½ c. minced onion
½ c. water	2 tsp. dried tarragon leaves
2 tblsp. butter or	1 tsp. garlic powder
regular margarine	4½ to 4¾ c. stirred
2 tblsp. sugar	whole wheat flour
1 tblsp. salt	Cooking oil
½ c. dairy sour cream	

Stir together flour and undissolved yeast in large mixing bowl.

Heat milk, water, butter, sugar and salt in saucepan until very warm (120-130⁰). Add liquid mixture to yeast-flour mixture. Beat with electric mixer at medium speed until smooth, about 3 minutes.

Add sour cream, mashed potatoes, onion, tarragon and garlic powder; beat until smooth. Stir in enough whole wheat flour to make a moderately stiff dough.

Turn dough out onto floured surface. Cover and let rest 4 minutes. Knead dough until smooth, 5 to 8 minutes. Place dough in greased bowl; turn over to grease top. Cover and let rise in warm place until doubled, about 45 minutes.

Punch down dough. Divide dough in half. Let rest 10 minutes. Shape each half into a loaf and place in 2 greased 8½ × 4½ × 2½-inch loaf pans.

Cover and let rise in warm place until almost doubled, 30 to 40 minutes.

Bake in 375⁰ oven 35 to 40 minutes, or until loaves sound hollow when tapped. Remove from pans; cool on racks. While still hot, brush tops of loaves with cooking oil. Makes 2 loaves.

Refrigerate Whole-Grain Flours

Whole-grain flours should be refrigerated in airtight containers, because the dark flours contain the oil-rich germ of the wheat kernel and can become rancid if improperly stored. It's best to freeze dark flours during the summer months, especially if you don't plan to do much baking. Then the flour will be fresh for fall and winter baking.

PERFECT BRAN BREAD

We received this unusual bran bread from a Florida woman who loves to cook and is always trying new bread recipes.

4¾ to 5 c. sifted flour	¼ c. shortening
1 pkg. active dry yeast	2 tsp. salt
2¼ c. milk	1½ c. 40% Bran Flakes
2 tblsp. sugar	cereal

Combine 2½ c. of the flour and undissolved yeast in large mixing bowl.

Scald milk in saucepan. Add sugar, shortening and salt. Cool to very warm (120-130°). Add liquid mixture to flour-yeast mixture. Beat with electric mixer at medium speed until smooth, about 3 minutes.

Stir in Bran Flakes and enough remaining flour to make a moderately stiff dough.

Turn dough out onto floured surface. Knead dough until smooth and satiny, 8 to 10 minutes. Place in greased bowl, turning once to grease top. Cover and let rise in warm place until doubled, about 1 hour.

Punch down dough. Divide in half. Let rest 10 minutes. Shape each half into a loaf. Place in 2 greased 8½ × 4½ × 2½-inch loaf pans. Let rise in warm place until doubled, about 1¼ hours.

Bake in 400° oven 30 minutes, or until loaves sound hollow when tapped. Remove from pans; cool on racks. Makes 2 loaves.

WHOLE WHEAT-PECAN BREAD

Mild, nutty-flavored whole wheat bread with chopped toasted pecans throughout—interesting flavor combination.

¾ c. chopped pecans	1 c. milk
1¾ to 2 c. sifted flour	¼ c. water
2 tblsp. brown sugar, packed	1 tblsp. butter or regular margarine
1 pkg. active dry yeast	1 c. stirred whole wheat flour
1 tsp. salt	

Arrange pecans in 8-inch square baking pan. Toast in 350° oven 10 to 12 minutes, stirring once after 5 minutes. Cool well.

Stir together 1 c. of the flour, brown sugar, undissolved yeast and salt in mixing bowl.

Heat milk, water and butter in 2-qt. saucepan until very warm (120-130°). Gradually add to flour-yeast mixture, beating with electric mixer until smooth, about 2 minutes. Add ½ c. more flour. Beat at high speed 2 minutes.

Stir in pecans, whole wheat flour and enough remaining flour to make a soft dough. (No kneading is necessary.) Cover and let rise in warm place until doubled, about 40 minutes.

Punch down dough. Let rest 10 minutes. Roll out to 12 × 8-inch rectangle on floured surface. Roll up like a jelly roll, starting at narrow end. Tuck ends under. Place in greased 8½ × 4½ × 2½-inch loaf pan. Cover and let rise until doubled, about 35 minutes.

Bake in 375° oven 30 minutes, or until loaf sounds hollow when tapped. Remove from pan; cool on rack. Makes 1 loaf.

THREE-FLAVORED BRAID

Whole wheat, rye and white bread all twisted together in one braided loaf. Excellent choice for buffets and picnics.

5 c. sifted flour	2 tblsp. molasses
2 tblsp. sugar	1 c. stirred whole
1 tblsp. salt	wheat flour
2 pkgs. active dry yeast	1 tsp. caraway seeds
¼ c. soft butter or	1 tblsp. baking cocoa
regular margarine	2 tblsp. molasses
2¼ c. very warm water	1 c. stirred rye flour
(120-130°)	

Combine 2¼ c. of the flour, sugar, salt and undissolved yeast in mixing bowl; mix well. Add butter and very warm water to the flour-yeast mixture. Beat with electric mixer at medium speed about 2 minutes, scraping bowl occasionally. Add 1 more c. of the flour. Beat at high speed 2 minutes, scraping bowl occasionally.

Divide dough into 3 parts. Add 2 tblsp. molasses and whole wheat flour to one third. If necessary, add a little flour to make a soft dough.

Turn dough out onto floured surface. Knead until smooth and satiny, about 5 minutes. Place in greased bowl; turning over once to grease top. Cover and set aside.

Add caraway seeds, cocoa, 2 tblsp. molasses and rye flour to one third. If necessary, add a little flour to make a soft dough.

Turn dough out onto floured surface. Knead until smooth and satiny, about 5 minutes. Place in greased bowl; turning over once to grease top. Cover and set aside.

Add enough remaining flour to remaining one third to make a soft dough.

Turn dough out onto floured surface. Knead until smooth and satiny, about 5 minutes. Place in greased bowl; turning over once to grease top. Cover. Place all 3 bowls in warm place. Let rise until doubled, about 1 hour.

Punch down doughs. Divide each dough into halves. Let rest 10 minutes. Roll each piece into 15-inch rope. Place 1 rye, 1 whole wheat and 1 white rope on greased baking sheet. Braid 3 ropes together; pinch ends to seal. Repeat with remaining ropes. Cover and let rise in warm place until doubled, about 1 hour.

Bake in 350° oven 35 minutes, or until loaves sound hollow when tapped. Remove from baking sheets; cool on racks. Makes 2 loaves.

OUTSTANDING RAISIN BREAD

The home economists in our Countryside Test Kitchens unanimously agreed that this was one of the best breads we've ever tested.

2 c. milk	½ c. lukewarm
⅔ c. sugar	water (110°)
2 tblsp. butter or	1 egg
regular margarine	1 tsp. ground cinnamon
1 tsp. salt	8 c. sifted flour
2 pkgs. active dry yeast	1 c. raisins

Scald milk in saucepan. Combine milk, sugar, butter and salt in large mixing bowl. Cool to lukewarm.

Sprinkle yeast over lukewarm water; stir to dissolve.

Add yeast mixture, egg, cinnamon and 4 c. of the flour to milk mixture. Beat with electric mixer at medium speed until smooth, about 2 minutes. Stir in raisins.

Gradually stir in enough remaining flour to make a stiff dough.

Turn dough out onto floured surface. Knead until smooth, about 8 minutes. Place dough in greased bowl, turning over once to grease top. Cover and let rise in warm place until doubled, about 1 hour.

Punch down dough. Divide dough in half. Let rest 10 minutes. Shape each half into a loaf. Place in 2 greased 9 × 5 × 3-inch loaf pans. Cover and let rise until doubled, about 1¼ hours.

Bake in 350° oven 40 minutes, or until loaves sound hollow when tapped. Remove from pans; cool on racks. Makes 2 loaves.

Streaky Bread
A bowl that is too heavily greased can cause streaking in a baked loaf of bread. When the dough is punched down and turned over, the grease is carried through the dough in streaks.

GOLDEN RAISIN LOAVES

An unusual raisin bread containing both whole wheat and white flour. You can substitute candied fruit for the raisins if you wish.

2 c. stirred whole	½ c. buttermilk
wheat flour	2 eggs
¼ c. sugar	1½ c. golden raisins
2 pkgs. active dry yeast	2¼ to 2¾ c. sifted flour
1 tsp. salt	Cooking oil
2 tsp. ground cinnamon	Vanilla Icing
¾ c. water	(recipe follows)
⅓ c. butter or	
regular margarine	

Tender Crust or Chewy Crust
If you want a shiny tender crust on your loaf of bread, rub the tops of the hot loaves with unsalted shortening. If you prefer a hard chewy crust, brush the warm crust with warm water.

Stir together 1¾ c. of the whole wheat flour, sugar, undissolved yeast, salt and cinnamon in large mixing bowl.

Heat water and butter in saucepan over low heat to very warm (120-130°). Remove from heat; stir in buttermilk. Add to flour-yeast mixture. Beat with electric mixer at medium speed until smooth, about 2 minutes.

Add eggs; beat 2 minutes more. Stir in raisins. Gradually stir in remaining ¼ c. whole wheat flour and enough remaining flour to make a stiff dough. Let rest 5 minutes.

Turn dough out onto floured surface. Knead until smooth, 5 to 8 minutes. Cover with a bowl and let rest 30 minutes.

Punch down dough. Divide dough in half. Let rest 10 minutes. Roll out each half to 12 × 7-inch rectangle. Beginning at narrow side, roll up tightly like a jelly roll. Seal edges. Tuck ends under to form rounded edges. (Loaf is about 7 × 3 inches.) Place on greased baking sheet. Brush with oil. Cover and let rise in warm place until almost doubled, about 30 minutes.

Bake in 375° oven 25 minutes, or until loaves sound hollow when tapped. Remove from baking sheet. Cool on racks 20 minutes. Frost with Vanilla Icing. Makes 2 loaves.

Vanilla Icing: Combine 2 c. sifted confectioners sugar, ¼ tsp. vanilla and 2½ tblsp. milk in bowl. Mix until smooth.

CINNAMON-RAISIN BREAD

Cinnamon-swirled loaf studded with lots of iron-rich raisins. You can ice it with a thin vanilla glaze if you like.

5½ to 6 c. sifted flour	1 egg
2 pkgs. active dry yeast	1 c. raisins
1 c. milk	1 c. sugar
¾ c. water	1 tblsp. ground cinnamon
¼ c. sugar	2 tblsp. melted butter or
¼ c. cooking oil	regular margarine
2 tsp. salt	

Stir together 2 c. of the flour and undissolved yeast in large mixing bowl.

Heat milk, water, ¼ c. sugar, oil and salt in saucepan over very low heat until very warm (120-130⁰). Add liquid mixture to flour-yeast mixture. Beat with electric mixer at medium speed until smooth, about 3 minutes. Blend in egg. Stir in raisins.

Gradually stir in enough remaining flour to make a moderately soft dough.

Turn dough out onto floured surface. Knead until smooth and satiny, about 10 minutes. Cover dough with bowl. Let rest 20 minutes.

Combine 1 c. sugar and cinnamon; set aside.

Punch down dough. Divide dough in half. Roll out each half on floured surface to 14×7-inch rectangle. Brush with melted butter. Sprinkle with half of sugar-cinnamon mixture. Beginning at narrow side, roll up tightly like a jelly roll. Press edges to seal. Fold ends under. Place in 2 greased $8\frac{1}{2} \times 4\frac{1}{2} \times 2\frac{1}{2}$-inch loaf pans. Brush tops of loaves with remaining butter. Cover and let rise in warm place until doubled, about 45 minutes.

Bake in 375⁰ oven 35 to 40 minutes, or until loaves sound hollow when tapped. Remove from pans immediately. Cool on racks. Makes 2 loaves.

DATE-RAISIN BREAD

This bread is a Christmas tradition in an Ohio family. Originally made with dried apples, it is now made with dates, raisins and nuts.

¾ c. raisins	2 pkgs. active dry yeast
½ c. water	1 c. lukewarm
1 c. milk, scalded	water (110⁰)
2 tsp. brown sugar,	5½ to 5¾ c. sifted flour
packed	¼ lb. dates, chopped
3 tblsp. butter or	1 c. chopped walnuts
regular margarine	Confectioners Sugar Icing
½ tsp. ground cinnamon	(recipe follows)
1¼ tsp. salt	

Combine raisins and ½ c. water in small saucepan. Simmer, covered, 5 minutes. Drain well and cool completely.

Pour scalded milk over brown sugar, butter, cinnamon and salt in mixing bowl. Cool to lukewarm.

Sprinkle yeast over 1 c. lukewarm water; stir to dissolve. Add 3 c. of the flour and yeast mixture to milk mixture. Beat with electric mixer at medium speed until smooth, about 2 minutes.

Stir in drained raisins, dates and walnuts. Add enough remaining flour to make a stiff dough.

Turn dough out onto floured surface. Knead until smooth, 8 to 10 minutes. Place dough in greased bowl, turning over once to grease top. Cover and let rise in warm place until doubled, about 1 hour.

Punch down dough. Divide dough in half. Let rest 10 minutes. Shape each half into a loaf. Place in 2 greased 8½ × 4½ × 2½-inch loaf pans. Cover and let rise until doubled, about 1 hour.

Bake in 350⁰ oven 35 minutes, or until loaves sound hollow when tapped. Remove from pans; cool on racks. When cooled, frost tops of loaves with Confectioners Sugar Icing. Makes 2 loaves.

Confectioners Sugar Icing: Combine 2½ c. sifted confectioners sugar, 1 tsp. vanilla and 3 tblsp. milk in bowl. Stir until smooth.

ANADAMA BREAD

This authentic American bread is made from cornmeal, which was readily available during colonial times. It has a molasses flavor.

7 to 7½ c. sifted flour	2¼ c. very warm water
1¼ c. yellow cornmeal	(120-130⁰)
2 pkgs. active dry yeast	⅔ c. molasses
2½ tsp. salt	
⅓ c. butter or	
regular margarine	

Stir together 2½ c. of the flour, cornmeal, undissolved yeast and salt in mixing bowl. Add butter.

Gradually add very warm water and molasses to flour-yeast mixture, beating with electric mixer at medium speed until smooth, about 2 minutes.

Stir in enough remaining flour to make a stiff dough.

Turn dough out onto floured surface. Knead until smooth and elastic, 8 to 10 minutes. Place dough in greased bowl, turning once to grease top. Cover and let rise in warm place until doubled, about 1 hour.

Punch down dough. Divide dough in half. Let rest 10 minutes. Roll out each half to 14 × 9-inch rectangle. Roll up like a jelly roll, starting at narrow side. Tuck ends under. Place in 2 greased 9 × 5 × 3-inch loaf pans. Cover and let rise in warm place until doubled, about 1 hour.

Bake in 375° oven 35 minutes, or until loaves sound hollow when tapped. Remove from pans; cool on racks. Makes 2 loaves.

SWISS CHEESE-MUSTARD BREAD

This bread is the perfect choice for ham sandwiches because of its nippy Swiss cheese and mustard flavor.

5½ to 6 c. sifted flour	2 tsp. salt
2 pkgs. active dry yeast	3 eggs
¾ c. milk	8 oz. shredded Swiss
½ c. water	cheese (2 c.)
¼ c. cooking oil	Melted butter or
2 tblsp. sugar	margarine
2 tblsp. prepared mustard	

Stir together 2 c. of the flour and undissolved yeast in large mixing bowl.

Heat milk, water, oil, sugar, mustard and salt in saucepan over low heat until very warm (120-130°). Add liquid mixture to flour-yeast mixture. Beat with electric mixer at medium speed until smooth, about 3 minutes. Blend in eggs and cheese.

Gradually stir in enough remaining flour to make a moderately soft dough.

Turn dough out onto floured surface. Knead until smooth and satiny, 5 to 10 minutes. Cover dough with bowl and let rest 30 minutes.

Punch down dough. Divide dough in half. Let rest 10 minutes. Shape each half into a ball. Place in 2 greased 1½-qt. round casseroles, turning to grease all sides. Let rise in warm place until doubled, about 1 hour.

Bake in 375° oven 25 to 30 minutes, or until loaves sound hollow when tapped. Remove from casseroles; brush with melted butter. Cool on racks. Makes 2 loaves.

Pan Selection
Loaf pans of glass, darkened metal or dull-finished aluminum are ideal for baking bread. They absorb heat and give a nice brown crust. To darken a shiny tin loaf pan, heat it for 5 hours in a 350° oven.

WELSH RAREBIT BREAD

Cheese-flavored bread with a hint of Worcestershire sauce. The bread is braided before placing in loaf pans.

5 to 5½ c. sifted flour	8 oz. American processed
2 pkgs. active dry yeast	cheese, cubed
2 tblsp. sugar	2 tblsp. butter or
2 tsp. salt	regular margarine
1 tsp. dry mustard	1 tblsp. Worcestershire
Dash of cayenne pepper	sauce
1½ c. milk	Cooking oil
½ c. water	

Stir together 2 c. of the flour, undissolved yeast, sugar, salt, mustard and pepper in large mixing bowl.

Heat milk, water, cheese and butter in saucepan over low heat to melt most of the cheese. Cool to very warm (120-130º). Add liquid mixture to flour-yeast mixture. Beat with electric mixer at medium speed until smooth, about 3 minutes. Stir in Worcestershire sauce and enough remaining flour to make a soft dough.

Turn dough out onto floured surface. Knead until smooth and satiny, about 8 minutes. Place dough in greased bowl; turn over to grease top. Cover and let rise in warm place until doubled, about 1 hour.

Punch down dough. Divide in half. Let rest 10 minutes. Roll out each half to 11 × 5-inch rectangle. Cut into 3 long strips. Braid 3 strips together, tucking ends under. Place in 2 greased 9 × 5 × 3-inch loaf pans. Brush with cooking oil. Cover and let rise in warm place until doubled, 45 to 60 minutes.

Bake in 350º oven 20 minutes. Cover with aluminum foil to prevent overbrowning. Bake 25 more minutes, or until loaves sound hollow when tapped. Remove from pans immediately; cool on racks. Makes 2 loaves.

Croutons
Cut day-old bread slices into small cubes. Arrange on baking sheet. Bake at 300° until golden brown, stirring occasionally. Serve as garnish for soups.

EASY BATTER BREADS

Batter breads are the easiest of all the yeast breads. If you have never attempted to bake a loaf of bread, making a batter bread would be a good way to begin.

These breads are made from doughs that are too soft to be kneaded. They're a cinch to mix and they rise very quickly. Many of them do not have to be shaped; the batter is just poured into the pan. Some, however, are stiff enough to be formed into attractive shapes.

You can beat your batter breads by hand or by an electric mixer, but the most important step in making batter breads is to beat very vigorously to start a good gluten formation. If you have a mixer, we suggest you use it—much easier on the arms! Beat your batter until it tends to slide away from the sides of the bowl and looks shiny and smooth.

In a batter bread, the yeast feeds on the sugar and forms carbon dioxide gas. The gluten framework that has been developed by stirring and beating traps this gas in its tiny openings and as the gas expands, the batter rises.

Rising of batter breads is extremely important, so follow the recipe directions very carefully. If the batter rises too long a time, the bread will fall or sag in the center.

If the recipe tells you to "stir down," stir the raised batter with a spoon until it is reduced to almost its original size.

Some batter breads are shaped and then allowed to rise until doubled. Test to see if they have risen enough, by pressing lightly with your little finger near the edge of the bread. If the small dent remains, the bread has risen enough and is ready for baking.

HERBED SOUR CREAM BATTER BREAD

This versatile batter bread can be served for lunch or dinner because its unusual herb flavor accents most meats and fish.

4¾ c. sifted flour	½ tsp. marjoram leaves
2 tblsp. sugar	½ tsp. oregano leaves
2 tsp. salt	½ tsp. parsley flakes
2 pkgs. active dry yeast	½ c. very warm water
1 c. warm dairy sour	(120-130°)
cream	2 eggs
6 tblsp. soft butter or	
regular margarine	

Combine 1 c. of the flour, sugar, salt, undissolved yeast, sour cream, butter, marjoram, oregano, parsley and water in bowl. Beat with electric mixer at medium speed 2 minutes. Add eggs and ½ c. of the flour; beat 2 minutes at high speed.

Stir in enough remaining flour to make a soft dough. Cover; let rise until doubled, about 35 minutes.

Stir down. Turn into 2 well-greased 1-qt. casseroles. Cover; let rise until doubled, about 50 minutes.

Bake in 375° oven 35 minutes, or until golden brown. Remove from casseroles; cool on racks. Makes 2 loaves.

RICH EGG BATTER BREAD

A basic white batter bread with lots of eggs to give it a pale yellow color, deep flavor and added protein.

6½ c. sifted flour	2 c. very warm water
2 tblsp. sugar	(120-130⁰)
2 tsp. salt	3 eggs
2 pkgs. active dry yeast	
2 tblsp. soft butter	
or regular margarine	

Mix together 1½ c. of the flour, sugar, salt and undissolved yeast in large bowl.

Add butter. Gradually add water to flour-yeast mixture. Beat with electric mixer at medium speed 2 minutes. Add eggs and ½ c. of the flour; beat 2 minutes at high speed.

Stir in enough remaining flour to make a soft dough. Cover; let rise in warm place until doubled, about 35 minutes.

Stir down. Turn into 2 well-greased 1½-qt. casseroles. Cover; let rise in warm place until doubled, about 40 minutes.

Bake in 375⁰ oven 35 minutes or until golden brown. Remove from casseroles; cool on racks. Makes 2 loaves.

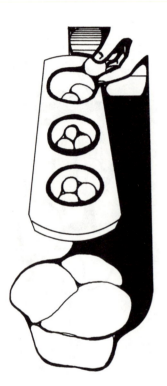

GOLDEN PARMESAN ROLLS

A sprinkling of sesame seeds dots the shiny tops of these attractive, clover-shaped, cheesy dinner rolls—perfect for company.

3¼ c. sifted flour	2 tsp. salt
2 pkgs. active dry yeast	1 egg
½ c. milk	1 c. grated Parmesan
½ c. water	cheese
½ c. butter or	1 egg yolk, slightly beaten
regular margarine	1 tsp. water
¼ c. sugar	Sesame seeds

Stir together 1 c. of the flour and undissolved yeast in mixing bowl.

Heat together milk, ½ c. water, butter, sugar and salt in saucepan to very warm (120-130⁰). Add to flour-yeast mixture all at once. Beat with electric mixer at medium speed 3 minutes or until smooth. Blend in egg, 1 c. flour and Parmesan cheese. Beat 2 more minutes.

Stir in enough remaining flour to make a soft dough. Cover and let rise in warm place until doubled, about 1 hour.

Divide dough into fourths. Let rest 10 minutes. With greased hands, shape each fourth into 9 balls. Place 3 balls in each greased 3-inch muffin-pan cup (see illustration). Brush tops with combined egg yolk and 1 tsp. water. Sprinkle with sesame seeds. Cover and let rise in warm place until almost doubled, about 30 minutes.

Bake in 325° oven 30 minutes or until golden brown. Makes 12.

RAISIN-CINNAMON BATTER LOAF

Batter breads are great timesavers when you want to serve fresh bread to your family and you don't have time to make conventional ones.

6 c. sifted flour	½ c. water
¼ c. sugar	½ c. butter or
2 tsp. salt	regular margarine
1 tsp. ground cinnamon	3 eggs
1 pkg. active dry yeast	1 c. raisins
1 c. milk	

Mix together 1½ c. of the flour, sugar, salt, cinnamon and undissolved yeast in large bowl.

Combine milk, water and butter in saucepan. Heat to very warm (120-130°). Gradually add to flour-yeast mixture. Beat with electric mixer at medium speed 2 minutes. Add eggs and ½ c. of the flour; beat 2 minutes at high speed.

Stir in raisins and enough remaining flour to make a soft dough. Cover; let rise until doubled, about 50 minutes.

Stir down. Turn into 2 well-greased 1½-qt. casseroles. Cover; let rise in warm place until doubled, about 40 minutes.

Bake in 375° oven 35 minutes or until done. Remove from casseroles; cool on racks. Makes 2 loaves.

Shell-top
Bread that is baked at too low a temperature will become too light before the oven heat sets the cell walls. Just a slight jar will cause the dough to fall. The baked loaf may look fine on the outside. When you cut into it, you will discover a huge hole right under the surface of the crust. This was caused by the collapsing dough.

APPLE CRUMB KUCHEN

This batter bread resembles old-fashioned German kuchen, but is so easy to make because you don't knead the dough.

2¼ c. sifted flour	2 eggs
½ c. sugar	4 medium apples, pared,
½ tsp. salt	cored and sliced
1 pkg. active dry yeast	Crumb Topping (recipe
¼ c. milk	follows)
¼ c. water	Vanilla Icing (recipe
⅓ c. butter or	follows)
regular margarine	

Mix together 1 c. of the flour, sugar, salt and undissolved yeast in large bowl.

Combine milk, water and butter in saucepan. Heat to very warm (120-130⁰). Gradually add to flour-yeast mixture, beating with electric mixer at medium speed until smooth, about 2 minutes. Add eggs and ½ c. of the flour; beat 2 minutes at high speed.

Stir in enough remaining flour to make a stiff batter. Spread in well-greased 9-inch square baking pan. Arrange apple slices in 4 rows on top. Sprinkle with Crumb Topping. Cover; let rise in warm place until doubled, about 1 hour.

Bake in 375⁰ oven 45 minutes, or until apples are tender. Cool in pan 10 minutes. Remove from pan; cool on rack. Drizzle with Vanilla Icing before serving. Makes 1 coffee cake.

Crumb Topping: Combine ⅓ c. sugar, ¼ c. flour, 2 tblsp. butter or regular margarine and 1 tsp. ground cinnamon in bowl. Mix until crumbly.

Vanilla Icing: Combine 1 c. sifted confectioners sugar, 1 tsp. vanilla and 1 tblsp. milk in bowl. Mix until smooth.

QUICK CARAMEL CRUNCH COFFEE CAKE

A delicious coffee cake with a flavorful walnut topping containing a hint of cocoa. It's a quick batter bread.

2¼ c. sifted flour	1 egg
¼ c. sugar	Caramel Nut Topping
1 pkg. active dry yeast	(recipe follows)
1 tsp. salt	Glaze (recipe follows)
¾ c. milk	
¼ c. butter or	
regular margarine	

Stir together 1 c. of the flour, sugar, undissolved yeast and salt in mixing bowl.

Heat milk and butter in small saucepan until very warm (120-130⁰). Add to flour-yeast mixture with egg all at once, beating with electric mixer at high speed 1 minute.

Beat in remaining flour, using electric mixer at medium speed. Spread batter in greased 9-inch square baking pan. Sprinkle with Caramel Nut Topping. Cover and let rise in warm place until doubled, about 1 hour.

Bake in 375⁰ oven 30 minutes or until golden brown. Serve warm, drizzled with Glaze. Makes 1 coffee cake.

Caramel Nut Topping: Combine ½ c. brown sugar (packed), ½ c. chopped walnuts, 1 tblsp. flour and 1 tblsp. baking cocoa in bowl. Cut in 2 tblsp. soft butter or regular margarine until mixture is crumbly.

Glaze: Combine ½ c. sifted confectioners sugar, 2 tblsp. melted butter or regular margarine, ½ tsp. vanilla and 1 to 2 tsp. milk in mixing bowl. Stir until smooth.

REGAL SAVARIN RING

A very light batter-type sweet bread featuring a cake-like texture and a delicate orange flavor. Delightful for drop-in holiday guests.

1 pkg. active dry yeast	½ tsp. salt
⅓ c. lukewarm water (110⁰)	3 eggs
1¾ c. sifted flour	2 tsp. grated orange rind
1 tblsp. sugar	¾ c. fresh orange juice
½ c. butter or regular margarine	½ c. water
½ c. sugar	⅔ c. sugar
	¾ c. warmed orange marmalade

Sprinkle yeast over ⅓ c. lukewarm water; stir to dissolve. Stir in ½ c. of the flour and 1 tblsp. sugar. Cover and let stand in warm place until bubbly, about 1 hour.

Cream together butter, ½ c. sugar and salt until fluffy, using electric mixer at medium speed. Add eggs, one at a time, beating after each addition. Add yeast mixture, remaining 1¼ c. flour and orange rind. Beat at medium speed 2 minutes. Turn into well-greased 1½-qt. ring mold. Cover and let rise in warm place until doubled, about 1 hour.

Bake in 350⁰ oven 35 minutes or until golden brown. Meanwhile, combine orange juice, ½ c. water and ⅔ c. sugar in saucepan. Bring to a boil, stirring constantly. Remove from heat.

Remove bread from pan immediately; place on rack. Brush with orange syrup until it is all absorbed (about 15 minutes). Brush with marmalade. Makes 1 coffee cake.

SALLY LUNN

An egg-rich batter bread that was traditionally served with hot tea. It's so flavorful, doesn't need a spread and is best served warm.

3½ to 4 c. sifted flour	½ c. water
⅓ c. sugar	½ c. butter or
1 pkg. active dry yeast	regular margarine
1 tsp. salt	3 eggs
½ c. milk	

Stir together 1¼ c. of the flour, sugar, undissolved yeast and salt in mixing bowl.

Heat milk, water and butter in saucepan over low heat until very warm (120-130°). Gradually add to flour-yeast mixture, beating with electric mixer at medium speed 2 minutes or until smooth. Add eggs and 1 c. of the flour. Beat at high speed 2 minutes, scraping bowl occasionally.

Gradually stir in enough remaining flour to make a stiff batter. Cover and let rise in warm place until doubled, about 1 hour. Stir down batter. Beat well with spoon ½ minute. Turn into well-greased and floured 9-inch tube pan. Cover; let rise in warm place until doubled, about 1 hour.

Bake in 350° oven 45 to 50 minutes or until golden brown. Remove from pan; cool slightly on rack. Best when served warm. Makes 1 coffee cake.

POLISH BABKA

This batter bread recipe makes a light and delicate coffee cake that is traditionally served at Easter time by Polish-Americans.

1 pkg. active dry yeast	1 tsp. vanilla
¼ c. lukewarm water	1 tsp. rum flavoring
(110°)	4 c. sifted flour
½ c. melted butter or	1 c. milk, scalded
regular margarine	and cooled
½ c. sugar	Dry bread crumbs
4 egg yolks	Confectioners sugar
1 tsp. salt	

Sprinkle yeast over lukewarm water; stir to dissolve.

Combine butter and sugar in mixing bowl. Add egg yolks. Beat with electric mixer at medium speed until well-blended, about 2 minutes. Add yeast mixture, salt, vanilla and rum flavoring.

Gradually add 3 c. of the flour alternately with milk, beating well after each addition, using electric mixer at low speed. Beat until batter is thick. Gradually stir in remaining flour, mixing well.

Generously butter 10-inch fluted tube pan. Coat pan with bread crumbs. Turn dough into prepared pan. Cover and let rise in warm place until doubled, about 1½ hours.

Bake in 350° oven 45 minutes or until golden brown. Cool in pan on rack 10 minutes. Remove from pan; cool on rack. Dust with confectioners sugar before serving. Serve warm or cold. Makes 1 coffee cake.

HOMEMADE FROZEN YEAST DOUGHS

Now you can make your very own frozen yeast doughs at home. They can be mixed, kneaded, shaped, wrapped in foil and stored in the freezer. When you want a loaf of homemade bread, simply let the dough thaw and rise. Then, pop it into the oven and you'll have homemade bread with no fuss.

No, you can't make these breads and bake them the same day. These doughs were especially developed to freeze now and bake later. You will notice there is a much higher amount of yeast added to the flour in these recipes compared to the conventional yeast doughs.

These doughs can be frozen up to a month. Do not thaw them in the refrigerator longer than overnight. If you do, they will develop a strong aroma and an unpleasant taste.

You will find that homemade doughs taste so much better than the supermarket version, and they will cost you less, too. We have given you a good variety from which to choose.

Freezer breads are not for spur-of-the-moment entertaining, because they do take several hours to thaw and rise. But they are great to have on hand for periods when you are just too busy to prepare a dough from scratch.

FREEZER WHITE BREAD

Frozen doughs are great timesavers because they can be made ahead. Your family can still enjoy fresh bread when you have busy days.

12½ to 13½ c. unsifted flour	4 pkgs. active dry yeast
½ c. sugar	¼ c. soft butter
2 tblsp. salt	or regular margarine
⅔ c. instant nonfat dry milk solids	4 c. very warm water (120-130⁰)

Mix together 4 c. of the flour, sugar, salt, dry milk and undissolved yeast in large bowl. Add butter.

Gradually add water to flour-yeast mixture. Beat with electric mixer at medium speed 2 minutes, scraping bowl occasionally. Add 1½ c. of the flour. Beat at high speed 2 minutes, scraping bowl occasionally.

Stir in enough remaining flour to make a stiff dough.

Turn dough out onto lightly floured board. Knead until smooth and elastic, about 15 minutes. Cover with a towel; let rest 15 minutes.

Divide dough into 4 equal parts. Form each piece into a mound 6 inches in diameter. Place on greased baking sheets. Cover with plastic wrap. Freeze until firm. Transfer to plastic bags. Freeze up to 4 weeks.

To bake, remove from freezer; place on ungreased baking sheet. Cover; let stand at room temperature until fully thawed, about 4 hours. Roll dough into 12 × 8-inch rectangle. Roll up like jelly roll, from 8-inch side. Pinch seam to seal. Place in greased 8½ × 4½ × 2½-inch loaf pan. Let rise in warm place, free from draft, until doubled in bulk, about 1½ hours.

Bake in 350⁰ oven 35 minutes, or until loaf sounds hollow when tapped. Remove from pan; cool on rack. Makes 4 loaves.

For round loaves: Let thawed dough rise on ungreased baking sheets until doubled, about 1 hour. Bake as above.

Bread Rounds
Cut homemade bread slices into 2-inch rounds with a sharp biscuit cutter. Brush both sides with melted butter. Arrange on top of casserole in place of biscuits.

FREEZER CINNAMON LOAVES

An advantage of freezer breads is you can make them ahead, bake them all at once or one at a time—you make the choice.

7¼ to 8¼ c. unsifted flour	¾ c. water
⅔ c. sugar	3 eggs
3 pkgs. active dry yeast	Melted butter or
1 tsp. salt	regular margarine
⅔ c. soft butter or	9 tblsp. sugar
regular margarine	1½ tsp. ground cinnamon
1 c. milk	

Combine 2 c. of the flour, ⅔ c. sugar, undissolved yeast and salt in 6-qt. bowl. Add butter.

Heat milk and water in saucepan until very warm (120-130°). Add to flour-yeast mixture. Beat with electric mixer at medium speed 2 minutes. Add eggs and 1 c. more flour. Beat at high speed 2 minutes or until thick and elastic.

Gradually stir in enough remaining flour to make a soft dough.

Turn dough out onto floured surface. Knead dough until smooth, about 10 minutes.

Divide into thirds. Let rest 10 minutes. Roll each third to 14 × 8-inch rectangle. Brush with melted butter. Sprinkle each with 3 tblsp. of the sugar and ½ tsp. of the cinnamon. Roll up tightly like jelly roll, from 8-inch side. Pinch seam to seal. Wrap in plastic wrap. Place in 3 ungreased 8½ × 4½ × 2½-inch loaf pans. Freeze until firm. Remove; wrap in aluminum foil. Freeze up to 4 weeks.

To bake, unwrap frozen loaf and place in greased 8½ × 4½ × 2½-inch loaf pan. Cover with plastic wrap. Thaw at room temperature about 2½ hours or overnight in refrigerator. Brush dough lightly with oil. Cover with towel. Let rise in warm place until the corners of the pan are filled and the dough is about 1 inch above center of the pan, about 2 hours.

Bake in 375° oven 25 to 30 minutes, or until loaf sounds hollow when tapped. If you wish, drizzle your favorite confectioners sugar icing over top of slightly warm loaf. Makes 3 loaves.

HONEY-WHEAT GERM BREAD

Because so many of our farm readers told us they liked our freezer bread recipes, we developed this whole wheat bread.

9½ to 10½ c. unsifted flour	2 c. milk
4 pkgs. active dry yeast	2 c. water
2 tblsp. salt	2 c. wheat germ
½ c. honey	
¼ c. soft butter or regular margarine	

Combine 4 c. of the flour, undissolved yeast and salt in 6-qt. bowl. Add honey and butter.

Heat milk and water in saucepan until very warm (120-130°). Add to flour-yeast mixture. Beat with electric mixer at medium speed 2 minutes. Add 2 c. flour. Beat at high speed 2 minutes or until thick and elastic. Stir in wheat germ.

Gradually stir in enough remaining flour to make a soft dough.

Turn dough out onto floured surface. Knead until smooth and elastic, about 10 minutes. Cover with plastic wrap and then a towel. Let rest 20 minutes.

Punch down dough. Divide into fourths. Let rest 10 minutes. Roll each fourth into 12 × 8-inch rectangle. Roll up tightly like jelly roll from 8-inch side. Seal lengthwise edge and ends well. Wrap in plastic wrap. Place in 4 ungreased 8½ × 4½ × 2½-inch loaf pans. Freeze until firm. Remove from pans; wrap in aluminum foil. Freeze up to 4 weeks.

To bake, unwrap frozen loaf and place in greased 8½ × 4½ × 2½-inch loaf pan. Cover with plastic wrap. Thaw at room temperature about 2 hours or overnight in refrigerator. Brush with oil. Cover with towel; let rise in warm place until the corners of pan are filled and dough is about 1 inch above center of pan, about 3 hours.

Bake in 350° oven 40 to 45 minutes, or until loaf sounds hollow when tapped. If bread browns too quickly, cover loosely with aluminum foil. Makes 4 loaves.

Cheese Bread Sticks
Cut crusts from loaf of unsliced day-old bread. Cut into ¾-inch slices lengthwise and then into 4 inch wide strips. Brush with melted butter. Sprinkle with grated cheese. Place on shallow baking sheet. Bake at 375° for 15 minutes or until brown.

ROUND PUMPERNICKEL LOAVES

You can freeze pumpernickel dough, too. These hearty loaves are just as good as those made conventionally.

7 to 8 c. unsifted flour	¼ c. molasses
3 c. stirred rye flour	2 (1-oz.) squares
2 tblsp. salt	unsweetened chocolate
4 large shredded wheat	1 tblsp. butter or
biscuits, broken up	regular margarine
¾ c. cornmeal	2 c. mashed potatoes
3 pkgs. active dry yeast	2 tsp. caraway seeds
3½ c. water	

Combine flours. Mix together 2 c. of the flour mixture, salt, shredded wheat biscuits, cornmeal and undissolved yeast in 6-qt. bowl.

Combine water, molasses, chocolate and butter in saucepan. Heat until very warm (120-130⁰). Add to flour-yeast mixture. Beat with electric mixer at medium speed 2 minutes. Add potatoes and 1 c. of the flour mixture. Beat at high speed 2 minutes. Stir in caraway seeds and enough remaining flour mixture to make a soft dough.

Turn dough out onto floured surface; cover with bowl. Let rest 15 minutes. Knead until smooth and elastic, about 15 minutes.

Divide into thirds. Form each into a ball. Place on greased baking sheet. Flatten to form 6-inch round. Cover with plastic wrap. Freeze until firm. Wrap in aluminum foil. Freeze up to 4 weeks.

To bake, unwrap loaf and place on greased baking sheet. Cover with plastic wrap. Thaw at room temperature 3½ hours. Remove plastic wrap; cover with towel. Let rise in a warm place until doubled, about 2 hours.

Bake in 375⁰ oven 35 minutes, or until loaf sounds hollow when tapped. Makes 3 loaves.

APRICOT BRAID

This flavorful coffee cake is made the freezer-method way. You freeze the dough, then thaw and bake. Perfect for the busy seasons.

5½ to 6½ c. unsifted flour	3 eggs
¾ c. sugar	Apricot Filling
1 tsp. salt	(recipe follows)
3 pkgs. active dry yeast	Crumb Topping
½ c. soft butter	(recipe follows)
or regular margarine	
1 c. very warm water	
(120-130⁰)	

Combine 1¼ c. of the flour, sugar, salt and undissolved yeast in large bowl. Add butter.

Gradually add water to flour-yeast mixture. Beat with electric mixer at medium speed 2 minutes, scraping bowl occasionally. Add eggs and ¼ c. of the flour. Beat at high speed 2 minutes, scraping bowl occasionally.

Stir in enough remaining flour to make a soft dough.

Turn dough out onto lightly floured board. Knead until smooth and elastic, about 8 to 10 minutes.

Divide dough into thirds. Roll each third into a 12 × 7-inch rectangle. Transfer to 3 greased baking sheets. Starting at narrow side, spread one third of the Apricot Filling down center third of each rectangle. Cut 1-inch-wide strips along both sides of filling, cutting from edges of dough to filling, making 12 strips on each side. Fold strips at an angle across filling, alternating from side to side (see illustration). Sprinkle with one third of the Crumb Topping. Cover sheets tightly with plastic wrap; place in freezer.

When firm, remove from baking sheets and wrap each coffee cake with plastic wrap, then with aluminum foil. Keep frozen up to 4 weeks.

To bake, remove from freezer. Unwrap and place on ungreased baking sheets. Let stand covered loosely with plastic wrap at room temperature until fully thawed, about 2 hours. Let rise in warm place until more than doubled in bulk, about 1½ hours.

Bake in 375⁰ oven 20 to 25 minutes or until golden brown. Remove from baking sheet; cool on racks. Makes 3 coffee cakes.

Apricot Filling: Combine 2¼ c. dried apricots (11-oz. pkg.) and 1½ c. water in saucepan. Bring to a boil; cook until liquid is absorbed and apricots are tender, about 20 minutes. Sieve; stir in 1½ c. brown sugar (packed). Cool.

Crumb Topping: Combine ½ c. unsifted flour, 3 tblsp. sugar and ¾ tsp. ground cinnamon in bowl. Mix in 3 tblsp. soft butter or margarine until mixture is crumbly.

FREEZER ORANGE BUNS

These orange-flavored sweet rolls are made by the freezer-dough method. They're shaped before freezing. To serve, just thaw and bake.

5½ to 6½ c. sifted flour	3 eggs
¾ c. sugar	Melted butter or
1 tsp. salt	regular margarine
3 pkgs. active dry yeast	Orange Sugar (recipe
½ c. soft butter or	follows)
regular margarine	
1 c. very warm water	
(120-130⁰)	

Combine 1¼ c. of the flour, sugar, salt and undissolved yeast in mixing bowl; mix thoroughly. Add soft butter.

Gradually add water to dry ingredients, beating with electric mixer at medium speed 2 minutes, scraping bowl occasionally. Add eggs and ¼ c. of the flour. Beat at high speed 2 minutes, scraping bowl occasionally.

Gradually stir in enough remaining flour to make a soft dough.

Turn dough out onto floured surface. Knead until smooth and elastic, 8 to 10 minutes.

Divide dough into thirds. Divide each third into 8 pieces. Form each piece into a ball. Dip each ball in melted butter and then coat with Orange Sugar. Place in 3 greased 8-inch round cake pans, 8 rolls in each pan. Cover pans tightly with plastic wrap, then with aluminum foil. Place in freezer. Can be frozen up to 4 weeks.

To bake, remove rolls from freezer. Let stand, loosely covered with plastic wrap, at room temperature until fully thawed, about 3 hours. Let rise in warm place until doubled, about 2¼ hours.

Bake in 350⁰ oven 25 to 30 minutes or until golden brown. Remove from pans; cool on racks. Makes 24.

Orange Sugar: Combine 1 c. sugar and 2 tblsp. grated orange rind in small bowl; mix well.

SOURDOUGH BREAD

"Sourdoughs" were the mountain men, sheepherders, pioneers, miners and prospectors of the Old West. Sourdough was taken to Alaska by the prospectors during the Gold Rush of the 1890s. They were called sourdoughs because wherever they traveled, they carried a ball of "starter" in their sack of flour. The starter was made of wild yeasts from the air combined with a mixture of flour and water, which began to ferment after several days. When it was fermented to the right stage, the men turned out biscuits, pancakes and loaves of bread over their campfire. On bitter cold nights, they took their starter to bed with them so that the yeast wouldn't be killed by the cold air.

In our Farm Journal Test Kitchens we perfected a starter that is a lot more reliable than the wild yeast method, however, and you don't have to depend on the yeasts from the air, as we used packaged yeast. The starter will keep indefinitely in the refrigerator.

Sourdough bread is even-textured with a thick brown crust. It has its own very distinctive flavor—a decided tanginess that we think is delicious. And it makes marvelous toast.

MODERN SOURDOUGH STARTER

This basic sourdough starter can be stored indefinitely if you replenish it. Use it to make Sourdough Bread and Golden Sourdough Biscuits.

2 pkgs. active dry yeast	**4 c. unsifted flour**
4 c. lukewarm	
water (110⁰)	

Place yeast in glass, stoneware or plastic bowl.* Add about ½ c. of the lukewarm water to yeast; stir to dissolve with wooden spoon. Add remaining water alternately with flour, mixing well after each addition with wooden spoon. Cover with towel. Place in warm place (85⁰) 6 hours or overnight.

The starter is ready to use in any of the following recipes. (It will look bubbly, and a clear liquid will rise to the top.) Stir before measuring. After removing needed amount of Modern Sourdough Starter, pour remaining mixture into stoneware crock or plastic container. Cover and refrigerate. (Can be stored indefinitely.)

Replenish Modern Sourdough Starter at least once a week by stirring in ½ c. warm water and ½ c. unsifted flour. Cover and let stand at room temperature overnight. Next morning, stir down mixture. Cover with lid; refrigerate.

*Note: Do not use metal utensils because prolonged contact with metal will drastically reduce the purity and change the taste of sourdough.

SOURDOUGH BREAD

Light, airy bread with a slightly yeasty flavor. It was rated "excellent" by the home economists in our Countryside Test Kitchens.

1 c. Modern Sourdough
   Starter (see recipe
   above)
2 c. lukewarm water (110°)
8¾ to 9 c. unsifted flour
1 c. milk
3 tblsp. butter or
   regular margarine

3 tblsp. sugar
2 tsp. salt
1 pkg. active dry yeast
¼ c. lukewarm
   water (110°)
1 tsp. baking soda
Melted butter or
   regular margarine

Pour Modern Sourdough Starter into glass, stoneware or plastic bowl. Add 2 c. lukewarm water alternately with 2½ c. of the flour, mixing well with wooden spoon. Cover with towel. Let stand in warm place (85°) overnight.

Scald milk in saucepan. Add butter, sugar and salt. Cool to lukewarm.

Sprinkle yeast over ¼ c. lukewarm water; stir to dissolve. Combine yeast with milk mixture. Add milk mixture and 2 c. of the flour to starter mixture, beating with wooden spoon until smooth. Sprinkle baking soda over batter; stir gently to mix well. Cover bowl with towel. Let rise in warm place (85°) until almost doubled, about 40 minutes.

Stir down batter. Gradually stir in enough remaining flour to make a soft dough that leaves the sides of the bowl.

Turn dough out onto floured surface. Knead dough 5 minutes or until smooth. Divide dough in half. Cover and let rest 10 minutes.

Shape each half into a loaf. Place in 2 greased 9 × 5 × 3-inch loaf pans. Brush tops with melted butter. Let rise in warm place until dough reaches tops of pans, about 1 hour.

Bake in 375° oven 50 minutes, or until loaves sound hollow when tapped. Makes 2 loaves.

Flour Changes
Flour tends to dry out during the summer months. When fall arrives, you might find that your recipe does not need as much flour as it did in the summer months.

GOLDEN SOURDOUGH BISCUITS

If you don't have time to bake these crusty biscuits with flaky centers just before serving, bake them ahead of time and reheat them.

2 c. unsifted flour	½ c. buttermilk
1 tsp. salt	1 c. Modern Sourdough
½ tsp. baking soda	Starter (see recipe above)
1 tsp. baking powder	Melted butter or
½ c. butter or	regular margarine
regular margarine	

Combine flour, salt, baking soda and baking powder in bowl. Cut in butter with pastry blender or two knives until mixture resembles cornmeal. Combine buttermilk and Modern Sourdough Starter; blend well. Stir into crumb mixture with a fork until mixture forms a soft dough.

Turn dough out onto floured surface; knead gently 30 seconds. Roll out to ½-inch thickness. Cut into biscuits with 3-inch biscuit or cookie cutter. Place on greased baking sheet. Brush with melted butter. Cover with towel; let stand in warm place 30 minutes.

Bake in 425° oven 12 to 15 minutes or until golden brown. Serve warm with butter. Makes 12 biscuits.

To reheat: Wrap biscuits in aluminum foil. Heat in 375° oven 15 minutes or until hot.

SOFT DINNER ROLLS

Very light and tender no-knead dinner rolls. Serve with lots of country fresh butter.

1 c. milk, scalded	3 pkgs. active dry yeast
1 c. sugar	1 c. lukewarm
6 tblsp. lard	water (110°)
¼ c. shortening	8½ to 9 c. sifted flour
1 tblsp. salt	5 eggs

Pour scalded milk over sugar, lard, shortening and salt in mixing bowl. Cool to lukewarm.

Sprinkle yeast over lukewarm water; stir to dissolve.

Add 3 c. flour, eggs and yeast mixture to milk mixture. Beat with electric mixer at medium speed until smooth, about 2 minutes.

Gradually stir in enough remaining flour to make a soft dough. (No kneading is necessary.)

Place dough in greased bowl, turning once to grease top. Cover and let rise in warm place until doubled, about 1 hour.

Punch down dough. Turn onto lightly floured surface. Divide dough into thirds. Let rest 10 minutes. Divide each third into 12 pieces. Shape each piece into a ball. Arrange rolls in 3 greased 8-inch square baking pans, 12 rolls equally spaced in each pan. Cover and let rise until doubled, about 50 minutes.

Bake in 375° oven 15 minutes or until golden brown. Remove from pans; cool on racks. Makes 36.

BASIC DINNER ROLLS

You have a choice of five different ways to shape these basic dinner rolls. The recipe yield depends on the shapes you select.

¾ c. milk, scalded	1 pkg. active dry yeast
¼ c. sugar	¾ c. lukewarm
2¼ tsp. salt	water (110°)
¼ c. shortening	4½ c. sifted flour

Pour scalded milk over sugar, salt and shortening in mixing bowl. Cool to lukewarm.

Sprinkle yeast over lukewarm water; stir to dissolve.

Add yeast mixture and 2¼ c. of the flour to milk mixture. Beat with electric mixer at medium speed 2 minutes.

Gradually stir in enough remaining flour to make a soft dough.

Turn dough out onto floured surface. Knead until smooth and elastic, 8 to 10 minutes.

Place dough in greased bowl, turning over once to grease top. Cover and let rise in warm place until doubled, about 1 hour 25 minutes.

Punch down dough. Shape dough into rolls (variations follow). Let rise and bake according to directions given in each variation.

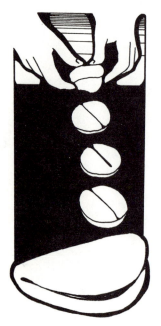

Variations:

Parker House Rolls: Divide dough in half. Let rest 10 minutes. Roll out each half on floured surface to ½-inch thickness. Cut into rounds with floured 2½-inch biscuit cutter (see illustration). Crease heavily through center with dull edge of knife. Brush lightly with melted butter or regular margarine. Fold in half, with top half overlapping bottom half. Place on greased baking sheets, about 1 inch apart. Cover and let rise in warm place until doubled, about 1 hour. Bake in 425° oven 20 minutes or until golden brown. Remove from baking sheets; cool on racks. Makes 24.

Pan Rolls: Divide dough in half. Let rest 10 minutes. Form each half into a roll about 9 inches long on floured surface. Cut with sharp knife into 12 equal pieces. Form each piece into a ball. Place in 2 greased 9-inch round cake pans, 12 rolls equally spaced in each pan (see illustration). Brush lightly with melted butter or regular margarine. Cover and let rise in warm place until doubled, about 1 hour. Bake in 425° oven 20 minutes or until golden brown. Remove from baking sheets; cool on racks. Makes 24.

Twin Roll-ups: Divide dough in half. Let rest 10 minutes. Roll out each half on floured surface into an 18 × 6-inch rectangle. Brush lightly with melted butter or regular margarine. Roll up like a jelly roll, starting from wide end. Cut with sharp knife into 2-inch pieces.

Place on greased baking sheets, about 1 inch apart. Crease heavily through center of each roll with dull edge of knife. Cover and let rise in warm place until doubled, about 1 hour. Bake in 425° oven 20 minutes or until golden brown. Remove from baking sheets; cool on racks. Makes 18.

Clover Leaf Rolls: Divide dough in half. Let rest 10 minutes. Form each half into a roll 9 inches long on floured surface. Cut roll into 9 (1-inch) pieces. Form each piece into 3 small balls (see illustration). Place 3 balls in each greased 3-inch muffin-pan cup. Brush with melted butter or regular margarine. Cover and let rise in warm place until doubled, about 1 hour. Bake in 425° oven 15 minutes or until golden brown. Remove from pans; cool on racks. Makes 18.

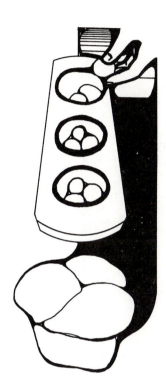

Crescents: Divide dough into thirds. Let rest 10 minutes. Roll each third on floured surface to 9-inch circle (see illustration). Cut with sharp knife into 8 wedges. Brush lightly with melted butter or regular margarine. Roll up, starting at wide end of wedge. Place, point side down, on greased baking sheets, about 2 inches apart. Curve each roll into a half circle. Cover and let rise in warm place until doubled, about 1 hour. Bake in 425° oven 20 minutes or until golden brown. Remove from baking sheets; cool on racks. Makes 24.

MELT-IN-YOUR-MOUTH ROLLS

"We make these golden brown dinner rolls again and again for church dinners," a Michigan farm woman wrote us.

2 c. milk	¼ c. lukewarm
¼ c. shortening	water (110°)
¼ c. sugar	7 c. sifted flour
2 tsp. salt	2 eggs
2 pkgs. active dry yeast	

Scald milk in saucepan. Pour over shortening, sugar and salt in large mixing bowl. Cool to lukewarm.

Sprinkle yeast over lukewarm water; stir to dissolve.

Add yeast mixture, 3 c. flour and eggs to milk mixture. Beat with electric mixer at medium speed until smooth, about 2 minutes.

Gradually stir in enough remaining flour to make a soft dough.

Turn dough out onto floured surface. Knead until smooth and satiny, 8 to 10 minutes. Place dough in greased bowl, turning over once to grease top. Cover and let rise in warm place until doubled, about 1 hour.

Punch down dough. Divide dough into thirds. Let rest 10 minutes. Divide each third into 12 pieces. Shape each piece into a ball. Place 12 balls, equally spaced, in 3 greased 9-inch round cake pans. Cover and let rise in warm place until doubled, 45 to 60 minutes.

Bake in 400° oven 12 to 15 minutes or until golden brown. Remove from pans; cool on racks. Makes 36.

POTATO YEAST ROLLS

Old-fashioned potato rolls with crusty tops and soft tender centers that have been baked in one family for several generations.

1¼ c. cubed, pared	1 pkg. active dry yeast
potatoes (½-inch cubes)	1 tsp. sugar
⅓ c. sugar	5¾ c. sifted flour
½ c. butter or	2 eggs
regular margarine	¼ c. melted butter or
1 tsp. salt	regular margarine

Place potatoes in 2-qt. saucepan. Add enough water to cover. Cook, covered, 15 minutes or until tender. Remove from heat. Drain potatoes, reserving cooking water. Add enough hot water to reserved cooking water to make 1¼ c.

Mash potatoes, using a vegetable masher. (You will need 1 c. mashed potatoes.)

Pour 1 c. of the hot potato water over ⅓ c. sugar, ½ c. butter and salt in mixing bowl. Cool to lukewarm.

Sprinkle yeast and 1 tsp. sugar over remaining ¼ c. lukewarm potato water (110⁰); stir to dissolve.

Add yeast mixture, 1 c. mashed potatoes and 2½ c. of the flour to butter mixture. Beat with electric mixer at medium speed until smooth, about 2 minutes. Add eggs; beat well.

Gradually stir in enough remaining flour to make a soft dough. (No kneading is necessary.) Place dough in greased bowl, turning over once to grease top. Cover and let rise in warm place until doubled, about 1¼ hours.

Punch down dough. Divide dough in half. Let rest 10 minutes. Roll out each half on floured surface to ⅜-inch thickness. Cut into rounds with 2½-inch biscuit or cookie cutter (see illustration). Brush tops of rounds with melted butter. Crease each roll in center with floured knife handle. Fold rolls over on the crease and press edges together lightly. Place rolls, with sides touching, on greased baking sheets. Brush with melted butter. Cover and let rise in warm place until doubled, about 45 minutes.

Bake in 400⁰ oven 12 to 15 minutes or until golden brown. Remove from baking sheets; cool on racks. Makes 48.

EASY PARKER HOUSE ROLLS

Choose these fast-fix dinner rolls on days when you have limited time to be in the kitchen.

1¼ c. milk, scalded	¼ c. lukewarm
3 tblsp. sugar	water (110⁰)
2 tblsp. butter or	4 to 5 c. sifted flour
regular margarine	2 tblsp. melted butter or
¾ tsp. salt	regular margarine
2 pkgs. active dry yeast	

Pour scalded milk over sugar, 2 tblsp. butter and salt in mixing bowl. Cool to lukewarm.

Sprinkle yeast over lukewarm water; stir to dissolve.

Add 2 c. of the flour and yeast mixture to milk mixture. Beat with electric mixer at medium speed until smooth, about 2 minutes.

Gradually add enough remaining flour to make a soft dough. Cover and let rest 15 minutes.

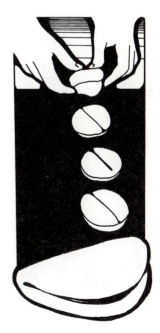

Knead dough a few times on lightly floured surface until no longer sticky. Roll out to ½-inch thickness. Cut into rounds, using floured biscuit cutter (see illustration). Brush rounds with remaining 2 tblsp. melted butter. Crease each roll in center with dull edge of knife. Fold rolls over on the crease and press edges together lightly. Place on greased baking sheets, about 3 inches apart. Cover and let rise in warm place until almost doubled, about 30 minutes.

Bake in 400⁰ oven 10 minutes or until golden brown. Remove from baking sheets; cool on racks. Makes 18.

CHRISTMAS MORNING BRIOCHE

These delightful topknot rolls have a hint of lemon flavor. Delicious for brunch or a special holiday breakfast.

¼ c. milk	¼ c. lukewarm
1 c. butter or	water (110⁰)
regular margarine	6 eggs
½ c. sugar	4½ c. sifted flour
½ tsp. salt	1 egg white, slightly beaten
2 tsp. grated lemon rind	1 tblsp. water
2 pkgs. active dry yeast	

Heat milk and butter over low heat until butter is melted. Pour over sugar, salt and lemon rind in bowl; cool to lukewarm.

Sprinkle yeast over ¼ c. lukewarm water; stir until dissolved.

Add eggs, 3 c. of the flour and yeast mixture to milk mixture. Beat with electric mixer at medium speed 4 minutes.

Gradually stir in enough remaining flour to make a soft dough. (No kneading is necessary.) Cover and let rise in warm place until doubled, about 1 hour.

Stir down dough. Cover with foil. Refrigerate overnight.

Divide dough into 32 pieces. With floured hands, shape 24 pieces into balls. Place in greased 3-inch fluted brioche pans or muffin-pan cups. Flatten and make an indentation in center of each. Divide each remaining piece into 3 parts. Shape into 24 teardrop shapes. Place in indentations pointed side down. Cover and let rise in warm place until doubled, about 45 minutes. Brush with combined egg white and 1 tblsp. water.

Bake in 375⁰ oven 12 to 15 minutes or until golden brown. Remove from pans; cool on racks. Makes 24.

To Measure Flour
To measure flour correctly, pile lightly into measuring cup and level off excess flour with a straight-edge knife or spatula. Never shake or tap the cup while you are measuring the flour.

REFRIGERATED YEAST ROLLS

You can store this refrigerated dough up to one week. These rolls are so light and tender.

1 c. boiling water	6½ c. sifted flour
¾ c. lard	1 c. prepared instant
½ c. sugar	mashed potatoes*
¾ tsp. salt	2 eggs
1 pkg. active dry yeast	
½ c. lukewarm	
water (110°)	

Combine boiling water, lard, sugar and salt in large mixing bowl. Cool to lukewarm.

Sprinkle yeast over lukewarm water; stir to dissolve.

Add yeast mixture, 1 c. of the flour, mashed potatoes and eggs to lard mixture. Beat with electric mixer at medium speed until smooth, about 2 minutes.

Gradually stir in remaining flour. (No kneading is necessary.) Place dough in greased 4-qt. bowl. Grease top of dough. Cover with aluminum foil. Refrigerate at least 2 hours. (Dough can be refrigerated up to 1 week.)

Punch down dough. Divide dough into fourths. Let rest 10 minutes. Roll out each fourth to 12-inch circle (see illustration). Cut in 12 wedges. Roll up each wedge, from wide end. Place, point side down, on greased baking sheets, about 3 inches apart. Shape into crescent. Cover and let rise in warm place until almost doubled, about 45 minutes.

Bake in 375° oven 15 minutes or until golden brown. Remove from baking sheets; cool on racks. Makes 48.

*Note: Add some additional potato flakes so potatoes are stiff.

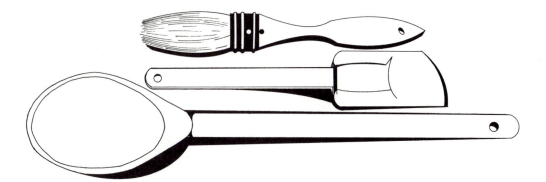

BACON-ONION ROLLS

"My husband likes these crusty onion-flavored rolls served with a stew or soup," says a New York farm homemaker.

8 strips bacon	¼ c. milk
4½ to 4¾ c. sifted flour	1 tblsp. melted butter or
¼ c. dry onion soup mix	regular margarine
2 pkgs. active dry yeast	Butter or regular
1 tblsp. sugar	margarine
1 (12 oz.) can beer	1 tblsp. cornmeal

Fry bacon in skillet until crisp. Remove bacon; drain on paper towels and crumble bacon. Reserve 2 tblsp. bacon drippings.

Stir together 1¾ c. of the flour, onion soup mix, undissolved yeast and sugar in mixing bowl.

Heat beer, milk and 1 tblsp. butter in saucepan over low heat until very warm (120-130°). (Mixture will look curdled.) Pour over flour-yeast mixture all at once. Beat with electric mixer at low speed ½ minute. Turn to high speed; beat 3 minutes more.

Stir in crumbled bacon and enough remaining flour to make a soft dough.

Turn dough out onto floured surface. Knead until smooth and elastic, about 5 minutes. Place in greased bowl, turning over once to grease top. Cover and let rise in warm place until doubled, about 45 minutes.

Punch down dough. Divide into 18 pieces. Let rest 10 minutes. Shape each piece into a ball. Place in greased 3-inch muffin-pan cups. Cover and let rise in warm place until doubled, about 30 minutes.

Brush tops of rolls with butter. Sprinkle with cornmeal.

Bake in 375° oven 18 minutes or until golden brown. Remove from pan; cool on racks. Makes 18.

Fancy Dessert
*Fruit and Cream Tart
(p. 325) is beautiful to look
at and simply scrumptious to
eat. Serve with pride at your
most special party.*

A Bevy of Baked Goods
Clockwise from left: Old-Fashioned Filled Cookies (p. 273), Coconut Crown Coffee Cake (p. 72), Cranberry Muffins (p. 114), Cocoa Chiffon Cake (p. 199) and elegant Greek Orange Braid (p. 76).

Assorted Baked Goods
Clockwise, starting at left: Apple Crunch Muffins (p. 119), Cherry Cream Pie (p. 313), No-Knead French Bread (p. 24), Refrigerated Yeast Rolls (p. 63), Basic White Bread (p. 25), Whole Wheat-Potato Bread (p. 32), Golden Cinnamon Loaves (p. 27), Refrigerator Chocolate Pinwheels (p. 255), Pennsylvania Dutch Cinnamon Buns (p. 96), Special Strawberry Sponge Cake (p. 192) and Pineapple Nut Bread (p. 124).

Double Berry Pie
Cranberry-Raspberry Pie (p. 289) combines tart cranberries with sweet raspberries for a perfect flavor combination. Great to serve for the holidays.

FAVORITE HAMBURGER OR FRANKFURTER BUNS

These hearty homemade buns won't get soggy no matter how much ketchup, onion, relish or mustard you load on.

2 c. milk	**1 tsp. sugar**
¾ c. sugar	**1 c. lukewarm**
⅔ c. lard	**water (110⁰)**
3 tsp. salt	**10½ to 11 c. sifted flour**
2 pkgs. active dry yeast	**2 eggs**

Scald milk in saucepan. Pour over ¾ c. sugar, lard and salt in large mixing bowl. Cool to lukewarm.

Sprinkle yeast and 1 tsp. sugar over lukewarm water; stir to dissolve. Let stand 10 minutes.

Add yeast mixture, 5 c. of the flour and eggs to milk mixture. Beat with electric mixer at medium speed until smooth, about 2 minutes.

Gradually stir in enough remaining flour to make a soft dough.

Turn dough out onto floured surface. Knead until smooth and satiny, 8 to 10 minutes. Place dough in greased bowl, turning over to grease top. Cover and let rise in warm place until doubled, about 1 hour.

Punch down dough. Divide dough into fourths. Let rest 10 minutes.

For hamburger buns: Divide each fourth into 9 pieces. Shape each piece into a ball. Place balls on greased baking sheets, about 3 inches apart. Flatten each to a 3-inch circle, pressing with palm of hand. Cover and let rise until doubled, about 45 minutes.

Bake in 350⁰ oven 18 minutes or until golden brown. Remove from baking sheets; cool on racks. Makes 36.

For frankfurter buns: Roll each fourth to 9 × 4-inch rectangle. Cut in 9 (4 × 1-inch) strips. Roll each strip on the counter top to form a 5½-inch cylinder. Place on greased baking sheets, about 3 inches apart. Flatten slightly with palm of hand. Cover and let rise until doubled, about 45 minutes. Bake as directed. Makes 36.

MINI HAMBURGER BUNS

These buns are just the right size for buffet entertaining. Split and fill with assorted sandwich fillings or small beef patties.

2 pkgs. active dry yeast	1 tblsp. salt
2 tsp. sugar	2 tblsp. cider vinegar
1 c. lukewarm	1½ c. water
water (110°)	8 to 10 c. sifted flour
½ c. sugar	
½ c. melted butter or	
regular margarine	

Sprinkle yeast and 2 tsp. sugar over lukewarm water; stir to dissolve. Let stand 10 minutes.

Combine ½ c. sugar, butter, salt, vinegar and water in mixing bowl. Add yeast mixture and 2 c. of the flour. Beat with electric mixer at medium speed until smooth, about 2 minutes.

Gradually stir in enough remaining flour to make a soft dough.

Turn dough out onto floured surface. Knead until smooth and no longer sticky, 8 to 10 minutes. Place dough in greased bowl, turning over once to grease top. Cover and let rise in warm place until doubled, about 1 hour.

Punch down dough. Cover and let rise again until doubled, about 45 minutes.

Punch down dough. Divide dough into fourths. Let rest 10 minutes. Divide each fourth into 12 equal pieces. Shape each piece into a ball. Place on greased baking sheets, about 3 inches apart. Cover and let rise until doubled, about 45 minutes.

Bake in 400° oven 15 minutes or until golden brown. Remove from baking sheets; cool on racks. Makes 48.

WHOLE WHEAT SANDWICH BUNS

Hearty whole wheat rolls that are perfect for all kinds of sandwich fillings as well as hamburger patties.

2 c. water	2 pkgs. active dry yeast
½ c. sugar	3 eggs
½ c. nonfat dry milk	3½ c. stirred whole
1 tblsp. salt	wheat flour
¾ c. cooking oil	Milk
4½ to 5 c. sifted flour	

Combine water, sugar, dry milk, salt and oil in saucepan. Heat to very warm (120-130°). Stir together 4 c. of the flour and undissolved yeast in bowl. Add very warm liquid and eggs. Beat with electric mixer at low speed ½ minute, scraping sides of bowl constantly. Beat at high speed 3 minutes, scraping bowl occasionally.

Stir in whole wheat flour by hand. Add enough remaining flour to make a moderately soft dough.

Turn dough out onto floured surface. Knead until smooth and elastic, about 5 minutes. Place in greased bowl, turning to grease top. Cover and let rise in warm place until doubled, about 1½ hours.

Punch down dough. Divide into thirds. Let rest 10 minutes.

Divide each third into 8 portions. Shape into balls. Place on greased baking sheets about 3 inches apart. Press down with palm of hand to make 3½-inch rounds. Cover and let rise in warm place until doubled, 30 to 45 minutes. Brush with milk.

Bake in 375° oven 12 minutes or until golden brown. Remove from baking sheets; cool on racks. Makes 24.

Avoid Excess Flour
Add just enough flour to a yeast dough at mixing and kneading time to prevent the dough from sticking. Try to keep the dough as soft as possible. Adding flour after the dough has risen may cause dark streaks and a coarse texture.

SOFT PRETZELS

Golden brown homemade pretzels make an unusual treat, especially when served warm and spread with mustard.

2 pkgs. active dry yeast	7½ c. sifted flour
1 c. lukewarm water (110⁰)	1 tblsp. baking soda
2 c. milk, scalded	1 egg, beaten
2 tblsp. sugar	1 tblsp. water
2 tsp. salt	Coarse salt

Sprinkle yeast over lukewarm water; stir to dissolve.

Pour scalded milk over sugar and salt in mixing bowl. Cool to lukewarm.

Add yeast mixture and 3 c. flour to milk mixture. Beat at medium speed with electric mixer 2 minutes. Stir in enough remaining flour to make a soft dough.

Turn dough out onto floured surface. Knead until smooth and satiny, about 10 minutes.

Place in greased bowl, turning over to grease top. Cover and let rise until doubled, about 1½ hours.

Punch down dough. Divide dough in half. Let rest 10 minutes. Roll into 12 × 10-inch rectangle. Cut into 10 (12-inch) strips. Roll each strip into 20-inch rope. To form pretzel, hold ends of rope (see illustration). Form a large loop, overlapping rope 3 inches from both ends. Twist rope once 3 inches from ends. Bring down ends of rope and pinch to opposite sides of pretzel. Place on lightly floured surface. Repeat with remaining dough. Let rise uncovered 30 minutes.

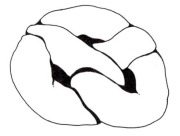

Heat 2 qt. water to boiling in Dutch oven during last 10 minutes of rising time. Add baking soda. Add pretzels to boiling water, two at a time. Boil 1 minute. Remove with slotted spoon. Let water drain off. Place pretzels on well-greased aluminum foil-covered baking sheets. Combine egg and 1 tblsp. water. Brush pretzels with egg mixture. Sprinkle with coarse salt.

Bake in 400⁰ oven 18 minutes or until golden brown. Serve warm. Makes 20 pretzels.

Note: Pretzels can be reheated. Wrap in aluminum foil; place in 400⁰ oven 10 minutes or until warm.

HOMEMADE ZWEIBACK TOAST

You can make zweiback or "twice-baked" bread at home. So crisp and crunchy. Great for snacks or a teething baby.

2 c. milk	½ c. soft butter or
2 pkgs. active dry yeast	regular margarine
1 c. sugar	8 to 8¼ c. sifted flour
2 tsp. salt	2 eggs

Scald milk in saucepan. Cool to lukewarm in large mixing bowl. Sprinkle yeast over lukewarm milk; stir to dissolve.

Add sugar, salt, butter, 4 c. of the flour and eggs to yeast mixture. Beat with electric mixer at medium speed until smooth, about 2 minutes.

Gradually stir in enough remaining flour to make a soft dough.

Turn dough out onto floured surface. Knead until smooth and satiny, 8 to 10 minutes. Place dough in greased bowl, turning over to grease top. Cover and let rise in warm place until doubled, about 1 hour.

Punch down dough. Divide dough into 16 pieces. Let rest 10 minutes. Shape each piece into 3 × 2-inch oval-shaped roll. Place rolls on greased baking sheets, about 3 inches apart. Cover and let rise in warm place until doubled, about 1 hour.

Bake in 350⁰ oven 20 minutes or until golden brown. Remove from baking sheets; cool on racks.

Slice each roll into ½-inch slices. Place on baking sheets. Return to 250° oven 1¼ hours or until slices are golden and dry, turning 2 or 3 times. Makes 2½ lbs.

HOMEMADE PIZZA

Now you can make homemade pizza that tastes better than what you buy. Freeze ahead for last-minute quick meals.

2 pkgs. active dry yeast	1 (8-oz.) can tomato sauce
1½ c. lukewarm water (110⁰)	½ c. finely chopped onion
4½ c. sifted flour	1 clove garlic, minced
2 tblsp. sugar	½ tsp. Worcestershire sauce
2 tblsp. plus 2 tsp. baking powder	½ tsp. Tabasco sauce
1½ tsp. salt	1 tsp. dried oregano leaves
1 tsp. cream of tartar	1 lb. ground beef
1 c. shortening	1 c. grated Parmesan cheese
1 (10½-oz.) can condensed cream of mushroom soup	12 oz. mozzarella cheese, shredded
1 c. ketchup	¾ c. sliced pimiento-stuffed olives

To make pizza dough: Sprinkle yeast over lukewarm water; stir to dissolve. Sift together flour, sugar, baking powder, salt and cream of tartar in mixing bowl. Cut in shortening with pastry blender until mixture resembles coarse meal. Add yeast mixture, stirring until dough forms.

Turn dough out onto lightly floured surface. Knead lightly 10 times. Divide dough into thirds. Roll out each third on floured surface to 15 × 12-inch rectangle. Place on 3 greased baking sheets, crimping up edges to form ½-inch rim.

To make pizza filling: Combine mushroom soup, ketchup, tomato sauce, onion, garlic, Worcestershire sauce, Tabasco sauce and oregano in bowl; mix well to blend.

Quickly brown ground beef in skillet, stirring often. Remove from heat; drain off excess fat.

Spread surface of each pizza with one third of tomato sauce mixture. Top with one third of browned ground beef, one third of Parmesan cheese, one third of mozzarella cheese and one third of sliced olives.

Bake in 425⁰ oven 15 minutes or until crust is golden brown. Cut into wedges and serve immediately. Makes 3 large pizzas.

Note: Prepared pizzas can be frozen for baking later. Place pizza on baking sheet in freezer. When frozen, remove from baking sheet. Wrap pizza in aluminum foil and return to freezer. When ready to bake, remove aluminum foil. Place on baking sheet. Do not thaw. Bake in 425⁰ oven 20 minutes or until crust is golden brown.

MAPLE BUTTER TWIST

This braided coffee ring is filled with slightly chewy Maple-Walnut Filling and iced with Maple Glaze. It's absolutely delicious.

¾ c. milk, scalded	1 egg
¼ c. sugar	3½ to 3¾ c. sifted flour
3 tblsp. butter or regular margarine	Maple-Walnut Filling (recipe follows)
1½ tsp. salt	Maple Glaze (recipe follows)
1 pkg. active dry yeast	
¼ c. lukewarm water (110°)	

Pour scalded milk over sugar, butter and salt in mixing bowl. Cool to lukewarm.

Sprinkle yeast over lukewarm water; stir to dissolve.

Add egg, 1 c. of the flour and yeast mixture to milk mixture. Beat with electric mixer at medium speed until smooth, about 2 minutes.

Gradually stir in enough remaining flour to make a stiff dough.

Turn dough out onto floured surface. Knead until smooth and satiny, about 5 minutes.

Place in greased bowl, turning dough over once to grease top. Cover and let rise in warm place until doubled, about 1½ hours.

Punch down dough. Divide dough in half. Let rest 10 minutes. Roll out each half to 14 × 8-inch rectangle. Spread each with one half of Maple-Walnut Filling. Roll up like a jelly roll, starting at wide end. Cut in half lengthwise. Join together at one end. Twist the two pieces around each other several times, keeping cut side up. Shape each into a ring in 2 well-greased 8-inch round cake pans. Cover and let rise in warm place until doubled, 45 to 60 minutes.

Bake in 350° oven 30 minutes or until golden brown. Remove from pans; cool on racks. While still warm, spread tops with Maple Glaze. Makes 2 coffee cakes.

Maple-Walnut Filling: Stir ¼ c. soft butter or regular margarine in bowl until creamy. Add ½ c. chopped walnuts, ⅓ c. sugar, ½ c. brown sugar (packed), 2 tblsp. flour and ½ tsp. ground cinnamon; mix well. Add ¼ c. maple-flavored syrup and ½ tsp. maple flavoring; mix well.

Maple Glaze: Combine 1 c. sifted confectioners sugar, 1 tblsp. soft butter or regular margarine, 1 tblsp. milk and ½ tsp. maple flavoring in bowl. Beat until smooth.

Watch That Salt
Too much salt in a yeast bread inhibits the yeast growth. Measure carefully.

COCONUT CROWN COFFEE CAKE

A bubble-type coffee ring with a chewy coconut and pecan filling throughout the loaf. It's topped with a vanilla glaze.

5 to 5½ c. sifted flour	2 eggs
2 pkgs. active dry yeast	½ tsp. grated lemon rind
½ c. sugar	Brown Sugar Syrup
1 tsp. salt	(recipe follows)
¾ c. milk	1 c. flaked coconut
½ c. water	½ c. chopped pecans
½ c. butter or	Vanilla Glaze
regular margarine	(recipe follows)

Stir together 1¾ c. of the flour, undissolved yeast, sugar and salt in mixing bowl.

Heat milk, water and butter in saucepan over low heat to very warm (120-130⁰). Add to flour-yeast mixture with eggs and lemon rind. Beat with electric mixer at low speed ½ minute. Beat at high speed 3 minutes.

Gradually add enough remaining flour to make a soft dough

Turn dough out onto floured surface. Knead until smooth, 5 to 7 minutes. Cover dough; let rest 20 minutes.

Meanwhile, prepare Brown Sugar Syrup.

Divide dough into pieces to make 1¼-inch balls. Sprinkle 2 tblsp. coconut into greased 10-inch tube pan. Drizzle with ¼ c. of Brown Sugar Syrup. Arrange a layer of balls over filling so they barely touch. Top with more coconut, drizzle with more Brown Sugar Syrup and half of pecans. Arrange remaining half of dough balls in a layer. Top with remaining coconut, remaining pecans and Brown Sugar Syrup. Cover and let rise in warm place until doubled, about 1 hour. (Dough should be 1 inch from top of pan.)

Bake in 375⁰ oven 20 minutes. Cover with aluminum foil to prevent overbrowning. Continue baking 40 more minutes or until golden brown. Remove from pan immediately; cool on rack, top side up. Drizzle with Vanilla Glaze before serving. Makes 1 coffee cake.

Brown Sugar Syrup: Combine 1½ c. brown sugar (packed), 6 tblsp. evaporated milk, 6 tblsp. butter or regular margarine and 2 tblsp. light corn syrup in saucepan. Heat over low heat just until sugar is dissolved and butter is melted, stirring constantly. Cool slightly.

Vanilla Glaze: Combine 1 c. sifted confectioners sugar, 2 tblsp. milk and ¼ tsp. vanilla in bowl; stir until smooth.

LEMON CUSTARD-FILLED CRESCENT

This recipe makes three crescent-shaped coffee cakes. The creamy filling is made with sweetened condensed milk and lemon juice.

4½ to 5 c. sifted flour	½ c. water
2 pkgs. active dry yeast	¼ c. cooking oil
½ c. sugar	2 eggs
1 tsp. salt	Creamy Lemon Filling
1 tsp. grated lemon rind	(recipe follows)
½ c. milk	1½ c. chopped walnuts

Stir together 1¼ c. flour, undissolved yeast, sugar, salt and lemon rind in mixing bowl.

Heat milk, water and oil in saucepan over low heat to very warm (120-130°). Add to flour-yeast mixture all at once, beating with electric mixer at medium speed until smooth, about 2 minutes. Beat in eggs and 1 c. flour. Beat at medium speed 1 more minute.

Gradually stir in enough remaining flour to make a moderately stiff dough.

Turn dough out onto floured surface. Knead until smooth and satiny, 8 to 10 minutes. Cover with bowl. Let stand 45 minutes.

Meanwhile, prepare Creamy Lemon Filling; set aside.

Divide dough into thirds. Roll each third into 13 × 12-inch rectangle. Spread one third of Creamy Lemon Filling on each. Sprinkle one third of walnuts over filling. Roll up like a jelly roll, starting from long side. Pinch seam to seal. Place on 3 greased baking sheets.

To shape coffee cake, curve rolled dough into crescent shape. With scissors or sharp knife, snip outside edge at 1-inch intervals, cutting about 1½ inches deep. Brush with cooking oil. Cover and let rise in warm place until doubled, 35 to 40 minutes.

Bake in 350° oven 25 minutes or until golden brown. Remove from baking sheets; cool on racks. While still warm, drizzle with your favorite glaze if you wish. Serve warm. Makes 3 coffee cakes.

Creamy Lemon Filling: Place 1 (14-oz.) can sweetened condensed milk in bowl. Gradually stir in ⅓ c. lemon juice, stirring until blended.

DANISH KRINGLE

This coffee cake has a flaky texture much like Danish pastry. The recipe was given to a Wisconsin farm woman by her grandmother.

4 c. sifted flour	4 egg yolks
2 tblsp. sugar	2 egg whites, stiffly beaten
1 tsp. salt	Almond Filling (recipe
1 c. shortening	follows)
1 c. milk, scalded	Vanilla Glaze (recipe
1 pkg. active dry yeast	follows)

Sift together flour, sugar and salt into mixing bowl. Cut in shortening until mixture looks like coarse meal.

Cool scalded milk to lukewarm. Sprinkle yeast over milk; stir to dissolve. Add egg yolks; beat with fork until blended.

Add milk mixture to flour mixture, mixing well with fork. (No kneading is necessary.)

Place dough in greased bowl, turning over once to grease top.

Cover and let rise in warm place until doubled, about 1½ hours.

Punch down dough. Divide dough into thirds. Let rest 10 minutes. Roll each third to 16 × 9-inch rectangle. Transfer to 3 greased baking sheets.

For each coffee cake, spread one third of beaten egg whites lengthwise in center of dough to within 2½ inches of long sides. Spoon one third of Almond Filling over egg whites. Fold one long side to center and then fold other side to center, overlapping 2 inches. Pinch edges to seal.

Cover and let rise in warm place until dough looks light, about 45 minutes.

Bake in 400° oven 18 minutes or until golden brown. Remove from baking sheets; cool on racks. Ice with Vanilla Glaze. Makes 3 coffee cakes.

Almond Filling: Combine 1½ c. ground blanched almonds, 1 c. sugar, ¾ c. soft butter or regular margarine and 1½ tsp. almond extract in bowl. Mix until blended.

Vanilla Glaze: Combine 1½ c. sifted confectioners sugar, 2 tblsp. milk and ½ tsp. vanilla in bowl. Stir until smooth.

Breads Made with Milk
Breads that are made with milk could take a little longer to bake than those made with water, because of the milk protein and milk solids. You may have to cover the loaves with brown wrapping paper during the last half of the baking period to prevent the surface from becoming too dark before the interior of the bread is done.

WHOLE WHEAT MAPLE RING

This whole wheat coffee cake has a hint of honey flavor. The pecan filling features brown sugar, cinnamon and maple flavoring.

3¼ to 3½ c. sifted flour	2 c. stirred whole wheat flour
2 pkgs. active dry yeast	
2 tsp. salt	3 tblsp. melted butter or regular margarine
½ tsp. ground nutmeg	
¾ c. milk	Pecan Filling (recipe follows)
½ c. water	
¼ c. cooking oil	Vanilla Glaze (recipe follows)
½ c. honey	
2 eggs	

Stir together 2 c. of the flour, undissolved yeast, salt and nutmeg in mixing bowl.

Heat milk, water, oil and honey in saucepan over low heat until very warm (120-130°). Gradually add to flour-yeast mixture, beating with electric mixer at medium speed 2 minutes. Beat in eggs and 1 c. of the whole wheat flour. Beat at medium speed 1 minute more. Let rest 5 minutes.

Gradually stir in remaining 1 c. whole wheat flour and enough remaining flour to make a soft dough.

Turn dough out onto floured surface. Knead until smooth and satiny, 8 to 10 minutes.

Place dough in greased bowl, turning once to grease top. Cover and let rise in warm place until doubled, about 1½ hours.

Punch down dough. Divide dough in half. Let rest 10 minutes. Roll out each half to 15 × 8-inch rectangle. Brush each with 1 tblsp. melted butter.

Prepare Pecan Filling. Sprinkle one half of Pecan Filling over each dough rectangle. Roll up like a jelly roll, starting at wide end. Pinch edge to seal.

Form into a ring and place on 2 greased baking sheets. With scissors or sharp knife, cut through ring almost to center at 1-inch intervals. Turn each slice over on its side. Brush both coffee cakes with remaining melted butter. Cover and let rise in warm place until doubled, 30 to 45 minutes.

Bake in 350° oven 25 minutes or until golden brown. Remove from baking sheets; cool on racks. While still warm, drizzle with Vanilla Glaze. Makes 2 coffee cakes.

Pecan Filling: Combine ½ c. brown sugar (packed), ½ c. chopped pecans, 1 tblsp. ground cinnamon and 1 tsp. maple flavoring in bowl; mix well.

Vanilla Glaze: Combine 1 c. sifted confectioners sugar, 1 tblsp. melted butter or regular margarine, 1½ tblsp. milk, 1 tsp. vanilla and pinch of salt in bowl. Mix until smooth.

GREEK ORANGE BRAID

Do not ice this bread if you plan to freeze it. Top with the tangy orange glaze after the coffee cake thaws.

5 to 5¼ c. sifted flour	2 eggs
1 pkg. active dry yeast	3 tblsp. orange juice
1 c. milk	1 tblsp. grated orange rind
½ c. butter or	Orange Icing (recipe
regular margarine	follows)
½ c. sugar	¼ c. toasted slivered
1 tsp. salt	almonds

Combine 1 c. of the flour and undissolved yeast in large mixing bowl.

Scald milk in saucepan. Add butter, sugar and salt. Cool to very warm (120-130º).

Add milk mixture to flour-yeast mixture. Beat with electric mixer at medium speed until smooth, about 2 minutes. Add eggs and 1 c. flour, orange juice and orange rind. Beat at high speed 2 minutes more.

Gradually stir in enough remaining flour to make a soft dough.

Turn dough out onto floured surface. Knead until smooth and satiny, 8 to 10 minutes. Place dough in greased bowl, turning over to grease top. Cover and let rise in warm place until doubled, 1¼ to 1½ hours.

Punch down dough. Divide in half. Let rest 10 minutes. Divide each half into 3 pieces. Roll each piece into 14-inch rope. Press ends of 3 ropes together; braid together. Braid remaining 3 ropes. Place on 2 greased baking sheets, tucking ends under. Cover and let rise in warm place until doubled, 50 to 60 minutes.

Bake in 375º oven 20 minutes or until golden brown. Remove from baking sheets; cool on racks. Drizzle with Orange Icing. Sprinkle with almonds. Makes 2 coffee cakes.

Orange Icing: Combine 1½ c. sifted confectioners sugar and 2 tblsp. orange juice in bowl. Beat with spoon until smooth.

SWEDISH TEA RING

An Indiana farm woman has traditionally made these lovely rings to give as Christmas gifts to relatives and friends for the last 10 years.

½ c. milk, scalded	4½ to 4¾ c. sifted flour
½ c. sugar	2 eggs
¼ c. butter or	3 tblsp. melted butter
regular margarine	or regular margarine
1½ tsp. salt	Pecan Filling (recipe
2 pkgs. active dry yeast	follows)
½ c. lukewarm	Vanilla Glaze (recipe
water (110°)	follows)

Pour scalded milk over sugar, ¼ c. butter and salt in large mixing bowl. Cool to lukewarm.

Sprinkle yeast over lukewarm water; stir to dissolve.

Add yeast mixture, 2 c. of the flour and eggs to milk mixture. Beat with electric mixer at medium speed until smooth, about 2 minutes.

Gradually stir in enough remaining flour to make a soft dough.

Turn dough out onto floured surface. Knead dough until smooth and satiny, about 8 minutes. Place dough in greased bowl, turning over to grease top. Cover and let rise in warm place until doubled, 1 to 1¼ hours.

Punch down dough. Divide in half. Let rest 10 minutes. Roll out each half to 14 × 7-inch rectangle. Brush each with one half of melted butter. Sprinkle with Pecan Filling. Roll up tightly like jelly roll, starting at wide end. Pinch edges to seal. With sealed edge down, shape in rings on 2 greased baking sheets. Pinch edges together. Snip dough with scissors from edge of circle two thirds of the way to center at 1-inch intervals. Turn cut pieces on their sides. Cover and let rise in warm place until doubled, about 45 minutes.

Bake in 350° oven 25 minutes or until golden brown. Remove from baking sheets; cool on racks. While still warm, frost with Vanilla Glaze. Makes 2 rings.

Pecan Filling: Combine ½ c. chopped pecans, ½ c. sugar and 1 tsp. ground cinnamon in bowl; mix well.

Vanilla Glaze: Combine 1½ c. sifted confectioners sugar, 2 tblsp. milk and ½ tsp. vanilla in bowl. Beat with spoon until smooth.

Fruits 'n' Nuts
Fruits and nuts add nutritive value and flavor to yeast breads. They often tend to make the mixture heavier so that the rising time may take longer.

RAISIN SPICE TEA RING

A popular coffee cake in our Countryside Test Kitchens—every last crumb disappeared in just a few minutes.

1½ c. milk, scalded	1½ c. quick-cooking oats
½ c. sugar	1 egg
¾ c. butter or regular margarine	¾ c. melted butter or regular margarine
2½ tsp. salt	Cinnamon-Raisin Filling (recipe follows)
2 pkgs. active dry yeast	Vanilla Icing (recipe follows)
½ c. lukewarm water (110⁰)	
5 c. sifted flour	

Pour scalded milk over sugar, ¾ c. butter and salt in large mixing bowl. Cool to lukewarm.

Sprinkle yeast over lukewarm water; stir to dissolve.

Add yeast mixture, 1 c. of the flour, oats and egg to milk mixture. Beat with electric mixer at medium speed until smooth, about 2 minutes.

Gradually stir in enough remaining flour to make a soft dough.

Turn dough out onto floured surface. Knead until smooth and satiny, 8 to 10 minutes. Place dough in greased bowl, turning over to grease top. Cover and let rise in warm place until doubled, about 1 hour.

Punch down dough. Divide dough in half. Let rest 10 minutes. Roll out each half to 18 × 12-inch rectangle. Brush each with ¼ c. melted butter. Sprinkle each with one half of Cinnamon-Raisin Filling. Roll up tightly like a jelly roll, starting at long side. Pinch edge to seal.

Form into a circle on greased baking sheet, pinching ends together. Snip dough with scissors from edge of circle two thirds of the way to center at 1-inch intervals. Turn cut pieces on their sides. Brush each ring with 2 tblsp. melted butter. Cover and let rise until doubled, about 1 hour.

Bake in 350⁰ oven 25 to 30 minutes or until golden brown. Remove from baking sheets; cool on racks. While still warm, drizzle with Vanilla Icing. Makes 2 rings.

Cinnamon-Raisin Filling: Combine ½ c. melted butter or regular margarine, 1 c. sugar, 1¾ c. raisins, 1 c. chopped pecans and 4 tsp. ground cinnamon in bowl. Mix well.

Vanilla Icing: Combine 1½ c. sifted confectioners sugar, 5 tsp. milk and ½ tsp. vanilla in bowl. Beat with spoon until smooth.

BRAIDED GERMAN SWEET BREAD

This extra-large lemon-scented coffee bread serves 30 people. You can stir raisins into the dough, too, if you like.

2 c. milk, scalded	2 tblsp. lemon juice
½ c. butter or	1 tsp. grated lemon rind
regular margarine	4 tsp. ground cinnamon
⅓ c. sugar	½ c. sugar
2 tsp. salt	¼ c. melted butter or
2 pkgs. active dry yeast	regular margarine
¼ c. lukewarm	Confectioners Sugar
water (110°)	Icing (recipe follows)
7 to 7¼ c. sifted flour	2 tblsp. chopped walnuts
2 eggs	Maraschino cherry halves

Pour scalded milk over ½ c. butter, ⅓ c. sugar and salt in large mixing bowl. Cool to lukewarm.

Sprinkle yeast over lukewarm water; stir to dissolve.

Add yeast mixture, 3 c. of the flour, eggs, lemon juice and lemon rind to milk mixture. Beat with electric mixer at medium speed until smooth, about 2 minutes.

Gradually stir in enough remaining flour to make a soft dough that is no longer sticky.

Turn dough out onto floured surface. Knead until smooth and satiny, about 10 minutes. Place dough in greased bowl, turning dough once to grease top. Cover and let rise in warm place until doubled, about 1 hour.

Combine cinnamon and ½ c. sugar; mix well. Set aside.

Punch down dough. Let rest 10 minutes. Roll out dough to 18 × 15-inch rectangle. Cut into thirds, making 3 (15 × 6-inch) rectangles. Brush with ¼ c. melted butter. Sprinkle with cinnamon-sugar mixture. Roll up each piece tightly like a jelly roll, starting at wide end.

To form braid, place 3 strips diagonally on greased baking sheet, joining at one end. Braid 3 strips together, tucking ends under. Cover and let rise in warm place until doubled, 20 to 30 minutes.

Bake in 350° oven 30 minutes or until golden brown. Remove from baking sheet; cool on rack. While still warm, ice with Confectioners Sugar Icing. Decorate with chopped walnuts and maraschino cherry halves. Makes 1 extra-large coffee cake.

Confectioners Sugar Icing: Combine 1½ c. sifted confectioners sugar, 5 tsp. milk and ½ tsp. vanilla in bowl. Beat with spoon until smooth.

CHRISTMAS EVE SAFFRON BRAID

Very tender yeast coffee cake with a pale yellow color because it's flavored with a little bit of saffron.

1 c. milk, scalded	1 egg
½ c. sugar	½ tsp. ground cardamom
2 tblsp. butter or regular margarine	4¼ c. sifted flour
	Icing (recipe follows)
½ tsp. salt	Candied red and green cherries
¹⁄₁₆ tsp. powdered saffron	
1 pkg. active dry yeast	Toasted slivered almonds
¼ c. lukewarm water (110⁰)	

Pour scalded milk over sugar, butter, salt and saffron in mixing bowl. Cool to lukewarm.

Sprinkle yeast over lukewarm water; stir to dissolve. Add yeast mixture, egg, cardamom and 1 c. of the flour to milk mixture. Beat with electric mixer at medium speed until smooth, about 2 minutes.

Gradually stir in enough remaining flour to make a soft dough.

Turn dough out onto floured surface. Knead until smooth and satiny, about 5 minutes. Place in lightly greased bowl, turning to grease top. Cover and let rise in warm place until doubled, about 1½ hours.

Punch down dough. Divide dough into thirds. Let rest 10 minutes. Shape each third into 21-inch rope. Place 3 ropes on greased baking sheet, joining at one end. Braid 3 ropes together; pinch ends to seal. Let rise in warm place until doubled, about 1 hour.

Bake in 350⁰ oven 25 minutes or until golden brown. Remove from baking sheet; cool on rack. While warm, drizzle with Icing. Decorate with cherries and almonds. Makes 1 loaf.

Icing: Combine 1 c. sifted confectioners sugar, 1 tblsp. milk and ½ tsp. vanilla in bowl. Beat until smooth.

Flour Storage
Store flour in a clean, airtight container in a cool dry place to maintain maximum freshness.

CHRISTMAS COFFEE RING

If you wish to give this coffee cake a special holiday look, decorate with bits of candied pineapple and leaves cut from green cherries.

1 c. buttermilk	2 eggs
¼ c. shortening	2 tblsp. melted butter
⅓ c. sugar	or regular margarine
1½ tsp. salt	Honey Filling (recipe
2 pkgs. active dry yeast	follows)
¼ c. lukewarm	Vanilla Glaze (recipe
water (110°)	follows)
4½ c. sifted flour	Red maraschino cherries

Heat buttermilk in saucepan until warm. Combine buttermilk, shortening, sugar and salt in mixing bowl.

Sprinkle yeast over lukewarm water; stir to dissolve. Add yeast mixture and 2 c. of the flour to buttermilk mixture. Beat with electric mixer at medium speed 2 minutes or until smooth. Blend in eggs.

Gradually add enough remaining flour to make a soft dough.

Turn dough out onto floured surface. Knead dough until smooth and satiny, about 5 minutes. Place in greased bowl, turning to grease top. Cover and let rise until doubled, about 1 hour.

Punch down dough. Divide in half. Let rest 10 minutes. Roll out one half to 10-inch square. Brush with butter. Top with one half of Honey Filling. Roll up like jelly roll; pinch edge. Cut in 1-inch slices. Layer slices, cut side down, in greased 10-inch tube pan with solid bottom. Repeat with remaining dough. Cover; let rise until dough reaches the top of pan, about 1 hour.

Bake in 350° oven 25 minutes. Cover with aluminum foil to prevent overbrowning. Bake 20 more minutes or until golden brown. Remove from pan; cool on rack. Drizzle with Vanilla Glaze; decorate with cherries. Makes 12 servings.

Honey Filling: Combine ⅓ c. raisins, ⅓ c. chopped walnuts, ¼ c. sugar, 1 tsp. ground cinnamon, 1 tblsp. grated orange rind, 1 tblsp. orange juice and ½ c. honey in bowl; mix well.

Vanilla Glaze: Combine 1 c. sifted confectioners sugar, 1 tblsp. milk and 1 tsp. vanilla in bowl; beat until smooth.

GRANDMA'S CINNAMON BUBBLE RING

"Whenever I make this pretty bubble coffee ring, it doesn't last too long. My family loves it," an Illinois farm woman assured us.

1½ c. milk, scalded	5½ c. sifted flour
½ c. sugar	1 egg
¼ c. butter or	¾ c. sugar
regular margarine	1 tblsp. ground cinnamon
½ tsp. salt	¼ c. melted butter or
1 pkg. active dry yeast	regular margarine
¼ c. lukewarm	
water (110°)	

Pour scalded milk over ½ c. sugar, ¼ c. butter and salt in mixing bowl. Cool to lukewarm.

Sprinkle yeast over lukewarm water; stir to dissolve.

Add yeast mixture, 3 c. of the flour and egg to milk mixture. Beat with electric mixer at medium speed 2 minutes, scraping bowl occasionally.

Gradually stir in enough remaining flour to make a soft dough. Cover and let rise in warm place until doubled, about 1 to 1½ hours.

Meanwhile, combine ¾ c. sugar and 1 tblsp. cinnamon in bowl; mix well. Set aside.

Punch down dough. Place dough on floured surface. Toss dough gently a few times to make dough easier to handle. Divide dough in half. Let rest 10 minutes. Cut each half into 28 equal-sized pieces. Shape each piece into a ball. Roll in ¼ c. melted butter and then coat with sugar-cinnamon mixture. Arrange balls in greased 10-inch tube pan with a solid bottom, making 2 to 3 layers. Cover and let rise in warm place until almost doubled, about 45 minutes.

Bake in 375° oven 40 minutes or until golden brown. Immediately remove from pan; cool on rack. Makes 1 coffee cake.

EXTRA-LARGE HONEY-MAPLE COFFEE CAKE

An Indiana farm woman has received two Purple Sweepstakes Ribbons and other prizes for this extra-special maple-flavored coffee cake.

1 pkg. active dry yeast	½ c. butter or
¼ c. lukewarm	regular margarine
water (110°)	2 tblsp. honey
1 c. heavy cream	6 tblsp. butter or
3 egg yolks,	regular margarine
slightly beaten	Maple-Cinnamon Filling
2 tsp. maple flavoring	(recipe follows)
3⅔ c. sifted flour	Honey Glaze (recipe
¼ c. sugar	follows)
1 tsp. salt	

Sprinkle yeast over lukewarm water in small bowl; stir to dissolve. Add heavy cream, egg yolks and maple flavoring; mix well.

Sift together flour, sugar and salt into mixing bowl. Cut in ½ c. butter with pastry blender until mixture forms coarse crumbs. Stir in cream mixture, mixing just until moistened. Cover with plastic wrap and refrigerate overnight.

Combine honey and 6 tblsp. butter in small saucepan. Heat over low heat until butter is melted. Remove from heat; cool to room temperature.

Prepare Maple-Cinnamon Filling; set aside.

Turn dough out onto floured surface. Divide dough into thirds. Remove one third of dough and keep remaining dough refrigerated. Roll out one third of dough into 12-inch circle. Place in greased 14-inch pizza pan or on baking sheet. Brush with one third of butter-honey mixture and sprinkle with one third of Maple-Cinnamon Filling. Roll out another one third of dough and place over first layer. Brush with butter-honey mixture and sprinkle with Maple-Cinnamon Filling. Repeat layers, ending with Maple-Cinnamon Filling.

Place a 2-inch cookie or biscuit cutter in center of dough to use as a cutting guide. Cut dough into 16 wedges, using sharp knife or scissors, from edge of circle to edge of cookie cutter in center. Be sure to cut through all three layers of dough. Seal wide ends of wedges by pinching dough layers together. Remove cookie cutter.

Picking up the wide end of 1 wedge, gently twist several times to form a corkscrew shape and lay down on pizza pan or baking sheet. Repeat this twisting procedure with all the wedges. Cover and let rise in warm place until almost doubled, about 1¼ hours.

Bake in 350° oven 25 minutes or until golden brown. Remove from pizza pan or baking sheet by loosening around edges with a metal spatula. Invert coffee cake on another baking sheet. Place cooling rack on bottom of coffee cake and turn it over so that coffee cake is right side up on cooling rack. While still warm, drizzle with Honey Glaze. Makes 1 large coffee cake.

Maple-Cinnamon Filling: Combine 1 c. sugar, ⅔ c. finely chopped pecans, 2 tsp. maple flavoring and 2 tsp. ground cinnamon in bowl; mix well.

Honey Glaze: Combine 1 c. sifted confectioners sugar, 2 tsp. honey, 1 tblsp. milk and 1 tsp. maple flavoring in bowl; beat until smooth.

RUSSIAN KULICH

A traditional Easter bread from Russia. It's baked in coffee cans and the top is said to resemble an old Russian church dome.

2¾ to 3 c. sifted flour	1 egg
¼ c. sugar	¼ c. chopped blanched
1 tsp. salt	almonds
1 tsp. grated lemon rind	¼ c. raisins
1 pkg. active dry yeast	Confectioners Sugar Icing
½ c. milk	(recipe follows)
¼ c. water	Multi-colored confection
2 tblsp. butter or	decorations
regular margarine	

Combine ¾ c. of the flour, sugar, salt, lemon rind and undissolved yeast in large mixing bowl; mix thoroughly.

Combine milk, water and butter in saucepan. Heat over low heat until very warm (120-130⁰). Gradually add to flour-yeast mixture, beating with electric mixer at medium speed 2 minutes, scraping bowl occasionally. Add egg and ¾ c. of the flour; beat at high speed 2 minutes.

Stir in almonds, raisins and enough remaining flour to make a soft dough.

Turn dough out onto lightly floured surface. Knead until smooth and elastic, about 10 minutes.

Place dough in greased bowl, turning over once to grease top. Cover and let rise in warm place until doubled, about 1 hour.

Punch down dough. Divide dough in half. Let rest 10 minutes. Shape each half into a ball. Place in 2 greased 1-lb. coffee cans. Cover and let rise until doubled, about 1 hour.

Bake in 350⁰ oven 30 to 35 minutes or until golden brown. Remove from cans; cool on racks.

When cool, frost tops of loaves with Confectioners Sugar Icing, letting icing drip down sides of kulich. Sprinkle top with multi-colored confection decorations. Serve warm or cold. Makes 2 loaves.

Confectioners Sugar Icing: Combine 1¼ c. sifted confectioners sugar, ¼ tsp. vanilla and 4 tsp. milk in bowl. Blend until smooth.

ITALIAN PANETTONE

This Italian coffee cake is also delicious toasted and spread with butter or cream cheese. It was very popular in our test kitchens.

4½ to 5½ c. sifted flour	3 eggs
½ c. sugar	½ c. mixed candied fruit
1 tsp. salt	½ c. raisins
2 pkgs. active dry yeast	1 egg, slightly beaten
½ c. milk	1 tblsp. water
½ c. water	
½ c. butter or	
regular margarine	

Combine 1½ c. of the flour, sugar, salt and undissolved yeast in mixing bowl; mix thoroughly.

Combine milk, ½ c. water and butter in saucepan. Heat to very warm (120-130⁰). Gradually add to flour-yeast mixture, beating with electric mixer at medium speed 2 minutes. Add 3 eggs and ½ c. of the flour. Beat at high speed 2 minutes. Stir in candied fruit and raisins.

Gradually add enough remaining flour to make a soft dough.

Turn dough out onto floured surface. Knead until smooth and elastic, about 8 to 10 minutes.

Place in greased bowl, turning over once to grease top. Cover and let rise in warm place until doubled, about 1 hour.

Punch down dough. Cover and let rise until doubled, about 30 minutes.

Punch down dough. Divide in half. Let rest 10 minutes. Form each half into a ball. Place on opposite corners of greased baking sheet. Cover and let rise in warm place until doubled, about 1 hour.

Beat together 1 egg and 1 tblsp. water. Brush egg mixture on top of loaves.

Bake in 350⁰ oven 30 to 35 minutes or until golden brown. Remove from baking sheet; cool on racks. Serve warm or cold. Makes 2 coffee cakes.

Measuring Liquids
To measure liquids, put the measuring cup on a level surface. Otherwise, the surface of the liquid will slant and give a wrong perspective. Bend down to measure at eye level and fill until the liquid flows to the correct mark.

FOUR-IN-ONE YEAST ROLLS

You can choose from four different flavored fillings when you make this sweet dough. Each filling is enough for one fourth of the dough.

3 pkgs. active dry yeast	⅓ c. sugar
⅓ c. sugar	4 tsp. salt
1 c. lukewarm water (110°)	1 c. water
	13 to 13½ c. sifted flour
2 c. milk	4 eggs
½ c. butter or regular margarine	Vanilla Icing (recipe follows)
¼ c. lard	

Combine yeast, ⅓ c. sugar and 1 c. lukewarm water in large mixing bowl. Mix well. Let stand 20 minutes in warm place until foamy.

Scald milk in saucepan. Stir in butter, lard, ⅓ c. sugar and salt. Stir until butter and lard are melted. Add 1 c. water; cool to lukewarm.

Add milk mixture to yeast mixture with 5 c. of the flour and eggs. Beat with electric mixer at medium speed until smooth, about 2 minutes.

Gradually add enough remaining flour to make a soft dough.

Turn dough out onto floured surface. Knead until smooth and satiny, 8 to 10 minutes.

Place dough in very large greased bowl (6-qt.), turning over once to grease top. Cover and let rise in warm place until doubled, about 1 hour. Punch down dough. Divide dough in fourths. Shape and fill dough as desired according to the variations that follow.

Cover and let rise in warm place until doubled, about 45 minutes.

Bake in 375° oven 15 minutes or until golden brown. Remove from baking sheets; cool on racks. Drizzle with Vanilla Icing. Makes 48.

Variations:

Raspberry/Almond Rolls: Divide one fourth of the dough into 12 equal-sized pieces. Roll each piece into a 14-inch rope, by rolling back and forth on floured surface, using your hands. Place one end of rope in center and wind dough pinwheel fashion. Place on greased baking sheets, about 2 inches apart. Tuck loose end under. Combine ¾ c. raspberry preserves and ¼ c. sliced almonds in small bowl; mix well. Make an impression in center of each roll by pulling dough gently with fingers. Fill with a teaspoonful of raspberry filling.

Pineapple Coconut Rolls: Using one fourth of dough, shape as directed in Raspberry/Almond variation. Combine ¾ c. pineapple preserves and ⅓ c. flaked coconut in bowl; mix well. Fill as directed in Raspberry/Almond variation.

Prune-filled Rolls: Combine ¾ c. chopped prunes and ¾ c. water in small saucepan. Bring to a boil. Simmer, uncovered, 10 minutes. Drain prunes well. Mash with fork until smooth. Stir in ⅓ c. brown sugar, packed. Cool completely. Using one fourth of the dough, shape and fill as directed for Raspberry/Almond variation.

Orange Butterfly Rolls: Roll out one fourth of the dough on floured surface to 12 × 9-inch rectangle. Combine ¼ c. flour, ⅓ c. sugar and 1 tblsp. grated orange rind in bowl; mix well. Cut in 3 tblsp. soft butter or regular margarine until mixture forms coarse crumbs. Sprinkle evenly over dough. Roll up like a jelly roll, starting at wide end. Cut into 12 (1-inch) slices. Do not turn rolls cut side down, but leave slice standing on end. Crease each roll heavily across center with dull edge of knife. Place on greased baking sheets, about 2 inches apart.

Vanilla Icing: Combine 3½ c. sifted confectioners sugar, 4 tblsp. milk and 1 tsp. vanilla in bowl; beat until smooth.

SWEET SQUASH BUNS

A Washington farm woman often serves these tender rolls for dinner without the thin confectioners sugar glaze.

1 c. milk, scalded	1 pkg. active dry yeast
1 (12-oz.) pkg. frozen mashed squash, thawed (1¼ c.)	¼ c. lukewarm water (110⁰)
1 c. sugar	6 to 6¼ c. sifted flour
¼ c. butter or regular margarine	1 tblsp. melted butter or regular margarine
½ tsp. salt	Confectioners Sugar Glaze (recipe follows)

Pour scalded milk over squash, sugar, ¼ c. butter and salt in mixing bowl. Let cool to lukewarm.

Sprinkle yeast over lukewarm water; stir to dissolve.

Add 2 c. of the flour and yeast mixture to milk mixture. Beat with electric mixer at medium speed until smooth, about 2 minutes.

Gradually stir in enough remaining flour to make a stiff dough. (No kneading is necessary.)

Place in greased bowl, turning once to grease top. Cover and let rise in warm place until doubled, about 1 hour.

Punch down dough. Turn out onto floured surface. Toss lightly until dough is no longer sticky.

Divide dough in half. Let rest 10 minutes. Shape each half into 12 balls. Place in 2 greased 9-inch round cake pans, 12 rolls equally spaced in each pan. Brush tops of rolls with 1 tblsp. melted butter. Cover and let rise in warm place until doubled, about 45 minutes.

Bake in 375⁰ oven 30 minutes or until golden brown. Remove from pans; cool on racks. While still warm, drizzle with Confectioners Sugar Glaze. Makes 24.

Confectioners Sugar Glaze: Combine 1 c. sifted confectioners sugar, ¼ tsp. vanilla and 1 tblsp. milk in bowl. Stir until smooth.

BOHEMIAN KOLACHES

"The secret to a good kolache is to have the dough as soft as possible, a quick oven and practice," a Nebraska woman of Czech descent said.

2 c. milk, scalded	7¾ c. sifted flour
¾ c. sugar	3 egg yolks
⅔ c. butter or regular margarine	Cottage Cheese Filling (recipe follows)
2 tsp. salt	Apricot Filling
2 pkgs. active dry yeast	(recipe follows)
¼ c. lukewarm water (110°)	

Pour scalded milk over sugar, butter and salt in mixing bowl. Let cool to lukewarm.

Sprinkle yeast over lukewarm water; stir to dissolve.

Add 2 c. of the flour, egg yolks and yeast mixture to milk mixture. Beat with electric mixer at medium speed until smooth, about 2 minutes. Cover and let rest in warm place until bubbly, about 40 minutes.

Gradually stir in enough remaining flour to form a soft dough.

Turn dough out onto floured surface. Knead until smooth and satiny, 8 to 10 minutes.

Place in greased bowl, turning over once to grease top. Cover and let rise until doubled, about 1½ hours.

Punch down dough. Divide dough into fourths. Let rest 10 minutes. Shape each fourth into 12 balls. Place on greased baking sheets, about 2 inches apart. Make a deep depression in center of each ball, using fingers. Fill with Cottage Cheese Filling or Apricot Filling. Cover and let rise in warm place until almost doubled, about 30 minutes.

Bake in 375° oven 15 minutes or until golden brown. Remove from baking sheets; cool on racks. Makes 48.

Cottage Cheese Filling: Combine 1½ c. large curd cottage cheese (12 oz.), 6 tblsp. sugar, 1 egg yolk, 1 tblsp. quick tapioca and ¾ tsp. lemon extract in bowl. Mix until blended. Place a few raisins in each roll (you will need 1 c. raisins). Top with a small teaspoonful of cheese filling. Makes enough filling for 48 rolls.

Apricot Filling: Combine ⅓ c. unsifted flour and ⅓ c. brown sugar (packed) in bowl. Cut in 2 tblsp. butter or regular margarine until mixture is crumbly. Fill each roll with 1 tsp. of apricot preserves (you will need 1 c. preserves). Sprinkle each with crumb mixture. Makes enough filling and topping for 48 rolls.

Greasing Pans
To grease pans, dip a pastry brush or a little crumpled paper into shortening and rub over inside of pan to cover bottom and corners well. Or use a butter wrapper for extra flavor and to use up every bit of butter.

BUTTERSCOTCH CRESCENT ROLLS

"I've been taking these delicious rolls to church suppers for 10 years now and I seldom ever get one to eat," a Kansas farm woman told us.

1 (3¾-oz.) pkg. butterscotch pudding and pie filling mix	4½ to 5 c. sifted flour
1 (13-oz.) can evaporated milk	1 tsp. salt
¼ c. butter or regular margarine	2 eggs
2 pkgs. active dry yeast	Coconut Filling (recipe follows)
¼ c. lukewarm water (110°)	Brown Sugar Glaze (recipe follows)

Combine pudding mix and evaporated milk in 2-qt. saucepan. Cook over medium heat, stirring constantly, until mixture thickens and comes to a boil. Remove from heat; add butter and cool to lukewarm.

Sprinkle yeast over lukewarm water in mixing bowl. Stir to dissolve.

Add cooled pudding, 1 c. of the flour, salt and eggs to yeast mixture. Beat with electric mixer at medium speed until smooth, about 2 minutes.

Gradually stir in enough remaining flour to make a soft dough.

Turn dough out onto floured surface. Knead until smooth and elastic, 5 to 8 minutes. Place in greased bowl, turning over once to grease top. Cover and let rise in warm place until doubled, about 1 hour.

Meanwhile, prepare Coconut Filling; set aside.

Punch down dough. Divide into fourths. Let rest 10 minutes. Roll each fourth to 9-inch circle. Cut each circle into 8 wedges. Place a rounded teaspoonful of Coconut Filling on each wedge. Roll up from wide end. Place point down on greased baking sheets, about 2 inches apart. Shape into crescents. Cover and let rise in warm place until almost doubled, about 30 to 45 minutes.

Bake in 375° oven 10 minutes or until golden brown. Remove from baking sheets; cool on racks. While still warm, frost with Brown Sugar Glaze. Makes 32.

Coconut Filling: Combine ½ c. flaked coconut, ⅔ c. brown sugar (packed), ⅓ c. chopped pecans, 2 tblsp. flour and ¼ c. melted butter or regular margarine in bowl. Mix until blended.

Brown Sugar Glaze: Combine ¼ c. brown sugar (packed), 2 tblsp. evaporated milk and 2 tblsp. butter or regular margarine in 1-qt. saucepan; mix well. Bring mixture to a boil, stirring constantly. Boil 1 minute. Remove from heat and stir in 1 c. sifted confectioners sugar and 1 more tblsp. evaporated milk. Beat until smooth.

CREAM CHEESE-FILLED ROLLS

These cream cheese-filled rolls hint of lemon and nutmeg. Not too sweet. They were well liked in our test kitchens.

1 c. milk, scalded	1 tsp. grated lemon rind
1 c. sugar	¼ tsp. ground nutmeg
⅔ c. butter or	3 eggs
regular margarine	Cream Cheese Filling
1 tsp. salt	(recipe follows)
2 pkgs. active dry yeast	1 egg white
¼ c. lukewarm	2 tsp. water
water (110⁰)	½ tsp. ground cinnamon
6¼ to 6½ c. sifted flour	½ c. sugar

Pour scalded milk over sugar, butter and salt in mixing bowl. Cool to lukewarm.

Sprinkle yeast over lukewarm water; stir to dissolve.

Add yeast mixture and 2 c. of the flour to milk mixture. Beat with electric mixer at medium speed until smooth, about 2 minutes. Add lemon rind, nutmeg and eggs. Beat 2 more minutes at medium speed.

Gradually stir in enough remaining flour to make a soft dough.

Turn dough out onto floured surface. Knead until smooth and elastic, about 8 minutes. Place dough in greased bowl, turning over once to grease top. Cover and let rise in warm place until doubled, about 1½ hours.

Meanwhile, prepare Cream Cheese Filling.

Punch down dough. Divide dough into thirds. Let rest 10 minutes. Roll out each third to 10½-inch square. Cut in 9 squares. Place dough on greased baking sheets, about 3 inches apart. Place a rounded teaspoonful of Cream Cheese Filling in center of each square. Fold one point over to form triangle. Press edges lightly to seal. Cover and let rise in warm place until doubled, about 30 minutes.

Beat together egg white and 2 tsp. water until blended. Brush tops of rolls with egg white mixture. Combine cinnamon and ½ c. sugar. Sprinkle over each roll.

Bake in 350⁰ oven 12 to 15 minutes or until golden brown. Remove from baking sheets; cool on racks. Serve warm or cold. Makes 27.

Cream Cheese Filling: Combine 1 (8-oz.) pkg. softened cream cheese, ¼ c. sugar and 1 egg in mixing bowl. Beat with electric mixer at medium speed until smooth and creamy, about 2 minutes.

VERSATILE POTATO ROLLS

This superb roll recipe can be made into lovely cinnamon rolls or festive sticky buns. Both are delicious.

2 pkgs. active dry yeast	5 eggs
2 c. lukewarm water (110°)	6 tblsp. butter or regular margarine, melted
2 c. warm mashed potatoes	1½ c. sugar
1 c. shortening, melted and cooled	1 tblsp. ground cinnamon
1 c. sugar	1½ c. raisins
1 tblsp. salt	Vanilla Icing (recipe follows)
12 to 13 c. sifted flour	

Sprinkle yeast over lukewarm water in large mixing bowl; stir to dissolve.

Add mashed potatoes, cooled shortening, 1 c. sugar, salt, 4 c. of the flour and eggs to yeast mixture. Beat with electric mixer at medium speed 2 minutes. Transfer to 6-qt. mixing bowl.

Gradually stir in enough remaining flour to make a soft dough. Cover and let rise in warm place until doubled, about 1 hour.

Punch down dough. Divide into thirds. Let rest 10 minutes. Roll each third into 14 × 10-inch rectangle. Brush each with one third of melted butter.

Combine 1½ c. sugar and cinnamon in small bowl. Sprinkle one third of mixture over each rectangle. Top each with one third of raisins. Roll up like jelly roll, starting at wide end. Pinch edges to seal. Cut each roll into 12 slices. Arrange slices in 3 greased 13 × 9 × 2-inch baking pans, 12 rolls equally spaced in each pan. Cover and let rise until doubled, about 1 hour.

Bake in 350° oven 40 minutes or until golden brown. Remove from pans; cool on racks 10 minutes. Drizzle with Vanilla Icing. Makes 36.

Vanilla Icing: Combine 3 c. sifted confectioners sugar, 1½ tsp. vanilla and 4 to 5 tblsp. milk in bowl. Beat until smooth.

Sticky Bun Variation: Combine 1 c. butter or regular margarine, 5 c. brown sugar (packed) and 1½ c. molasses in 2-qt. saucepan. Heat over low heat until butter is melted. Stir until smooth. Divide molasses syrup among 3 greased 13 × 9 × 2-inch baking pans. Proceed with basic recipe as above, placing rolls on top of syrup in prepared pans. After baking, remove from pans immediately and cool on racks.

PINEAPPLE CINNAMON BUNS

Light, puffy sweet rolls swirled with a tasty pineapple, almond and red maraschino cherry filling and just a dash of cinnamon.

½ c. milk, scalded
⅓ c. sugar
¼ c. shortening
¾ tsp. salt
1 pkg. active dry yeast
½ c. lukewarm
   water (110⁰)
1 egg
3¼ c. sifted flour
2 tblsp. melted butter or
   regular margarine

¼ c. sugar
½ tsp. ground cinnamon
1 (8½-oz.) can crushed
   pineapple, drained
⅓ c. toasted slivered
   almonds
¼ c. chopped red
   maraschino cherries

Pour scalded milk over ⅓ c. sugar, shortening and salt in mixing bowl. Cool to lukewarm.

Sprinkle yeast over lukewarm water; stir to dissolve.

Add yeast mixture, egg and 1 c. of the flour to milk mixture. Beat with electric mixer at medium speed until smooth, about 2 minutes.

Gradually stir in enough remaining flour to make a soft dough.

Turn dough out onto floured surface. Knead until smooth and satiny, 8 to 10 minutes. Place dough in greased bowl, turning over once to grease top. Cover and let rise in warm place until doubled, about 1 hour.

Punch down dough. Cover and let rise again until doubled, about 45 minutes.

Punch down dough. Let rest 10 minutes. Roll dough out on floured surface to 15 × 10-inch rectangle. Brush with melted butter. Sprinkle with ¼ c. sugar, cinnamon, pineapple, almonds and cherries. Roll up like a jelly roll, starting at narrow side. Cut into 12 (1-inch) slices. Place slices equally spaced, cut side down, in greased 13 × 9 × 2-inch baking pan. Cover and let rise in warm place until doubled, about 30 minutes.

Bake in 350⁰ oven 25 minutes or until golden brown. Remove from pan; cool on rack. While still warm, frost with your favorite confectioners sugar icing, if you wish. Makes 12.

COUNTRY-STYLE STICKY BUNS

A little molasses gives these tender sticky buns a different flavor.
They're best when served warm with butter.

¾ c. milk, scalded	4 c. sifted flour
⅓ c. sugar	¼ c. molasses
⅓ c. butter or	½ c. brown sugar, packed
regular margarine	⅓ c. butter or
1 tsp. salt	regular margarine
2 pkgs. active dry yeast	½ c. chopped pecans
⅓ c. lukewarm	1 c. brown sugar, packed
water (110°)	½ c. raisins
1 egg	1 tsp. ground cinnamon

Pour scalded milk over sugar, ⅓ c. butter and salt in mixing bowl. Cool to lukewarm.

Sprinkle yeast over lukewarm water; stir to dissolve.

Add yeast mixture, egg and 1 c. of the flour to milk mixture. Beat with electric mixer at medium speed until smooth, about 2 minutes.

Gradually add enough remaining flour to make a soft dough.

Turn dough out onto floured surface. Knead until smooth and satiny, 8 to 10 minutes. Place dough in greased bowl, turning over once to grease top. Cover and let rise in warm place until doubled, about 1 hour.

Meanwhile, combine molasses, ½ c. brown sugar and ⅓ c. butter in saucepan. Heat over low heat until butter melts. Spread mixture in 2 greased 9-inch round cake pans. Sprinkle each with one half of pecans.

Combine 1 c. brown sugar, raisins and cinnamon; mix well. Set aside.

Punch down dough. Divide dough in half. Let rest 10 minutes. Roll out each half into 12 × 8-inch rectangle. Sprinkle each with one half of raisin mixture. Roll up like a jelly roll, starting at long side. Pinch edges to seal. Cut each roll into 12 (1-inch) slices. Arrange slices, cut side down, in prepared pans, 12 rolls equally spaced in each pan. Cover and let rise in warm place until doubled, about 30 minutes.

Bake in 350° oven 25 minutes or until golden brown. Remove from pans; cool on racks. Makes 24.

NO-KNEAD STICKY BUNS

"My mother remembers these rolls baking in the wood cookstove when she came home from school," a young Wisconsin girl wrote.

1 c. milk, scalded	Cooking oil
¼ c. shortening	Brown Sugar Topping
¼ c. sugar	(recipe follows)
1 tsp. salt	⅔ c. pecan halves
1 pkg. active dry yeast	½ c. sugar
¼ c. lukewarm	2 tsp. ground cinnamon
water (110°)	2 tblsp. melted butter or
3¾ c. sifted flour	regular margarine
1 egg	

Pour scalded milk over shortening, ¼ c. sugar and salt in large mixing bowl. Cool to lukewarm.

Sprinkle yeast over lukewarm water; stir to dissolve.

Add yeast mixture, 2 c. of the flour and egg to milk mixture. Beat with electric mixer at medium speed until smooth, about 2 minutes.

Gradually stir in remaining flour. (No kneading is necessary.) Brush top of dough with oil. Cover and let rise in warm place until doubled, 1 to 1½ hours.

Prepare Brown Sugar Topping. Pour into 2 (9-inch) round cake pans. Sprinkle half of pecan halves in each pan.

Combine ½ c. sugar and cinnamon; set aside.

Punch down dough. Divide in half. Let rest 10 minutes. Roll out each half to 12 × 8-inch rectangle. Brush each with half of melted butter. Sprinkle with half of sugar-cinnamon mixture. Roll up tightly like a jelly roll, starting at wide side. Pinch edges to seal. Cut each roll into 8 slices. Arrange 8 slices, equally spaced, in each prepared pan. Flatten slightly. Cover and let rise in warm place until almost doubled, about 45 minutes.

Bake in 375° oven 20 minutes or until golden brown. Invert pans on racks and remove pans. Serve warm or cold. Makes 16.

Brown Sugar Topping: Combine ½ c. brown sugar (packed), ¼ c. butter or regular margarine and 1 tblsp. light corn syrup in 2-qt. saucepan. Cook over low heat, stirring constantly, until butter is melted and mixture starts to boil. Remove from heat.

CINNAMON COFFEE ROLLS

You can serve freshly baked yeast rolls for breakfast. Just stir up the dough the night before and refrigerate.

1 pkg. active dry yeast	1 c. milk, scalded and
¼ c. lukewarm	cooled to lukewarm
water (110⁰)	(110⁰)
4 c. sifted flour	¼ c. sugar
¼ c. sugar	¾ tsp. ground cinnamon
1 tsp. salt	2 tblsp. melted butter or
1 c. butter or	regular margarine
regular margarine	Vanilla Frosting
3 egg yolks,	(recipe follows)
slightly beaten	

Sprinkle yeast over lukewarm water; stir to dissolve.

Combine flour, ¼ c. sugar and salt in mixing bowl; mix thoroughly. Cut in 1 c. butter with pastry blender until mixture resembles cornmeal. Add yeast mixture, egg yolks and milk. Stir with fork until well blended. (No kneading is necessary.) Cover with aluminum foil and chill in refrigerator overnight.

Combine ¼ c. sugar and cinnamon; mix well. Set aside.

Roll out dough on floured surface to 15 × 10-inch rectangle. Brush with 2 tblsp. melted butter. Sprinkle with sugar-cinnamon mixture. Roll up like jelly roll, starting at wide end. Pinch edges to seal. Cut into 15 (1-inch) slices. Place rolls, equally spaced, cut side down, in greased 13 × 9 × 2-inch baking pan. Cover and let rise in warm place until almost doubled, about 1 hour.

Bake in 375⁰ oven 20 to 25 minutes or until golden brown. Remove from pan; cool on rack. Frost with Vanilla Frosting. Makes 15.

Vanilla Frosting: Combine 1½ c. sifted confectioners sugar, 2 tblsp. soft butter or regular margarine, 1½ tsp. vanilla and 1 tblsp. hot water in bowl. Beat until smooth. Add 1 more tblsp. hot water, if necessary, to make a frosting of spreading consistency.

PENNSYLVANIA DUTCH CINNAMON BUNS

These extra-delicious cinnamon swirl buns frosted with Confectioners Sugar Icing are perfect for breakfast or brunch.

5¼ to 5¾ c. sifted flour	2 eggs
¼ c. sugar	¾ c. sugar
2 pkgs. active dry yeast	1 tsp. ground cinnamon
1 tsp. salt	3 tblsp. melted butter or
1 c. milk	regular margarine
½ c. water	Confectioners Sugar Icing
¼ c. butter or	(recipe follows)
regular margarine	

Stale Flour

Old flour can produce an inferior loaf of bread. It may smell rancid or musty. That means that the gluten could have deteriorated and you will not be able to make a satisfactory loaf of bread. Buy a fresh bag of flour for your bread making.

Combine 1¾ c. of the flour, ¼ c. sugar, undissolved yeast and salt in mixing bowl; mix thoroughly.

Combine milk, water and ¼ c. butter in saucepan. Heat over very low heat until very warm (120-130°). Gradually add to flour-yeast mixture, beating with electric mixer at medium speed 2 minutes, scraping bowl occasionally. Add eggs and ½ c. of the flour. Beat at high speed 2 minutes, scraping bowl occasionally.

Gradually stir in enough remaining flour to make a soft dough.

Turn dough out onto floured surface. Knead until smooth and elastic, 8 to 10 minutes. Place dough in greased bowl, turning over once to grease top. Cover and let rise in warm place until doubled, about 45 minutes.

Meanwhile combine ¾ c. sugar and cinnamon; mix well. Set aside.

Punch down dough. Divide dough into thirds. Let rest 10 minutes. Roll out each third on lightly floured surface to 14 × 8-inch rectangle. Brush each with 1 tblsp. melted butter and sprinkle with one third of sugar-cinnamon mixture. Roll up like a jelly roll, starting at narrow side. Pinch edges to seal. Cut each roll into 8 (1-inch) slices. Place slices, equally spaced, cut side down in greased 3-inch muffin-pan cups. Cover and let rise in warm place until doubled, about 30 minutes.

Bake in 350° oven 20 to 25 minutes or until golden brown. Remove from pans; cool on racks 20 minutes. Drizzle with Confectioners Sugar Icing. Makes 24.

Confectioners Sugar Icing: Combine 1½ c. sifted confectioners sugar, ¼ tsp. vanilla and 2 tblsp. milk in bowl; beat until smooth.

EXTRA-SPECIAL CINNAMON ROLLS

The Kansas woman who sent us this recipe emphasized that these rolls were worth the extra trouble. She was absolutely right!

2 c. raisins	½ c. shortening
Boiling water	2½ c. brown sugar, packed
2 pkgs. active dry yeast	8 tsp. ground cinnamon
1 tblsp. sugar	½ c. melted butter or
2½ c. lukewarm	regular margarine
water (110°)	1 c. heavy cream
½ c. sugar	½ c. brown sugar, packed
2 tsp. salt	½ tsp. vanilla
¼ tsp. ground ginger	1 tsp. ground cinnamon
8½ to 9 c. sifted flour	Vanilla Glaze (recipe
2 eggs	follows)

Place raisins in bowl; add enough boiling water to cover. Let stand 5 minutes to plump. Drain off water; reserve raisins.

Sprinkle yeast and 1 tblsp. sugar over lukewarm water in large mixing bowl; stir to dissolve. Add ½ c. sugar, salt, ginger, 3 c. of the flour and eggs. Beat with electric mixer at medium speed 2 minutes, scraping bowl occasionally. Cover and let stand in warm place until foamy, about 40 minutes.

Add raisins and shortening to yeast mixture; mix well. Gradually stir in enough remaining flour to make a soft dough.

Turn dough out onto floured surface. Knead until smooth, about 10 minutes. Place dough in greased bowl, turning over once to grease top. Cover and let rise in warm place until doubled, about 1 hour.

Meanwhile, combine 2½ c. brown sugar and 8 tsp. cinnamon in bowl; set aside.

Punch down dough. Divide dough in fourths. Let rest 10 minutes. Roll out each fourth on floured surface to 18 × 8-inch rectangle. Spread each with one fourth of melted butter. Sprinkle each with one fourth of brown sugar-cinnamon mixture. Roll up like a jelly roll, starting at wide end. Pinch edges to seal. Cut each roll in 18 (1-inch) slices. Place slices, equally spaced, cut side down, in 3 greased 13 × 9 × 2-inch baking pans, 24 rolls in each pan. Cover and let rise in warm place until doubled, about 45 minutes.

Meanwhile, combine heavy cream, ½ c. brown sugar, vanilla and 1 tsp. cinnamon in bowl; mix until blended. Spread one-third of cream mixture over each pan of rolls after they have doubled.

Bake in 375° oven 25 minutes or until golden brown. Remove from pans immediately. Cool on racks. While still warm, drizzle with Vanilla Glaze. Makes 72.

Vanilla Glaze: Combine 3 c. sifted confectioners sugar, dash of salt, 3 tblsp. melted butter or regular margarine, 1 tsp. vanilla and 2 tblsp. hot milk in bowl; beat until smooth. Add a little more milk, if necessary, to make a thin glaze.

HELEN'S DANISH-STYLE ROLLS

"Baking is a hobby of mine. I developed this version of a delicious Danish pastry and won a ribbon at the fair," an Ohio woman said.

½ c. milk	1 egg
⅓ c. evaporated milk	1 egg yolk
¼ c. butter or regular margarine	½ c. soft butter or regular margarine
⅓ c. sugar	¼ c. sugar
½ tsp. salt	¼ c. finely chopped walnuts
1 pkg. active dry yeast	
¼ c. lukewarm water (110⁰)	1 tsp. ground cinnamon
	½ c. raspberry preserves
3 to 3¼ c. sifted flour	Icing (recipe follows)

Scald milk and evaporated milk in saucepan. Pour over ¼ c. butter, ⅓ c. sugar and salt in large mixing bowl. Cool to lukewarm.

Sprinkle yeast over lukewarm water; stir to dissolve.

Add yeast mixture, 1 ½ c. of the flour, egg and egg yolk to milk mixture. Beat with electric mixer at medium speed until smooth, about 2 minutes.

Gradually stir in enough remaining flour to make a soft dough. Cover with aluminum foil. Chill in refrigerator 3 hours.

Roll out dough on lightly floured surface to 18 × 14-inch rectangle. Spread with ½ c. soft butter. Fold dough into thirds, starting at the long side, overlapping in the center. Then fold in half, starting at narrow side. (Dough will now have six layers.)

Wrap in aluminum foil. Chill in refrigerator 3 hours or overnight.

Meanwhile, combine ¼ c. sugar, walnuts and cinnamon in pie plate; mix well. Set aside.

Cut dough in half. Roll out each half on lightly floured surface to 14 × 9-inch rectangle. Cut into 12 strips, 9 inches long. Coat each strip with cinnamon-walnut mixture. Hold each strip at both ends and twist once, turning one hand toward you and the other hand away from you. To shape into roll, place one end of twisted strip on baking sheet and coil into circle. Tuck end under. Place on greased baking sheets, about 2 inches apart. Cover and let rise in warm place until doubled, about 1 hour.

Top each roll with about 1 tsp. of the raspberry preserves.

Bake in 350⁰ oven 15 minutes or until golden brown. Remove from baking sheets and cool on racks. While still warm, drizzle with Icing. Makes 24.

Icing: Combine 1 c. sifted confectioners sugar, 1 tsp. cornstarch, 1 tblsp. milk and ½ tsp. vanilla in bowl; beat until smooth.

MOCK DANISH-STYLE PASTRIES

"These flaky rolls have become so popular that I'm often asked to bring them to special occasions," wrote a Wisconsin farm wife.

1 c. milk	¼ tsp. vanilla
¼ c. shortening	¼ tsp. lemon extract
⅓ c. sugar	¼ tsp. ground mace
1 tsp. salt	1 c. shortening
1 pkg. active dry yeast	½ c. raspberry,
¼ c. lukewarm	strawberry or apricot
water (110⁰)	preserves
4¾ c. sifted flour	Confectioners Sugar
2 eggs	Frosting
	(recipe follows)

Scald milk in saucepan. Pour over ¼ c. shortening, sugar and salt in large mixing bowl. Cool to lukewarm.

Sprinkle yeast over lukewarm water; stir to dissolve.

Add yeast mixture, 3 c. of the flour, eggs, vanilla, lemon extract and mace to milk mixture. Beat with electric mixer at medium speed until smooth, about 2 minutes.

Gradually stir in enough remaining flour to make a soft dough.

Turn dough out onto floured surface. Knead until smooth and satiny, about 10 minutes. Place dough in greased bowl, turning over once to grease top. Cover and let rise in warm place until doubled, about 1 hour.

Roll out dough on floured surface to 15 × 12-inch rectangle. Dot surface of dough with ½ c. of the shortening. Fold in half, starting from narrow side, making 12 × 7½-inch rectangle. Dot surface of dough with remaining ½ c. shortening. Fold in thirds, starting at narrow side, and overlap in center (makes 6 layers). Pinch ends together. Let rest 20 minutes.

Cut dough in half. Roll out each half to 11 × 6-inch rectangle. Cut in 12 (6-inch) strips. Hold each strip at both ends and twist once, turning one hand toward you and the other hand away from you. Then form twisted strip into a ring, tucking ends under. Place rings on greased baking sheets, about 3 inches apart. Cover and let rise in warm place 30 minutes.

Bake in 375⁰ oven 20 to 25 minutes or until golden brown. Remove from baking sheets; cool on racks. While still warm, spoon 1 tsp. preserves in center of each pastry. Drizzle with Confectioners Sugar Frosting. Makes 24 pastries.

Confectioners Sugar Frosting: Combine 2 c. sifted confectioners sugar, 2 tblsp. milk and 1 tsp. vanilla in bowl. Beat with spoon until smooth.

HOT CROSS BUNS

These rolls were first baked in England to honor the Goddess of Spring. With the coming of Christianity, the crosses were added.

6 to 6½ c. sifted flour	3 eggs
½ c. sugar	1¼ c. currants
¾ tsp. salt	1 egg yolk
2 tsp. ground cinnamon	2 tblsp. water
2 pkgs. active dry yeast	Icing (recipe follows)
1½ c. milk	
6 tblsp. butter or regular margarine	

Combine 2 c. of the flour, sugar, salt, cinnamon and undissolved yeast in mixing bowl; mix thoroughly.

Combine milk and butter in saucepan. Heat until very warm (120-130°). Add to flour-yeast mixture, beating with electric mixer at medium speed 2 minutes. Add 3 eggs and 1 c. of the flour; beat 2 minutes. Stir in currants and enough flour to make a soft dough.

Turn dough out on lightly floured surface. Knead until smooth and elastic, about 10 minutes. Place in greased bowl, turning over once to grease top. Cover and let rise in warm place until doubled, about 1 hour.

Punch down dough. Let rest 10 minutes. Divide in 18 pieces; shape each piece into a ball. Place equally spaced in greased 13 × 9 × 2-inch baking pan. Combine egg yolk and water; mix well. Brush with egg yolk mixture. Cover and let rise in warm place until doubled, about 45 minutes.

Bake in 375° oven 20 to 25 minutes or until golden brown. Remove from pan; cool on rack. Frost with icing before serving. Best if served warm. Makes 18.

Icing: Combine 1 c. sifted confectioners sugar, 1 tblsp. milk and ½ tsp. vanilla in bowl; beat until smooth. Drip icing from spoon over center of each bun both lengthwise and crosswise to form crosses.

Expiration Date on Yeast
Be sure that your yeast is fresh. Check the date on the packet of active dry yeast. If the expiration date has passed, don't risk ruining a loaf of bread.

WHAT WENT WRONG WITH MY YEAST BREAD?

My bread had cracks on the top of the loaves—why?

The dough wasn't kneaded correctly. Or maybe it had too short a rising time or the loaves cooled too quickly in a draft.

My bread was heavy instead of light and stringy with a nice texture—why?

You may have killed some of the yeast by dissolving it in water that was too hot. Or you may have added too little flour. Or the kitchen may have been too cool for the yeast to work at full speed and make the bread rise enough.

The surface of my bread had heavy dark streaks—why?

Such streaks are a sign that you undermixed the dough or that you worked too much flour in the dough when you shaped it into loaves.

My bread was dry and crumbly when I sliced it—why?

Maybe your dough was too stiff or contained too much flour. Or the dough may not have been kneaded enough. Baking bread in an oven that is not hot enough can also make it dry and crumbly.

My bread was soggy—why?

You either added too much liquid or not enough flour. Or the bread was not fully baked when removed from the oven. Did it sound hollow when you tapped it?

The top of my bread was flat instead of nicely rounded—why?

The pans were placed too close together in the oven. Or the bread might have been cooled in a draft or the dough was too stiff, which indicates that too much flour had been added.

Chapter 3

Best Country Quick Breads

Quick breads are just that—quick, easy-to-make breads. They are leavened with either baking powder or baking soda plus an acid such as buttermilk or sour cream. Muffins, biscuits, tea breads and coffee cakes all belong to the quick bread family.

Muffins are the speediest of all to whip together. But even though they are simple, many women do complain that their muffins always have big tunnels and high-peaked tops.

The most important rule to remember in making muffins is *don't overstir the batter*. Extra beating overdevelops the gluten in the flour, which makes the muffins tough and causes huge tunnels inside them. Stir the batter only until all of the dry ingredients are moistened.

Some muffins are made using the "cake" method. The shortening and sugar are creamed before the dry ingredients are added. These muffins look and taste more like cake with a very fine-grained texture. When you make a muffin by this method, the "stir lightly" rule doesn't apply.

Biscuits, the second member of the quick bread family, are simple to make, too. The secret to making a perfect biscuit is to handle the dough with a very light touch. It's also important to cut the shortening into the dry ingredients until it looks like coarse corn meal. Done correctly, this step produces a light, tender biscuit with lots of flaky layers to capture the butter that you spread on the piping hot biscuit. Kneading also helps produce a light, flaky textured biscuit. But the important word to remember for kneading biscuits is *gently*, 10 to 15 times. The dough should always be soft, never stiff. Overkneading results in a tough, heavy biscuit.

When you cut out the biscuits with a biscuit cutter, press the cutter straight down. If you twist the cutter, you will end up with a lopsided biscuit. For a change, eliminate the cutting step and just cut the dough into squares or triangles with a sharp knife.

Tea breads and coffee cakes are made either by the "cake" method or by the "muffin" method, with just a quick stirring of the ingredients. Cracks in the top surface of a tea bread are fairly typical, so don't be disturbed if there are small cracks in yours.

Now that you have read about how to make a perfect biscuit or muffin, you may want to try some of the time-tested country recipes in this chapter. Many are heirlooms, passed lovingly down through generations, such as the Basic Sweet Muffins from a Missouri farm woman. She always presents this recipe to a new bride in the family. A top favorite in the wintertime in an Oregon ranch home is Candied Orange Rind Bread. It tastes even better after it mellows a day or two.

There are eight happy kids in an Iowa farm home when Mom makes her Applesauce Bread. If you're planning to entertain, do make the Brown Sugar Coffee Cake (it's so good that a Texas homemaker auctioned one off at a local fair for $100). These are just a few samplings from a chapter brimming with breads to bake in a hurry.

STEPS FOR MAKING BISCUITS

Follow these steps for making perfect biscuits:

Step 1—Sift the dry ingredients together into a large mixing bowl.

Step 2—Cut the shortening into the flour mixture with a pastry blender just until the mixture looks like coarse meal.

Step 3—Add the liquid all at once, stirring with a fork just enough to form a soft dough. Avoid overmixing as this will overdevelop the gluten in the flour and cause tough biscuits.

Step 4—Knead the dough on a lightly floured board very gently, quickly and lightly. Knead about 10 times or no longer than half a minute. This gentle kneading helps produce good volume, fine flaky texture and a good shape and crust. Overkneading with a heavy hand will give your biscuits a tough texture. Or it may cause the biscuits to fall over on the side and be lopsided.

Step 5—Roll out the biscuit dough on a lightly floured board to the thickness specified in the recipe. (If the biscuit is rolled too thin, it will be dry and unpleasant.) Cut the biscuits with a cutter, dipped in flour. Make one clean straight down cut with the cutter. If you turn or twist the cutter, the biscuits won't rise high and tall and may be lopsided. Push the leftover dough trimmings together lightly and roll them out with as little handling as possible. The biscuits from this dough won't be quite as tender as the "first cuts," but they will be acceptable.

Step 6—Transfer the biscuit dough with the spatula to a greased baking sheet. Place them an inch apart if you like crusty-sided biscuits; nestle them next to each other if you like soft-sided biscuits.

Step 7—Place baking sheet in the middle of the preheated oven and bake biscuits until they are golden brown. Lift them right from the baking sheet into a napkin-lined basket and serve them piping hot.

EXTRA-GOOD BASIC BISCUITS

No need to re-roll dough when making these biscuits because they're cut in triangles instead of rounds.

2 c. sifted flour	½ c. milk
2 tblsp. sugar	1 egg
3 tsp. baking powder	Milk
1 tsp. salt	Sugar
⅓ c. shortening	

Sift together flour, 2 tblsp. sugar, baking powder and salt into mixing bowl. Cut in shortening with pastry blender until mixture resembles coarse meal.

Combine ½ c. milk and egg in small bowl; beat with fork. Add to dry ingredients all at once, stirring just enough to make a soft dough that sticks together.

Turn dough onto lightly floured surface and knead gently 10 times. Roll out to 9-inch square. Cut in 9 (3-inch) squares. Cut each square in half diagonally forming 2 triangles. Place about 1 inch apart on greased baking sheet. Brush each with milk and sprinkle with sugar.

Bake in 450° oven 12 minutes or until golden brown. Serve warm. Makes 18.

Flaky Biscuits
Knead biscuit dough gently for a lovely, layered, flaky texture. Overkneading with a heavy hand results in a tough, leaden biscuit.

Don't Twist Biscuit Cutter
For straight, even sides on a biscuit, cut straight down with the cutter. Don't twist the cutter or you'll have lopsided biscuits.

MILE-HIGH BISCUITS

"These light flaky biscuits can't be beat when served with a spoonful of honey," says a Montana rancher.

3 c. sifted flour	¾ tsp. salt
2 tblsp. sugar	¾ c. shortening
4½ tsp. baking powder	1 egg, beaten
¾ tsp. cream of tartar	1 c. milk

Sift together flour, sugar, baking powder, cream of tartar and salt into bowl.

Cut in shortening with pastry blender until mixture resembles coarse meal.

Combine egg and milk; beat with fork. Add to flour mixture all at once, stirring just enough with fork to make a soft dough that sticks together.

Turn onto lightly floured surface and knead gently 15 times. Roll to 1-inch thickness. Cut with floured 2-inch cutter and place about 1 inch apart on ungreased baking sheet.

Bake in 450° oven 12 to 15 minutes or until golden brown. Serve warm. Makes 16.

FLAKY BAKING POWDER BISCUITS

Surprise a neighbor with a napkin-lined basket of these light, tender biscuits—especially appreciated by older folks.

2 c. sifted flour	½ c. shortening
1 tblsp. sugar	1 egg, beaten
4 tsp. baking powder	⅔ c. milk
½ tsp. salt	

Sift together flour, sugar, baking powder and salt into bowl.

Cut in shortening with pastry blender until mixture resembles coarse meal.

Combine egg and milk; beat with fork. Add to flour mixture all at once, stirring just enough with fork to make a soft dough that sticks together.

Turn onto lightly floured surface and knead gently 15 times. Roll to ¾-inch thickness. Cut with floured 2-inch cutter and place about 1 inch apart on ungreased baking sheet.

Bake in 425° oven 12 minutes or until golden brown. Serve warm. Makes 16.

Coarse Textured Biscuits
Undermixing biscuits results in coarse texture and dark spots on the crust. The acid in the baking powder hasn't been distributed enough to allow proper reaction with the baking soda.

Measure Liquid Carefully
In biscuits, too much liquid makes the dough sticky and too little makes the dough coarse and dry.

Perfect Biscuits
A perfect biscuit is fluffy, light and tender. Creamy white inside with a rich golden brown top crust.

OLD-FASHIONED BISCUIT PINWHEELS

Baked in a vanilla-flavored milk sauce, these crusty, sugar-glazed pinwheels can be served for breakfast or dessert.

2 c. sifted flour	2 tsp. vanilla
3 tsp. baking powder	¼ c. butter or
½ tsp. salt	regular margarine
3 tblsp. shortening	⅔ c. sugar
¾ c. buttermilk	2 c. milk
½ c. soft butter or	1 tsp. vanilla
regular margarine	Ground nutmeg
⅓ c. sugar	

Sift together flour, baking powder and salt into mixing bowl. Cut in shortening with pastry blender until mixture is crumbly. Add buttermilk, stirring just enough with fork to make a soft dough that sticks together.

Turn dough onto lightly floured surface and knead gently 10 times. Roll out to 12-inch square. Spread with ½ c. soft butter. Stir together ⅓ c. sugar and 2 tsp. vanilla in small bowl. Sprinkle mixture over butter. Roll up dough like a jelly roll. Cut into 1-inch slices. Place in greased 12 × 8 × 2-inch glass baking dish (2-qt.). Dot surface with ¼ c. butter. Sprinkle with ⅔ c. sugar. Combine milk and 1 tsp. vanilla. Pour milk mixture over biscuits.

Bake in 350° oven 50 minutes, basting 4 times with sauce during baking. Sprinkle with nutmeg. Serve warm. Makes 12 servings.

APPLE HONEY BUNS

Absolutely delicious apple sticky buns with a raisin-honey filling. These are best served warm.

Honey Topping (recipe
  follows)
36 pecan halves
2 c. sifted flour
2 tsp. baking powder
½ tsp. salt
½ tsp. ground cinnamon
3 tblsp. shortening
3 tblsp. butter or
  regular margarine
½ c. finely chopped,
  pared apple
⅔ c. milk
3 tblsp. melted butter
  or regular margarine
2 tblsp. applesauce
1 tblsp. honey
½ c. brown sugar, packed
3 tblsp. raisins

Prepare Honey Topping. Divide evenly into 12 ungreased 3-inch muffin-pan cups. Arrange 3 pecan halves in each cup.

Sift together flour, baking powder, salt and cinnamon into mixing bowl. Cut in shortening and 3 tblsp. butter with pastry blender until mixture is crumbly. Add apple; mix well. Add milk all at once, stirring with fork to make a soft dough that sticks together.

Turn dough onto lightly floured surface and knead gently about 30 seconds. Roll out to 12 × 8-inch rectangle.

Combine 3 tblsp. melted butter, applesauce and honey in small bowl. Spread on dough. Sprinkle with brown sugar and raisins. Roll up like a jelly roll, starting at wide end. Seal edges. Cut in 12 (1-inch) slices. Place slice, cut side down, on top of Honey Topping in each muffin-pan cup.

Bake in 425° oven 15 to 25 minutes or until lightly browned. Let cool in pan on rack 1 minute. Turn upside down on serving plate and remove pan. Best if served warm. Makes 12.

Honey Topping: Combine ¼ c. brown sugar (packed), 2 tblsp. melted butter or regular margarine, 2 tblsp. water and ¼ c. honey in small bowl; mix well.

BUTTERSCOTCH BISCUIT SWIRLS

An extra-special biscuit swirled with butterscotch filling. Just right with scrambled eggs for Sunday breakfast.

2 c. sifted flour	¾ c. milk
5 tsp. baking powder	½ c. melted butter or
½ tsp. salt	regular margarine
¼ c. butter or	1 c. brown sugar, packed
regular margarine	

Sift together flour, baking powder and salt into mixing bowl. Cut in ¼ c. butter with pastry blender until crumbs form. Add milk to dry ingredients all at once, stirring just enough with fork to make a soft dough that sticks together.

Turn out onto lightly floured surface and knead gently 10 times. Roll out to 12 × 10-inch rectangle. Brush with ½ c. melted butter. Sprinkle with brown sugar. Roll up like a jelly roll, starting at wide side. Cut in 12 slices. Place slice, cut side down, in each greased 3-inch muffin-pan cup.

Bake in 400° oven 18 minutes or until golden brown. Place a piece of aluminum foil under pan to catch drips during baking. Serve warm. Makes 12.

Biscuits and Honey
Split day-old biscuits. Spread with softened butter and run under the broiler, until hot and bubbly. Add a drizzle of honey and a tiny pinch of cinnamon just before you serve them.

PARMESAN CHEESE CRESCENTS

These golden brown crescents, rich in Parmesan cheese flavor, are so simple to prepare and elegant enough for company.

2 c. sifted flour	2 tblsp. grated Parmesan
3 tsp. baking powder	cheese
1 tsp. salt	1 tblsp. minced fresh
½ c. shortening	parsley
¾ c. milk	Milk
1 tblsp. melted butter or	
regular margarine	

Sift together flour, baking powder and salt into bowl. Cut in shortening with pastry blender until crumbly. Add ¾ c. milk to flour mixture all at once, stirring just enough with fork to make a soft dough that sticks together.

Turn onto lightly floured surface and knead gently 10 times. Roll into 13-inch circle. Brush with melted butter. Sprinkle with Parmesan cheese and parsley. Cut into 12 wedges. Roll up each from wide end. Place crescents, point down, on greased baking sheet. Brush with milk.

Bake in 425° oven 25 minutes or until golden brown. Serve warm. Makes 12.

MAKE-AHEAD BISCUIT MIX

If you keep this handy homemade biscuit mix on your shelf, you can serve hot tender biscuits with little trouble.

9 c. sifted flour	**4 tsp. salt**
1 c. nonfat dry milk	**1¾ c. shortening**
⅓ c. baking powder	

Stir together flour, dry milk, baking powder and salt in large bowl. Cut in shortening with pastry blender or two knives until mixture resembles coarse meal. Store mix in airtight container in a cool place up to 6 months. Makes about 12 cups.

To Make Basic Biscuits: Combine 2 c. Make-Ahead Biscuit Mix and ½ c. water in bowl. Mix with fork just enough to make a soft dough that sticks together.

Turn onto lightly floured surface and knead gently 15 times. Roll to ½-inch thickness. Cut with floured 2-inch cutter and place about 1 inch apart on ungreased baking sheet.

Bake in 425° oven 12 minutes or until golden brown. Serve warm. Makes 10.

ALL-PURPOSE BAKING MIX

Now you can make your own homemade baking mix and turn out delicious biscuits, muffins and crumb-topped coffee cakes.

10 c. sifted flour
1¾ c. sifted confectioners sugar
1⅓ c. instant nonfat dry milk

¼ c. baking powder
2 tblsp. salt
1 c. shortening

Combine flour, confectioners sugar, dry milk, baking powder and salt in very large mixing bowl. Cut in shortening with pastry blender or two knives until mixture resembles cornmeal.

Store mix in airtight containers in a cool place up to 6 months. Makes about 12 cups.

To use: Stir mix with large spoon before measuring. Spoon lightly into measuring cup and level off.

Cheddar Cheese Biscuits: Combine 2 c. All-Purpose Baking Mix, ½ c. shredded Cheddar cheese and ⅔ c. water. Mix with fork until moistened. Turn out on floured surface and knead gently 8 times. Roll out to ¾-inch thickness. Cut with floured 2-inch biscuit cutter. Place rounds, 2 inches apart, on greased baking sheet.

Bake in 400° oven 12 minutes or until golden brown. Serve warm. Makes 10 biscuits.

Golden Muffins: Combine 2 c. All-Purpose Baking Mix, 1 beaten egg and ¾ c. water. Stir only enough to moisten. Spoon mixture into greased 2½-inch muffin-pan cups, filling two-thirds full.

Bake in 425° oven 18 minutes or until golden brown. Serve warm. Makes 8 muffins.

Quick Coffee Cake: Combine 2 c. All-Purpose Baking Mix, ¾ c. sugar, 1 beaten egg, 3 tblsp. shortening, ¾ c. milk and 1 tsp. vanilla. Beat with electric mixer at medium speed 4 minutes. Spread batter in greased 9-inch square baking pan.

Combine ½ c. brown sugar (packed), 1 tblsp. flour, 1 tblsp. butter or regular margarine and ½ tsp. ground cinnamon in small bowl; mix until crumbly. Sprinkle over batter.

Bake in 350° oven 30 minutes or until golden brown. Serve warm. Makes 9 servings.

Curry Biscuits
Add about ¼ tsp. curry powder to the dry ingredients of a basic biscuit before they are sifted. Split the curry-scented biscuits open and use as a base for creamed chicken or shrimp.

Sage Biscuits
Add ½ tsp. powdered sage or poultry seasoning to sifted dry ingredients of a basic biscuit. Split hot biscuits open and top with creamed chicken or turkey.

Muffins
Back in the Gay Nineties, muffins were called "gems." When tender, light and hot from the oven, that's just what they are.

STEPS FOR MAKING MUFFINS

Muffins are among the simplest of all breads. Here is the basic method:

Step 1—Sift together the dry ingredients into a large mixing bowl.

Step 2—Combine the liquids and add all at once to the dry ingredients.

Step 3—Stir just enough to moisten. The batter must be stirred, never beaten. The mixture will appear rough and lumpy and that's exactly how it should look. (Overstirring or beating will result in a very poor product. The muffins will be small with very little volume. They will have high peaked tops and a pale smooth crust. When the muffin is broken in half, you'll see long tunnels running from the bottom up through the center. The texture will be tough and rubbery and even the flavor will suffer.)

Step 4—Fill each muffin cup two-thirds full. Follow specific recipes for greasing muffin pans or using paper cupcake liners. As soon as you have spooned the last of the batter into the pan, put it right into center of the preheated oven. The leavening action of the baking powder and soda begins as soon as the ingredients become moist. In order not to lose some of the power of the leavening gas, the muffins should be baked right away for best results. If you cannot bake them immediately, place them in the refrigerator. They should not be held longer than 30 minutes at the very most.

Step 5—Bake until golden brown. Or insert a cake tester or wooden pick in the center of the muffin; if it comes out clean, the muffin is done. Remove pans to cooling rack. Loosen and lift out muffins with a small spatula. Serve piping hot.

BASIC SWEET MUFFINS

"I sometimes serve these muffins for a quick supper along with scrambled eggs, sausage and fried apples," a Missouri farm woman said.

1¾ c. sifted flour	1 egg, slightly beaten
¼ c. sugar	3 tblsp. cooking oil
3 tsp. baking powder	1 c. milk
½ tsp. salt	

Sift together flour, sugar, baking powder and salt into mixing bowl.

Combine egg, oil and milk in small bowl; blend well. Add all at once to dry ingredients, stirring just enough to moisten. Spoon batter into greased 2½-inch muffin-pan cups, filling two-thirds full.

Bake in 400° oven 20 minutes or until golden brown. Serve warm. Makes 12.

PECAN CINNAMON MUFFINS

Richly-browned breakfast muffins with a hint of cinnamon and lots of pecans. Brown sugar adds much to the flavor.

1½ c. sifted flour	½ tsp. ground cinnamon
¼ c. sugar	1 egg, slightly beaten
¼ c. brown sugar, packed	½ c. cooking oil
2 tsp. baking powder	½ c. milk
½ tsp. salt	½ c. chopped pecans

Sift together flour, sugar, brown sugar, baking powder, salt and cinnamon into mixing bowl.

Combine egg, oil and milk in small bowl; blend well. Add all at once to dry ingredients, stirring just enough to moisten. Stir in pecans. Spoon batter into greased 2½-inch muffin-pan cups, filling two-thirds full.

Bake in 400⁰ oven 20 minutes or until golden brown. Serve warm. Makes 12.

Muffins In A Basket
Match the mood of your mealtime by using a variety of pretty napkins to line a muffin basket. For a picnic, choose a red and white checked napkin; for special dinners, use your finest linen napkins, and for Christmas, of course, a bright red napkin.

CRANBERRY MUFFINS

At holiday time, bake these muffins in 1¾-inch muffin-pan cups at 400° about 12 minutes. Just re-heat and serve with mugs of coffee.

2¼ c. sifted flour	¾ c. buttermilk
¼ c. sugar	¼ c. cooking oil
¾ tsp. baking soda	1 c. chopped raw
¼ tsp. salt	cranberries
1 egg, slightly beaten	½ c. sugar

Sift together flour, ¼ c. sugar, baking soda and salt into bowl.

Combine egg, buttermilk and oil in small bowl; blend well. Add all at once to dry ingredients, stirring just enough to moisten. Combine cranberries and ½ c. sugar; stir into batter.

Spoon batter into greased 2½-inch muffin-pan cups, filling two-thirds full.

Bake in 400⁰ oven 20 minutes or until golden brown. Serve warm. Makes 12.

HIGH-PROTEIN MUFFINS

These whole-grain muffins have a pleasant nutty flavor and are high in protein and roughage. The raisins are a good source of iron, too.

2½ c. 40% **Bran Flakes** cereal	4 tsp. baking powder
1½ c. raisins	1½ tsp. ground nutmeg
1¾ c. milk	¾ tsp. salt
1 c. stirred whole wheat flour	4 eggs, slightly beaten
1 c. soy flour	⅔ c. honey
1 c. toasted wheat germ	⅔ c. cooking oil
	¼ c. dark molasses

Combine Bran Flakes, raisins and milk in large mixing bowl.

Stir together whole wheat flour, soy flour, wheat germ, baking powder, nutmeg and salt; set aside.

Combine eggs, honey, oil and molasses in small bowl; blend well. Add egg mixture to soaked bran flakes; mix well.

Add dry ingredients all at once to bran mixture, stirring just enough to moisten. Spoon batter into paper-lined 3-inch muffin-pan cups, filling two-thirds full.

Bake in 350° oven 25 minutes or until golden brown. Serve warm. Makes 30.

SPICY APRICOT OAT MUFFINS

When you break open these hot muffins, you'll find them chock-full of bright orange apricots and chopped walnuts.

2 c. sifted flour	1 c. chopped dried apricots
½ c. sugar	½ c. chopped walnuts
3 tsp. baking powder	2 eggs, slightly beaten
1 tsp. salt	1⅓ c. milk
2 tsp. pumpkin pie spice	¼ c. cooking oil
½ c. quick-cooking oats	

Sift together flour, sugar, baking powder, salt and pumpkin pie spice into large mixing bowl. Stir in oats, apricots and walnuts.

Combine eggs, milk and oil in small bowl; blend well. Add all at once to dry ingredients, stirring just enough to moisten. Spoon batter into greased 3-inch muffin-pan cups, filling two-thirds full.

Bake in 350° oven 30 minutes or until golden brown. Serve warm. Makes 18.

Cheese Muffins
Fold ½ cup grated, sharp yellow cheese into a basic muffin recipe with the last few strokes of mixing. Serve with scrambled eggs and bacon for a special breakfast.

BACON AND ONION MUFFINS

Since these unusually flavored muffins are not too sweet, they're the perfect bread accompaniment for brunches and suppers.

½ lb. bacon, diced	½ tsp. salt
¼ c. chopped onion	2 eggs, slightly beaten
2¼ c. sifted flour	⅓ c. milk
2 tblsp. sugar	1 c. dairy sour cream
3 tsp. baking powder	Sesame seeds
½ tsp. baking soda	

Fry bacon until crisp in skillet. Remove with slotted spoon and drain on paper towels.

Sauté onion in 1 tblsp. of bacon drippings until tender (do not brown). Set aside to cool.

Sift together flour, sugar, baking powder, baking soda and salt into bowl.

Combine eggs, milk and sour cream in small bowl; blend well. Add all at once to dry ingredients, stirring just enough to moisten. Stir in bacon and sautéed onion.

Spoon batter into greased 2½-inch muffin-pan cups, filling two-thirds full. Sprinkle with sesame seeds.

Bake in 375° oven 18 to 20 minutes or until golden brown. Serve warm. Makes 18.

Surprise Muffins
Follow the recipe for Basic Muffins, except fill the muffin cups one-third full of batter. Drop ½ tsp. of your favorite jelly in center of batter. Add batter to fill cup two-thirds full. Kids will love these. And so will you.

GOLDEN CORNMEAL MUFFINS

Cornmeal muffins are an all-time American favorite. So good served with creamy butter and a spoon of homemade strawberry preserves.

1½ c. sifted flour	2 eggs, slightly beaten
¾ c. cornmeal	3 tblsp. melted butter or
½ c. sugar	regular margarine
4 tsp. baking powder	1 c. milk
1 tsp. salt	

Sift together flour, cornmeal, sugar, baking powder and salt into mixing bowl.

Combine eggs, butter and milk in small bowl; blend well. Add all at once to dry ingredients, stirring just enough to moisten. Spoon batter into greased 3-inch muffin-pan cups, filling two-thirds full.

Bake in 400° oven 15 minutes or until golden brown. Serve warm. Makes 12.

PUMPKIN OAT MUFFINS

Brown sugar, pumpkin, oatmeal and raisins are combined in this old-fashioned, moist muffin. It has a delightful crumb topping.

1 c. sifted flour	1 egg, slightly beaten
2 tsp. baking powder	¼ c. milk
1 tsp. pumpkin pie spice	¼ c. cooking oil
¼ tsp. baking soda	1 c. quick-cooking oats
½ tsp. salt	½ c. raisins
¾ c. canned mashed pumpkin	Crumb Topping (recipe follows)
½ c. brown sugar, packed	

Sift together flour, baking powder, pumpkin pie spice, baking soda and salt; set aside.

Combine pumpkin, brown sugar, egg, milk, oil, oats and raisins in bowl; blend well. Add dry ingredients all at once, stirring just enough to moisten. Spoon batter into greased 3-inch muffin-pan cups, filling two-thirds full. Sprinkle with Crumb Topping.

Bake in 400° oven 18 to 20 minutes or until golden brown. Serve warm. Makes 12.

Crumb Topping: Combine ½ c. brown sugar (packed), 1 tblsp. flour, ¼ tsp. pumpkin pie spice and 2 tblsp. butter or regular margarine in bowl. Mix until crumbly.

PUMPKIN MUFFINS

Feathery-light muffins with a hint of pumpkin flavor. These were judged "excellent" by our test kitchen home economists.

1 c. sifted flour	⅔ c. sugar
2 tsp. baking powder	1 egg
¼ tsp. salt	½ c. canned mashed pumpkin
¼ tsp. ground cinnamon	
¼ c. shortening	2 tblsp. milk

Sift together flour, baking powder, salt and cinnamon; set aside.

Cream together shortening and sugar in mixing bowl until light and fluffy, using electric mixer at medium speed. Beat in egg.

Combine pumpkin and milk in small bowl. Add dry ingredients alternately with pumpkin mixture to creamed mixture, stirring well after each addition. Spoon batter into paper-lined 2½-inch muffin-pan cups, filling two-thirds full.

Bake in 350° oven 20 minutes or until golden brown. Serve warm. Makes 12.

OATMEAL MUFFINS

A Wisconsin farmer thinks these cake-like oatmeal muffins are better than any other muffins he's ever eaten.

1 c. quick-cooking oats	1 tsp. salt
1 c. buttermilk	⅓ c. butter or
1 c. sifted flour	regular margarine
1 tsp. baking powder	½ c. brown sugar, packed
½ tsp. baking soda	1 egg

Combine oats and buttermilk in small bowl. Mix well and let stand 1 hour.

Sift together flour, baking powder, baking soda and salt; set aside.

Cream together butter and brown sugar in mixing bowl, using electric mixer at medium speed. Add egg; beat until light and fluffy.

Add dry ingredients alternately with oat mixture to creamed mixture, blending well after each addition. Spoon batter into greased 2½-inch muffin-pan cups, filling two-thirds full.

Bake in 400° oven 20 minutes or until golden brown. Serve warm. Makes 16.

BANANA-NUT MUFFINS

These delightful banana-flavored muffins are especially good when spread with soft butter and drizzled with warm honey.

2 c. sifted flour	2 eggs
3 tsp. baking powder	1⅓ c. mashed
½ tsp. salt	ripe bananas
½ c. shortening	(3 medium)
1 c. sugar	1 c. chopped walnuts

Sift together flour, baking powder and salt; set aside.

Cream together shortening and sugar in bowl until light and fluffy, using electric mixer at medium speed. Beat in eggs, one at a time, blending well after each addition. Stir in mashed bananas.

Add dry ingredients all at once, stirring just enough to moisten. Gently mix in chopped nuts. Spoon batter into greased 3-inch muffin-pan cups, filling two-thirds full.

Bake in 350° oven 20 minutes or until golden brown. Serve warm. Makes 18.

HEIRLOOM RAISIN MUFFINS

A California family has treasured this old-fashioned muffin recipe for several generations.

1 c. raisins	¾ c. sugar
1 c. water	2 eggs
½ c. soft butter or	1½ c. sifted flour
regular margarine	1 tsp. baking powder

Combine raisins and water in saucepan. Bring to a boil; reduce heat and cover. Simmer 20 minutes. Drain raisins, reserving liquid. Add enough water to reserved liquid to make ½ c. Cool well.

Cream together butter and sugar in bowl until fluffy, using electric mixer at medium speed. Add eggs; beat 2 more minutes.

Sift together flour and baking powder. Add flour mixture alternately with ½ c. raisin liquid to creamed mixture, beating well after each addition. Stir in raisins. Spoon batter into greased 3-inch muffin-pan cups, filling two-thirds full.

Bake in 400° oven 18 minutes or until golden brown. Serve warm. Makes 12.

Coconut Muffins
Add 1 c. shredded coconut to a basic muffin batter with the last few strokes of mixing. For a snack, serve Coconut Muffins with a glass of orange juice.

APPLE CRUNCH MUFFINS

These moist muffins with a crunchy pecan topping were a county winner in a state grange baking contest.

1½ c. sifted flour	1 egg, slightly beaten
½ c. sugar	½ c. milk
2 tsp. baking powder	1 c. shredded, unpared
½ tsp. salt	tart apples
½ tsp. ground cinnamon	Nut Crunch Topping
¼ c. shortening	(recipe follows)

Sift together flour, sugar, baking powder, salt and cinnamon into mixing bowl.

Cut in shortening with pastry blender until fine crumbs form. Combine egg and milk. Add to dry ingredients all at once, stirring just enough to moisten. Stir in apples. Spoon batter into paper-lined 2½-inch muffin-pan cups, filling two-thirds full. Sprinkle with Nut Crunch Topping.

Bake in 375° oven 25 minutes or until golden brown. Serve warm. Makes 12.

Nut Crunch Topping: Mix together ¼ c. brown sugar (packed), ¼ c. chopped pecans and ½ tsp. ground cinnamon in small bowl.

COUNTRY BRAN MUFFINS

The North Dakota farm woman who sent us this recipe sometimes refrigerates the batter for a few days so she can serve fresh muffins daily.

1 c. 40% Bran Flakes cereal	½ c. shortening
1 c. boiling water	1½ c. sugar
2½ c. sifted flour	2 eggs
2½ tsp. baking soda	2 c. All-Bran cereal
½ tsp. salt	2 c. buttermilk

Combine Bran Flakes and boiling water in bowl. Let stand 10 minutes.

Sift together flour, baking soda and salt; set aside.

Cream together shortening and sugar in large mixing bowl until light and fluffy, using electric mixer at medium speed. Add eggs, one at a time, beating well after each addition.

Stir in Bran Flakes mixture and All-Bran into creamed mixture. Add dry ingredients alternately with buttermilk to creamed mixture, mixing just enough to moisten. Spoon batter into well-greased 2½-inch muffin-pan cups, filling two-thirds full.

Bake in 400° oven 25 minutes or until golden brown. Serve warm. Makes 32.

Chive Muffins
Fold ¼ c. chives into the batter of basic muffins with the last few strokes of mixing. So good with steak and salad.

MOLASSES REFRIGERATOR MUFFINS

Tender, cake-like muffins flavored with five different spices. The batter can be stored up to three weeks and makes three dozen muffins.

4 c. sifted flour	¼ tsp. ground nutmeg
2 tsp. baking soda	1⅓ c. shortening
1 tsp. salt	1 c. sugar
1 tsp. ground cinnamon	4 eggs, slightly beaten
1 tsp. ground ginger	1 c. molasses
¼ tsp. ground cloves	1 c. buttermilk
¼ tsp. ground allspice	1 c. raisins

Sift together flour, baking soda, salt, cinnamon, ginger, cloves, allspice and nutmeg; set aside.

Cream together shortening and sugar in mixing bowl until light and fluffy, using electric mixer at medium speed. Add eggs; beat well. Blend in molasses and buttermilk. Add dry ingredients all at once, stirring just enough to moisten. Stir in raisins. Spoon batter into greased 3-inch muffin-pan cups, filling one-half full.

Bake in 350° oven 20 minutes or until golden brown. Serve warm. Makes 36.

To store: Store in covered container in refrigerator up to 3 weeks.

DATE-NUT BRAN MUFFINS

You can store this muffin batter up to six weeks and make five dozen date and walnut-filled muffins. They're nutritious, too.

5 c. sifted flour	2 c. chopped dates
2 c. sugar	2 c. coarsely chopped
5 tsp. baking soda	walnuts
1 tsp. salt	1 c. cooking oil
2 c. All-Bran cereal	4 eggs, slightly beaten
2 c. toasted wheat germ	2 c. water
2 c. 40% Bran Flakes	1 qt. buttermilk
cereal	

Sift together flour, sugar, baking soda and salt; set aside.

Combine All-Bran, wheat germ, Bran Flakes, dates, walnuts, oil, eggs, water and buttermilk in 6-qt. mixing bowl; mix well. Add dry ingredients all at once, stirring just enough to moisten. Spoon batter into greased 3-inch muffin-pan cups, filling two-thirds full.

Bake in 400° oven 20 minutes or until golden brown. Serve warm. Makes 60.

To store: Store in covered container in refrigerator up to 6 weeks.

OLD-FASHIONED BRAN MUFFINS

"Whenever I bring these delicious muffins to a church supper or a family reunion, they are a big hit," a Michigan farm woman wrote us.

3 c. Bran Buds	½ c. shortening
1 c. boiling water	1½ c. sugar
2½ c. sifted flour	2 eggs
2½ tsp. baking soda	2 c. milk
1 tsp. salt	

Combine 1 c. of the Bran Buds and boiling water in small bowl; let stand until mixture is cool.

Sift together flour, baking soda and salt; set aside.

Cream together shortening and sugar in large mixing bowl until light and fluffy, using electric mixer at medium speed. Add eggs, one at a time, beating well after each addition. Blend in milk, cooled bran mixture and remaining 2 c. Bran Buds. Add dry ingredients all at once to creamed mixture, stirring just enough to moisten. Spoon batter into greased 2½-inch muffin-pan cups, filling one-half full.

Bake in 400° oven 18 minutes or until golden brown. Serve warm. Makes 36.

To store: Store in covered container in refrigerator up to 3 weeks.

TEA BREADS AND COFFEE CAKES

The closest relatives to muffins in the quick bread family are the sweetened fruit and nut "tea" breads and spicy coffee cakes. They are made by either the muffin method or the cake method, depending upon the recipe.

Tea breads are the only members of the quick bread family that are never served hot. In fact, many of the breads are much easier to slice and have a richer, more mellow flavor if they are allowed to stand overnight.

These breads are a welcome treat for breakfast, for a between-meal snack or as a simple dessert for the family.

PURPLE RIBBON PRUNE BREAD

This prized recipe combines prunes with honey, orange rind, walnuts and two spices: cinnamon and nutmeg.

1½ c. chopped prunes	⅓ c. honey
1 c. boiling water	1 egg, beaten
2½ c. sifted flour	1 tsp. vanilla
⅔ c. sugar	2 tblsp. cooking oil
1 tsp. baking soda	1 tsp. grated orange rind
1 tsp. salt	1 c. chopped walnuts
1 tsp. ground cinnamon	1 tblsp. flour
½ tsp. ground nutmeg	

Combine prunes and boiling water in bowl. Cover and let stand 20 minutes.

Sift together 2½ c. flour, sugar, baking soda, salt, cinnamon and nutmeg into bowl.

Add honey, egg and vanilla to prunes; mix well. Add prune mixture, oil and orange rind to dry ingredients, stirring just until moistened. Combine walnuts with 1 tblsp. flour; stir into batter. Pour batter into greased 9 × 5 × 3-inch loaf pan.

Bake in 325⁰ oven 1 hour and 10 minutes, or until cake tester or wooden pick inserted in center comes out clean. Cool in pan on rack 10 minutes. Remove from pan; cool on rack. Makes 1 loaf.

GRAND CHAMPION PUMPKIN BREAD

This superb tea loaf, flavored with pumpkin pie spice and chopped dates, has won the Grand Champion Ribbon twice.

3⅓ c. sifted flour	⅔ c. cooking oil
4 tsp. pumpkin pie spice	4 eggs
2 tsp. baking soda	1 (1-lb.) can mashed
1 tsp. baking powder	pumpkin (2 c.)
1½ tsp. salt	⅔ c. water
2⅔ c. sugar	⅔ c. chopped dates

Sift together flour, pumpkin pie spice, baking soda, baking powder and salt; set aside.

Beat together sugar and oil in bowl until light and fluffy, using electric mixer at high speed. Add eggs, one at a time, beating well after each addition. Beat in pumpkin.

Add dry ingredients alternately with water to sugar mixture, beating well after each addition, using electric mixer at low speed. Stir in dates. Pour batter into 2 greased 9 × 5 × 3-inch loaf pans.

Bake in 325° oven 55 minutes, or until cake tester or wooden pick inserted in center comes out clean. Cool in pans on racks 10 minutes. Remove from pans; cool on racks. Makes 2 loaves.

LEMON TEA BREAD

To further enhance the tangy lemon flavor of this tea bread, wrap it in aluminum foil and let stand for several days.

1½ c. sifted flour	1 tsp. lemon extract
1½ tsp. baking powder	1½ tsp. grated
1 tsp. salt	lemon rind
1 c. sugar	½ c. milk
⅓ c. butter or	½ c. chopped pecans
regular margarine,	½ c. sugar
melted	¼ c. lemon juice
2 eggs	

Sift together flour, baking powder and salt; set aside.

Combine 1 c. sugar, butter, eggs, lemon extract and lemon rind in mixing bowl. Beat with electric mixer at medium speed 2 minutes.

Add dry ingredients alternately with milk, beating well after each addition. Stir in pecans. Pour batter into greased 9 × 5 × 3-inch loaf pan.

Bake in 350° oven 50 minutes, or until cake tester or wooden pick inserted in center comes out clean. Cool in pan on rack 10 minutes. Mix together ½ c. sugar and lemon juice. Prick holes in bread, using fork. Pour lemon juice mixture over top. When cooled, remove from pan. Wrap in aluminum foil. Let stand overnight. (Loaf slices better after standing.) Makes 1 loaf.

PINEAPPLE-NUT BREAD

A sturdy tea bread chock-full of pineapple bits, raisins and pecans. This can be made ahead and stored in the freezer.

2 c. sifted flour	¼ c. shortening, melted
½ c. sugar	and cooled
1 tsp. baking powder	1 (8¼-oz.) can crushed
½ tsp. baking soda	pineapple in syrup
½ tsp. salt	1 c. golden raisins
1 egg, slightly beaten	½ c. chopped pecans
¼ c. milk	

Sift together flour, sugar, baking powder, baking soda and salt.

Combine egg, milk, shortening, undrained pineapple, raisins and pecans in mixing bowl; mix well. Add dry ingredients all at once, stirring just until moistened. (Batter will be stiff.) Spread mixture in greased 9 × 5 × 3-inch loaf pan.

Bake in 350⁰ oven 55 minutes, or until cake tester or wooden pick inserted in center comes out clean. Cool in pan on rack 10 minutes. Remove from pan; cool on rack. Makes 1 loaf.

BANANA-CARROT TEA LOAF

This moist and tasty loaf combines carrots and bananas. The banana flavor develops more fully when stored overnight.

2 c. sifted flour	¾ c. cooking oil
1 tsp. baking soda	2 eggs
½ tsp. salt	1 c. finely grated pared
½ tsp. ground cinnamon	carrots
1 c. mashed ripe bananas	½ c. chopped pecans
1 c. sugar	

Sift together flour, baking soda, salt and cinnamon; set aside.

Combine bananas, sugar, oil and eggs in mixing bowl. Beat with electric mixer at medium speed 2 minutes. Stir in dry ingredients. Fold in carrots and pecans. Spread mixture in greased and floured 9 × 5 × 3-inch loaf pan.

Bake in 350⁰ oven 55 minutes, or until cake tester or wooden pick inserted in center comes out clean. Cool in pan on rack 10 minutes. Remove from pan; cool on rack. Wrap in aluminum foil. Let stand overnight. (Loaf will slice better after standing.) Makes 1 loaf.

CARROT-WALNUT BREAD

Nicely textured quick bread with shreds of carrot and lots of walnuts. Cinnamon and nutmeg add a gentle spicy flavor.

1½ c. sifted flour	¾ c. cooking oil
1 tsp. baking soda	2 eggs
½ tsp. ground cinnamon	1½ c. shredded, pared
¼ tsp. ground nutmeg	carrots
¼ tsp. salt	½ c. chopped walnuts
1 c. sugar	

Sift together flour, baking soda, cinnamon, nutmeg and salt; set aside.

Combine sugar, oil and eggs in mixing bowl. Beat with electric mixer at medium speed 2 minutes. Add dry ingredients, stirring just until moistened. Stir in carrots and walnuts. Pour batter into greased 9 × 5 × 3-inch loaf pan.

Bake in 350⁰ oven 1 hour, or until cake tester or wooden pick inserted in center comes out clean. Cool in pan on rack 10 minutes. Remove from pan; cool on rack. Makes 1 loaf.

BANANA-WALNUT BREAD

Be sure to use ripe bananas when mixing up this recipe. Look for bananas sporting brown-flecked skins.

1¾ c. sifted flour	½ c. sugar
2 tsp. baking powder	2 eggs
¼ tsp. baking soda	1 c. mashed, ripe bananas
½ tsp. salt	½ c. chopped walnuts
⅓ c. shortening	1 tblsp. flour

Sift together 1¾ c. flour, baking powder, baking soda and salt; set aside.

Cream together shortening and sugar in bowl until light and fluffy, using electric mixer at medium speed. Add eggs, one at a time, beating well after each addition.

Add dry ingredients alternately with bananas to creamed mixture, beating well after each addition, using electric mixer at low speed. Combine walnuts and 1 tblsp. flour; stir into batter. Pour batter into greased 9 × 5 × 3-inch loaf pan.

Bake in 350⁰ oven 1 hour, or until cake tester or wooden pick inserted in center comes out clean. Cool in pan on rack 10 minutes. Remove from pan; cool on rack. Wrap in aluminum foil. Let stand overnight. (Loaf will slice better after standing.) Makes 1 loaf.

CANDIED ORANGE RIND BREAD

Lovely saffron yellow-colored tea bread flecked with slivers of candied orange rind—delightful orange flavor.

4 medium oranges	¼ c. butter or
1 c. water	regular margarine
1 c. sugar	½ c. sugar
4 c. sifted flour	2 eggs
6 tsp. baking powder	2 c. milk
½ tsp. salt	

Thinly peel oranges, using a vegetable parer. Cut orange rind into thin slivers. (Reserve oranges for another use.)

Combine orange rind and 1 c. water in 2-qt. saucepan. Bring to a boil; reduce heat. Cover and simmer 15 minutes, or until orange rind is tender. Add 1 c. sugar. Continue cooking, uncovered, until mixture is syrupy, about 15 minutes. Cool to room temperature.

Sift together flour, baking powder and salt.

Cream together butter and ½ c. sugar in mixing bowl until light and fluffy, using electric mixer at medium speed. Add eggs; beat well. Blend in cooled orange rind mixture.

Add dry ingredients alternately with milk to creamed mixture, beating well after each addition. Pour batter into 2 greased 9 × 5 × 3-inch loaf pans.

Bake in 350° oven 50 minutes, or until cake tester or wooden pick inserted in center comes out clean. Cool in pans on rack 10 minutes. Remove from pans; cool on rack. Wrap in aluminum foil. Let stand overnight. (Loaves slice better after standing.) Makes 2 loaves.

SPICY APPLESAUCE BREAD

Moist, spicy tea bread studded with lots of raisins and chopped walnuts. Delicious when spread with softened cream cheese.

1 c. raisins	½ c. butter or
½ c. water	regular margarine
1 c. applesauce	1 c. sugar
1½ c. sifted flour	1 egg
1 tsp. baking soda	1 tsp. vanilla
½ tsp. ground cinnamon	½ c. chopped walnuts
⅛ tsp. ground cloves	

Combine raisins and water in small saucepan. Bring mixture to a boil; reduce heat. Cover and simmer 1 minute. Remove from heat. Stir in applesauce. Cool to lukewarm.

Sift together flour, baking soda, cinnamon and cloves.

Cream together butter and sugar in mixing bowl until light and fluffy, using electric mixer at medium speed. Beat in egg and vanilla.

Add dry ingredients alternately with applesauce mixture to creamed mixture, beating well after each addition. Stir in walnuts. Turn mixture into greased and waxed paper-lined 9 × 5 × 3-inch loaf pan.

Bake in 350⁰ oven 1 hour, or until cake tester or wooden pick inserted in center comes out clean. Cool in pan on rack 10 minutes. Remove from pan; cool on rack. Makes 1 loaf.

FESTIVE CRANBERRY LOAF

Perfect choice for holiday entertaining and gift-giving. This loaf combines two favorites: cranberries and oranges.

2 c. sifted flour	¾ c. fresh orange juice
1 c. sugar	1 tblsp. grated orange rind
1½ tsp. baking powder	1 c. coarsely chopped
1 tsp. salt	raw cranberries
½ tsp. baking soda	¼ c. chopped walnuts
¼ c. shortening	1 tblsp. flour
1 egg, beaten	

Sift together 2 c. flour, sugar, baking powder, salt and baking soda into bowl. Cut in shortening until crumbs form, using a pastry blender. Combine egg, orange juice and orange rind. Add to crumb mixture all at once; stir until moistened.

Combine cranberries, walnuts and 1 tblsp. flour. Stir into batter. Pour into greased and waxed paper-lined 8½ × 4½ × 2½-inch loaf pan.

Bake in 350⁰ oven 1 hour, or until cake tester or wooden pick inserted in center comes out clean. Cool in pan on rack 10 minutes. Remove from pan; cool on rack. Wrap in aluminum foil. Let stand overnight. (Loaf slices better after standing.) Makes 1 loaf.

HONEY CORN BREAD

Leftover squares of corn bread can be split in half and then toasted under the broiler. So good with a cup of hot coffee.

1 c. sifted flour	¼ c. honey
¾ c. cornmeal	2 tblsp. butter or regular
3 tsp. baking powder	margarine, melted
½ tsp. salt	1 c. milk
1 egg, beaten	

Sift together flour, cornmeal, baking powder and salt into bowl.

Combine egg, honey, butter and milk in another bowl. Add to dry ingredients, stirring just enough to moisten. Pour batter into greased 8-inch square baking pan.

Bake in 400° oven 30 minutes, or until cake tester or wooden pick inserted in center comes out clean. Cool in pan on rack. Serve warm with honey, if you wish. Makes 9 servings.

SKILLET CORN BREAD

This bacon-flavored corn bread bakes in a skillet. Just cut in wedges and serve piping hot with lots of creamy butter.

½ lb. bacon	1 tsp. baking soda
1 c. sifted flour	1 tsp. salt
1 c. yellow cornmeal	2 eggs
3 tblsp. sugar	1 c. buttermilk
3 tsp. baking powder	

Fry bacon in 10-inch heavy skillet with heat-proof handle until crisp. Remove bacon and drain on paper towels. Crumble bacon. Reserve ¼ c. bacon drippings. Do not wash skillet.

Sift together flour, cornmeal, sugar, baking powder, baking soda and salt into a mixing bowl.

Combine eggs, buttermilk and ¼ c. bacon drippings in another bowl. Beat with rotary beater until well blended. Add to dry ingredients. Stir just until moistened. Stir in crumbled bacon. Pour batter into same skillet.

Bake in 425° oven 20 minutes, or until cake tester or wooden pick inserted in center comes out clean. Cut in wedges. Serve warm. Makes 10 servings.

Beautiful Easter Breads
Treat your family and make these lovely breads during Lent and for Easter morning breakfast. Clockwise from top: Polish Babka (p. 46), Russian Kulich (p. 84), Hot Cross Buns (p.100) and Italian Panettone (p.85).

A Novel Bread
In Philadelphia it's the custom to spread lots of mustard on warm-from-the-oven salt-sprinkled Soft Pretzels (p. 68). Good without the mustard, too.

Great Grandmother's Treasures

Clockwise from left: Amish Oatmeal Cookies (p. 234), Heirloom Raisin Muffins (p. 119) and Heritage Dutch Apple Pie (p. 294).

Easy Batter Breads
No-fuss, no-knead breads for the novice baker to try first. Clockwise: Apple Crumb Kuchen (p. 44), Rich Egg Batter Bread (p. 42) and Herbed Sour Cream Batter Bread (p. 41).

WHOLE WHEAT RAISIN BREAD

A Wisconsin woman bakes several batches of this bread and freezes them. Her menfolks like it in their lunch boxes.

2 c. boiling water	2 tsp. baking powder
2 c. raisins	2 tsp. baking soda
1 c. sifted flour	1 tsp. salt
2 c. stirred whole wheat	2 eggs
flour	1½ c. sugar

Pour boiling water over raisins in small bowl. Let stand until cooled.

Stir together flour, whole wheat flour, baking powder, baking soda and salt.

Beat together eggs and sugar in mixing bowl until light and lemon-colored, using electric mixer at medium speed. Stir in raisin mixture. Add dry ingredients all at once, stirring just until moistened. Pour mixture into 5 greased (1-lb.) vegetable cans.

Bake in 350⁰ oven 40 minutes, or until cake tester or wooden pick inserted in center comes out clean. Remove from cans; cool on racks. Makes 5 small loaves.

SWISS CHEESE-WHOLE WHEAT LOAF

Whole wheat flour and shredded Swiss cheese are combined in this unusual quick bread. Its texture resembles a bran muffin.

2 c. stirred whole wheat	2 eggs
flour	1½ c. milk
¾ c. sifted flour	⅓ c. cooking oil
3 tsp. baking powder	¼ c. brown sugar, packed
1 tsp. baking soda	1 tblsp. dried onion flakes
1½ tsp. salt	1 c. shredded Swiss cheese

Stir together whole wheat flour, flour, baking powder, baking soda and salt in mixing bowl.

Combine eggs, milk, oil, brown sugar and onion flakes in another bowl; mix well. Stir in Swiss cheese. Add cheese mixture all at once to dry ingredients, stirring just until moistened. Turn into greased and waxed paper-lined 8½ × 4½ × 2½-inch loaf pan.

Bake in 375⁰ oven 1 hour, or until cake tester or wooden pick inserted in center comes out clean. Cover with aluminum foil during the last 15 minutes of baking to prevent overbrowning. Cool in pan on rack 10 minutes. Remove from pan; cool on rack. Makes 1 loaf.

WALNUT BROWN BREAD

Rich, dark bread that resembles Boston brown bread, but these loaves are baked instead of steamed.

3 c. raisins	4 tsp. baking soda
3 c. water	2 tsp. salt
¼ c. shortening	2 eggs, slightly beaten
5½ c. sifted flour	1 c. chopped walnuts
2 c. sugar	

Combine raisins and water in 3-qt. saucepan. Bring to a boil. Boil, uncovered, 5 minutes. Remove from heat. Add shortening. Cool mixture to lukewarm.

Sift together flour, sugar, baking soda and salt into mixing bowl. Add eggs, walnuts and raisin mixture. Stir just until moistened. Spoon batter into 6 greased (1-lb.) vegetable cans.

Bake in 350° oven 1 hour, or until cake tester or wooden pick inserted in center comes out clean. Cover with aluminum foil during the last 15 minutes of baking to prevent overbrowning. Cool in cans on racks 10 minutes. Remove from cans; cool on racks. Makes 6 loaves.

IRISH SODA BREAD

"It seems we are out of yeast and bread whenever we are snow-bound in the winter, so I make this often," says an Illinois woman.

4½ c. sifted flour	¼ c. butter or
½ c. sugar	regular margarine
1 tsp. baking powder	2 c. currants
1 tsp. baking soda	1 egg
1 tsp. salt	1½ c. buttermilk
1 tblsp. caraway seeds	1 egg yolk, beaten

Sift together flour, sugar, baking powder, baking soda and salt into mixing bowl. Stir in caraway seeds.

Cut in butter with pastry blender until mixture resembles coarse meal. Stir in currants.

Beat together 1 egg and buttermilk in small bowl. Add to dry ingredients. Stir just until moistened. Turn out on floured surface and knead until smooth. Form dough into a ball. Place in greased 2-qt. casserole. Cut a cross in top of loaf, about ½-inch deep. Brush bread with beaten egg yolk.

Bake in 350° oven 1 hour 20 minutes, or until cake tester or wooden pick inserted in center comes out clean. Cover top of loaf with aluminum foil after the first 50 minutes of baking to prevent overbrowning. Remove from casserole; cool on rack. Serve warm or cold. Makes 1 loaf.

QUICK CRUMB COFFEE CAKE

So quick and easy to make because the crumb topping is reserved from the basic coffee cake mixture.

2 c. sifted flour	½ tsp. salt
1 c. sugar	2 eggs
¾ c. butter or	¾ c. milk
regular margarine	2 tblsp. sugar
2 tsp. baking powder	1 tsp. ground cinnamon

Sift together flour and 1 c. sugar into bowl. Cut in butter with pastry blender until crumbs form. Remove 1 c. of mixture; set aside.

Add baking powder, salt, eggs and milk to remaining crumb mixture. Stir just until moistened. Pour batter into greased 8-inch square baking pan.

Combine reserved 1 c. crumb mixture, 2 tblsp. sugar and cinnamon; mix well. Sprinkle over batter.

Bake in 375° oven 40 minutes or until golden brown. Cool in pan on rack. Can be served warm or cold. Makes 6 to 8 servings.

BUTTER-RICH COFFEE CAKE

An Iowa family of German descent has been enjoying this quick country-style coffee cake for over five generations.

4½ c. sifted flour	1 tsp. vanilla
3 tsp. baking powder	1½ c. milk
¾ tsp. salt	½ c. butter or
3 c. sugar	regular margarine,
¾ c. butter or	melted
regular margarine	1½ c. sugar
6 eggs	1½ tsp. ground cinnamon

Sift together flour, baking powder and salt.

Cream together 3 c. sugar and ¾ c. butter in bowl until light and fluffy, using electric mixer at medium speed. Add eggs, one at a time, beating well after each addition. Beat in vanilla.

Add dry ingredients alternately with milk to creamed mixture, beating well after each addition. Pour batter into 2 greased 9-inch square baking pans.

Pour ½ c. melted butter over batter, dividing it evenly. Combine 1½ c. sugar and cinnamon. Sprinkle one half of mixture over each.

Bake in 350° oven 35 minutes or until golden brown. Cool in pans on racks. Can be served warm or cold. Makes 18 servings.

EASY CINNAMON COFFEE CAKE

"When each child in this family can read, he or she is allowed to make this coffee cake," an Iowa homemaker wrote us.

2¼ c. sifted flour	1 c. milk
1 c. sugar	1 tsp. vanilla
3 tsp. baking powder	¼ c. butter or
½ tsp. salt	regular margarine
¼ c. butter or	½ c. brown sugar, packed
regular margarine	1 tsp. ground cinnamon

Sift together flour, sugar, baking powder and salt into mixing bowl.

Cut in ¼ c. butter with pastry blender until crumbs form. Add milk and vanilla; stir just until moistened. Spread batter in greased 8-inch square pan. Dot batter with ¼ c. butter. Mix together brown sugar and cinnamon. Sprinkle over top of batter.

Bake in 350° oven 35 minutes or until golden brown. Cool in pan on rack. Can be served warm or cold. Makes 6 to 8 servings.

ALMOND BRUNCH COFFEE CAKE

An attractive coffee cake filled with chocolate chips and toasted almonds—just perfect for a mid-morning snack.

1 c. sifted cake flour	⅓ c. fresh orange juice
1¼ tsp. baking powder	¼ c. chopped blanched
½ tsp. salt	almonds
⅓ c. shortening	¼ c. semisweet chocolate
½ c. sugar	pieces
1 egg	Sifted confectioners sugar
1½ tsp. grated orange rind	

Sift together cake flour, baking powder and salt.

Cream together shortening and sugar in bowl until light and fluffy, using electric mixer at medium speed. Blend in egg and orange rind.

Add dry ingredients alternately with orange juice to creamed mixture, beating well after each addition. Pour batter into greased 8-inch round cake pan. Sprinkle almonds and chocolate pieces over batter.

Bake in 375° oven 25 to 30 minutes or until golden brown. Cool in pan on rack. Can be served warm or cold. Dust with confectioners sugar before serving. Makes 6 to 8 servings.

SOUR CREAM COFFEE CAKE

Velvety-crumbed coffee cake with a crunchy sugar-nut filling and topping.

2 c. sifted flour	3 eggs
1 tsp. baking powder	1 tsp. vanilla
1 tsp. baking soda	1 c. dairy sour cream
¼ tsp. salt	½ c. chopped walnuts
½ c. butter or	½ c. sugar
regular margarine	1 tsp. ground cinnamon
1 c. sugar	

Sift together flour, baking powder, baking soda and salt.

Cream together butter and 1 c. sugar in bowl until light and fluffy, using electric mixer at medium speed. Add eggs, one at a time, beating well after each addition. Blend in vanilla.

Add dry ingredients alternately with sour cream to creamed mixture, beating well after each addition. Spread one half of batter in greased 9-inch tube pan.

Combine walnuts, ½ c. sugar and cinnamon in small bowl. Sprinkle one half of mixture over batter. Carefully spread remaining batter on top. Sprinkle with remaining walnut mixture.

Bake in 350° oven 45 minutes or until golden brown. Cool in pan on rack 15 minutes. Remove from pan; cool on rack. Can be served warm or cold. Makes 10 servings.

BROWN SUGAR COFFEE CAKE

"This coffee cake brought in $105 at a school auction," wrote a young Texas woman when she sent in the recipe.

2¾ c. sifted flour	½ c. chopped pecans
¾ c. sugar	1 tsp. baking powder
1 tsp. salt	1 tsp. baking soda
1 tsp. ground cinnamon	1 c. buttermilk
1 c. brown sugar, packed	1 egg
¾ c. cooking oil	1 tsp. vanilla

Sift together flour, sugar, salt and cinnamon into mixing bowl. Stir in brown sugar until well mixed. Add oil; stir with fork until blended. Remove 1 c. of mixture and stir in pecans; set aside.

Dissolve baking powder and baking soda in buttermilk. Add buttermilk mixture and egg to remaining brown sugar mixture. Beat with electric mixer at medium speed 3 minutes; blend in vanilla. Pour batter into greased 13 × 9 × 2-inch baking pan. Sprinkle with reserved pecan mixture.

Bake in 350° oven 40 minutes or until golden brown. Cool in pan on rack. Can be served warm or cold. Makes 16 servings.

POPPY SEED COFFEE CAKE

Filled with lots of poppy seeds, this tender-crumbed coffee cake is a bit different. And it's not too sweet.

3 c. sifted flour	1 (13-oz.) can evaporated
1½ tsp. baking soda	milk
1 tsp. salt	⅓ c. poppy seeds
3 eggs	½ c. chopped walnuts
2 c. sugar	Sifted confectioners sugar
1 c. cooking oil	

Sift together flour, baking soda and salt.

Combine eggs, sugar and oil in mixing bowl. Beat with electric mixer at medium speed 3 minutes.

Add dry ingredients alternately with evaporated milk to egg mixture, beating well after each addition. Stir in poppy seeds and walnuts. Pour batter into ungreased 10-inch tube pan.

Bake in 325° oven 1 hour 25 minutes or until done. Cool in pan on rack. Dust with confectioners sugar before serving. Makes 16 servings.

QUICK PEACH KUCHEN

This sour cream-topped peach kuchen with its buttery shortbread-type crust is perfectly suitable for breakfast or dessert.

1 c. sifted flour	½ c. brown sugar, packed
2 tblsp. sugar	½ tsp. ground cinnamon
½ tsp. salt	2 eggs
½ c. butter or	1 c. dairy sour cream
regular margarine	¼ c. chopped unblanched
1 (1-lb. 13-oz.) can	almonds
sliced peaches, drained	

Sift together flour, sugar and salt into mixing bowl.

Cut in butter with pastry blender until crumbs form. Pat crumb mixture into bottom and one-half way up sides of ungreased 9-inch square baking pan.

Bake in 400° oven 10 minutes.

Arrange drained peaches on baked crust. Sprinkle with combined brown sugar and cinnamon. Return to oven. Bake 5 minutes more.

Meanwhile, beat eggs in bowl until thick and lemon-colored, using electric mixer at high speed. Beat in sour cream. Pour over peach layer. Sprinkle with almonds.

Bake in 400° oven 20 minutes, or until knife comes out clean when inserted in center of custard. Cool in pan on rack. Makes 6 to 8 servings.

APPLE COFFEE CAKE

"Since this recipe is so easy, I make it often for my family. Sometimes, I use home-canned apples," says a Wisconsin woman.

2 c. sifted flour	½ c. sugar
1 c. sugar	1 tsp. ground cinnamon
2 tsp. baking powder	2 tblsp. butter or
½ tsp. salt	regular margarine,
2 tblsp. shortening	melted
1 c. water	
3 c. sliced, pared tart	
apples	

Sift together flour, 1 c. sugar, baking powder and salt into mixing bowl.

Cut in shortening with pastry blender until mixture resembles coarse meal. Add water. Stir with fork until moistened. Spread mixture in greased 13 × 9 × 2-inch baking pan.

Arrange apple slices on batter. Combine ½ c. sugar and cinnamon. Sprinkle over apples. Drizzle with melted butter.

Bake in 350° oven 35 minutes or until apples are tender. Cool in pan on rack. Can be served slightly warm or cold. Makes 16 servings.

SOUR CREAM-PEAR COFFEE CAKE

"My daughter entered this coffee cake in the county 4-H fair and received a Blue Ribbon," an Iowa farm woman told us.

1½ c. sifted flour	1 egg
½ c. sugar	1 (8½-oz.) can pear halves,
2 tsp. baking powder	drained and diced (⅔ c.)
½ tsp. salt	1 egg, slightly beaten
¾ tsp. ground cinnamon	½ c. dairy sour cream
¼ c. butter or regular	¼ c. sugar
margarine	¼ tsp. ground cinnamon
½ c. evaporated milk	⅓ c. chopped walnuts

Sift together flour, ½ c. sugar, baking powder, salt and ¾ tsp. cinnamon into mixing bowl. Add butter, evaporated milk and 1 egg. Beat with electric mixer at medium speed 2 minutes. Stir in drained pears. Pour batter into greased 9-inch baking pan.

Combine slightly beaten egg with sour cream in small bowl; blend well. Spread over top of batter. Combine ¼ c. sugar, ¼ tsp. cinnamon and walnuts; sprinkle over sour cream layer.

Bake in 375° oven 30 minutes or until golden brown. Cool in pan on rack. Serve warm. Makes 9 servings.

WHAT WENT WRONG WITH MY QUICK BREADS?

My muffins turned out very pale with peaked tops—why?

You probably overmixed the batter, or the muffins might have been baked at too low a temperature.

My muffins were very dry and crumbly—why?

The oven temperature was too high and they overbaked. Perhaps your oven needs checking. Or too much flour was added to the batter. Did you sift and measure correctly?

My muffins were very tight in texture and had huge holes—why?

The muffins were definitely overmixed.

My muffins were very tough instead of light and tender—why?

You probably overmixed them, or you could have added too much flour.

My biscuits had brown spots on the surface—why?

This is a definite sign that the ingredients were not mixed together thoroughly. The spots are due to the soda in the baking powder. When the liquid isn't mixed completely with the baking powder, it leaves some soda in the leavening and that is what causes the spots.

The bottom crusts of my biscuits were very dark brown—why?

Did you use a shiny baking sheet? Shiny metal baking sheets are best because they reflect the heat away from the biscuits and keep the undercrust from browning too much.

My biscuits had a bitter taste—why?

You probably used too much baking powder or didn't measure it carefully. Or you didn't mix the dough thoroughly.

My biscuits were soggy and heavy—why?

Underbaking is the main cause of sogginess. Underbaking can also make a biscuit heavy. Too much flour, too much liquid and overmixing are other causes.

Chapter 4

Beautiful Country Cakes

Just about anyone who bakes is happy and proud to serve a beautiful cake. A light-as-a-feather, velvety-crumbed birthday cake. . . a sturdy cake full of raisins and nuts for a picnic. . . a rich, golden pound cake dusted with sugar for a company dinner. . . a sumptuous fruitcake, laden with candied cherries, nuts and citron, for the holidays.

While there are many farm homemakers who make perfect cakes, some so perfect they have won countless Blue Ribbons at the fair, many women have told us that of all the baked goods, cakes give them the most problems and they often have less-than-perfect results.

Cake making is a game you play by the rules. If you cheat even just a little bit, it will make a big difference in how your cake turns out. Cakes are created by a delicate balance of ingredients put together in just the right way.

Perhaps you haven't bothered to sift the flour because you thought it didn't matter that much. Our angel food cakes call for sifting the flour and dry ingredients together four times! And that's an important direction. Two or three times won't do. Not if you want to have a tall, beautiful, tender cake.

Maybe you beat your cake at the wrong time. In many conventional-type butter cakes, the beating is done before the dry and liquid ingredients are combined. After that, it's gentle stirring, unless the recipe specifies beating. Overbeating creates a cake that is coarse, with long tunnels. It's edible, but certainly not beautiful.

Basically, cakes fall into two general categories. First are the shortening-type cakes made with a shortening of some kind. They are often called butter cakes, too, because originally they were all made with country-fresh butter. The second category is the sponge or foam-type cake made without any shortening. There are a few "borderline" cakes, such as chiffon, but these are the two basic types.

In the conventional shortening-type cakes, the fat is creamed with the sugar. Then, the sifted dry ingredients are added alternately with the liquids to the creamed mixture. Sometimes the eggs are beaten into the creamed mixture; in other recipes, they are separated and the whites are folded into the batter at the last minute.

There are several variations of the conventional-type cake method. The one-bowl method eliminates the creaming step, which is a timesaver. Judging by the cake recipes sent to us from our farm and ranch friends, however, they prefer the basic creaming method. It does result in a lovely, fine-grained, tender-crumbed cake.

Other variations of the shortening cake are the pound cake and fruitcake. Each is handled a bit differently. Pound cakes used to be made from a pound of each major ingredient—flour, eggs and butter. These cakes were beaten for a very long time until they were light and fluffy. No leavening was used, since the air beaten into the batter made these cakes rise. Today's pound cakes are often helped out a bit with baking powder as a leavening, but beating in eggs one at a time is still an important part of making a pound cake. And you must beat very well after each egg is added. It is most helpful if you own an electric mixer—unless you really enjoy the exercise of beating!

Fruitcakes are made by the creaming method, but they are weighted with fruits, they often bake longer and their pans are lined with waxed paper and, in some cases, brown paper. This makes it easier to take this heavy cake out of the pan. Fruitcakes also need to be mellowed for several weeks before they develop their fine taste.

True sponge or foam cakes are made without any fat. Foams depend mainly on the air beaten into them for leavening. However, sponge cakes, like the pound cakes, often do have some baking powder added.

Angel food is a member of the foam-cake family. This light and lovely cake depends entirely upon the air beaten into the batter for leavening.

In most of our foam-type cakes, we use cake flour instead of all-purpose flour. Cake flour is made from soft wheat and has a very delicate gluten, which, in turn, results in the more delicate texture that characterizes foam cakes. Some cookbooks do give rules for substituting all-purpose flour for cake flour. Basically, you use 2 tablespoons less per cup of all-purpose flour. However, we feel that the cake flour gives a far superior cake.

We have a great many excellent cakes in this chapter and they are suited to every occasion. If you would like to try a layer cake first, consider the Coconut Pecan Layer Cake. It's three layers, filled and iced with a thick cream cheese frosting full of chopped pecans. When an Alabama farm woman sent us this recipe, she told us her family is positive there is not another cake in the world as delicious as this.

Another layer cake, Date-Walnut Cake, has been made for 40 years without a failure, according to the Idaho ranch woman who mailed us the recipe. Filled and topped with whipped cream, we think this cake is truly special.

If you like peanut butter, you'll love the Peanut Butter Squares. They're chock-full of peanuts, even to the topping. A Washington ranch woman told us we couldn't stop at one piece. She's right! We've never seen a cake disappear so fast from our kitchen.

Whether you are just a beginner at cakes or have been making them for years, we think these cakes will please you. Just follow our step-by-step directions carefully and you will have a beautiful cake each time.

BASIC CAKE INGREDIENTS

Flour, eggs, sugar, leavening, shortening and liquid are the basic cake ingredients. Here is how each functions:

Flour. This forms the framework of cake. A protein in the flour called gluten absorbs the liquid in the batter. It begins to swell and with the help of leavening in the cake and the heat from baking in the oven, it forms the cellular structure of the cake.

There are two types of flour used in cake baking—all-purpose and cake flour. A blend of hard and soft wheats, all-purpose is the most used of all flours in baking and is used in most of the recipes in this chapter. Cake flour is milled from soft wheat and contains less gluten than all-purpose. Rub a little between your fingers and you will feel the difference. It's much more velvety and soft to the touch than all-purpose flour. Cake flour is used primarily in the "foam-type" cakes, such as angel food, sponge and chiffon. These are very light, tender, delicate cakes.

When a recipe calls for "flour," all-purpose is the flour to use. Cake flour will be specified in those recipes which require this kind of flour.

Eggs. Eggs add flavor, color and texture to cakes and strengthen the framework of the cell walls. When beaten, they supply air for leavening. Eggs beat up more quickly and produce a higher volume if they are at room temperature. But it is much easier to separate eggs when they are cold. There's less chance of some of the egg yolk seeping into the egg white. If there is just one little bit of yolk in the egg white, it will not beat into peaks that are so important in some cake batters—angel food, for example.

When egg whites are beaten separately and folded into cake batter at the last minute, do not beat the batter afterward. Beating will break down the air cells and decrease or destroy the leavening action of the whites.

Sugar. Adds sweetness, tenderness and flavor. It also affects the browning of the cake. Use granulated sugar unless a different type is specified in the recipe.

Leavening. There are three things that make cakes light and porous—air, steam and carbon dioxide. When a cake rises, the action is usually caused by a combination of these three. Air is beaten into the batter by mixing; steam is formed from the liquid during baking and the carbon dioxide is released by the reaction between the baking powder and the moisture in the cake or by the action of baking soda with an acid, such as sour milk or molasses.

Invented early in the 19th century, baking powder is a combination of baking soda and an acid which reacts with the liquid in the batter to produce carbon dioxide. The carbon dioxide is what makes the cake rise. All of our recipes were tested with double-acting baking powder. Double-acting baking powder does just what it says—it acts twice. Some of the action takes place in the batter while it is still in the bowl, and the remaining action takes place while the batter is baking in the oven.

Another leavening, baking soda, is usually added to a recipe when it includes an acid ingredient, such as buttermilk, molasses, chocolate or fruit juice. The baking soda reacts with the acid and gives off carbon dioxide. Baking soda works quickly, so don't delay putting a cake that uses it as a leavening into the oven. There is no double action as there is in baking powder.

Always sift baking soda or baking powder with dry ingredients so as to distribute it evenly throughout the flour.

Shortening. Adds richness and makes a cake tender. It also prolongs freshness and distributes flavor. Butter, margarine, vegetable shortening and oil all give good results. However, be sure to use the type of shortening specified in the recipe. Do not use whipped butter or the soft, tub-type margarine in recipes that call for butter or margarine. Be sure to have shortening at room temperature. Foam cakes, angel and sponge cakes do not have shortening as an ingredient.

Liquids. These help all the other ingredients do their work. They help to dissolve the sugar and salt, develop the starch and gluten in the flour and form steam.

THE FROSTING ON THE CAKE

When you have made a beautiful cake, you need to "dress it up" with a handsome icing. All of our cake recipes have frosting "mates" to go along with them unless they taste best served plain or have their own baked or broiled-on icing.

There are probably thousands of variations of frostings—some full of nuts or flecked with chocolate, maraschino cherries and other fruits; others made with cream cheese instead of butter; and others that give a hint of flavor, such as mocha, almond or citrus. But basically there are three categories of frostings:

1. Fluffy Cooked Frostings, such as Seven-Minute and Sea Foam, are beaten over simmering hot water in the top of a double boiler. These icings spread easily and will mound and swirl into peaks and make a cake look very glamorous indeed. Seven-Minute frosted cakes are not the best choice to carry to a picnic as they are sticky and are best left uncovered for at least two hours after you have frosted them. After several days, they may develop a thin sugary crust. But more than likely, your cake won't last that long!

2. Cooked Fudge Frostings are really soft fudges spread on cakes. The mixture is cooked to temperature (usually soft ball stage), cooled and beaten until creamy. You need a strong arm just as you do for fudge. It isn't the easiest frosting to work with because it does tend to set quickly. If it does, place the bowl of frosting over a pan of hot water and beat in a teaspoon or two of water. If you're a beginner, don't tackle this frosting first, especially if you have just made your first cake. Instead, try our third type, the butter cream frosting.

3. Butter Cream Frostings are uncooked and are very popular because they are easy to make, taste good and travel well. They are made with confectioners sugar, a very fine pulverized sugar. The sugar is added gradually to the butter and beaten to a good spreading consistency, and then the liquid is stirred in. The consistency should not be so thin that the mixture runs off the cake or so thick that it tears the cake.

To frost a cake, always cool it thoroughly first. Brush away any loose crumbs from the sides of the cake. Place strips of waxed paper around the edge of the plate before placing the first layer of cake on the plate. Or if it is a tube- or oblong-type cake, place cake on waxed paper. The waxed paper catches the stray frosting drips or smears and can be pulled out easily when the cake is frosted.

Place the first cake layer on the plate. With a flexible metal spatula, spread frosting or filling, starting at the center, completely to the edge of the cake. Let frosting or filling set a few minutes, then place the second layer, bottom side down, on the filling.

Now frost the sides of both layers, using upward strokes. Pile the rest of the frosting on the top of the cake and spread to the edges. With the back of a spoon, make swirls and ripples for a pretty effect.

CUTTING THE CAKE

You must have a thin, pointed, very sharp knife to cut your cake easily. A serrated knife or scalloped-edge knife is particularly good for the light foam cakes.

To cut a layer cake, insert the point of the knife into the center of the cake and, deepening the point angled down slightly, saw through the cake with a gentle back and forth motion. Put very little pressure on the knife. If you do, you will squash the layers that you worked so hard to make light and fluffy. If you are cutting quite a few pieces of cake, dip the cake knife in hot water now and then to remove excess frosting.

SHORTENING OR BUTTER CAKES

Butter cakes, so-called because they were originally made with all butter, can be put together in several different ways.

The first method is the conventional method, which gives a cake a velvety, feathery texture. The ingredients are creamed together and the dry ingredients are added alternately with the liquid.

The second basic method for mixing this type of cake is a speedy one called the one-bowl method. The pattern for putting the one-bowl cakes together varies, as you will notice in our recipes.

Because the conventional butter cake does take more care and time, we have given you a step-by-step method for making it. It does take more time than the one-bowl method but we feel that you end up with a more beautiful cake. The one-bowl method does produce an acceptable cake, but the texture isn't as fine-grained and velvety as the conventional butter cake.

STEPS FOR MAKING A CONVENTIONAL-TYPE BUTTER CAKE

Here are the basic steps used in making a conventional-type butter cake.

Step 1—Prepare pans. All cakes should be baked in bright shiny metal pans. Bright pans reflect the heat away from the cake and produce the light, tender-brown crust that is just perfect. Don't use dark metal pans. Too much heat is absorbed and the cake will be too brown and crusty. Before you begin to mix your cake batter, you should grease your pans according to the directions in each recipe.

Some cake pans are simply greased such as the 13 × 9 × 2 ones, especially if the cake will be cooled and frosted right in the pan. Many layer cakes will need greased and waxed paper-lined pans. They are very delicate and might stick to the pan without the waxed paper.

Be sure to use the pan specified in the recipe. Pans that are too small may cause your cake to fall. Too big a pan may produce a cake with poor volume.

Step 2—Measure all ingredients. All ingredients should be ready when you start making the cake. For best volume, use shortening, eggs and milk that are at room temperature.

Step 3—Cream the shortening and sugar together. In a mixer bowl, cream the shortening and sugar together until the mixture is light and fluffy. Don't short-cut this step. The creaming incorporates air into the mixture and helps dissolve the sugar; done thoroughly, creaming will result in an even-grained cake with a moist, velvety texture. We used an electric mixer set at medium speed. It takes about 8 to 10 minutes for the mixture to become light and fluffy. If you are beating by hand, it will take about 150 strokes to equal one minute of electric mixer beating time.

Step 4—Add eggs. Depending upon the specific recipe, the eggs are either added one at a time and beaten well (at medium speed) after each addition or, in some cases, they are separated and the yolks are beaten in one at a time. Then the egg whites are beaten until they are stiff, but not dry, and folded into the batter after the dry ingredients have been added.

Step 5—Add the dry ingredients and liquid. Reduce the speed of the mixer to low and add the dry ingredients to the creamed mixture alternately with the liquid in five steps: dry, liquid, dry, liquid, dry. If the liquid is added first, the mixture tends to curdle.

Beat at low speed after each addition until the ingredients are well blended. This should take about 225 strokes by hand for the entire process. Be sure ingredients are thoroughly mixed, but no more. Undermixed cakes are coarse-textured and become dry and crumbly very quickly. If the batter is overmixed, the cake will be heavy and tough with a tight, compact texture.

Step 6—Pour the batter into the pans. If you have prepared a layer cake, divide the batter evenly between pans. Spread the batter evenly in the pan or pans with a rubber spatula. Tap the bottoms of the pans lightly on a counter top to remove large air bubbles.

Step 7—Place pans in preheated oven. To allow air to circulate freely in oven, place pans so that they do not touch each other or the sides of the oven. Do not open the oven door to peek at the cake while it is baking. The cake might collapse or have a deep depression in the center.

Step 8—Test for doneness. The cake is done when a wooden pick or a cake tester is inserted in the center of the cake and it comes out dry and clean.

Step 9—Remove cake from oven. Take the cakes from the oven and place them on wire racks. Cool the cakes in the pans for 10 minutes. Warm cake is very fragile. If it is allowed to stand for 10 minutes, it becomes firm enough to withstand handling. Don't let cake layers sit in the pans any longer, however, because then they might stick and become difficult to remove from the pans. To remove cakes from pans, loosen edges with a spatula. Turn out onto rack. Pull off waxed paper immediately. Invert on a second rack so that the cake is right side up. Cool. (Some of our cakes are cooled right in the pan. These are specified in the recipes.)

BASIC WHITE LAYER CAKE

Our taste panel members liked this white cake very much. It has a fine velvety texture that's so good with penuche frosting.

Easy Cake Decoration
Little silver candies or any small, colored hard candies may be used to decorate a cake. Use a toothpick to draw or space out a simple design on the frosting. Place candies carefully on design. Use tweezers, if necessary, to place each candy in position.

2⅔ c. sifted cake flour	4 egg whites
2¼ tsp. baking powder	1 tsp. vanilla
½ tsp. salt	⅔ c. cold water
1 c. butter or regular margarine	7-Minute Penuche Frosting (recipe follows)
1¼ c. sugar	

Sift together cake flour, baking powder and salt; set aside.

Cream together butter and sugar in mixing bowl until light and fluffy, using electric mixer at medium speed. Add egg whites, one at a time, beating well after each addition. Blend in vanilla.

Add dry ingredients alternately with cold water to creamed mixture, beating well after each addition, using electric mixer at low speed. Pour batter into 2 greased and waxed paper-lined 9-inch round cake pans.

Bake in 325° oven 25 to 30 minutes, or until cake tester or wooden pick inserted in center comes out clean. Cool in pans on racks 10 minutes. Remove from pans; cool on racks.

Spread the top of one layer with 7-Minute Penuche Frosting. Place second layer on top. Spread sides and top of cake with remaining frosting. Makes 12 servings.

7-Minute Penuche Frosting: Combine 2 egg whites, ¾ c. sugar, ¾ c. brown sugar (packed), ⅓ c. water and ¼ tsp. cream of tartar in top of double boiler. Beat 1 minute, using electric mixer at high speed. Place over simmering water. Cook 7 minutes, beating constantly with electric mixer at high speed, until soft glossy peaks form. Remove from hot water. Blend in 1 tsp. vanilla.

WHITE LAYER CAKE WITH ORANGE FROSTING

"Every time I showed this cake at a fair, it won a Blue Ribbon," a Missouri farm woman wrote across the bottom of the recipe.

3 c. sifted flour	**1 tsp. vanilla**
3 tsp. baking powder	**1 c. milk**
½ tsp. salt	**6 egg whites**
¾ c. butter or	**½ c. sugar**
** regular margarine**	**Orange Butter Frosting**
1½ c. sugar	** (recipe follows)**

Sift together flour, baking powder and salt; set aside.

Cream together butter and 1½ c. sugar in mixing bowl until light and fluffy, using electric mixer at medium speed. Blend in vanilla.

Add dry ingredients alternately with milk to creamed mixture, beating well after each addition, using electric mixer at low speed. (Batter will be stiff.)

Beat egg whites in another bowl until foamy, using electric mixer at high speed. Gradually beat in ½ c. sugar, beating until stiff peaks form. Fold batter into egg whites. Spread batter in 3 greased and waxed paper-lined 9-inch round cake pans.

Bake in 350° oven 20 to 25 minutes, or until cake tester or wooden pick inserted in center comes out clean. Cool in pans on racks 10 minutes. Remove from pans; cool on racks.

Spread top of one cake layer with Orange Butter Frosting. Place second layer on top. Spread with frosting. Place third layer on top. Spread sides and top of cake with frosting. Makes 16 servings.

Orange Butter Frosting: Combine 1 (1-lb.) box confectioners sugar (sifted), ½ c. soft butter or regular margarine, 1 tblsp. grated orange rind and 4 tblsp. orange juice in bowl. Beat with electric mixer at medium speed until smooth and creamy. Add 1 more tblsp. orange juice, if necessary, to make frosting of spreading consistency.

YELLOW LAYER CAKE WITH CHERRY FROSTING

A Missouri farm woman told us that this recipe has been popular since the Civil War. Try it and you'll know why.

2½ c. sifted flour	3 eggs
2 c. sugar	1 c. sour milk*
1 tsp. baking powder	Creamy Cherry Frosting
1 tsp. baking soda	(recipe follows)
⅔ c. butter or	¼ c. chopped red
regular margarine	maraschino cherries

Sift together flour, sugar, baking powder and baking soda into mixing bowl. Add butter, eggs and sour milk. Beat with electric mixer at low speed ½ minute. Turn mixer to medium speed and beat 3 more minutes. Pour batter into 2 greased and waxed paper-lined 9-inch round cake pans.

Bake in 350⁰ oven 25 minutes, or until cake tester or wooden pick inserted in center comes out clean. Cool in pans on racks 10 minutes. Remove from pans; cool on racks.

Spread the top of one layer with Creamy Cherry Frosting. Sprinkle with chopped cherries. Place second layer on top. Spread sides and top of cake with remaining frosting. Makes 12 servings.

Creamy Cherry Frosting: Combine 5½ c. sifted confectioners sugar, ¾ c. soft butter or regular margarine, 6 tblsp. juice drained from maraschino cherries, 2 drops red food coloring and ½ tsp. vanilla in bowl. Beat with electric mixer at medium speed until smooth and creamy. Add 1 more tblsp. cherry juice, if necessary to make frosting of spreading consistency.

*Note: To sour milk, place 1 tblsp. vinegar in measuring cup, add enough milk to make 1 c.

BOSTON CREAM PIE

Not really a pie, but a yellow cake filled with a velvety custard and topped with a thin chocolate glaze.

2 c. sifted cake flour	3 drops yellow food
1¼ c. sugar	coloring
2½ tsp. baking powder	1 egg
1 tsp. salt	Custard Cream Filling
⅓ c. shortening	(recipe follows)
1 c. milk	Chocolate Glaze
1 tsp. vanilla	(recipe follows)

Sift together cake flour, sugar, baking powder and salt into mixing bowl. Add shortening, milk, vanilla and yellow food coloring. Beat 2 minutes, using electric mixer at medium speed.

Add egg; beat 2 more minutes. Pour batter into 2 greased and waxed paper-lined 9-inch round cake pans.

Bake in 350° oven 25 to 30 minutes, or until cake tester or wooden pick inserted in center comes out clean. Cool in pans on racks 10 minutes. Remove from pans; cool on racks.

Prepare Custard Cream Filling. Spread the top of one cake layer with Custard Cream Filling. Top with second cake layer.

Prepare Chocolate Glaze. Quickly spread Chocolate Glaze evenly over top of cake. Refrigerate until serving time. Makes 10 servings.

Creamy Custard Filling: Combine ⅓ c. sugar, 4 tblsp. flour and ⅛ tsp. salt in 2-qt. saucepan. Gradually stir in 1½ c. milk and 3 drops yellow food coloring. Cook over medium heat, stirring constantly, until mixture comes to a boil. Cook 2 minutes, stirring constantly. Remove from heat. Beat 4 egg yolks in small bowl. Stir a small amount of hot mixture into egg yolks; blend well. Stir all of egg mixture into hot mixture, blending well. Return to low heat and cook, stirring constantly, 2 more minutes. Remove from heat. Stir in 2 tsp. vanilla. Cool completely.

Chocolate Glaze: Melt 1 (1-oz.) square unsweetened chocolate in small saucepan over very low heat. Remove from heat. Stir in ½ c. sifted confectioners sugar and ½ tsp. vanilla. Add 4 tsp. hot water, 1 tsp. at a time, blending well with spoon after each addition. Mixture should be smooth and satiny.

Blanching Almonds
Cover 1 c. of almonds with cold water. Bring to a boil. Drain. Quickly slip off skins by pressing with thumb and forefinger. For sliced or slivered almonds, cut with sharp knife while warm.

Simple Cake Design
Place a paper doily on top of unfrosted dark-colored cake. Sprinkle confectioners sugar over the doily. Remove doily.

COCONUT-PECAN LAYER CAKE

"My family and friends tell me that this is the best cake they've ever eaten," an Alabama farm woman wrote us.

2 c. sifted flour	1 tsp. vanilla
1 tsp. baking soda	1 c. buttermilk
½ c. butter or regular margarine	1⅓ c. flaked coconut
½ c. shortening	1 c. chopped pecans
2 c. sugar	Creamy Pecan Frosting (recipe follows)
5 eggs, separated	

Sift together flour and baking soda; set aside.

Cream together butter, shortening and sugar in mixing bowl until light and fluffy, using electric mixer at medium speed. Add egg yolks; beat well. Blend in vanilla.

Add dry ingredients alternately with buttermilk to creamed mixture, beating well after each addition, using electric mixer at low speed. Stir in coconut and pecans.

Beat egg whites in another bowl until stiff peaks form, using electric mixer at high speed. Fold into cake batter. Pour batter into 3 greased and waxed paper-lined 9-inch round cake pans.

Bake in 350° oven 25 minutes, or until cake tester or wooden pick inserted in center comes out clean. Cool in pans on racks 10 minutes. Remove from pans; cool on racks.

Spread the top of one layer with Creamy Pecan Frosting. Place second layer on top. Spread with frosting. Top with third layer. Frost sides and top of cake with frosting. Makes 12 servings.

Creamy Pecan Frosting: Cream together 1 (8-oz.) pkg. cream cheese and ¼ c. soft butter or regular margarine in bowl until smooth, using electric mixer at medium speed. Add 1 (1-lb.) box confectioners sugar (sifted), alternately with 3 tblsp. milk, beating well after each addition, using electric mixer at low speed. Blend in 1 tsp. vanilla. Stir in ½ c. chopped pecans.

Pretty Cake Borders
Sprinkle chopped nuts, shredded coconut, grated chocolate, or crushed peppermint stick in a 2-inch border around top of frosted cake.

APPLESAUCE LAYER CAKE

Here's a great applesauce cake for those who like a spicy cake, but don't care for raisins and nuts.

2 c. sifted flour	2 eggs
1 tsp. baking soda	1½ c. sugar
1 tsp. baking powder	½ c. cooking oil
1 tsp. salt	1 c. applesauce
1 tsp. ground cinnamon	Butter Cream Filling
¼ tsp. ground cloves	(recipe follows)

Sift together flour, baking soda, baking powder, salt, cinnamon and cloves; set aside.

Combine eggs and sugar in mixing bowl. Beat with electric mixer at medium speed 3 minutes. Blend in oil.

Add dry ingredients alternately with applesauce to oil mixture, beating well after each addition, using electric mixer at low speed. Pour batter into 2 greased and waxed paper-lined 9-inch round cake pans.

Bake in 350⁰ oven 30 minutes, or until cake tester or wooden pick inserted in center comes out clean. Cool in pans on racks 10 minutes. Remove from pans; cool on racks.

Spread the top of one layer with one half of Butter Cream Filling. Place second layer on top. Spread top with remaining filling. Makes 12 servings.

Butter Cream Filling: Combine 2 c. sifted confectioners sugar, 3 tblsp. soft butter or regular margarine, 1½ tsp. vanilla and 2 tblsp. milk in bowl. Beat until smooth and fluffy, using electric mixer at high speed.

Polka Dot Decorations
Dot a frosted cake with walnut halves or tiny colored gum drops. An easy but attractive touch.

OLD-FASHIONED COCONUT LAYER CAKE

This extra-special cake looks elegant when cut. It's three layers high and sprinkled with lots of coconut.

3½ c. sifted cake flour	1 tsp. vanilla
2 tsp. cream of tartar	1 c. milk
1 tsp. baking soda	1 c. flaked coconut
½ tsp. salt	½ c. sugar
1 c. butter or	7-Minute Frosting
regular margarine	(recipe follows)
1½ c. sugar	1⅓ c. flaked coconut
5 eggs, separated	

Sift together cake flour, cream of tartar, baking soda and salt; set aside.

Cream together butter and 1½ c. sugar until light and fluffy, using electric mixer at medium speed. Add egg yolks and vanilla; beat well.

Add dry ingredients alternately with milk to creamed mixture, beating well after each addition, using electric mixer at low speed. Stir in 1 c. coconut.

Beat egg whites in another bowl until foamy, using electric mixer at high speed. Gradually add ½ c. sugar, beating until stiff peaks form. Fold batter into egg whites. Spread batter in 3 greased and waxed paper-lined 9-inch round cake pans.

Bake in 350⁰ oven 20 minutes, or until cake tester or wooden pick inserted in center comes out clean. Cool in pans on racks 10 minutes. Remove from pans; cool on racks.

Spread top of one cake layer with 7-Minute Frosting. Place second cake layer on top. Spread with frosting. Top with third layer. Spread sides and top of cake with remaining frosting. Sprinkle sides and top of cake with 1⅓ c. coconut. Makes 12 servings.

7-Minute Frosting: Combine 2 egg whites, 1½ c. sugar, ⅓ c. water and ¼ tsp. cream of tartar in top of double boiler. Beat with electric mixer at high speed 1 minute. Place over simmering water. Cook 7 minutes, beating constantly with electric mixer at high speed until soft glossy peaks form. Remove from hot water. Beat in 1 tsp. vanilla.

STRAWBERRIES AND CREAM SPECTACULAR

This elegant dessert combines two American favorites: fresh strawberries and whipped cream. Festive and lovely for spring.

2½ c. sifted cake flour	½ tsp. vanilla
1⅔ c. sugar	5 egg yolks
4 tsp. baking powder	2 pt. fresh strawberries
1 tsp. salt	Whipped Cream (recipe
½ c. shortening	follows)
1¼ c. milk	¾ c. red currant jelly
1 tsp. lemon flavoring	

Sift together cake flour, sugar, baking powder and salt into mixing bowl. Add shortening and half of milk. Beat with electric mixer at medium speed 2 minutes, scraping bowl occasionally. Add remaining milk, lemon flavoring, vanilla and egg yolks. Beat with electric mixer 2 more minutes. Pour batter into 2 greased and waxed paper-lined 9-inch round cake pans.

Bake in 350⁰ oven 30 minutes, or until cake tester or wooden pick inserted in center comes out clean. Cool in pans on racks 10 minutes. Remove from pans; cool on racks.

Wash and hull strawberries. Chop enough strawberries to make 1 c.; reserve remaining berries.

Prepare Whipped Cream. Remove 1 c. cream; refrigerate remaining whipped cream. Fold 1 c. chopped strawberries into 1 c. cream.

Place one cake layer, top side down, on serving plate. Spread with strawberry/cream filling. Top with second cake layer, top side up.

Slice remaining strawberries. Arrange sliced strawberries on top of cake, starting at outer edge. (Place berries with point along edge of cake.) After first circle of berries is completed, continue placing strawberries in this manner until top is covered. Refrigerate 10 minutes.

Melt currant jelly in small saucepan over low heat, stirring constantly. Carefully spoon or brush hot jelly over strawberries.

Spread some of remaining Whipped Cream on sides of cake. Spoon the rest of the whipped cream into decorating bag. Using cake decorating tube with rosette tip 190, pipe rosettes between strawberry points around top edge of cake. Change to star tip 24, fill in spaces. Change to tip 71, pipe border around bottom edge of cake. If you do not wish to decorate cake with decorating tips, spoon remaining cream in small puffs on top of cake between strawberries. Refrigerate until serving time. Makes 12 servings.

Whipped Cream: Whip 2 c. heavy cream in chilled bowl until it begins to thicken, using electric mixer at high speed. Gradually beat in ¼ c. sugar and 1 tsp. vanilla. Beat until soft peaks form. (Do not overbeat.)

Note: Cake is best if served the same day.

To Line Cake Pans
Place the pan on a large piece of waxed paper. Trace around bottom of pan with point of scissors or sharp knife. Cut out. Place waxed paper in bottom of greased cake pan.

LEMON-FILLED LAYER CAKE

When an Alabama woman sent us this recipe, she said that it was one of her husband's favorite cakes.

3 c. sifted cake flour	1½ tsp. vanilla
2½ tsp. baking powder	1¼ c. milk
1 tsp. salt	Lemon Filling (recipe
⅔ c. butter or	follows)
regular margarine	Fluffy Frosting (recipe
1¾ c. sugar	follows)
2 eggs	⅔ c. flaked coconut

Sift together cake flour, baking powder and salt; set aside.

Cream together butter and sugar in bowl until light and fluffy, using electric mixer at medium speed. Add eggs, one at a time, beating well after each addition. Blend in vanilla.

Add dry ingredients alternately with milk to creamed mixture, beating well after each addition, using electric mixer at low speed. Pour batter into 2 greased and waxed paper-lined 9-inch round cake pans.

Bake in 350° oven 30 minutes, or until cake tester or wooden pick inserted in center comes out clean. Cool in pans on racks 10 minutes. Remove from pans; cool on racks.

Spread top of one cake layer with Lemon Filling. Place second layer on top. Spread sides and top of cake with Fluffy Frosting. Sprinkle coconut on top of cake. Makes 12 servings.

Lemon Filling: Combine ¾ c. sugar, 2 tblsp. cornstarch and dash of salt in small saucepan. Combine 2 egg yolks, ¾ c. water and 3 tblsp. lemon juice in small bowl. Beat with fork until blended. Gradually stir into cornstarch mixture. Cool over low heat, stirring constantly, until mixture thickens, about 10 minutes. Remove from heat; cool well.

Fluffy Frosting: Combine 2 egg whites, 1½ c. sugar, ¼ tsp. cream of tartar, ⅓ c. water and dash of salt in top of double boiler. Beat with electric mixer at high speed 1 minute. Place over simmering water. Cook 7 minutes, beating constantly with electric mixer at high speed, until soft glossy peaks form. Remove from heat. Blend in 1 tsp. vanilla.

To Beat Eggs Slightly
With a fork, mix whole eggs, yolks or whites just until texture is broken up.

DATE-WALNUT CAKE

"I have used this recipe for over 40 years and have never had a failure," wrote an Idaho woman.

1 c. cut-up pitted dates	1 c. sugar
1 c. boiling water	1 egg
1½ c. sifted flour	1 tsp. vanilla
1 tsp. baking soda	1 c. chopped walnuts
½ tsp. salt	Sweetened Vanilla Cream
1 tblsp. butter or	(recipe follows)
regular margarine	

Place dates in a small bowl; cover with boiling water. Let stand until completely cooled.

Sift together flour, baking soda and salt; set aside.

Combine butter, sugar and egg in mixing bowl. Beat with electric mixer at medium speed until well blended. Stir in date mixture.

Gradually stir in dry ingredients and vanilla. Stir in walnuts. Spread batter in 2 greased and waxed paper-lined 8-inch round cake pans.

Bake in 350° oven 20 minutes, or until cake tester or wooden pick inserted in center comes out clean. Cool in pans on racks 10 minutes. Remove from pans; cool on racks.

Spread top of one cake layer with one half of Sweetened Vanilla Cream. Place second layer on top. Spread top of cake with remaining cream. Refrigerate cake before serving. Makes 10 servings.

Sweetened Vanilla Cream: Combine 1 c. heavy cream, 2 tblsp. sugar and 1 tsp. vanilla in chilled bowl. Beat with electric mixer at high speed until soft peaks form.

Beating Eggs
Eggs give better volume if removed from the refrigerator long enough in advance to warm to room temperature before beating. If whites and yolks are to be beaten separately, separate the eggs as soon as they come from the refrigerator—they separate more easily when chilled.

CHOCOLATE VELVET CAKE

Tender, light cake layers swirled with an unusual coffee-flavored butter frosting and decorated with a melted chocolate drip.

3 (1-oz.) squares unsweetened chocolate	1 tsp. vanilla
1 c. water	1 c. buttermilk
2½ c. sifted cake flour	Creamy Coffee Frosting (recipe follows)
1½ tsp. baking soda	1 (1-oz.) square unsweetened chocolate
½ c. butter or regular margarine	1 tsp. butter or regular margarine
2 c. sugar	
3 eggs	

Combine 3 squares chocolate and water in small saucepan. Heat over medium heat until it comes to a boil. Remove from heat; cool completely.

Sift together cake flour and baking soda; set aside.

Cream together ½ c. butter and sugar in mixing bowl until light and fluffy, using electric mixer at medium speed. Add eggs, one at a time, beating well after each addition. Blend in vanilla.

Add dry ingredients alternately with buttermilk to creamed mixture, beating well after each addition, using electric mixer at low speed. Beat in chocolate mixture. Pour batter into 2 greased and waxed paped-lined 9-inch round cake pans.

Bake in 350° oven 35 minutes, or until cake tester or wooden pick inserted in center comes out clean. Cool in pans on racks 10 minutes. Remove from pans; cool on racks.

Spread top of one cake layer with Creamy Coffee Frosting. Place second cake layer on top. Spread sides and top of cake with remaining frosting.

Melt 1 square chocolate and 1 tsp. butter in small saucepan over very low heat; stir occasionally. Cool slightly. Remove from heat. Spoon chocolate around edge of top of cake, allowing it to drip down sides. Makes 12 servings.

Creamy Coffee Frosting: Combine 2 tsp. instant coffee granules and 2 tblsp. hot water in cup; set aside. Combine ¾ c. soft butter or regular margarine, 6 c. sifted confectioners sugar, 1 tsp. vanilla, 4 tblsp. milk and coffee mixture in large bowl. Beat with electric mixer at high speed until smooth and creamy.

SUNDAY CAKE SQUARES

An Ohio woman makes these for her great-grandchildren. The recipe was originally given to her mother over 70 years ago.

2½ c. sifted flour	3 eggs
3 tsp. baking powder	1 tsp. vanilla
½ tsp. salt	1 c. milk
⅛ tsp. ground nutmeg	⅓ c. sugar
1 c. shortening	1½ tsp. ground cinnamon
2 c. sugar	

Sift together flour, baking powder, salt and nutmeg; set aside.

Cream together shortening and 2 c. sugar in mixing bowl until light and fluffy, using electric mixer at medium speed. Add eggs, one at a time, beating well after each addition. Blend in vanilla.

Add dry ingredients alternately with milk to creamed mixture, beating well after each addition, using electric mixer at low speed. Spread batter in 2 greased 13 × 9 × 2-inch baking pans.

Combine ⅓ c. sugar and cinnamon; sprinkle over top of batter.

Bake in 350° oven 15 minutes, or until cake tester or wooden pick inserted in center comes out clean. Cool in pans on racks. Cut each pan into 24 servings. Makes 48 servings.

PEANUT BUTTER CAKE SQUARES

The perfect picnic treat: a moist peanut butter-flavored cake topped with a broiled-on peanut frosting. Delicious!

2¼ c. sifted cake flour	¾ c. smooth peanut butter
3 tsp. baking powder	3 eggs
¾ tsp. salt	½ tsp. vanilla
¾ c. butter or	1 c. milk
regular margarine	Broiled Peanut Butter
2¼ c. brown sugar, packed	Frosting (recipe follows)

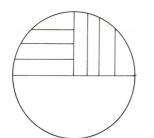

Sift together cake flour, baking powder and salt; set aside.

Cream together butter, brown sugar and peanut butter in mixing bowl until light and fluffy, using electric mixer at medium speed. Add eggs, one at a time, beating well after each addition. Blend in vanilla.

Add dry ingredients alternately with milk to creamed mixture, beating well after each addition, using electric mixer at low speed. Pour batter into greased 13 × 9 × 2-inch baking pan.

Bake in 350° oven 45 minutes, or until cake tester or wooden pick inserted in center comes out clean. Cool in pan on rack 20 minutes.

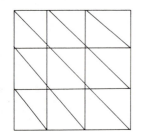

Meanwhile, prepare Broiled Peanut Butter Frosting. Spread over warm cake. Place under broiler, 3 inches from source of heat, until golden brown and bubbly, about 1 minute. Remove from broiler; cool on rack. Makes 16 servings.

Broiled Peanut Butter Frosting: Combine 1 c. brown sugar (packed), ⅓ c. butter or regular margarine, ⅔ c. smooth peanut butter and ¼ c. milk in 2-qt. saucepan; mix to blend. Cook over medium heat until butter melts and mixture is warm, stirring constantly. Remove from heat; stir in ⅔ c. chopped peanuts. Immediately spread over warm cake.

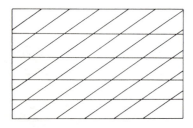

BANANA-WALNUT BARS

Mild-flavored banana bars that are perfect to pack into lunches because there's no sticky frosting to worry about.

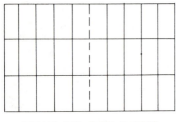

WAYS TO CUT CAKES

1¾ c. sifted flour	1 tsp. vanilla
2 tsp. baking powder	1 c. mashed ripe
½ tsp. salt	bananas (3 medium)
¼ c. shortening	½ c. chopped walnuts
1 c. sugar	Sifted confectioners sugar
2 eggs	

Sift together flour, baking powder and salt; set aside.

Cream together shortening and sugar in mixing bowl until light and fluffy, using electric mixer at medium speed. Add eggs, one at a time, beating well after each addition. Blend in vanilla.

Add dry ingredients alternately with mashed bananas to creamed mixture, beating well after each addition, using electric mixer at low speed. Stir in walnuts. Spread batter in greased 13 × 9 × 2-inch baking pan.

Bake in 350° oven 20 to 25 minutes, or until cake tester or wooden pick inserted in center comes out clean. Cool in pan on rack. Sprinkle with sifted confectioners sugar and cut into 32 (3¼ × 1½-inch) bars. Makes 32.

PINEAPPLE-CARROT CAKE

"This moist, old-fashioned cake is always a hit at picnic get-togethers," an Oregon woman wrote on the bottom of the recipe.

2½ c. sifted flour	1 c. grated, pared carrots
2 tsp. baking soda	1 (8¼-oz.) can crushed
1 tsp. salt	pineapple, drained
2 tsp. ground cinnamon	1 c. flaked coconut
1½ c. cooking oil	1 c. chopped walnuts
3 eggs	Vanilla Glaze
2 c. sugar	(recipe follows)
2 tsp. vanilla	

Sift together flour, baking soda, salt and cinnamon; set aside.

Combine cooking oil, eggs and sugar in mixing bowl. Beat with electric mixer at medium speed 2 minutes. Blend in vanilla.

Add dry ingredients, carrots, pineapple, coconut and walnuts to oil mixture, stirring to blend well. Pour into ungreased 13 × 9 × 2-inch baking pan.

Bake in 350° oven 55 minutes, or until cake tester or wooden pick inserted in center comes out clean. Place pan on rack. Immediately pour Vanilla Glaze over cake. Cool completely. Makes 16 servings.

Vanilla Glaze: Combine 1 c. sugar, 1 tsp. baking soda, ¼ c. butter or regular margarine, 1 tblsp. light corn syrup, ½ c. sour milk* and 1 tsp. vanilla in 2-qt. saucepan. Cook over medium heat, stirring constantly, until mixture comes to a boil. Simmer over low heat 5 minutes. Remove from heat; immediately pour over hot cake.

*Note: To sour milk, place 1½ tsp. vinegar in measuring cup. Add enough milk to make ½ c.

CARROT-PECAN CAKE

Flecked with shredded carrots and chopped walnuts, this tender cake is swirled with an unusual browned butter frosting.

3 c. sifted flour	2 c. sugar
2 tsp. baking powder	4 eggs
½ tsp. salt	1 tsp. vanilla
1 tsp. ground cinnamon	1 c. milk
¼ tsp. ground ginger	1 c. shredded, pared
¼ tsp. ground nutmeg	carrots
1 c. butter or	½ c. chopped pecans
regular margarine	Browned Butter Frosting
	(recipe follows)

Sift together flour, baking powder, salt, cinnamon, ginger and nutmeg; set aside.

Cream together butter and sugar in mixing bowl until light and fluffy, using electric mixer at medium speed. Add eggs, one at a time, beating well after each addition. Blend in vanilla.

Add dry ingredients alternately with milk to creamed mixture, beating well after each addition, using electric mixer at low speed. Stir in carrots and pecans. Pour batter into greased 13 × 9 × 2-inch baking pan.

Bake in 375° oven 40 minutes, or until cake tester or wooden pick inserted in center comes out clean. Cool in pan on rack.

Frost cake with Browned Butter Frosting. Makes 16 servings.

Browned Butter Frosting: Heat ¼ c. butter or regular margarine in small saucepan over low heat until butter is slightly browned. Remove from heat. Combine browned butter, 2⅓ c. sifted confectioners sugar, ½ tsp. vanilla and 2 tblsp. milk in bowl. Stir until smooth and creamy.

To Tint Coconut
Toss together ¾ c. shredded coconut and 1½ tsp. grated orange rind until tinted. Use to decorate frosted cupcakes or cakes.

DANISH PRUNE CAKE

This light, tender yellow cake is topped with cooked prune halves and then spread with a thin lemony glaze.

1 c. whole pitted prunes	⅔ c. sugar
¾ c. water	2 eggs
1 c. sifted flour	½ tsp. grated lemon rind
½ tsp. baking powder	3 tsp. lemon juice
½ tsp. salt	2 tblsp. sugar
¼ tsp. ground nutmeg	Lemon Glaze (recipe
½ c. butter or	follows)
regular margarine	

Combine prunes and water in small saucepan. Bring to a boil;

reduce heat and simmer 2 minutes. Remove from heat. Cover and let stand until completely cooled. Drain well and cut prunes in halves.

Sift together flour, baking powder, salt and nutmeg; set aside.

Cream together butter and ⅔ c. sugar in mixing bowl until light and fluffy, using electric mixer at medium speed. Add eggs, one at a time, beating well after each addition. (Mixture may look curdled.)

Stir dry ingredients into creamed mixture; blend well. Add lemon rind and 1 tsp. of the lemon juice; mix well. Spread batter in well-greased 9-inch springform pan. Arrange prune halves on top of batter, cut side down. Combine remaining 2 tsp. of the lemon juice with 2 tblsp. sugar; mix well. Sprinkle over prune layer.

Bake in 350⁰ oven 55 minutes, or until cake tester or wooden pick inserted in center comes out clean. Cool in pan on rack 10 minutes. Remove sides of pan and cool completely. Spread with Lemon Glaze. Cut in wedges. Makes 6 to 8 servings.

Lemon Glaze: Combine 1 c. sifted confectioners sugar, 1 tsp. melted butter or regular margarine, 1 tsp. lemon juice and 2½ tsp. water in mixing bowl. Beat until smooth.

ORANGE-RAISIN CAKE

An Oregon woman jotted this cake recipe on the back of an envelope in 1950 and it's still a family favorite.

1 thin-skinned whole orange	½ tsp. salt
	½ c. shortening
1 c. raisins	1 c. sugar
2 c. sifted flour	2 eggs
1 tsp. baking soda	1 c. milk
1 tsp. baking powder	Sifted confectioners sugar

Cut orange in quarters. Remove seeds but do not peel. Grind orange and raisins in food grinder, using medium blade. (You should have 1¼ c. orange-raisin mixture.)

Sift together flour, baking soda, baking powder and salt; set aside.

Cream together shortening and sugar in mixing bowl until light and fluffy, using electric mixer at medium speed. Add eggs, one at a time, beating well after each addition.

Add dry ingredients alternately with milk to creamed mixture, beating well after each addition, using electric mixer at low speed. Stir in orange-raisin mixture. Pour batter into greased 13 × 9 × 2-inch baking pan.

Bake in 350⁰ oven 30 minutes, or until cake tester or wooden pick inserted in center comes out clean. Cool in pan on rack. Sprinkle with sifted confectioners sugar. Makes 16 servings.

SPICY APPLESAUCE CAKE

"I loved this spicy, moist cake when I was a child. My grandma gave me the recipe when I got married," wrote a Michigan woman.

2 c. sifted flour	1 c. sugar
2 tsp. baking soda	2 eggs
⅛ tsp. salt	1½ c. applesauce
1 tsp. ground cinnamon	¼ c. water
½ tsp. ground nutmeg	1 c. raisins
¼ tsp. ground cloves	1 c. chopped walnuts
¼ tsp. ground ginger	Sweetened whipped cream
½ c. butter or regular margarine	

Sift together flour, baking soda, salt, cinnamon, nutmeg, cloves and ginger; set aside.

Cream together butter and sugar in mixing bowl until light and fluffy, using electric mixer at medium speed. Add eggs, one at a time, beating well after each addition. Blend in applesauce.

Add dry ingredients alternately with water to creamed mixture, beating well after each addition, using electric mixer at low speed. Stir in raisins and walnuts. Pour batter into greased 13 × 9 × 2-inch baking pan.

Bake in 375° oven 35 minutes, or until cake tester or wooden pick inserted in center comes out clean. Cool in pan on rack. Top each serving with sweetened whipped cream. Makes 16 servings.

CRUMB-TOPPED APPLE CAKE

"My son's teacher asked each student to make this when he was in sixth grade. Now his wife bakes it," wrote an Ohio woman.

1½ c. sifted flour	1 egg
1 c. sugar	2 c. finely chopped,
1 tsp. baking soda	pared apples
½ tsp. baking powder	½ c. milk
¼ tsp. salt	Cinnamon-Pecan Topping
½ c. shortening	(recipe follows)

Sift together flour, sugar, baking soda, baking powder and salt into mixing bowl. Add shortening, egg, apples and milk. Beat with electric mixer at medium speed 3 minutes. Pour batter into greased 13 × 9 × 2-inch baking pan. Sprinkle with Cinnamon-Pecan Topping.

Bake in 350° oven 40 minutes, or until cake tester or wooden pick inserted in center comes out clean. Cool in pan on rack. Makes 16 servings.

Cinnamon-Pecan Topping: Combine ½ c. brown sugar (packed) and 2 tsp. ground cinnamon in bowl. Cut in 2 tblsp. soft butter or regular margarine until crumbly, using pastry blender. Stir in ½ c. finely chopped pecans.

SLICED APPLE CAKE

"My mother baked this apple cake several times a week during the apple season when we were children," a Minnesota woman told us.

1½ c. sifted flour	½ c. milk
2 tsp. baking powder	6 c. sliced, pared
½ tsp. salt	apples
¼ c. butter or	Cinnamon Crumb
regular margarine	Topping (recipe follows)
¾ c. sugar	Sweetened whipped cream
1 egg	

Sift together flour, baking powder and salt; set aside.

Cream together butter and sugar in mixing bowl until light and fluffy, using electric mixer at medium speed. Beat in egg.

Add dry ingredients alternately with milk to creamed mixture, beating well after each addition, using electric mixer at low speed. Spread batter in greased 13 × 9 × 2-inch baking pan. Arrange apple slices in rows, leaving a small space between slices. Sprinkle Cinnamon Crumb Topping over apples.

Bake in 375° oven 40 minutes, or until apples are tender and a cake tester or wooden pick inserted into center comes out clean. Cool in pan on rack. Best if served warm, topped with a dollop of sweetened whipped cream. Makes 16 servings.

Cinnamon Crumb Topping: Combine 1¼ c. sugar, 2 tblsp. flour and 1 tsp. cinnamon in bowl. Cut in 2 tblsp. butter or regular margarine until crumbly, using a pastry blender.

Fresh Eggs Sink
A fresh egg sinks when placed in cold water. When the egg is cracked open, the yolk is firm and the white is thick.

Don't Wash Eggs
The protective coating on the shell helps preserve eggs until you are ready to use them.

OLD-FASHIONED RAISIN CAKE

"I couldn't find this recipe of my mother's for years. Then I finally discovered it in my cousin's recipe file," wrote a Michigan woman.

1½ c. raisins	1½ c. sugar
1½ tsp. baking soda	3 eggs
1½ c. boiling water	1 tsp. vanilla
2¼ c. sifted flour	½ c. chopped walnuts
1 tsp. baking powder	Seafoam Frosting (recipe
½ tsp. salt	follows)
1 c. shortening	

Grind raisins in food grinder, using medium blade. Combine ground raisins, baking soda and boiling water in bowl. Cool to lukewarm.

Sift together flour, baking powder and salt; set aside.

Cream together shortening and sugar in mixing bowl until light and fluffy, using electric mixer at medium speed. Add eggs, one at a time, beating well after each addition. Blend in vanilla.

Add dry ingredients alternately with raisin mixture to creamed mixture, beating well after each addition, using electric mixer at low speed. Stir in walnuts. Pour batter into greased and waxed paper-lined 13 × 9 × 2-inch baking pan.

Bake in 375° oven 35 to 40 minutes, or until cake tester or wooden pick inserted in center comes out clean. Cool in pan on rack 10 minutes. Remove from pan; cool on rack.

Frost sides and top with Seafoam Frosting. Makes 16 servings.

Seafoam Frosting: Combine 2 egg whites, 1½ c. brown sugar (packed), ⅓ c. water, ⅛ tsp. cream of tartar and ⅛ tsp. salt in top of double boiler. Beat 1 minute, using electric mixer at high speed. Place over simmering water. Cook 7 minutes, beating constantly with electric mixer at high speed, until soft glossy peaks form. Remove from hot water. Blend in 1 tsp. vanilla.

SURPRISE RAISIN CAKE

The surprise ingredient in this spicy cake is tomato juice. It adds moistness and richness to the cake.

3½ c. sifted flour	2 c. sugar
1 tsp. baking soda	2 c. tomato juice
1 tsp. salt	2 c. raisins
3 tsp. ground cinnamon	Rich Penuche Frosting
½ tsp. ground cloves	(recipe follows)
¾ c. shortening	

Sift together flour, baking soda, salt, cinnamon and cloves; set aside.

Cream together shortening and sugar in mixing bowl until light and fluffy, using electric mixer at medium speed.

Blend in tomato juice. Gradually beat in dry ingredients, using electric mixer at low speed. Stir in raisins. Spread batter in greased 13 × 9 × 2-inch baking pan.

Bake in 350⁰ oven 40 minutes, or until cake tester or wooden pick inserted in center comes out clean. Cool in pan on rack.

Frost top of cake with Rich Penuche Frosting. Makes 16 servings.

Rich Penuche Frosting: Combine 2 c. brown sugar (packed), ½ c. light cream and 3 tblsp. butter or regular margarine in heavy 2-qt. saucepan. Cook over medium heat, stirring constantly, until mixture comes to a boil. Continue cooking, without stirring, until temperature reaches 234⁰ on candy thermometer. Remove from heat. Cool to 110⁰. Beat with electric mixer at high speed until mixture is thick enough to spread, about 10 minutes.

FOOLPROOF CHOCOLATE CAKE

A simple-to-make deep fudgy cake with a chewy coconut topping that's spread over the warm cake and placed under the broiler.

½ c. baking cocoa	2 eggs
1 tsp. baking soda	1 tsp. vanilla
½ c. boiling water	2½ c. sifted flour
½ c. butter or	1 c. buttermilk
regular margarine	Broiled Icing (recipe
2 c. sugar	follows)

Combine cocoa, baking soda and boiling water in bowl; stir well to blend. Set aside.

Cream together butter and sugar in mixing bowl until light and fluffy, using electric mixer at medium speed. Add eggs, one at a time, beating well after each addition. Blend in vanilla.

Add flour alternately with buttermilk to creamed mixture, beating well after each addition, using electric mixer at low speed. Blend in cocoa mixture. Pour batter into greased 13 × 9 × 2-inch baking pan.

Bake in 350⁰ oven 35 minutes, or until cake tester or wooden pick inserted in center comes out clean. Cool in pan on rack 5 minutes. Spread with Broiled Icing. Place under broiler, about 5 inches from the source of heat, 2 minutes or until golden brown and bubbly. Cool in pan on rack. Cut into squares. Makes 16 servings.

Broiled Icing: Combine ⅔ c. brown sugar (packed), ⅓ c. melted butter or regular margarine, ¼ c. half-and-half and 1 c. flaked coconut in bowl; mix until blended.

CHOCO-DATE CAKE

The Minnesota woman who sent us this recipe said she originally added the oatmeal by mistake, and it's been a hit ever since.

8 oz. pitted dates, chopped	1 c. sugar
1¼ c. water	2 eggs
1¼ c. sifted flour	1 tsp. vanilla
1¼ tsp. baking soda	½ c. quick-cooking oats
½ tsp. salt	1 (6-oz.) pkg. semisweet
¾ c. butter or regular	chocolate pieces
margarine	Sweetened whipped cream

Combine dates and water in saucepan. Bring to a boil; reduce heat. Cover and simmer 10 minutes. Remove from heat; cool completely.

Sift together flour, baking soda and salt; set aside.

Cream together butter and sugar in mixing bowl until light and fluffy, using electric mixer at medium speed. Add eggs, one at a time, beating well after each addition. Beat in vanilla.

Stir flour mixture into creamed mixture, mixing well. Stir in date mixture, oats and chocolate pieces; blend well. Pour batter into greased 13 × 9 × 2-inch baking pan.

Bake in 350° oven 35 minutes, or until cake tester or wooden pick inserted in center comes out clean. Cool in pan on rack. Serve cake topped with sweetened whipped cream. Makes 16 servings.

CHOCOLATE SPICE CAKE

At Christmastime, a Texas woman makes this spicy chocolate cake instead of the usual fruitcake or coconut cake.

2 c. sifted flour	4 eggs
2 tsp. cream of tartar	3 (1-oz.) squares
1 tsp. baking soda	unsweetened chocolate,
1 tsp. ground cinnamon	melted and cooled
½ tsp. ground cloves	½ c. dairy sour cream
¼ tsp. ground nutmeg	1 c. chopped walnuts
1 c. butter or regular	8 oz. pitted dates, chopped
margarine	Cream Cheese Frosting
2 c. sugar	(recipe follows)
1 c. warm mashed	
potatoes*	

Sift together flour, cream of tartar, baking soda, cinnamon, cloves and nutmeg; set aside.

Cream together butter and sugar in mixing bowl until light and fluffy, using electric mixer at medium speed. Beat in mashed potatoes. Add eggs, one at a time, beating well after each addition.

Blend in chocolate.

Add dry ingredients alternately with sour cream to creamed mixture, beating well after each addition, using electric mixer at low speed. Stir in walnuts and dates. Pour batter into greased 13 × 9 × 2-inch baking pan.

Bake in 350⁰ oven 40 minutes, or until cake tester or wooden pick inserted in center comes out clean. Cool in pan on rack.

Frost with Cream Cheese Frosting. Makes 16 servings.

Cream Cheese Frosting: Beat 1 (3-oz.) pkg. cream cheese in mixing bowl with electric mixer at medium speed until smooth. Gradually beat in 5 tblsp. milk. Blend in 2 (1-oz.) squares unsweetened chocolate, melted and cooled. Gradually add 2 c. sifted confectioners sugar and dash of salt; beat until smooth, using electric mixer at low speed.

*Note: Prepare 2 servings instant mashed potatoes according to package directions, or use regular mashed potatoes.

Chopping Sticky Fruits
Raisins and other sticky fruits can be chopped easily by dipping knife or scissors in warm water.

PREACHER CHOCOLATE CAKE

"This recipe received its name because my grandmother made it when the preacher came for dinner," a Missouri woman said.

2 c. sifted flour	2 eggs
½ c. baking cocoa	1 tsp. vanilla
2 tsp. baking soda	½ c. sour milk*
½ tsp. salt	1 c. boiling water
½ c. shortening	Cocoa Creme Frosting
1 c. sugar	(recipe follows)
1 c. brown sugar, packed	

Sift together flour, cocoa, baking soda and salt; set aside.

Cream together shortening, sugar and brown sugar in mixing bowl until light and fluffy, using electric mixer at medium speed. Add eggs, one at a time, beating well after each addition. Blend in vanilla.

Add dry ingredients alternately with sour milk to creamed mixture, beating well after each addition, using electric mixer at low speed. Slowly blend in boiling water. (Batter is thin.) Pour batter into greased 13 × 9 × 2-inch baking pan.

Bake in 350° oven 40 minutes, or until cake tester or wooden pick inserted in center comes out clean. Cool in pan on rack. Frost with Cocoa Creme Frosting. Makes 16 servings.

Cocoa Creme Frosting: Combine 1 c. sugar and 1 tblsp. baking cocoa in 2-qt. saucepan. Gradually stir in ¼ c. milk and 6 tblsp. butter or regular margarine. Cook over medium heat, stirring constantly, until mixture comes to a boil. Boil 1 minute, stirring constantly. Remove from heat and stir in 1 tsp. vanilla. Cool to 120° on candy thermometer. Beat mixture with electric mixer at medium speed until frosting is of spreading consistency.

*Note: To sour milk, place 1½ tsp. vinegar in measuring cup. Add enough milk to make ½ c.

Toasting Almonds
Spread the blanched nuts in a shallow pan and heat in 250° oven 15 to 20 minutes or until lightly browned. Or brown the almonds in a little butter in a skillet over low heat, stirring or shaking to brown them evenly.

PINEAPPLE-TOPPED COCOA CAKE

Very dark, fudgy cake with a luscious pineapple and chocolate topping. Everyone in our test kitchens thought it was extra-good.

¾ c. baking cocoa	2 eggs, separated
1 c. boiling water	1 tsp. vanilla
2½ c. sifted flour	1 c. cold water
1 tsp. baking soda	Pineapple Topping (recipe
1 tsp. salt	follows)
½ c. shortening	Cocoa Icing (recipe
2 c. sugar	follows)

Combine cocoa and 1 c. boiling water in bowl; cool completely. Sift together flour, baking soda and salt; set aside.

Cream together shortening and sugar in mixing bowl until light and fluffy, using electric mixer at medium speed. Add egg yolks; beat well. Blend in vanilla.

Add dry ingredients alternately with 1 c. cold water to creamed mixture, beating well after each addition, using electric mixer at low speed. Blend in cooled cocoa mixture.

Beat egg whites in another bowl until stiff peaks form, using electric mixer at high speed. Fold egg whites into chocolate mixture. Pour batter into greased 13 × 9 × 2-inch cake pan.

Bake in 375° oven 30 to 35 minutes, or until cake tester or wooden pick inserted in center comes out clean. Cool in pan on rack.

Spread cooled cake with Pineapple Topping. Drizzle with Cocoa Icing. Makes 16 servings.

Pineapple Topping: Combine 1 tblsp. cornstarch, ½ c. sugar and ¹⁄₁₆ tsp. salt in 2-qt. saucepan. Stir in 1 (8¼-oz.) can crushed pineapple, undrained. Cook over medium heat, stirring constantly, until mixture boils. Remove from heat and cool completely.

Cocoa Icing: Combine ⅔ c. sifted confectioners sugar, 4 tsp. baking cocoa and 4 tsp. milk in bowl; beat until smooth.

PEANUT BUTTER-CHOCOLATE CHIP CAKE

Even a child can make this simple recipe. Both the cake and the topping are made from the same basic crumb mixture.

2¼ c. sifted flour	½ tsp. baking soda
2 c. brown sugar, packed	1 c. milk
1 c. smooth peanut butter	1 tsp. vanilla
½ c. soft butter or regular margarine	3 eggs
1 tsp. baking powder	1 (6-oz.) pkg. semisweet chocolate pieces

Combine flour, brown sugar, peanut butter and butter in mixing bowl. Beat with electric mixer at low speed until mixture is crumbly. Remove 1 c. crumb mixture and reserve.

Add baking powder, baking soda, milk, vanilla and eggs to remaining crumb mixture. Beat at low speed until blended. Then beat 3 minutes at medium speed. Pour batter into greased 13 × 9 × 2-inch baking pan. Sprinkle with reserved 1 c. crumbs and chocolate pieces.

Bake in 350° oven 40 minutes, or until cake tester or wooden pick inserted in center comes out clean. Cool in pan on rack. Makes 16 servings.

MARBLE SQUARES A LA MODE

This recipe is from the collection of a Kansas woman who has been gathering recipes for years.

⅔ c. sifted flour	1½ tsp. vanilla
½ tsp. baking powder	1 (1-oz.) square
¼ tsp. salt	unsweetened chocolate,
½ c. butter or	melted and cooled
regular margarine	Vanilla ice cream
¾ c. sugar	Fudge Sauce (recipe
2 eggs	follows)

Sift together flour, baking powder and salt; set aside.

Cream together butter and sugar in bowl until light and fluffy, using electric mixer at medium speed. Add eggs, one at a time, beating well after each addition. Blend in vanilla.

Gradually add dry ingredients to creamed mixture, beating well after each addition, using electric mixer at low speed.

Spoon one half of cake mixture into another bowl. Stir in cooled chocolate. Drop chocolate mixture and vanilla mixture alternately (like a checkerboard) in greased 8-inch square baking pan. Zigzag metal spatula through batter to marble.

Bake in 350° oven 25 to 30 minutes, or until cake tester or wooden pick inserted in center comes out clean. Cool in pan on rack. Cut in squares. When ready to serve, top each square with a scoop of vanilla ice cream. Spoon Fudge Sauce over top. Makes 9 servings.

Fudge Sauce: Combine ¾ c. sugar, 3 tblsp. baking cocoa and dash of salt in 2-qt. saucepan. Blend in 2 tblsp. water, stirring until cocoa is dissolved. Stir in ⅔ c. evaporated milk. Cook over medium heat, stirring constantly, until mixture boils. Boil over low heat 3 to 4 minutes, stirring constantly, until sauce thickens. Remove from heat. Stir in 2 tblsp. butter or regular margarine and 1 tsp. vanilla. Cool to lukewarm. Makes 1 cup.

CHOCOLATE-APPLESAUCE CAKE

No need to frost this moist applesauce cake since it's sprinkled with chocolate pieces and walnuts before baking.

2 c. sifted flour	2 eggs
2 tblsp. baking cocoa	2 tsp. vanilla
1½ tsp. baking soda	2 c. applesauce
½ tsp. salt	1 (6-oz.) pkg. semisweet
½ c. shortening	chocolate pieces
1½ c. sugar	½ c. chopped walnuts

Sift together flour, cocoa, baking soda and salt; set aside.
Cream together shortening and sugar in mixing bowl until light

and fluffy, using electric mixer at medium speed. Add eggs, one at a time, beating well after each addition. Blend in vanilla.

Add dry ingredients alternately with applesauce to creamed mixture, beating well after each addition, using electric mixer at low speed. Pour batter into greased 13 × 9 × 2-inch baking pan. Sprinkle with chocolate pieces and walnuts.

Bake in 350⁰ oven 35 minutes, or until cake tester or wooden pick inserted in center comes out clean. Cool in pan on rack. Makes 16 servings.

CHOCOLATE-RAISIN CAKE

A home-style snacking cake that can be eaten out-of-hand. Just right for picnics and barbecues.

1 c. raisins	1 c. sugar
1 c. hot water	2 eggs
1 tsp. baking soda	1 tsp. vanilla
2 c. sifted flour	1 (6-oz.) pkg. semisweet
¼ tsp. salt	chocolate pieces
1 c. butter or regular margarine	½ c. chopped walnuts

Combine raisins, hot water and baking soda in bowl. Cool to room temperature.

Sift together flour and salt; set aside.

Cream together butter and sugar in mixing bowl until light and fluffy, using electric mixer at medium speed. Add eggs, one at a time, beating well after each addition. Blend in vanilla.

Add dry ingredients alternately with raisin mixture to creamed mixture, beating well after each addition, using electric mixer at low speed. Stir in one half of chocolate pieces. Pour batter into greased 13 × 9 × 2-inch baking pan. Sprinkle with remaining chocolate pieces and walnuts.

Bake in 350⁰ oven 40 minutes, or until cake tester or wooden pick inserted in center comes out clean. Cool in pan on rack. Makes 16 servings.

Checkerboard Cake
Frost half a square or oblong cake with a light frosting, and the other half with a dark frosting. Cut in squares. Place a walnut half in the center of each square. Alternate squares of light and dark frosted cake on a serving tray.

CHOCOLATE DATE CAKE

"I first enjoyed this moist date cake at a sewing class 20 years ago,"
a New York woman told us.

1¼ c. boiling water	1 c. sugar
1 c. chopped dates	2 eggs
2 c. sifted flour	1 (6-oz.) pkg. semisweet
2 tblsp. baking cocoa	chocolate pieces
1 tsp. baking soda	½ c. chopped walnuts
½ tsp. salt	¼ c. sugar
¾ c. butter or regular	
margarine	

Pour boiling water over dates in small bowl. Cool to room temperature.

Sift together flour, baking cocoa, baking soda and salt; set aside.

Cream together butter and 1 c. sugar in mixing bowl until light and fluffy, using electric mixer at medium speed. Add eggs, one at a time, beating well after each addition.

Add dry ingredients alternately with date mixture to creamed mixture, beating well after each addition, using electric mixer at low speed. Pour into greased 13 × 9 × 2-inch baking pan. Combine chocolate pieces, walnuts and remaining ¼ c. sugar in small bowl; mix well. Sprinkle over batter.

Bake in 350° oven 35 minutes, or until cake tester or wooden pick inserted in center comes out clean. Cool in pan on rack. Makes 16 servings.

CHERRY-CHOCOLATE CAKE

Even if you don't have a lot of baking experience, you will be able to make this easy cake, and you don't need a mixer.

1 (18½-oz.) box dark	2 eggs
chocolate cake mix	1 tsp. almond flavoring
1 (21-oz.) can cherry pie	Deep Chocolate Frosting
filling	(recipe follows)

Combine cake mix, cherry pie filling, eggs and almond flavoring in mixing bowl. Stir until mixture is well blended, using wooden spoon. Spread batter in greased 13 × 9 × 2-inch cake pan.

Bake in 350° oven 35 minutes, or until cake tester or wooden pick inserted in center comes out clean. Cool in pan on rack 15 minutes. Meanwhile, prepare Deep Chocolate Frosting. Spread on warm cake. Cool completely. Makes 16 servings.

Deep Chocolate Frosting: Combine 1 c. sugar, 5 tblsp. butter or regular margarine and ⅓ c. milk in 2-qt. saucepan. Cook over medium heat, stirring constantly, until mixture comes to a boil. Boil for 1 minute. Remove from heat. Stir in 1 (6-oz.) pkg. semisweet chocolate pieces. Stir until smooth.

QUICK-FIX CHOCOLATE CAKE

This cake is extra-moist because it's made with prepared chocolate pudding from a mix and a chocolate cake mix.

1 (4-oz.) pkg. chocolate
    pudding and pie filling
    mix
2 c. milk
1 (18½-oz.) pkg. milk
    chocolate cake mix

⅔ c. cooking oil
1 (6-oz.) pkg. semisweet
    chocolate pieces
½ c. chopped pecans

Combine pudding mix and milk in 2-qt. saucepan. Cook according to package directions for pudding. Remove from heat. Cool to room temperature.

Combine cake mix and oil in mixing bowl. Beat with electric mixer at medium speed until blended.

Add cooled pudding to cake batter and beat at medium speed 2 minutes. Pour into greased 13 × 9 × 2-inch baking pan. Sprinkle with chocolate pieces and pecans.

Bake in 350⁰ oven 40 minutes, or until cake tester or wooden pick inserted in center comes out clean. Cool in pan on rack. Makes 16 servings.

To Flour Pans
Sprinkle each greased pan with a little flour; shake pan to coat it evenly. Remove excess flour by gently knocking inverted pan on work surface.

HEIRLOOM SPICE CAKE

This spice cake has always been baked in a cast-iron skillet for three generations in one Ohio family.

2 c. sifted flour	1 c. sugar
1 tsp. baking soda	1 egg
½ tsp. salt	1 c. sour milk*
1 tsp. ground cinnamon	1 c. chopped walnuts
½ tsp. ground nutmeg	1 c. raisins
¼ tsp. ground cloves	Sifted confectioners sugar
1 c. butter or	
regular margarine	

Sift together flour, baking soda, salt, cinnamon, nutmeg and cloves; set aside.

Cream together butter and sugar in mixing bowl until light and fluffy, using electric mixer at medium speed. Beat in egg.

Add dry ingredients alternately with sour milk to creamed mixture, beating well after each addition, using electric mixer at low speed. Stir in walnuts and raisins. Pour batter into greased 13 × 9 × 2-inch baking pan.

Bake in 350⁰ oven 40 minutes, or until cake tester or wooden pick inserted in center comes out clean. Sprinkle with sifted confectioners sugar. Makes 16 servings.

*Note: To sour milk, place 1 tblsp. vinegar in measuring cup. Add enough milk to make 1 c.

FROSTED COFFEE BARS

Flavored with coffee and studded with raisins and walnuts, these cake-like bars were a favorite in our test kitchens.

½ c. raisins	¼ c. shortening
Boiling water	1 c. brown sugar, packed
1½ c. sifted flour	1 egg
½ tsp. baking soda	1 tsp. vanilla
½ tsp. baking powder	½ c. hot coffee
½ tsp. salt	¼ c. chopped walnuts
½ tsp. ground cinnamon	Glaze (recipe follows)

Place raisins in a bowl. Add enough boiling water to cover; cool completely. Drain off water.

Sift together flour, baking soda, baking powder, salt and cinnamon; set aside.

Cream together shortening and brown sugar in mixing bowl until light and fluffy, using electric mixer at medium speed. Add egg and vanilla; beat well.

Add dry ingredients alternately with hot coffee to creamed mixture, beating well after each addition, using electric mixer at low speed. Stir in walnuts and raisins. Pour into greased 13 × 9 × 2-inch baking pan.

Bake in 350⁰ oven 20 minutes, or until cake tester or wooden pick inserted in center comes out clean. Cool in pan on rack 10 minutes. While still warm, pour Glaze over cake. Cut into 32 (3¼ × 1½-inch) bars. Makes 32 bars.

Glaze: Combine 1 c. sifted confectioners sugar, 1 tblsp. butter or regular margarine, 2 tblsp. milk and ½ tsp. vanilla in bowl; beat until smooth.

NUTMEG CAKE WITH LEMON SAUCE

A very rich brown sugar cake spiced with nutmeg. It's at its best served slightly warm with a spoon of extra-lemony sauce.

2 c. sifted cake flour	1 egg
2 c. brown sugar, packed	1 c. dairy sour cream
½ c. butter or regular margarine	½ c. chopped pecans
1 tsp. baking soda	Tangy Lemon Sauce (recipe follows)
1 tsp. ground nutmeg	

Combine cake flour and brown sugar in bowl. Cut in butter until coarse crumbs form, using pastry blender. Press one half of crumb mixture into greased 9-inch square baking pan.

Add baking soda and nutmeg to remaining crumb mixture; mix well. Stir in egg and sour cream; stirring well. Spread mixture in pan. Sprinkle with pecans.

Bake in 350⁰ oven 35 minutes, or until cake tester or wooden pick inserted in center comes out clean. Cool in pan on rack. Serve warm with Tangy Lemon Sauce. Makes 9 servings.

Tangy Lemon Sauce: Combine ¾ c. sugar, 1½ tblsp. cornstarch and ⅛ tsp. salt in 2-qt. saucepan; mix well. Stir in 1 c. water and 2 tblsp. lemon juice. Cook over medium heat, stirring constantly, until mixture thickens and comes to a boil. Boil 1 minute. Remove from heat; stir in 1 tsp. grated lemon rind, dash of ground mace, 2 tblsp. butter or regular margarine and 1 drop of yellow food coloring. Spoon over squares of warm cake.

MARBLE MOLASSES CAKE SQUARES

"I remember watching my mother make this marble cake every Saturday. It's so pretty," a Minnesota woman told us.

Whipped Cream-Frosted Cakes
If a cake has a whipped cream filling or frosting, serve at once. Or store in refrigerator until served. After serving, return to refrigerator.

1½ c. sifted flour	1 tsp. ground cinnamon
2 tsp. baking powder	1 tsp. ground nutmeg
½ tsp. salt	½ tsp. ground cloves
½ c. butter or	½ tsp. salt
regular margarine	½ c. butter or
½ c. sugar	regular margarine
3 eggs, separated	½ c. sugar
½ tsp. vanilla	½ c. molasses
½ c. milk	½ c. sour milk*
1½ c. sifted flour	Sifted confectioners sugar
1 tsp. baking soda	

To make vanilla batter: Sift together 1½ c. flour, baking powder and ½ tsp. salt; set aside.

Cream together ½ c. butter and ½ c. sugar in mixing bowl until light and fluffy, using electric mixer at medium speed. Beat in egg whites and vanilla.

Add dry ingredients alternately with milk to creamed mixture, beating well after each addition, using electric mixer at low speed. Set aside.

To make molasses batter: Sift together 1½ c. flour, baking soda, cinnamon, nutmeg, cloves and ½ tsp. salt; set aside.

Cream together ½ c. butter and ½ c. sugar in mixing bowl until light and fluffy, using electric mixer at medium speed. Beat in egg yolks and molasses.

Add dry ingredients alternately with sour milk to creamed mixture, beating well after each addition, using electric mixer at low speed.

Drop molasses batter and vanilla batter alternately (like a checkerboard) in greased and waxed paper-lined 13 × 9 × 2-inch baking pan.

Bake in 350° oven 35 minutes, or until cake tester or wooden pick inserted in center comes out clean. Cool in pan on rack 10 minutes. Remove from pan; cool on rack. Sprinkle with sifted confectioners sugar before serving. Makes 16 servings.

*Note: To sour milk, place 1½ tsp. vinegar in measuring cup. Add enough milk to make ½ c.

HEIRLOOM GINGERBREAD

Deep, dark gingerbread with a rich molasses flavor. Superb served slightly warm with a puff of whipped cream.

2½ c. sifted flour	½ c. butter or
1½ tsp. baking soda	regular margarine
½ tsp. salt	½ c. sugar
1 tsp. ground cinnamon	1 egg
1 tsp. ground ginger	1 c. molasses
¼ tsp. ground cloves	1 c. hot water

Sift together flour, baking soda, salt, cinnamon, ginger and cloves; set aside.

Cream together butter and sugar in mixing bowl until light and fluffy, using electric mixer at medium speed. Add egg; beat well. Gradually beat in molasses.

Add dry ingredients alternately with hot water to creamed mixture, beating well after each addition, using electric mixer at low speed. Pour batter into greased 13 × 9 × 2-inch baking pan.

Bake in 350⁰ oven 25 minutes, or until cake tester or wooden pick inserted in center comes out clean. Cool in pan on rack. Makes 16 servings.

CRUMB-TOPPED GINGERBREAD

An easy-mix gingerbread that doesn't even require beating. Turns out a light, tender cake every time.

2 c. sifted flour	1 egg
1 c. sugar	2 tblsp. molasses
1½ tsp. ground ginger	1 tsp. baking soda
1 tsp. ground cinnamon	½ tsp. salt
½ c. shortening	1 c. sour milk*

Sift together flour, sugar, ginger and cinnamon in mixing bowl. Cut in shortening with pastry blender until mixture is crumbly. Remove ½ c. crumb mixture; set aside.

Add egg, molasses, baking soda, salt and sour milk to remaining crumb mixture; stir well to blend. Pour batter into greased 8-inch square baking pan. Sprinkle with reserved ½ c. crumb mixture.

Bake in 350⁰ oven 45 minutes, or until cake tester or wooden pick inserted in center comes out clean. Cool in pan on rack. Makes 9 servings.

*To Sour Milk: Place 1 tblsp. vinegar in measuring cup. Add enough milk to make 1 c.

OLD-FASHIONED GINGERBREAD

Surround each cake square with sliced fresh peaches, top with a scoop of vanilla ice cream and dust with cinnamon.

2½ c. sifted flour	½ c. shortening
1½ tsp. baking soda	½ c. sugar
1 tsp. ground ginger	1 egg
1 tsp. ground cinnamon	1 c. dark molasses
½ tsp. salt	½ c. hot water

Sift together flour, baking soda, ginger, cinnamon and salt; set aside.

Cream together shortening and sugar in mixing bowl until light and fluffy, using electric mixer at medium speed. Beat in egg and molasses.

Add dry ingredients alternately with hot water to creamed mixture, beating well after each addition, using electric mixer at low speed. Pour batter into greased 9-inch square baking pan.

Bake in 350° oven 45 minutes, or until cake tester or wooden pick inserted in center comes out clean. Cool in pan on rack. Makes 9 servings.

BASIC SPICY GINGERBREAD

If you like an extra-spicy gingerbread, this recipe is for you. Great to eat out-of-hand, warm from the oven, with butter.

1 c. sifted flour	½ c. molasses
1 tsp. baking soda	1 egg
½ tsp. salt	¼ c. sugar
½ tsp. ground cinnamon	¼ c. melted shortening
½ tsp. ground nutmeg	½ c. hot water
¼ tsp. ground cloves	

Sift together flour, baking soda, salt, cinnamon, nutmeg and cloves; set aside.

Combine molasses, egg and sugar in mixing bowl. Beat with electric mixer at medium speed until well blended.

Add dry ingredients to molasses mixture, beating well, using electric mixer at low speed. Blend in melted shortening and hot water; beat well. Pour batter into greased and floured 8-inch square baking pan.

Bake in 350° oven 30 to 35 minutes, or until cake tester or wooden pick inserted in center comes out clean. Cool in pan on rack. Makes 9 servings.

PINEAPPLE UPSIDE-DOWN CAKE

One of the popular cakes tested in our Countryside Test Kitchens this year. Sour cream gives it a unique flavor.

½ c. butter or regular
   margarine
1 c. brown sugar, packed
1 (8¼-oz.) can crushed
   pineapple
2 c. sifted flour
2 tsp. baking powder
½ tsp. salt

⅔ c. butter or
   regular margarine
1½ c. sugar
3 eggs
½ tsp. almond extract
1 c. dairy sour cream
Sweetened whipped
   cream

Beating Cakes By Hand
150 strokes is equivalent to one minute of beating time with electric mixer.

Combine ½ c. butter and brown sugar in 2-qt. saucepan. Cook over medium heat, stirring constantly, until mixture is bubbly. Immediately pour into ungreased 12 × 8 × 2-inch glass baking dish (2-qt.). Spoon undrained pineapple over all. Set aside.

Sift together flour, baking powder and salt; set aside.

Cream together ⅔ c. butter and sugar in mixing bowl until light and fluffy, using electric mixer at medium speed. Add eggs, one at a time, beating well after each addition. Blend in almond extract.

Add dry ingredients alternately with sour cream to creamed mixture, beating well after each addition, using electric mixer at low speed. Pour batter into prepared baking dish.

Bake in 325° oven 55 minutes, or until cake tester or wooden pick inserted in center comes out clean. Invert pan on rack; cool on rack. Best if served warm with a puff of sweetened whipped cream. Makes 12 servings.

SKILLET PINEAPPLE UPSIDE-DOWN CAKE

"My husband is always asking me to make this luscious pineapple upside-down cake," a Kansas farm woman wrote on the recipe.

2 (8¼-oz.) cans sliced pineapple in heavy syrup	8 pecan halves
¼ c. butter or regular margarine	1 c. sifted flour
⅓ c. sugar	¾ c. sugar
⅓ c. brown sugar, packed	1½ tsp. baking powder
7 red maraschino cherries, halved	½ tsp. salt
	¼ c. shortening
	1 egg

Drain pineapple, reserving ½ c. syrup. Set aside.

Melt butter in 10-inch ovenproof skillet. Stir in ⅓ c. sugar and brown sugar until blended. Arrange pineapple slices, maraschino cherries and pecan halves in syrup in skillet. Set aside.

Sift together flour, ¾ c. sugar, baking powder and salt into large bowl. Add shortening and reserved ½ c. pineapple syrup. Beat 2 minutes, using electric mixer at medium speed. Add egg; beat 2 more minutes. Pour batter evenly into prepared skillet.

Bake in 350° oven 40 minutes, or until cake tester or wooden pick inserted in center comes out clean. Cool in skillet on rack 5 minutes. Loosen around edges of cake with metal spatula. Invert onto cooling rack. Best if served warm. Makes 10 servings.

FRUITCAKES

Fruitcakes date back to pre-Colonial days. The English made fruitcakes bursting with raisins, candied fruits and nuts. They aged and ripened these Christmas specials just as we do today.

Fruitcakes are made just like the conventional butter cakes, but they take a long time to bake and are baked at lower temperatures. Be sure not to overbake these fruit-studded cakes or they will be dry and crumbly.

Make your fruitcakes ahead—even a month ahead is none too soon. Then let them ripen and mellow in an airtight container (or wrapped in cloths soaked in brandy or apple juice) in a cool place. If you can't find a cool spot in your home, put them in the refrigerator to ripen until the flavors marry together to produce a moist cake that is easy to cut and delicious to eat.

BEST-EVER FRUITCAKE

This recipe makes two large lightly-glazed fruitcakes studded with dates, currants, raisins and flavored with currant jelly.

3 c. raisins	½ tsp. ground nutmeg
2½ c. dried currants	¼ tsp. ground cloves
8 oz. pitted dates, chopped	1¼ c. shortening
1 c. halved red maraschino cherries, drained	2 c. sugar
	2 tblsp. light corn syrup
1 c. chopped citron	1 c. red currant jelly
2 c. chopped walnuts	6 eggs
2 c. chopped pecans	1 c. orange juice
5 c. sifted flour	2 tblsp. light corn syrup
1 tsp. baking soda	¼ c. sugar
1 tsp. baking powder	¼ c. water
1 tsp. salt	4 tsp. lemon juice
1 tsp. ground cinnamon	

Combine raisins, currants, dates, maraschino cherries, citron, walnuts and pecans in 6-qt. mixing bowl; set aside.

Sift together flour, baking soda, baking powder, salt, cinnamon, nutmeg and cloves; set aside.

Cream together shortening and 2 c. sugar in mixing bowl until light and fluffy, using electric mixer at medium speed. Beat in 2 tblsp. light corn syrup and currant jelly. Add eggs, one at a time, beating well after each addition.

Add dry ingredients alternately with orange juice to creamed mixture, beating well after each addition, using electric mixer at low speed. Pour batter over fruit-nut mixture; mix well with wooden spoon. Spread batter in 2 greased and floured 10-inch tube pans.

Bake in 275° oven 2 hours, or until cake tester or wooden pick inserted in center comes out clean. Cool in pans on racks 10 minutes. Remove from pans; cool on racks.

Combine 2 tblsp. light corn syrup, ¼ c. sugar, water and lemon juice in small saucepan. Cook over medium heat, stirring constantly, until mixture comes to a boil. Remove from heat; cool 5 minutes. Brush syrup over warm fruitcakes. Cool completely. Makes 2 fruitcakes.

To Store: Wrap cooled fruitcakes in aluminum foil and store in cool dry place for 1 to 2 months.

MINIATURE FRUITCAKES

A Michigan woman found this recipe in a magazine several years ago. She's changed it so much, she feels it's a new recipe.

1 (6-oz.) can frozen orange juice concentrate, thawed	1¼ c. sifted flour
	⅛ tsp. baking soda
½ c. dark corn syrup	½ tsp. ground cinnamon
1 (15-oz.) box golden raisins	¼ tsp. ground nutmeg
	⅛ tsp. ground allspice
1 c. dried currants	⅛ tsp. ground cloves
4 oz. red candied cherries, halved	½ c. butter or regular margarine
4 oz. green candied cherries, halved	⅔ c. sugar
	3 eggs
8 oz. diced candied pineapple	1 c. coarsely chopped pecans

Combine orange juice concentrate, dark corn syrup, raisins and currants in 3-qt. saucepan. Cook over medium heat, stirring occasionally, until mixture comes to a boil. Reduce heat and simmer 5 minutes. Remove from heat.

Reserve 33 of the red candied cherry halves and 33 of the green candied cherry halves to decorate each fruitcake; set aside.

Stir remaining candied cherries and pineaplle into raisin mixture; set aside.

Sift together flour, baking soda, cinnamon, nutmeg, allspice and cloves; set aside.

Cream together butter and sugar in mixing bowl until light and fluffy, using electric mixer at medium speed. Add eggs, one at a time, beating well after each addition. Gradually stir in dry ingredients. Add fruit mixture and pecans; mix well. Spoon batter into paper-lined 1¾-inch muffin-pan cups, filling three-fourths full. Top each with candied cherry half.

Bake in 350⁰ oven 20 to 25 minutes, or until cake tester or wooden pick inserted in center comes out clean. Remove from pans; cool on racks. Makes 66 miniature fruitcakes.

To Store: Place fruitcakes in tightly-covered container and store in cool, dry place for at least 1 week to improve flavor.

GOLDEN FRUITCAKE LOAVES

A Kansas family looks forward to this no-citron fruitcake every Christmas. It's filled with dates, cherries and citrus peel.

8 oz. chopped candied pineapple	3½ c. sifted flour
8 oz. pitted dates, chopped	1½ tsp. baking powder
4 oz. red candied cherries	1 tsp. salt
4 oz. green candied cherries	1 tsp. ground cinnamon
4 oz. chopped candied orange peel	¾ c. shortening
4 oz. chopped candied lemon peel	1 c. brown sugar, packed
1½ c. raisins	1 c. dark corn syrup
2 c. chopped walnuts	½ c. milk
	1 tsp. vanilla
	4 eggs

Combine pineapple, dates, red and green cherries, orange peel, lemon peel, raisins, walnuts and 1½ c. of the flour in 6-qt. mixing bowl; set aside.

Sift together remaining 2 c. flour, baking powder, salt and cinnamon; set aside.

Cream together shortening and brown sugar in mixing bowl until light and fluffy, using electric mixer at medium speed. Beat in corn syrup, milk and vanilla; mix well. Add eggs, one at a time, beating well after each addition.

Gradually add dry ingredients to creamed mixture, mixing well with wooden spoon after each addition. Pour batter over fruit-nut mixture; mix well. Spread batter evenly in 3 greased and waxed paper-lined 8½ × 4½ × 2½-inch loaf pans.

Bake in 275° oven 2 hours 10 minutes, or until cake tester or wooden pick inserted in center comes out clean. Cool in pans on racks 10 minutes. Remove from pans; cool on racks. Makes 3 loaves.

To Store: Wrap cooled fruitcakes in aluminum foil and store in cool dry place for 1 to 2 months.

Cracking Whole Walnuts
Hold the walnut so it stands on its flat end. With a hammer, strike the pointed end with a sharp blow Or, use a nutcracker if you have one. While you're cracking, do a whole pound of walnuts at once. Store kernels in covered jar or plastic bag in refrigerator or freezer.

RICH FRUITCAKE

Very dark fruitcake with real molasses flavor. It's filled with lots of dates and raisins.

½ tsp. instant coffee powder	½ c. butter or regular margarine
½ c. boiling water	1 c. brown sugar, packed
2½ c. sifted flour	3 eggs
1 tsp. baking soda	½ c. molasses
½ tsp. salt	2½ c. raisins
1 tsp. ground cinnamon	1 c. mixed candied fruit
½ tsp. ground nutmeg	
½ tsp. ground allspice	1 c. chopped pitted dates
¼ tsp. ground cloves	½ c. chopped pecans

Dissolve coffee powder in boiling water; set aside to cool.

Sift together flour, baking soda, salt, cinnamon, nutmeg, allspice and cloves; set aside.

Cream together butter and brown sugar in bowl until light and fluffy, using electric mixer at medium speed. Add eggs, one at a time, beating well after each addition.

Combine coffee and molasses. Add dry ingredients alternately with coffee-molasses mixture to creamed mixture, beating well after each addition, using electric mixer at low speed. Stir in raisins, candied fruit, dates and pecans. Spread batter in 2 greased and waxed paper-lined 8½ × 4½ × 2½-inch loaf pans.

Add enough hot tap water to a 13 × 9 × 2-inch baking pan or a roasting pan to fill 1 inch deep. Place on lower rack in oven. This helps to moisten cake.

Bake in 275° oven on top rack 2 hours, or until cake tester or wooden pick inserted in center comes out clean. Remove from pans; cool on racks. Makes 2 loaves.

To Store: Wrap cooled fruitcakes in aluminum foil and store in a cool, dry place for 1 to 2 months.

POUND CAKES

Our great-great-grandmothers made their pound cakes with a pound of every ingredient—flour, butter and eggs. The leavening in these pound cakes was the air that was beaten into them. They were beaten and beaten until your arm was so tired you couldn't beat another stroke.

Today's pound cakes can be made with an electric mixer and do not require ingredients by the pound. Baking powder is the leavening, but the eggs are beaten in separately and beaten very well after each addition.

In fact, many of the younger cooks have never tasted a real old-fashioned pound cake made without any leavening but air. When they do, they are often disappointed and prefer the modern version. It's lighter and not as dense and compact as the old-fashioned pound.

OLD-FASHIONED POUND CAKE

Since this pound cake is leavened only by the air beaten into the batter, it's very important to beat the full 10 minutes.

1 c. butter or regular margarine	1 tsp. vanilla
1⅔ c. sugar	2 c. sifted flour
5 eggs	½ c. milk

Cream together butter and sugar in mixing bowl until light and fluffy, using electric mixer at medium speed. Add eggs, one at a time, beating well after each addition. Blend in vanilla (total beating time: 10 minutes).

Add flour alternately with milk to creamed mixture, beating well after each addition, using electric mixer at low speed. Pour batter into greased 10-inch fluted tube pan.

Bake in 350⁰ oven 1 hour, or until cake tester inserted in center comes out clean or top springs back when lightly touched with finger. Cool in pan on rack 10 minutes. Remove from pan; cool on rack. Makes 12 servings.

CONFECTIONERS SUGAR POUND CAKE

This yellow pound cake makes the perfect shortcake base, ladled with sweetened, sliced strawberries and topped with cream.

2½ c. sifted flour	1 (1-lb.) box confectioners
1 tsp. baking powder	sugar, sifted
½ tsp. salt	6 eggs
1½ c. butter or	2 tsp. vanilla
regular margarine	Sifted confectioners sugar

Sift together flour, baking powder and salt; set aside.

Cream together butter and 1 lb. confectioners sugar in mixing bowl until light and fluffy, using electric mixer at medium speed. Add eggs, one at a time, beating well after each addition. Blend in vanilla (total beating time: 10 minutes).

Add dry ingredients, one-third at a time to creamed mixture, beating well after each addition. Pour batter into greased 10-inch tube pan.

Bake in 350° oven 1 hour, or until cake tester inserted in center comes out clean or top springs back when lightly touched with finger. Cool in pan on rack 10 minutes. Remove from pan; cool on rack. Sprinkle with sifted confectioners sugar. Makes 12 servings.

WALNUT POUND CAKE

Delicately flavored with ground walnuts, this cake is made with a favorite heirloom recipe of a Maryland woman.

3 c. sifted flour	3 eggs
½ tsp. baking powder	2 tsp. vanilla
½ tsp. baking soda	1 c. sour milk*
¾ tsp. salt	½ c. finely ground
1 c. butter or	walnuts
regular margarine	Sifted confectioners sugar
2 c. sugar	

Sift together flour, baking powder, baking soda and salt; set aside.

Cream together butter and sugar in mixing bowl until light and fluffy, using electric mixer at medium speed. Add eggs, one at a time, beating well after each addition. Blend in vanilla (total beating time: 10 minutes).

Add dry ingredients alternately with sour milk to creamed mixture, beating well after each addition, using electric mixer at low speed. Stir in walnuts. Pour batter into greased 10-inch tube pan.

Bake in 350° oven 1 hour, or until cake tester inserted in center comes out clean or top springs back when lightly touched with finger. Cool in pan on rack 10 minutes. Remove from pan; cool on

rack. Sprinkle with sifted confectioners sugar. Makes 12 servings.
*Note: To sour milk, place 1 tblsp. vinegar in measuring cup. Add enough milk to make 1 c.

GRANDMA'S CHOCOLATE POUND CAKE

A Mississippi woman received this recipe from her grandmother. The cake has a very mild chocolate flavor.

3 c. sifted flour	½ c. shortening
4 tblsp. baking cocoa	2 c. sugar
½ tsp. baking powder	5 eggs
½ tsp. salt	1½ tsp. vanilla
1 c. butter or regular margarine	1 c. milk
	Sifted confectioners sugar

Sift together flour, cocoa, baking powder and salt; set aside.

Cream together butter, shortening and sugar in bowl until light and fluffy, using electric mixer at medium speed. Add eggs, one at a time, beating well after each addition. Blend in vanilla (total beating time: 10 minutes).

Add dry ingredients alternately with milk to creamed mixture, beating well after each addition. Pour batter into greased 10-inch tube pan.

Bake in 325° oven 1 hour 20 minutes, or until cake tester inserted in center comes out clean or top springs back when lightly touched with finger. Cool in pan on rack 10 minutes. Remove from pan; cool on rack. Sprinkle with sifted confectioners sugar. Makes 12 servings.

Chopped Walnut Decoration
Take a big handful of chopped walnuts and press against the frosted sides of a cake. Repeat until cake sides are blanketed with nuts. Leave top plain or decorate with walnut halves.

PUMPKIN POUND CAKE

"My husband enjoys growing the pumpkins for this cake, which is his favorite pound cake," a North Carolina woman told us.

3 c. sifted flour	2 eggs
4 tsp. baking powder	1 c. canned or mashed,
¼ tsp. baking soda	cooked pumpkin
½ tsp. salt	1 tsp. lemon extract
1 c. butter or	½ c. milk
regular margarine	1 c. chopped walnuts
1 c. sugar	Sifted confectioners sugar
1 c. brown sugar, packed	

Sift together flour, baking powder, baking soda and salt; set aside.

Cream together butter, sugar and brown sugar in mixing bowl until light and fluffy, using electric mixer at medium speed. Add eggs, one at a time, beating well after each addition. Blend in pumpkin and lemon extract (total beating time: 10 minutes).

Add dry ingredients alternately with milk to creamed mixture, beating well after each addition, using electric mixer at low speed. Stir in walnuts. Pour batter into greased 10-inch tube pan.

Bake in 325° oven 1 hour 20 minutes, or until cake tester inserted in center comes out clean or top springs back when lightly touched with finger. Cool in pan on rack 10 minutes. Remove from pan; cool on rack. Sprinkle with sifted confectioners sugar. Makes 12 servings.

MARY'S SUGAR POUND CAKE

"Although I have not won any prizes with this cake, it has won the hearts of my family and friends," wrote a Wisconsin woman.

4 tsp. sugar	3 c. sugar
3 c. sifted flour	5 eggs
½ tsp. salt	1 tblsp. vanilla
1 c. butter or	¾ c. evaporated milk
regular margarine	¼ c. water
½ c. shortening	

Generously grease a 10-inch fluted tube pan; sprinkle with 4 tsp. sugar to coat.

Sift together flour and salt; set aside.

Cream together butter, shortening and 3 c. sugar in mixing bowl until light and fluffy, using electric mixer at medium speed. Add eggs, one at a time, beating well after each addition. Blend in vanilla (total beating time: 10 minutes).

Add dry ingredients alternately with evaporated milk and water to creamed mixture, beating well after each addition. Pour batter into prepared pan.

Bake in 350° oven 1 hour 25 minutes, or until cake tester inserted in center comes out clean or top springs back when lightly touched with finger. Cool in pan on rack 20 minutes. Remove from pan; cool on rack. Makes 12 servings.

FOAM CAKES

The foam cakes are the beauties of the "cake bunch." They are primarily leavened by air that is beaten into the egg whites and/or egg yolks.

There are three foam cakes: angel food, sponge and chiffon. Each one differs from the other, but the same principles of cake making apply to all three.

We have chosen to give you step-by-step directions for making an angel food cake, because all three foam cakes are based on this basic method of beating eggs to incorporate air and folding in flour to keep in the air.

Angel food cakes are always baked in ungreased pans. They need to climb the sides of the pan and grease would make them slide down and collapse. When sponge cakes are baked in tube pans, the pans are never greased; but if they are made by one of the alternate methods for sponges, the pans are greased. A Chiffon cake, just like the angel food cakes, is always put into an ungreased pan. It is the only one of the three foams that contains fat.

STEPS FOR MAKING ANGEL FOOD CAKE

Here are the basic steps used in making an angel food cake:

Step 1—Separate the Eggs. Separate eggs while still cold. Let egg whites come to room temperature before beating for better volume.

Step 2—Sift Dry Ingredients. Sift together the cake flour and sugar four times. Cake flour is used because it is a delicate flour that is made from soft wheat and doesn't contain as much gluten as the all-purpose flour. The dry ingredients are sifted four times so that the flour will be feathery light with air and thoroughly mixed with nary a tiny lump.

Step 3—Beat the Eggs. Beat the egg whites with the cream of tartar, flavoring and salt with an electric mixer at high speed in a large bowl, until it is foamy. The cream of tartar helps to stabilize the egg whites and also makes the cake a snowy white. If the cream of tartar isn't used, the interior of the cake tends to be a creamy color rather than the pure white which is so characteristic of a lovely angel food cake. Now the sugar is added very gradually and the egg whites are beaten until they are stiff but not dry. At this point the egg whites are still moist and glossy and if you tipped the bowl, they would float slowly to the side. If the egg whites aren't beaten enough, the cake will be very low in volume and very tough. If the eggs are beaten too much so that they are stiff and dry, the cake will have huge holes, coarse texture and low volume.

Step 4—Add Flour Mixture. Add the flour in four parts, folding 15 gentle but thorough strokes with each addition. This step is always done by hand with a rubber spatula or a wire whisk. The air must be kept in the batter. A heavy stirring motion or overfolding will release all the air and the batter will lose its volume. By "folding," we mean an under-and-over movement. Slide your spatula under the mass of egg whites, bring it up over the flour and fold the flour into the egg whites.

Step 5—Fill the Pan. Push the batter into an ungreased tube pan. Do this very gently. Don't press down on the batter. Very gently smooth and level the batter around the center tube and sides so that it can cling and rise high. With a metal spatula, carefully cut through the batter once to remove any air pockets.

Step 6—Place Cake in Oven. Place it in the oven on the lower rack. Do not open the door until it's time to check your cake.

Step 7—Test for Doneness. If the cake is golden brown and crusty with deep dry cracks on the top and leaves no impression when touched lightly with a fingertip, it's done. You can test with a cake tester, too. (A wooden toothpick will be too short.) The cake is done when the tester is inserted in the center and it comes out dry and clean.

Step 8—Let Cake Cool. Immediately turn the cake upside down and place the tube of the pan over a funnel or a bottle. Let it hang until the cake is completely cool, at least 2 hours. If you remove the cake before it's thoroughly cool, it might collapse in a soggy heap.

PARTY ANGEL FOOD CAKE

Tall and lovely, this angel food looks so special when covered with fluffy frosting and decorated with maraschino cherries.

1 c. plus 2 tblsp. sifted cake flour	1 c. sugar
¾ c. sugar	1 tsp. vanilla
1⅔ c. egg whites (about 12)	½ tsp. almond extract
1½ tsp. cream of tartar	10 red maraschino cherries, cut up
½ tsp. salt	½ c. chopped pecans

Don't Grease Angel Food Cake Pans
Never grease the pans for angel food and true sponge cakes. These batters need to cling to the sides of the pans in order to rise to their full height. Greasing also causes these cakes to fall out of the pans while cooling.

Sift together cake flour and ¾ c. sugar 4 times; set aside.

Beat egg whites, cream of tartar and salt in large mixing bowl until foamy, using electric mixer at high speed. Gradually add 1 c. sugar, 2 tblsp. at a time, until stiff glossy peaks form. Blend in vanilla and almond extract.

Add flour mixture in 4 parts, folding about 15 strokes after each addition. Fold in cut-up cherries and pecans. Turn batter into ungreased 10-inch tube pan. Pull metal spatula through batter once to break up large air bubbles.

Bake in 350° oven 45 minutes, or until top springs back when lightly touched with finger. Invert tube pan on funnel or bottle to cool. When completely cooled, remove from pan. Frost with your favorite fluffy white frosting and decorate with red maraschino cherries with stems, if you wish. Makes 12 servings.

PEPPERMINT ANGEL FOOD CAKE

This pink-and-white marbled angel food is a bit different and so lovely when swirled with the two-tone pink frosting.

1 c. sifted cake flour	1 c. sugar
1 c. sifted confectioners sugar	1 tsp. vanilla
⅔ c. egg whites (about 12)	½ tsp. peppermint extract
1½ tsp. cream of tartar	12 drops red food color
¼ tsp. salt	Two-Toned Swirl Frosting (recipe follows)

Luscious Dessert
Slice an angel food cake or a sponge cake. Top each slice with a scoop of vanilla ice cream, some fresh sliced strawberries. Add a dollop of whipped cream.

Sift together cake flour and confectioners sugar 4 times; set aside.

Beat egg whites, cream of tartar and salt in large mixing bowl until foamy, using electric mixer at high speed. Gradually add sugar, 2 tblsp. at a time, until stiff glossy peaks form.

Add flour mixture in 4 parts, folding about 15 strokes after each addition. Divide batter in half. Fold vanilla into one half. Fold peppermint extract and red food color into other half. Drop batter by alternate spoonfuls into ungreased 10-inch tube pan. Pull metal spatula through batter, swirling gently.

Bake in 325° oven 50 minutes, or until top springs back when lightly touched with finger. Invert tube pan on funnel or bottle to cool. When completely cooled, remove from pan.

Frost with Two-Toned Swirl Frosting. Makes 12 servings.

Two-Toned Swirl Frosting: Prepare your favorite 7-minute frosting or see index of this book for 7-Minute Frosting recipe. Add 2 drops peppermint extract to prepared 7-minute frosting. Tint frosting pale pink with red food color. Remove ½ c. of frosting and tint dark pink by adding more red food color. Frost cake with pale pink frosting. Using a spoon, swirl dark pink frosting over cake.

ALMOND-FLAVORED ANGEL FOOD CAKE

Excellent, light angel food with a hint of almond flavoring. Delicious with just a light dusting of confectioners sugar.

1 c. sifted cake flour	1½ tsp. vanilla
¾ c. sugar	¼ tsp. almond extract
1½ c. egg whites (about	¼ tsp. salt
11 large eggs)	¾ c. sugar
1½ tsp. cream of tartar	

Sift together cake flour and ¾ c. sugar three times; set aside.

Beat egg whites, cream of tartar, vanilla, almond extract and salt in large bowl until foamy, using electric mixer at high speed. Gradually add ¾ c. sugar, 1 tblsp. at a time, until stiff glossy peaks form.

Add flour mixture in 4 parts, folding about 15 strokes after each addition. Spoon batter into ungreased 10-inch tube pan. Pull metal spatula through batter once to break large air bubbles.

Bake in 375° oven 30 minutes, or until top springs back when lightly touched with finger. Invert tube pan on funnel or bottle to cool. When completely cooled, remove from pan. Makes 12 servings.

SPONGE CAKES

There are many variations of the sponge cake and many methods for making it. Some are made with egg yolks and whites; some, with just egg yolks. Some recipes have no liquid, while others call for hot water, cold water or hot milk.

The main leavening in sponge cake is air, but many recipes call for baking powder, too. The air is beaten into the egg yolks. They are beaten until they are thick, creamy and pale yellow. Beating is the most important feature of a sponge cake. If you underbeat the yolks, you will not have the lovely, airy texture—even with the help of the baking powder.

Sponge cakes are sometimes put into tube pans, but they can also be put into square pans or layer pans. The well-known jelly roll is a sponge baked in a long thin pan.

In some recipes the pans are greased, but when the conventional tube pan is used, it is never greased and is cooled upside down on a funnel or bottle, just like the angel food cake.

The sponge cake that is baked in a tube pan follows all of the same principles as the angel food cake.

SPECIAL STRAWBERRY SPONGE CAKE

You'll make a hit when you serve this very lovely strawberry short-cake. It's made with square sponge layers and whipped cream.

1½ c. sifted flour	2 tsp. vanilla
1 tsp. baking powder	½ tsp. cream of tartar
½ tsp. salt	½ c. sugar
6 eggs, separated	1 pt. fresh strawberries
1 c. sugar	Vanilla Whipped Cream
6 tblsp. water	(recipe follows)

Sift together flour, baking powder and salt; set aside.

Beat egg yolks in medium bowl until thick and lemon-colored, using electric mixer at high speed, about 5 minutes. Gradually add 1 c. sugar, beating well. Blend in water and vanilla, using electric mixer at low speed. Beat in dry ingredients.

Beat egg whites and cream of tartar in large bowl until foamy, using electric mixer at high speed. Gradually add ½ c. sugar, beating until stiff peaks form.

Gently fold egg yolk mixture into egg whites. Pour batter into 2 greased and waxed paper-lined 8-inch square baking pans.

Bake in 350° oven 25 minutes, or until top springs back when touched lightly with finger. Invert pans and cool 15 minutes. Remove from pans; cool on racks.

Wash and hull strawberries. Reserve 16 whole strawberries. Chop

Decorated Cakes
Even if you've never held a pastry tube in your hands, you'll find these make-ahead decorations easy to master. Then decorate the cakes. Clockwise from top: Floral Basket Cake (p. 211), Flowered Cupcakes (p. 212) and spring-like Pink-Flowered Sheet Cake (p. 212).

Special Occasion Cakes
For birthdays, showers and important parties, delight your guests with a Peppermint Angel Food Cake (p. 190). It's light as a feather with a hint of peppermint.

Taste of Spring
A homemade strawberry shortcake, Strawberries and Cream Spectacular (p. 151) is made with a cake base instead of biscuits. Frosted with whipped cream and topped with sliced strawberries, this dessert is perfect to welcome spring.

Gold Rush Favorites
*Sourdough Bread (p. 55)
and Golden Sourdough Bis-
cuits (p. 56) are made with a
modern starter—much more
reliable than the pioneer version. A hearty bread with a
tangy flavor.*

remaining strawberries; set aside.

Prepare Vanilla Whipped Cream. Remove 1 c. of the Vanilla Whipped Cream and fold in chopped strawberries.

Spread the top of one layer with strawberry-cream mixture. Top with second cake layer.

Remove 1 c. Vanilla Whipped Cream and reserve for decoration of top. Spread sides and top of cake with the remaining Vanilla Whipped Cream. Decorate top of cake with 1 c. reserved Vanilla Whipped Cream by spooning 12 puffs evenly spaced around the edge of the cake. Place a whole strawberry in the center of each puff of cream. Cut 4 remaining whole strawberries in half lengthwise. Place a strawberry half on both sides of each corner of the cake. Refrigerate until serving time. Makes 12 servings.

Vanilla Whipped Cream: Whip 2 c. heavy cream in chilled bowl until it begins to thicken, using electric mixer at high speed. Gradually beat in ¼ c. sugar and 2 tsp. vanilla. Beat just until soft peaks form. Do not overbeat.

To Beat Eggs until Thick and Lemon-colored
Beat whole eggs or egg yolks thoroughly, until they thicken and color changes to a pale yellow.

FIVE-EGG SPONGE CAKE

"This cake was originally baked in a wood cookstove. I make it for special occasions," an Ohio farm woman said.

1½ c. sifted cake flour	½ c. water
1 tsp. baking powder	1 tsp. vanilla
¼ tsp. salt	¾ tsp. cream of tartar
5 eggs, separated	Sifted confectioners sugar
1½ c. sugar	

Sift together cake flour, baking powder and salt; set aside.

Beat egg yolks in medium bowl until thick and lemon-colored, using electric mixer at high speed, about 3 minutes. Gradually beat in sugar and water. Blend in vanilla and dry ingredients.

Combine egg whites and cream of tartar in large bowl. Beat with electric mixer at high speed until soft peaks that hold their shape are formed.

Fold egg yolk mixture into egg whites. Pour into ungreased 9-inch tube pan. Pull metal spatula through batter once to break large air bubbles.

Bake in 325° oven 1 hour, or until top springs back when touched lightly with finger. Invert tube pan on funnel or bottle to cool. When completely cooled, remove from pan.

Sprinkle with sifted confectioners sugar. Makes 10 servings.

LAZY DAISY CAKE

"This quick cake is best when served warm from the oven," wrote the Kentucky farm woman who sent in the recipe.

1 c. sifted flour	2 eggs
1 tsp. baking powder	1 c. sugar
¼ tsp. salt	1 tsp. vanilla
2 tblsp. butter or	Coconut-Pecan Topping
regular margarine	(recipe follows)
½ c. milk	

Sift together flour, baking powder and salt; set aside.

Heat butter and milk over low heat until butter melts. Keep milk mixture warm.

Beat together eggs and sugar in bowl 2 minutes, using electric mixer at medium speed. Gradually beat in dry ingredients and vanilla, using electric mixer at low speed. Add hot milk mixture to egg mixture, beating until blended. Pour into greased 9-inch square baking pan.

Bake in 375° oven 20 minutes, or until top springs back when lightly touched with finger. Cool in pan on rack 10 minutes. Spread with Coconut-Pecan Topping. Place under broiler, 3 inches from the source of heat, until lightly browned and bubbly. Cool in pan on rack. Makes 9 servings.

Coconut-Pecan Topping: Combine ½ c. butter or regular margarine, ¾ c. brown sugar (packed), 1 c. flaked coconut, ½ c. chopped pecans and 4 tblsp. light cream in small saucepan. Bring to a boil over medium heat. Remove from heat.

PRALINE-TOPPED SPONGE SQUARES

These sponge-type cake squares are so easy to make and perfect to tote to potlucks, picnics and other parties.

2 c. sifted flour	4 eggs
2 tsp. baking powder	1¾ c. sugar
1 tsp. salt	1 tsp. vanilla
2 tblsp. butter or	**Broiled Praline Topping**
regular margarine	**(recipe follows)**
1 c. milk	

Sift together flour, baking powder and salt; set aside.

Heat butter and milk in saucepan over low heat until butter melts. Keep milk mixture warm.

Beat eggs in large mixing bowl 3 minutes, using electric mixer at high speed. Gradually add sugar, beating until thick and lemon-colored, about 5 minutes. Blend in dry ingredients, using electric mixer at low speed.

Slowly add hot milk mixture and vanilla, beating until blended. Pour batter into greased 15½ × 10½ × 1-inch jelly roll pan.

Bake in 325° oven 20 minutes, or until top springs back when lightly touched. Remove from oven; carefully spread hot cake with Broiled Praline Topping. Place under broiler, 6 inches from source of heat, until lightly browned and bubbly. Cool in pan on rack. Makes 24 servings.

Broiled Praline Topping: Combine ½ c. butter or regular margarine, 4 tblsp. light corn syrup, 1 c. brown sugar (packed) and 2 tblsp. milk in 2-qt. saucepan; mix to blend. Bring to a boil; cook 2 minutes. Remove from heat. Stir in 1 c. flaked coconut and ½ c. coarsely chopped cashews.

To Beat Whites Until Stiff
Be sure there is not one speck of yolk in the whites. Beat with a rotary beater or electric mixer until mass is stiff but not dry. At this point, the cells are white and very small and the egg whites will flow slowly in one mass when the bowl is tipped.

STRAWBERRY-FILLED CAKE ROLL

Extra-special cake roll swirled with strawberry filling. Whipped cream can be used instead of non-dairy whipped topping.

⅔ c. sifted cake flour	Sifted confectioners sugar
1 tsp. baking powder	3 c. sliced fresh
¼ tsp. salt	strawberries (about
4 eggs, separated	1½ pt.)
¼ c. sugar	1 (9-oz.) container non-
½ tsp. vanilla	dairy whipped topping
½ c. sugar	

Sift together cake flour, baking powder and salt; set aside.

Beat egg yolks in mixing bowl until thick and lemon-colored, using electric mixer at high speed. Gradually beat in ¼ c. sugar. Blend in vanilla.

Beat egg whites in another bowl until frothy, using electric mixer at high speed. Gradually beat in ½ c. sugar, beating until stiff glossy peaks form.

Fold egg yolk mixture into egg white mixture. Then carefully fold in dry ingredients. Spread batter in greased and waxed paper-lined 15½ × 10½ × 1-inch jelly roll pan.

Bake in 375° oven 10 to 12 minutes, or until top springs back when lightly touched with finger. Loosen cake around edges with metal spatula. Turn out on dish towel sprinkled with sifted confectioners sugar. Trim off browned crust along edges. Roll up, starting at narrow side, rolling towel up with cake. Cool completely.

Stir strawberries into non-dairy whipped topping in bowl. Unroll cake. Spread strawberry mixture on cake. Reroll cake, using towel to help make a tight roll, placing seam side down. Refrigerate until serving time. Makes 10 servings.

PINEAPPLE CREAM ROLL

An unusual cake roll filled with a creamy, vanilla-flavored pudding flecked with red maraschino cherries and pineapple.

¾ c. sifted cake flour	1 tsp. vanilla
¾ tsp. baking powder	Sifted confectioners sugar
¼ tsp. salt	Pineapple Cream Filling
4 eggs	(recipe follows)
¾ c. sugar	

Sift together cake flour, baking powder and salt; set aside.

Beat eggs in mixing bowl until thick and lemon-colored, using electric mixer at high speed, about 5 minutes. Gradually add sugar, beating well after each addition. Blend in vanilla.

Fold dry ingredients into egg mixture. Spread batter in waxed paper-lined 15½ × 10½ × 1-inch jelly roll pan.

Bake in 375⁰ oven 13 minutes, or until top springs back when lightly touched with finger. Loosen cake around edges with metal spatula. Turn cake out on linen dish towel sprinkled with sifted confectioners sugar. Trim off browned crust along edges. Roll up cake, starting at wide end, rolling towel up with cake. Cool cake while preparing Pineapple Cream Filling.

Unroll cake and spread with Pineapple Cream Filling to within ½ inch of edges. Reroll cake, using towel to help make a tight roll. Place cake roll, open end down. Cool completely. Then refrigerate until serving time. Makes 8 servings.

Pineapple Cream Filling: Combine ½ c. sugar, 2 tblsp. cornstarch, 2 tblsp. flour and ¼ tsp. salt in small saucepan. Gradually stir in 2 c. milk. Cook over medium heat, stirring constantly, until mixture thickens. Mix some of the hot pudding mixture with 2 beaten egg yolks. Then stir egg mixture into remaining hot mixture. Cook 1 more minute. Add 1 (8½-oz.) can crushed pineapple (drained), 8 red maraschino cherries (quartered) and 1 tsp. vanilla. Cool completely.

MY FAVORITE JELLY ROLL

A light cake roll with a bright orange apricot preserves center and dusted with confectioners sugar.

HOW TO FOLD EGG WHITES

¾ c. sifted cake flour	½ tsp. almond extract
¾ tsp. baking powder	Sifted confectioners sugar
¼ tsp. salt	1 c. apricot preserves, or
5 eggs	any other jam or jelly
¾ c. sugar	

Sift together cake flour, baking powder and salt; set aside.

Combine eggs, sugar and almond extract in mixing bowl. Beat with electric mixer at high speed until thick and lemon-colored, about 5 minutes.

Fold dry ingredients into egg mixture. Spread batter in greased and waxed paper-lined 15½ × 10½ × 1-inch jelly roll pan.

Bake in 350⁰ oven 20 minutes, or until top springs back when lightly touched with finger. Loosen cake around edges with metal spatula. Turn cake out on linen dish towel dusted with sifted confectioners sugar. Trim off browned crust along edges. Roll up, starting at narrow end, rolling towel up with cake. Cool completely.

Unroll cake and spread with apricot preserves to within ½ inch of edges. Reroll cake, using towel to help make a tight roll. Place cake roll, open end down. Makes 8 servings.

LEMON SPONGE CAKE

An extra-light and tender basic sponge cake. It's delicious with just a dusting of confectioners sugar.

8 eggs, separated	**1¼ c. sifted flour**
½ c. sugar	**½ tsp. cream of tartar**
2 tblsp. cold water	**½ tsp. salt**
½ tsp. vanilla	**1 c. sugar**
½ tsp. almond extract	**Sifted confectioners sugar**
½ tsp. lemon extract	

Combine egg yolks, ½ c. sugar, water, vanilla, almond extract and lemon extract in mixing bowl. Beat with electric mixer at high speed until thick and lemon-colored, about 5 minutes. Stir in flour all at once.

Beat egg whites, cream of tartar and salt until foamy, using electric mixer at high speed. Gradually add 1 c. sugar, beating until stiff peaks form.

Gradually fold egg yolk mixture into egg whites. Pour batter into ungreased 10-inch tube pan. Pull metal spatula through batter once to break large air bubbles.

Bake in 325° oven 60 to 65 minutes, or until top springs back when lightly touched with finger. Invert tube pan on funnel or bottle to cool. When completely cooled, remove from pan. Sprinkle with sifted confectioners sugar. Makes 12 servings.

Star Cake
Invert a small star mold on a frosted layer cake. Sprinkle chopped nuts thickly around mold. Remove mold.

CHIFFON CAKES

Chiffon cakes are made entirely different from other foam cakes.

A well is made in the sifted dry ingredients in a bowl. Into the well go the oil, egg yolks, water and flavoring. After this mixture has been beaten until smooth, it is poured over the egg whites, which have been beaten to a thick, white cloud. Then the egg yolk mixture is gently folded into the whites.

The batter is poured into an ungreased tube pan and the cake bakes to a high, towering beauty.

COCOA CHIFFON CAKE

One of our favorite Farm Journal standbys. We are often asked for copies of this recipe because the cake is so sensational.

½ c. baking cocoa	1¾ c. sugar
¾ c. boiling water	1½ tsp. baking soda
8 eggs, separated	1 tsp. salt
½ tsp. cream of tartar	½ c. cooking oil
1¾ c. sifted cake flour	2 tsp. vanilla

Combine cocoa and boiling water in small bowl; stir to blend. Cool completely.

Beat egg whites and cream of tartar in mixing bowl until very stiff peaks form, using electric mixer at high speed. Set aside.

Sift together cake flour, sugar, baking soda and salt into another mixing bowl. Make a well in the center. Add oil, vanilla, egg yolks and cocoa mixture. Beat with electric mixer at low speed 1 minute. (Or beat with spoon until smooth.)

Gradually pour chocolate mixture over egg whites, folding just until blended. Pour batter into ungreased 10-inch tube pan. Pull metal spatula through batter once to break large air bubbles.

Bake in 325° oven 55 minutes. Increase temperature to 350° and bake 10 minutes longer, or until top springs back when lightly touched with finger. Invert tube pan on funnel or bottle to cool. When completely cooled, remove from pan. Frost with your favorite fluffy chocolate frosting. Makes 12 servings.

Chocolate Drizzle
Melt 1-oz. square of unsweetened chocolate with 1 tsp. butter over low heat and drizzle over the surface of a fluffy white frosting. Or, with a small paint brush, paint a name, a greeting or a design onto a frosting with the chocolate.

CHOCOLATE CHIFFON LAYER CAKE

Light-textured milk chocolate confection filled and frosted with a delicate cocoa-flavored whipped cream.

1¾ c. sifted flour	1 tsp. vanilla
1 c. sugar	2 (1-oz.) squares
¾ tsp. baking soda	unsweetened chocolate,
¾ tsp. salt	melted and cooled
⅓ c. cooking oil	½ c. sugar
1 c. sour milk*	Cocoa Cream Frosting
2 eggs, separated	(recipe follows)

Sift together flour, 1 c. sugar, baking soda and salt into large bowl. Add oil and one half of sour milk. Beat with electric mixer at medium speed until well blended. Add egg yolks, vanilla, cooled chocolate and remaining sour milk. Beat well.

Beat egg whites in another large bowl until frothy, using electric mixer at high speed. Gradually add ½ c. sugar, beating until stiff peaks form. Fold egg whites into chocolate mixture. Pour into 2 greased and waxed paper-lined 9-inch cake pans.

Bake in 350⁰ oven 25 minutes, or until top springs back when lightly touched with finger. Cool in pans on racks 10 minutes. Remove from pans; cool on racks. Spread top of one cake layer with Cocoa Cream Frosting. Top with second layer. Frost sides and top of cake with remaining frosting. Refrigerate until serving time. Makes 12 servings.

Cocoa Cream Frosting: Combine 2 c. heavy cream, 1 c. sifted confectioners sugar, ¼ c. baking cocoa and ¹⁄₁₆ tsp. salt in chilled mixing bowl. Beat with electric mixer at high speed until mixture forms soft peaks. Do not overbeat.

*Note: To sour milk, place 1 tblsp. vinegar in measuring cup; add enough milk to make 1 c.

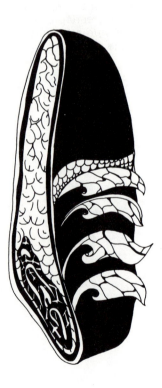

SPICY CHIFFON CAKE

When frosted with 7-minute or seafoam frosting this spicy cake is elegant indeed. (See index for choice of recipes.)

2 c. sifted flour	½ tsp. ground allspice
1½ c. sugar	½ tsp. ground cloves
3 tsp. baking powder	½ c. cooking oil
1 tsp. salt	7 eggs, separated
1 tsp. ground cinnamon	¾ c. cold water
½ tsp. ground nutmeg	½ tsp. cream of tartar

Sift together flour, sugar, baking powder, salt, cinnamon, nutmeg, allspice and cloves into bowl. Make a well in the center. Add oil, egg yolks and water. Beat with electric mixer at low speed 1 minute. (Or beat with spoon until smooth.)

Beat egg whites and cream of tartar in another bowl until stiff peaks form, using electric mixer at high speed.

Gradually pour egg yolk mixture over whites, folding just until blended. Pour into ungreased 10-inch tube pan. Pull metal spatula through batter once to break large air bubbles.

Bake in 325° oven 55 minutes, then increase heat to 350° and bake 10 to 15 minutes more, or until top springs back when touched lightly with finger. Invert tube pan on funnel or bottle to cool. When completely cooled, remove from pan. Makes 12 servings.

ORANGE CHIFFON CAKE

This tender cake makes a perfect base for strawberry shortcake. The light orange flavor blends nicely with strawberries.

2 c. sifted flour	8 eggs, separated
1½ c. sugar	¾ c. cold water
3 tsp. baking powder	2 tblsp. grated orange rind
1 tsp. salt	½ tsp. cream of tartar
½ c. cooking oil	

Sift together flour, sugar, baking powder and salt into bowl. Make a well in the center. Add oil, egg yolks, water and orange rind. Beat with electric mixer at low speed 1 minute. (Or beat with spoon until smooth.)

Beat egg whites and cream of tartar in another bowl, until stiff peaks form, using electric mixer at high speed. Gradually pour egg yolk mixture over whites, folding just until blended. Pour batter into ungreased 10-inch tube pan. Pull metal spatula through batter once to break large air bubbles.

Bake in 325° oven 1 hour 5 minutes, or until top springs back when touched lightly with finger. Invert tube pan on funnel or bottle to cool. When completely cooled, remove from pan. Makes 12 servings.

BANANA CUSTARD CHIFFON CAKE

To make this cake extra-fancy, split into three layers. Frost between layers and on sides with sweetened whipped cream.

2¼ c. sifted cake flour	¾ c. mashed bananas
1½ c. sugar	(2 medium)
3 tsp. baking powder	1 tblsp. lemon juice
1 tsp. salt	1 tsp. vanilla
½ c. cooking oil	1 c. egg whites (7 or 8)
5 egg yolks	½ tsp. cream of tartar

Sift together cake flour, sugar, baking powder and salt into bowl. Make a well in the center. Add oil, egg yolks, bananas, lemon juice and vanilla. Beat with electric mixer at low speed 1 minute. (Or beat with spoon until smooth.)

Beat egg whites and cream of tartar in another bowl until stiff peaks form, using electric mixer at high speed. Gradually pour egg yolk mixture over whites, folding just until blended. Pour batter into ungreased 10-inch tube pan. Pull metal spatula through batter once to break large air bubbles.

Bake in 325° oven 50 to 60 minutes, or until top springs back when lightly touched with finger. Invert pan on funnel or bottle to cool. When completely cooled, remove from pan. Makes 12 servings.

Toasted Cake
Cut leftover cake into wedges or squares. Split and spread cut surface with softened butter. Sprinkle with sugar and cinnamon. Broil about 3 inches from heat for 1 or 2 minutes or until bubbly.

BLUE RIBBON PEPPERMINT CHIFFON

Marbled pink and yellow cake that's so attractive and tasty it doesn't need a frosting—just dust with confectioners sugar.

2½ c. sifted cake flour	½ c. cold water
1½ c. sugar	1½ tsp. peppermint extract
3 tsp. baking powder	½ tsp. vanilla
1 tsp. salt	½ tsp. cream of tartar
½ c. cooking oil	15 drops red food color
7 eggs, separated	

Sift together cake flour, sugar, baking powder and salt into bowl. Make a well in the center. Add oil, egg yolks, water, peppermint extract and vanilla. Beat with electric mixer at low speed 1 minute. (Or beat with spoon until smooth.)

Beat egg whites and cream of tartar in another bowl until stiff peaks form, using electric mixer at high speed. Gradually pour egg yolk mixture over whites, fold just until blended. Pour one-third of batter into another bowl. Tint pink with red food color.

Alternate large spoonfuls of pink and plain batter in ungreased 10-inch tube pan. Carefully pull a spatula through batter to create a swirled effect.

Bake in 325° oven 55 minutes; increase heat to 350° and bake 15 minutes more, or until top springs back when lightly touched with finger. Invert tube pan on funnel or bottle to cool. When completely cooled, remove from pan. Makes 12 servings.

CHUNKY CHOCOLATE CUPCAKES

These vanilla cupcakes are filled with chunks of chocolate and then swirled with a creamy, rich, orange-flavored frosting.

1 c. sifted flour	¼ c. milk
1 c. sugar	1½ (1-oz.) squares
1½ tsp. baking powder	unsweetened chocolate,
½ tsp. salt	chopped
2 eggs	Creamy Orange Frosting
¼ c. cooking oil	(recipe follows)
1 tsp. vanilla	

Sift together flour, sugar, baking powder and salt into mixing bowl.

Combine eggs, oil, vanilla and milk in another bowl; beat with electric mixer at medium speed until well blended.

Add egg mixture to dry ingredients; beat with electric mixer at medium speed until well mixed. Stir in chocolate. Spoon batter into paper-lined 2½-inch muffin-pan cups, filling two-thirds full.

Bake in 400° oven 20 to 25 minutes, or until cake tester or wooden pick inserted in center comes out clean. Remove from pans; cool on racks.

Frost with Creamy Orange Frosting. Makes 12.

Creamy Orange Frosting: Combine 2½ c. sifted confectioners sugar, 3 tblsp. soft butter or regular margarine, 1 tsp. grated orange rind and 2 tblsp. orange juice in bowl. Beat until smooth.

Chop and Measure Nuts
Measure nuts after they are chopped. Ground or finely chopped nuts should be the consistency of coarse meal. Finely chopped, the size of a peppercorn. Medium chopped, about the size of a cranberry.

LIGHT CHOCOLATE BROWNIE CUPCAKES

These chewy cupcakes are more like a brownie than a cake. Perfect to tuck into children's lunch boxes.

4 (1-oz.) squares semisweet	1 tsp. vanilla
chocolate	1 c. sifted flour
1 c. butter or	1¾ c. sugar
regular margarine	4 eggs
1 c. chopped walnuts	

Melt chocolate and butter in small saucepan over very low heat. Remove from heat. Stir in walnuts and vanilla.

Sift together flour and sugar into mixing bowl. Add eggs; beat until blended, using electric mixer at medium speed. Stir in chocolate mixture. Spoon batter into paper-lined 2½-inch muffin-pan cups, filling one-half full.

Bake in 325° oven 35 minutes, or until cake tester or wooden pick inserted in center comes out clean. Remove from pans; cool on racks. Makes 24.

BLACK BOTTOM CUPCAKES

Each walnut-topped chocolate cupcake has a surprise center made of sweetened cream cheese and chocolate pieces.

2 (3-oz.) pkgs. cream cheese	¼ c. baking cocoa
1 egg	1 tsp. baking soda
⅓ c. sugar	½ tsp. salt
⅛ tsp. salt	1 c. water
1 (6-oz.) pkg. semisweet chocolate pieces	⅓ c. cooking oil
1½ c. sifted flour	1 tblsp. vinegar
1 c. sugar	1 tsp. vanilla
	2 tblsp. sugar
	½ c. chopped walnuts

Beat cream cheese in bowl until smooth, using electric mixer at medium speed. Add egg, ⅓ c. sugar and ⅛ tsp. salt. Beat until blended. Stir in chocolate pieces; set aside.

Sift together flour, 1 c. sugar, cocoa, baking soda and ½ tsp. salt into mixing bowl.

Combine water, oil, vinegar and vanilla in small bowl; mix well. Add oil mixture to cocoa mixture. Beat with electric mixer at medium speed until well blended. Spoon batter into paper-lined 2½-inch muffin-pan cups, filling one-third full. Top each with a large teaspoonful of cheese mixture.

Combine 2 tblsp. sugar and walnuts in bowl; mix well. Sprinkle each cupcake with sugar-walnut mixture.

Bake in 350⁰ oven 35 minutes, or until cake tester or wooden pick inserted in center comes out clean. Remove from pans; cool on racks. Makes 18.

MILK CHOCOLATE CUPCAKES

Light chocolate cupcakes swirled with a mocha frosting. So good for after-school snacks or afternoon coffee breaks.

¾ c. sifted flour	1 (1-oz.) square
1¼ tsp. baking powder	unsweetened chocolate,
¼ tsp. salt	melted and cooled
¼ c. shortening	⅓ c. milk
¾ c. sugar	Cocoa-Coffee Frosting
2 egg yolks	(recipe follows)
1 tsp. vanilla	

Sift together flour, baking powder and salt; set aside.

Cream together shortening and sugar in mixing bowl until light and fluffy, using electric mixer at medium speed. Blend in egg yolks, vanilla and cooled chocolate.

Add dry ingredients alternately with milk to creamed mixture, beating well after each addition, using electric mixer at low speed. Spoon batter into paper-lined 2½-inch muffin-pan cups, filling one-half full.

Bake in 350° oven 20 minutes, or until cake tester or wooden pick inserted in center comes out clean. Remove from pans; cool on racks. Frost with Cocoa-Coffee Frosting. Makes 12 cupcakes.

Cocoa-Coffee Frosting: Combine 1½ c. sifted confectioners sugar, 3 tblsp. soft butter or regular margarine, 3 tblsp. baking cocoa, 1 tblsp. strong coffee, 1 tblsp. milk and ½ tsp. vanilla in bowl. Beat with electric mixer at medium speed until smooth.

LEMON CRUNCH CUPCAKES

No need to frost these delicate cupcakes because they are sprinkled with a sugar-lemon mixture before baking.

2 c. sifted flour	3 eggs
1 c. sugar	1 tblsp. grated lemon rind
2½ tsp. baking powder	¼ c. sugar
½ tsp. salt	1 tblsp. grated lemon rind
⅔ c. shortening	½ tsp. ground nutmeg
⅔ c. milk	

Sift together flour, 1 c. sugar, baking powder and salt into mixing bowl. Add shortening and milk; beat with electric mixer at medium speed 3 minutes. Add eggs, one at a time, beating well after each addition. Add 1 tblsp. lemon rind.

Combine ¼ c. sugar, 1 tblsp. lemon rind and nutmeg in small bowl; mix well. Set aside.

Spoon batter into paper-lined 2½-inch muffin-pan cups, filling two-thirds full. Sprinkle each with sugar-lemon mixture.

Bake in 375⁰ oven 20 to 25 minutes, or until cake tester or wooden pick inserted in center comes out clean. Remove from pans; cool on racks. Makes 24.

COCOA-RAISIN CUPCAKES

Old-fashioned, moist cupcakes combining raisins, applesauce, cocoa and walnuts. Spiced with cinnamon and nutmeg.

¼ c. butter or regular margarine	¼ tsp. ground nutmeg
¼ c. baking cocoa	¼ tsp. salt
¾ c. applesauce	1 egg
1¼ c. sifted flour	½ c. raisins
1 c. sugar	½ c. chopped walnuts
¾ tsp. baking soda	Butter Frosting (recipe
½ tsp. ground cinnamon	follows)

Melt butter in small saucepan over low heat. Remove from heat. Stir in cocoa and applesauce; set aside.

Sift together flour, sugar, baking soda, cinnamon, nutmeg and salt into mixing bowl. Add applesauce mixture and egg. Stir with spoon just until moistened. Stir in raisins and walnuts. (Batter is very thick.) Spoon batter into paper-lined 3-inch muffin-pan cups, filling one-half full.

Bake in 350⁰ oven 20 minutes, or until cake tester or wooden pick inserted in center comes out clean. Remove from pans; cool on racks. Frost with Butter Frosting. Makes 18 cupcakes.

Butter Frosting: Combine 1½ c. sifted confectioners sugar, 3 tblsp. soft butter or regular margarine, 1 tblsp. milk and ½ tsp. vanilla in bowl. Beat with electric mixer until frosting is smooth and of spreading consistency.

ORANGE CUPCAKES

A hot orange syrup is spooned over these cupcakes when they're removed from the oven—keeps them moist and adds flavor.

2 c. sifted cake flour	1 egg
1 tsp. baking soda	1 tsp. grated orange rind
½ tsp. baking powder	⅔ c. buttermilk
¼ tsp. salt	1 c. sugar
½ c. shortening	½ c. orange juice
1 c. sugar	

Sift together cake flour, baking soda, baking powder and salt; set aside.

Cream together shortening and 1 c. sugar in mixing bowl until light and fluffy, using electric mixer at medium speed. Add egg and orange rind; beat well.

Add dry ingredients alternately with buttermilk to creamed mixture, beating well after each addition, using electric mixer at low speed. Spoon batter into paper-lined 2½-inch muffin-pan cups, filling two-thirds full.

Bake in 350° oven 20 to 25 minutes, or until cake tester or wooden pick inserted in center comes out clean.

Meanwhile, combine 1 c. sugar and orange juice in small saucepan. Cook over medium heat, stirring constantly, until sugar dissolves. Remove cupcakes from pans. Spoon hot syrup over hot cupcakes. Cool on racks. Makes 18.

SPICY RAISIN CUPCAKES

These nutty raisin-filled cupcakes taste even better when spread with a creamy butter frosting. They're rich in iron, too.

1 (1-lb.) box raisins	¼ tsp. salt
2 c. water	1 c. butter or
2⅓ c. sifted flour	regular margarine
2 tsp. baking soda	1½ c. sugar
2 tsp. ground nutmeg	2 eggs
2 tsp. ground cinnamon	1 c. chopped walnuts

Combine raisins and water in small saucepan. Bring to a boil, reduce heat; simmer 10 minutes. Drain and reserve cooking liquid. Add water, if necessary, to cooking liquid to make 1 c.

Sift together flour, baking soda, nutmeg, cinnamon and salt; set aside.

Cream together butter and sugar in mixing bowl until light and fluffy, using electric mixer at medium speed. Add eggs, one at a time, beating well after each addition.

Add dry ingredients alternately with 1 c. reserved cooking liquid to creamed mixture, beating well after each addition, using electric mixer at low speed. Stir in raisins and walnuts. Spoon batter into paper-lined 2½-inch muffin-pan cups, filling two-thirds full.

Bake in 375° oven 20 to 25 minutes, or until cake tester or wooden pick inserted in center comes out clean. Remove from pans; cool on racks. Makes 36.

MAKE-AHEAD CAKE DECORATIONS

We have developed some very simple cake decorations that you can make and keep on hand until you are ready to use them.

All you'll need are a few basic decorating tools: two decorating bags; paste food colors; three standard size decorating tubes (shell, star and leaf) and two tube couplers. (The couplers allow you to change decorating tubes without changing bags.)

The first step is to make a batch of Basic Cake Frosting (recipe follows). Be sure to use paste colors for tinting the frosting because liquid colors thin it. Because the frosting stays soft, it's great for practicing; you can scrape up your first efforts and reuse them.

Begin by practicing the shell border on a baking sheet. Once you've mastered this, you can go on to the pretty drop flowers and leaves.

Now you're ready to do the Make-Ahead Cake Decorations (recipe follows). This icing hardens on standing, so the flowers can be kept on hand indefinitely for special occasions. One batch makes enough attractive decorations for several cakes and dozens of cupcakes. You'll have fun decorating cakes like the ones we show here, as well as creating your own.

MAKE-AHEAD CAKE DECORATIONS

You can store these decorations up to one year. Keep on hand for last-minute decorative touches to cakes and other desserts.

1 (1-lb.) box confectioners sugar	1 tsp. cream of tartar
3 egg whites	1 tsp. vanilla
	Paste food colors

Sift confectioners sugar into mixing bowl. Add egg whites, cream of tartar and vanilla. Beat with electric mixer at low speed until moistened. Beat at high speed until stiff, glossy peaks form. Keep frosting covered with wet paper towels or cloth at all times so it doesn't dry out. Tint with paste colors as desired.

Fill decorating bag no more than one-half full. (Do not overfill.) Twist bag closed, forcing icing down into the tube.

Make drop flowers, using star tube, working on waxed paper-lined baking sheets. Add leaves, using leaf tube. (See Figure 3.) Let flowers and leaves dry out completely. Remove from waxed paper. Layer flowers in airtight containers; cover. Store up to 1 year in dry place.

To Store: Unused frosting also can be stored in covered plastic container in refrigerator for 2 weeks. To use, bring to room temperature and beat until stiff peaks form.

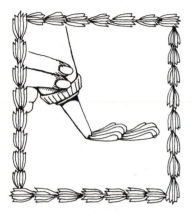

Figure 1: Shell Border
Use any shell tube (we used #98). Hold bag at 45° angle, with tube touching work surface and back end of bag aimed at your chest. Squeeze bag using heavy pressure, lifting tube slightly until frosting fans out. Now relax pressure as you pull tube down, bringing shell to a point. Stop pressure. Start at tail of shell and make another shell. Continue until you have a row of shells. Always work toward yourself.

BASIC CAKE FROSTING

This very creamy frosting is perfect for fancy decorated cakes because it's so easy to smooth out with a hot spatula.

2¼ c. sifted confectioners sugar	¼ c. milk
1 c. shortening	½ tsp. vanilla

Combine confectioners sugar, shortening, milk and vanilla in mixing bowl. Beat with electric mixer at low speed until moistened. Beat at high speed 5 minutes.

This frosting stays soft and creamy. It's perfect for frosting cakes that are to be decorated, because it can be smoothed so that the decorations stand out against it. You also can use this frosting to make borders.

To frost cake for decorating:

For layer cakes, place one layer, bottom side down, on serving plate. Spread with frosting, using metal spatula. Top with second layer, top side down. If there are any gaps between layers, fill with frosting.

Frost sides of cake first. Spread frosting on sides, working from bottom toward top. Use long even strokes, building up edges a bit higher than cake top.

Cover top of cake with frosting and spread out to built-up edges.

Dip metal spatula in very hot water. Shake off excess water. Place spatula on cake. Press down very lightly and smooth out frosting. Keep dipping spatula in water as needed.

Smooth out sides of cake in the same way. This takes a little practice, so don't get discouraged.

For sheet cakes, use the same procedure as for layer cakes.

Note: Frosting can be made ahead. Cover and store in refrigerator up to 3 weeks. Stir before using.

FLORAL BASKET CAKE

A lovely cake for birthdays, Mother's Day and Easter. It's topped with a lovely spring bouquet of make-ahead flowers.

1 recipe Basic Cake Frosting	Assorted Make-Ahead Cake Decorations
Paste food colors	
2 (9-inch) baked round cake layers	

Tint one half of Basic Cake Frosting pale yellow. Frost cake layers, following directions for frosting layer cake (see Basic Cake Frosting).

Tint one fourth of Basic Cake Frosting apricot, using red and yellow paste food colors. Fill decorating bag no more than one-half full. (Do not overfill.)

Use a shell tube. (We used # 98.) Make bottom shell border. (See Figure 1.) Proceed as shown, holding bag at 45° angle so tip of bag is pointed into the space where the cake meets the cake plate. Turn cake as you go, always working towards yourself.

Change to a star tube. (We used #30.) Make top star flower border. (See Figure 2.) Proceed as shown for star flower, making stars close together along top edge of cake.

Tint remaining frosting bright yellow. Fill decorating bag no more than one-half full. (Do not overfill.) Use a shell tube. (We used #98.) With a toothpick sketch out a small basket on top of cake, about 2½ inches high, 3¼ inches wide at top tapering to 1¼ wide at bottom. (See photo.)

Make basket, starting at top. Hold bag at 45° angle, making 7 horizontal lines. Change to round tube. (We used #2.) Add vertical lines over horizontal lines at regular intervals to resemble basket. (See photo.)

Arrange Make-Ahead Cake Decorations above basket.

Figure 2: Drop Flowers
Use any star tubes (we used #30 and #27). Star Flowers: Hold tube perpendicular to work surface. Squeeze out a star flower. Stop pressure. Lift up tube. Swirled Flowers (see diagram): Hold tube perpendicular to work surface with your hand turned as far left as possible. As you squeeze, turn your hand to the right as far as possible and stop pressure. (See arrow.)

PINK-FLOWERED SHEET CAKE

You can make this picture-perfect cake even if you've never decorated one before. Change the colors to suit your party.

1 recipe Basic Cake Frosting	**16 large pink Make-Ahead Flowers**
Paste Food Colors	
1 (13 × 9 × 2-inch) baked sheet cake	

Frost cake with Basic Cake Frosting, following directions for frosting a sheet cake (see Basic Cake Frosting).

Tint half of remaining Basic Cake Frosting bright apple green.* Fill decorating bag no more than one-half full. (Do not overfill.) Use a star tube. (We used #30.)

Mark off top of cake into 16 rectangles, using string.

Make star flower border on dividing lines between rectangles and top border. (See Figure 2.) Proceed as shown for star flower, making stars close together to form a border.

Place one large Make-Ahead Flower in center of each rectangle.

Note: Cover and refrigerate remaining frosting. Store up to 3 weeks.

Figure 3: Stand-Up Leaf
Use any leaf tube (we used #67). Hold bag at 45° angle to work surface with back of bag pointed at your chest. Squeeze with heavy pressure to build up base of leaf. Pull tube straight up and away from surface as you relax pressure. Draw leaf to a point. Stop pressure.

FLOWERED CUPCAKES

So elegant, but simple to decorate. Just frost cupcakes and top with Make-Ahead Cake Decorations.

1 recipe Basic Cake Frosting	**Paste food colors**
24 baked cupcakes	**Make-Ahead Cake Decorations**

Frost tops of cupcakes with Basic Cake Frosting. Or tint a pale color and frost cupcakes.

Arrange Make-Ahead Cake Decorations on top of each cake.

WHAT WENT WRONG WITH MY CAKE?

My layer cake was humped and cracked in the center—why?

There was probably too much flour in the batter. Did you measure and sift the flour carefully? Or the oven was too hot and the batter rose too quickly? Perhaps your oven is not registering the correct temperature.

My cake was very pale—why?

Perhaps you skimped on the sugar or didn't measure it correctly. Or the pan was too big. Did you use the pan size specified in the recipe?

My cake was too brown—why?

The two most common reasons for overbrowning are too hot an oven or baking a cake too long. However, too much sugar can also cause overbrowning.

My cake had large holes and a crumbly texture—why?

Holes that are large and unevenly distributed are almost always a sign that you didn't mix the cake batter enough. Or a cake can crumble if it is too tender, which is caused by too much shortening or too much sugar. Accurate measuring and thorough mixing of cake batter are very important.

My cake was gummy—why?

A gummy cake is the result of underbaking or using too much sugar or shortening. Always be sure to measure very accurately when you make a cake. The ingredients are carefully balanced to produce perfect results.

My cake really sank in the middle—why?

If your sunken cake is also too brown, it didn't have enough liquid or it had too much sugar, baking powder or shortening. If your cake is only sunken, it didn't bake long enough. Did you test carefully for doneness?

My angel food cake was low and heavy with a very tight crumb—why?

The egg whites were not beaten enough or you didn't fold in the dry ingredients gently enough and knocked out precious air that is used for leavening.

213

Chapter 5

Fun-to-Eat Country Cookies

In a great many farm and ranch kitchens, the very first bit of "cooking" that a child does is helping Mom make cookies. Even the smallest youngster can stand on tiptoe and shake a little colored sugar on a cookie.

And in many country homes, there are wonderful memories of Grandma's cookie jar. Sometimes it was a big, fat glass container. Other times, it was a homey brown earthenware jar. But whatever the shape or color, it was always filled with the grandchildren's favorite cookies—ready for them when they came to visit.

Our farm and country women sent us lovely letters along with their cookie recipes. The letters were nostalgic and the cookie recipes were great. It's our pleasure, here, to share many of these recipes and, often, the comments of their contributors.

Cookies are divided into six types. They're classified by the way they're formed: drop, bar, molded, rolled, refrigerator and pressed. And we discovered that every type is made often in country kitchens. A farm wife may make the easiest—bar and drop cookies—as often as several times a week, especially during the harvest and planting seasons. During those times, the men's favorites are the ones that are piled high in the cookie jars—so good with a big pitcher of lemonade or hot coffee during a late afternoon break in the field.

If you have never baked at all, we would suggest that cookies be your first project. You can't fail, as they are the easiest to make of all the baked goods.

Why not start with the tangy Lemon Square Bars sent to us from a good cook in Michigan? She tells us everyone is disappointed if she shows up at a church supper with another contribution instead of these good bars. They have a rich, buttery layer on the bottom and a tart, lemony layer on the top. They are so simple to make but look like they came from a very fancy bake shop.

Or make an heirloom treasure, old-fashioned Date-Filled Cookies. A Montana woman remembers racing home from school as a child to find the fragrant smell of these cookies permeating her mother's big farm kitchen. The cookies were made jumbo size for the children to eat with a glass of milk, and regular size for family snacking.

If you're planning a special party, borrow a Minnesota farm woman's prized recipe for Cherry-Walnut Bars. She makes them often for showers, graduations and small weddings.

For a coffee break, try the Raspberry Jam Squares—they are just perfect with a cup of steaming hot coffee or tea for a quick pick-me-up.

We've given you tips for making all six types of cookies. Once you start to make these wonderful country cookies, we think your cookie jar will always be full to the brim—but it will empty fast.

BASIC TIPS FOR ALL TYPES OF COOKIES

Measure flour carefully. Too much flour will result in a dry, tough cookie. Too little flour makes them spread and lose their shape.

Use shiny metal baking sheets so heat is reflected away from cookies. To assure delicate, even browning, the sheets should be two inches smaller all around than your oven. When you bake one batch at a time, place baking sheet on rack in center of oven. If baking two batches at the same time, divide the oven into thirds with the racks and place a baking sheet on each rack. Always use cool baking sheets. Cookie dough will melt and spread on a hot one. Follow recipe directions for greasing baking sheets. Some cookies are so high in fat that the sheets do not need to be greased.

Check cookies for doneness at end of the shortest baking time given in the recipe. Overbaking makes cookies dry.

Remove cookies from baking sheet with wide spatula at once unless recipe specifies otherwise. When left on the baking sheet for even a few minutes, they continue to cook. Spread cookies in a single layer on cooling racks. When cooling bar cookies, set the pan on a rack.

Crisp Cookies. Store in a container with a loose-fitting lid. If they do soften, spread them on a baking sheet before serving and heat them 3 to 5 minutes at 300°.

Soft Cookies. Store in a container with a tight-fitting lid.

Bar Cookies. It is often convenient to store them in the pan in which they baked. Place a piece of plastic wrap over top of cookies; cover pan with its own lid or snugly with foil.

MIXING AND SHAPING COOKIES

Cookies may be made by hand or with an electric mixer. We used an electric mixer in all of our recipes.

Every recipe in this cookbook gives precise directions for mixing the dough, but here are a few general directions that apply to most of the cookies: use the electric mixer at medium speed for creaming fats (usually butter or margarine) and to beat in the eggs and flavoring. You can beat them by hand until they are light and fluffy, if you wish. The dry ingredients are added gradually and mixed at low speed on the mixer or stirred in with a wooden spoon by hand.

DROP COOKIES

The dough for drop cookies is soft enough to drop from a spoon. Use an ordinary teaspoon rather than a measuring spoon. Use slightly rounded spoonfuls rather than level ones, unless, of course, your recipe specifies otherwise. Push the dough off the spoon with a rubber spatula or another spoon. Make the drops all the same size so they will bake evenly. Bake them just until done. Remove immediately from baking sheet. If cookies are left for only a few minutes on a hot sheet, they will continue to bake and will be overdone and dry.

SOUR CREAM DROP COOKIES

This heirloom cookie was originally made with homemade sour cream stored in a crock in the basement.

2¾ c. sifted flour	1½ c. sugar
1½ tsp. baking powder	2 eggs
½ tsp. baking soda	½ c. dairy sour cream
½ tsp. salt	½ tsp. lemon extract
¼ tsp. ground nutmeg	Sugar
1 c. butter or	
regular margarine	

Sift together flour, baking powder, baking soda, salt and nutmeg; set aside.

Cream together butter and 1½ c. sugar in bowl until light and fluffy, using electric mixer at medium speed. Add eggs, one at a time, beating well after each addition. Blend in sour cream and lemon extract.

Gradually stir dry ingredients into creamed mixture, blending well. Drop mixture by rounded teaspoonfuls, about 3 inches apart, on greased baking sheets. Sprinkle each with sugar.

Bake in 375° oven 8 minutes, or until golden brown around the edges. Remove from baking sheets; cool on racks. Makes 5½ dozen.

Cookie Tree
A cookie tree from which guests may help themselves is a fun way to serve cookies at a Christmas Party. Ball-shaped cookies may be wrapped in plastic wrap and tied onto the branches with bright colored ribbons. Use small artificial tree or a real one.

AMISH SUGAR COOKIES

"These cookies are so delicious that they melt in your mouth," a *Kansas farm woman wrote us when she sent in the recipe.*

4½ c. sifted flour
1 tsp. baking soda
1 tsp. cream of tartar
1 c. butter or
   regular margarine
1 c. cooking oil
1 c. sugar

1 c. sifted confectioners
   sugar
2 eggs
1 tsp. vanilla
1 c. chopped walnuts
Sugar

Sift together flour, baking soda and cream of tartar; set aside.

Cream together butter, oil, 1 c. sugar and confectioners sugar in mixing bowl until light and fluffy, using electric mixer at medium speed. Add eggs, one at a time, beating well after each addition. Blend in vanilla.

Gradually stir dry ingredients into creamed mixture, mixing well. Add walnuts. Drop mixture by rounded teaspoonfuls, about 3 inches apart, on greased baking sheets. Flatten each with bottom of greased drinking glass dipped in sugar.

Bake in 375° oven 10 minutes, or until lightly browned around the edges. Remove from baking sheets; cool on racks. Makes 7 dozen.

Cheer a Sick Boy
Make a batch of cookies and pile them in a bright shiny toy dump truck. Plastic wrap and wait for the delighted smile.

FROSTED CHRISTMAS BUTTER COOKIES

These rich, buttery cookies are special enough for Christmas. So easy, too, because they don't need to be rolled out.

3 c. sifted flour	1 c. brown sugar,
1 tsp. baking soda	packed
1 tsp. cream of tartar	3 eggs
1 c. butter or	1 c. dairy sour cream
regular margarine	Vanilla Frosting
1 c. sugar	(recipe follows)

Sift together flour, baking soda and cream of tartar; set aside.

Cream together butter, sugar and brown sugar in bowl until light and fluffy, using electric mixer at medium speed. Add eggs, one at a time, beating well after each addition.

Add dry ingredients alternately with sour cream to creamed mixture, beating well after each addition, using electric mixer at low speed. Drop mixture by rounded teaspoonfuls, about 3 inches apart, on greased baking sheets.

Bake in 350° oven 8 to 10 minutes, or until edges are browned. Remove from baking sheets; cool on racks. Frost with Vanilla Frosting. Makes 7 dozen.

Vanilla Frosting: Combine 4 c. sifted confectioners sugar, 1 tsp. vanilla and 4 tblsp. milk in bowl. Beat until smooth. Add 1 more tblsp. milk, if necessary, to make frosting of spreading consistency.

BROWN-RIM BUTTER COOKIES

Extra-thin vanilla wafers that are perfect with ice cream or sherbet.

2½ c. sifted flour	½ c. shortening
1 tsp. salt	⅔ c. sugar
½ c. butter or	2 eggs
regular margarine	1 tsp. vanilla

Sift together flour and salt; set aside.

Cream together butter, shortening and sugar in bowl until light and fluffy, using electric mixer at medium speed. Add eggs, one at a time, beating well after each addition. Blend in vanilla.

Gradually stir dry ingredients into creamed mixture, blending well. Drop mixture by teaspoonfuls, about 3 inches apart, on greased baking sheets. Flatten each with bottom of drinking glass dipped in water to 2¾-inch rounds.

Bake in 375° oven 8 minutes, or until lightly browned around the edges. Remove from baking sheets; cool on racks. Makes 4 dozen.

DROP SUGAR COOKIES

"This soft cookie recipe is one of my husband's favorites," a Pennsylvania woman wrote us.

4 c. sifted flour	3 eggs
2 tsp. baking powder	1 c. dairy sour cream
1 tsp. baking soda	1 tsp. vanilla
1 tsp. salt	3 tblsp. sugar
1 c. lard	½ tsp. ground cinnamon
2 c. sugar	

Sift together flour, baking powder, baking soda and salt; set aside.

Cream together lard and 2 c. sugar in bowl until light and fluffy, using electric mixer at medium speed. Add eggs, one at a time, beating well after each addition. Blend in sour cream and vanilla.

Gradually stir dry ingredients into creamed mixture, blending well. Drop mixture by rounded teaspoonfuls, about 3 inches apart, on greased baking sheets. Combine 3 tblsp. sugar and cinnamon. Sprinkle sugar-cinnamon mixture over each cookie.

Bake in 375° oven 10 minutes or until golden brown. Remove from baking sheets; cool on racks. Makes 5 dozen.

BUTTERSCOTCH-OATMEAL COOKIES

"Mom always stored these cookies in a big earthenware jug. She got the recipe from a Scottish friend," wrote a New York woman.

¾ c. sifted flour	½ c. brown sugar,
¾ tsp. baking soda	packed
⅛ tsp. salt	½ c. sugar
¼ tsp. ground cinnamon	1 egg
½ c. shortening	1 c. quick-cooking oats

Sift together flour, baking soda, salt and cinnamon; set aside.

Cream together shortening, brown sugar and sugar in bowl until light and fluffy, using electric mixer at medium speed. Add egg; beat well.

Gradually stir dry ingredients into creamed mixture, blending well. Stir in oats. Drop mixture by rounded teaspoonfuls, about 3 inches apart, on greased baking sheets.

Bake in 325° oven 15 minutes or until golden brown. Remove from baking sheets; cool on racks. Makes 2½ dozen.

FARMHOUSE WALNUT COOKIES

An Arkansas woman told us that these sandy-textured cookies are very popular at bake sales in her area.

5 c. sifted flour	2 c. sugar
4 tsp. baking powder	2 eggs
½ tsp. baking soda	1 c. dairy sour cream
½ tsp. salt	2 tsp. vanilla
1 c. butter or	¾ c. chopped walnuts
regular margarine	Sugar

Sift together flour, baking powder, baking soda and salt; set aside.

Cream together butter and 2 c. sugar in bowl until light and fluffy, using electric mixer at medium speed. Add eggs, one at a time, beating well after each addition. Blend in sour cream and vanilla.

Gradually stir dry ingredients into creamed mixture, blending well. Stir in walnuts. Drop mixture by rounded teaspoonfuls, about 3 inches apart, on greased baking sheets. Flatten cookies with bottom of greased drinking glass dipped in sugar to ¼-inch thickness.

Bake in 375° oven 12 minutes or until golden brown. Remove from baking sheets; cool on racks. Makes about 6 dozen.

To Store Soft Cookies
Store soft cookies in a container with a tight-fitting lid. Place sheets of waxed paper between layers to prevent cookies from sticking together.

RAISIN-MOLASSES COOKIES

These cookies are extra-crunchy on the outside and slightly chewy on the inside. They make good lunchbox treats.

2 c. sifted flour	½ c. shortening
1½ tsp. baking powder	¼ c. sugar
¼ tsp. baking soda	1 egg
½ tsp. salt	¾ c. molasses
1 tsp. ground cinnamon	1 c. golden raisins
1 tsp. ground ginger	

Sift together flour, baking powder, baking soda, salt, cinnamon and ginger; set aside.

Cream together shortening and sugar in bowl until light and fluffy, using electric mixer at medium speed. Add egg and molasses, beating well.

Gradually stir dry ingredients into creamed mixture, blending well. Stir in raisins. Drop mixture by teaspoonfuls, about 3 inches apart, on greased baking sheets.

Bake in 350° oven 12 to 14 minutes, or until no imprint remains when cookies are lightly touched with finger. Remove from baking sheets; cool on racks. Makes 3 dozen.

SPICY APPLESAUCE DROP COOKIES

A grandmother from Oregon sent in this recipe. She told us she keeps these cookies on hand for her many grandchildren.

2 c. sifted flour	1 c. sugar
1 tsp. baking soda	1 egg
½ tsp. baking powder	1 c. applesauce
¼ tsp. salt	1 tsp. vanilla
1 tsp. ground cinnamon	½ c. raisins
1 tsp. ground nutmeg	½ c. chopped walnuts
½ c. butter or regular margarine	Sifted confectioners sugar

Sift together flour, baking soda, baking powder, salt, cinnamon and nutmeg; set aside.

Cream together butter and sugar in bowl until light and fluffy, using electric mixer at medium speed. Add egg, applesauce and vanilla, beating well.

Gradually stir dry ingredients into creamed mixture, blending well. Stir in raisins and walnuts. Drop mixture by teaspoonfuls, about 3 inches apart, on greased baking sheets.

Bake in 350° oven 12 minutes or until golden brown. Remove from baking sheets; cool on racks. When completely cooled, sprinkle cookies with sifted confectioners sugar. Makes 4 dozen.

CHOCOLATE CHIP-OATMEAL COOKIES

"Ten times better than regular oatmeals," is her family's comment each time a Michigan farm wife serves these cookies.

2 c. sifted flour	1 c. sugar
1 tsp. baking powder	2 eggs
1 tsp. baking soda	1 tsp. vanilla
½ tsp. salt	2 c. quick-cooking oats
1 c. shortening	1 (12-oz.) pkg. semisweet chocolate pieces
1 c. brown sugar, packed	½ c. chopped walnuts

Sift together flour, baking powder, baking soda and salt; set aside.

Cream together shortening, brown sugar and sugar in bowl until light and fluffy, using electric mixer at medium speed. Add eggs, one at a time, beating well after each addition. Blend in vanilla.

Gradually stir dry ingredients into creamed mixture, blending well. Stir in oats, chocolate pieces and walnuts. Drop mixture by teaspoonfuls, about 2 inches apart, on greased baking sheets.

Bake in 350⁰ oven 12 to 15 minutes or until golden brown. Remove from baking sheets; cool on racks. Makes 6 dozen.

CHEWY COCONUT MACAROONS

Crispy on the outside, these pretty beige-colored macaroons are quick and easy to make.

⅓ c. sifted flour	¾ c. sugar
¼ tsp. baking powder	1 tblsp. butter or
⅛ tsp. salt	regular margarine,
2 eggs	melted
1 tsp. vanilla	2⅔ c. flaked coconut

Sift together flour, baking powder and salt; set aside.

Beat together eggs and vanilla in bowl until foamy, using electric mixer at high speed. Gradually beat in sugar. Continue beating at high speed until thick and lemon-colored. Blend in butter.

Gradually add dry ingredients to egg mixture, using electric mixer at low speed. Fold in coconut. Drop mixture by rounded teaspoonfuls, about 2 inches apart, on greased baking sheets.

Bake in 325⁰ oven 15 minutes, or until golden brown around the edges. Remove from baking sheets; cool on racks. Makes 2½ dozen.

To Store Crisp Cookies
Store crisp cookies in a container with a loose-fitting cover. If cookies become soft, place in single layer on ungreased baking sheet and heat at 300° for about 5 minutes.

CHOCOLATE-RAISIN OAT COOKIES

You seldom see an oat cookie with chocolate pieces—the flavors blend so well. Your family will request these often.

1 c. sifted flour	1 egg
¾ tsp. baking powder	¾ c. quick-cooking oats
½ c. butter or	½ c. raisins
regular margarine	½ c. semisweet
¾ c. brown sugar,	chocolate pieces
packed	

Sift together flour and baking powder; set aside.

Cream together butter and brown sugar in bowl until light and fluffy, using electric mixer at medium speed. Beat in egg.

Gradually stir dry ingredients into creamed mixture, blending well. Stir in oats, raisins and chocolate pieces. (Dough will be stiff.) Drop mixture by rounded teaspoonfuls, about 2 inches apart, on greased baking sheets.

Bake in 375° oven 8 to 10 minutes or until golden brown. Remove from baking sheets; cool on racks. Makes 3½ dozen.

COCONUT-OATMEAL COOKIES

This hand-me-down recipe was a favorite in our test kitchens. Makes a soft, chewy cookie.

1¼ c. sifted flour	½ c. sugar
1 tsp. baking powder	2 eggs
1 tsp. baking soda	1 tsp. vanilla
½ tsp. salt	1 tblsp. milk
½ c. shortening	1 c. flaked coconut
½ c. brown sugar,	1 c. quick-cooking oats
packed	

Cooling Cookies
Place cookies in a single layer on wire rack to cool. Placing cookies on top of each other will cause them to stick together.

Sift together flour, baking powder, baking soda and salt; set aside.

Cream together shortening, brown sugar and sugar in bowl until light and fluffy, using electric mixer at medium speed. Add eggs, one at a time, beating well after each addition. Blend in vanilla and milk.

Gradually stir dry ingredients into creamed mixture, blending well. Stir in coconut and oats. Drop mixture by rounded teaspoonfuls, about 3 inches apart, on greased baking sheets.

Bake in 350° oven 10 to 12 minutes or until golden brown. Remove from baking sheets; cool on racks. Makes about 3½ dozen.

RAISIN DROP COOKIES

Just the kind of soft, chewy cookie that makes the perfect snack after a hard day's work outdoors.

1½ c. raisins	¾ c. sugar
1 c. water	¾ c. brown sugar,
3 c. sifted flour	packed
1 tsp. baking soda	2 eggs
¾ tsp. baking powder	1 tsp. vanilla
1 tsp. salt	
1 c. butter or	
regular margarine	

Combine raisins and water in small saucepan. Bring to a boil, reduce heat and simmer 10 minutes. Remove from heat; cool completely. Drain raisins, reserving ½ c. cooking liquid. Set aside.

Sift together flour, baking soda, baking powder and salt; set aside.

Cream together butter, sugar and brown sugar in bowl until light and fluffy, using electric mixer at medium speed. Add eggs, one at a time, beating well after each addition. Blend in vanilla.

Add dry ingredients alternately with reserved ½ c. cooking liquid to creamed mixture, beating well after each addition and using electric mixer at low speed. Stir in raisins. Drop mixture by rounded teaspoonfuls, about 3 inches apart, on greased baking sheets.

Bake in 375° oven 6 to 8 minutes or until golden brown. Remove from baking sheets; cool on racks. Makes 5½ dozen.

CRISP OATMEAL COOKIES

These oatmeal cookies are pretty enough to decorate any holiday cookie plate. Try green candied cherries on some.

1 c. sifted flour	1 egg
½ tsp. baking soda	⅓ c. water
1 tsp. salt	1 tsp. vanilla
¾ c. shortening	3 c. quick-cooking oats
1 c. brown sugar, packed	30 red candied cherries, cut in half
½ c. sugar	

Sift together flour, baking soda and salt; set aside.

Cream together shortening, brown sugar and sugar in mixing bowl until light and fluffy, using electric mixer at medium speed. Add egg, water and vanilla, beating well.

Gradually stir dry ingredients into creamed mixture, blending well. Stir in oats. Drop mixture by rounded teaspoonfuls, about 3 inches apart, on greased baking sheets. Press a candied cherry half in center of each cookie.

Bake in 350° oven 15 minutes or until golden brown. Remove from baking sheets; cool on racks. Make 5 dozen.

Drop Cookies
A snap to make! Some are chewy with a cake-like texture; others are crisp and thin. No end to the variety you can make.

OLD-FASHIONED RAISIN DROP COOKIES

"I sent these to my son overseas. Although they arrived four months later, they were still fresh," wrote a Wisconsin woman.

2 c. raisins	¼ tsp. ground nutmeg
1 c. water	¼ tsp. ground allspice
1 tsp. baking soda	1 c. shortening
4 c. sifted flour	2 c. sugar
1 tsp. baking powder	3 eggs
2 tsp. salt	1 tsp. vanilla
1½ tsp. ground cinnamon	1 c. chopped walnuts

Combine raisins and water in 2-qt. saucepan. Bring to a boil. Cover and simmer 5 minutes. Remove from heat. Drain cooking liquid, reserving ½ c. Combine raisins with ½ c. reserved liquid. Cool to lukewarm and stir in baking soda; set aside.

Sift together flour, baking powder, salt, cinnamon, nutmeg and allspice; set aside.

Cream together shortening and sugar in bowl until light and fluffy, using electric mixer at medium speed. Add eggs, one at a time, beating well after each addition. Blend in vanilla and raisin mixture.

Gradually stir dry ingredients into creamed mixture, mixing well. Stir in walnuts. Drop mixture by rounded teaspoonfuls, about 3 inches apart, on greased baking sheets.

Bake in 400° oven 8 to 10 minutes or until golden brown. Remove from baking sheets; cool on racks. Makes 6½ dozen.

CHOCOLATE DROP COOKIES

"I have fond memories of these cookies and my Aunt Annie, who baked them when we were children," said a New York woman.

2⅔ c. sifted flour	2 eggs
1 tsp. baking soda	2 tsp. vanilla
½ tsp. salt	4 (1-oz.) squares
½ c. shortening	unsweetened chocolate,
½ c. butter or	melted and cooled
regular margarine	1 c. sour milk*
1½ c. brown sugar, packed	

Sift together flour, baking soda and salt; set aside.

Cream together shortening, butter and brown sugar in bowl until light and fluffy, using electric mixer at medium speed. Add eggs, one at a time, beating well after each addition. Blend in vanilla and chocolate.

Add dry ingredients alternately with sour milk to creamed mixture, beating well after each addition and using electric mixer at low speed. Drop mixture by rounded teaspoonfuls, about 2 inches apart, on greased baking sheets.

Bake in 350° oven 8 minutes, or until no imprint remains when cookies are lightly touched with finger. Remove from baking sheets; cool on racks. Makes about 8 dozen.

*Note: To sour milk, place 1 tblsp. vinegar in measuring cup. Add enough milk to make 1 c.

TEXAS RANGER COOKIES

"These cookies won me my first Blue Ribbon at a local fair," a Texas homemaker wrote us.

2 c. sifted flour	1 c. brown sugar,
1 tsp. baking soda	packed
½ tsp. baking powder	2 eggs
½ tsp. salt	1 tsp. vanilla
1 c. shortening	1 c. flaked coconut
1 c. sugar	1 c. chopped pecans

Oven Spacing
If you're baking one sheet of cookies at a time, place oven rack in center of oven. If you're baking two sheets at a time, place racks so that they divide oven into thirds.

To Drop Cookies
Use kitchen teaspoons, not measuring teaspoons, to drop cookie dough onto baking sheet.

Sift together flour, baking soda, baking powder and salt; set aside.

Cream together shortening, sugar and brown sugar in bowl until light and fluffy, using electric mixer at medium speed. Add eggs, one at at time, beating well after each addition. Blend in vanilla.

Gradually stir dry ingredients into creamed mixture, blending well. Stir in coconut and pecans. Drop mixture by rounded teaspoonfuls, about 3 inches apart, on ungreased baking sheets.

Bake in 375° oven 10 minutes or until golden brown. Remove from baking sheets; cool on racks. Makes 6 dozen.

APPLESAUCE OATMEAL COOKIES

Soft, puffy cake-like cookies filled with raisins. They are flavored with applesauce and spiced with cinnamon and cloves.

1¾ c. sifted flour	1 c. sugar
1 tsp. baking soda	1 egg
½ tsp. baking powder	1 c. applesauce
½ tsp. salt	½ c. raisins
1 tsp. ground cinnamon	1 c. quick-cooking oats
½ tsp. ground cloves	
½ c. butter or	
regular margarine	

Sift together flour, baking soda, baking powder, salt, cinnamon and cloves; set aside.

Cream together butter and sugar in bowl until light and fluffy, using electric mixer at medium speed. Add egg and applesauce, beating well.

Gradually stir dry ingredients into creamed mixture, blending well. Stir in raisins and oats. Drop mixture by teaspoonfuls, about 3 inches apart, on greased baking sheets.

Bake in 375° oven 15 minutes or until golden brown. Remove from baking sheets; cool on racks. Makes 4 dozen.

ORANGE-CHOCOLATE COOKIES

Start with a basic cookie dough and stir in chocolate bits, fresh orange juice and grated rind for a tasty flavor combination.

2 c. sifted flour	1 egg
½ tsp. baking powder	1 tblsp. grated orange
½ tsp. baking soda	rind
½ tsp. salt	1 tsp. orange juice
¼ tsp. ground nutmeg	½ c. sour milk*
½ c. butter or	1 (6-oz.) pkg. semisweet
regular margarine	chocolate pieces
1 c. sugar	

Sift together flour, baking powder, baking soda, salt and nutmeg; set aside.

Cream together butter and sugar in bowl until light and fluffy, using electric mixer at medium speed. Add egg, orange rind and orange juice; blend well.

Add dry ingredients alternately with sour milk to creamed mixture, beating well after each addition and using electric mixer at low speed. Stir in chocolate pieces. Drop mixture by rounded teaspoonfuls, about 3 inches apart, on greased baking sheets.

Bake in 350° oven 15 minutes or until golden brown. Remove from baking sheets; cool on racks. Makes 4 dozen.

*Note: To sour milk, place 1½ tsp. vinegar in measuring cup. Add enough milk to make ½ c.

APPLE-PECAN DROP COOKIES

*Country-style soft apple cookies sprinkled with confectioners sugar.
Walnuts can be used instead of pecans.*

3 c. sifted flour	2 tsp. vanilla
2 tsp. baking powder	½ c. dairy sour cream
1 tsp. baking soda	2 c. finely chopped,
¼ c. shortening	pared apples
1 c. brown sugar,	½ c. chopped pecans
packed	Sifted confectioners
1 c. sugar	sugar
3 eggs	

Baking Sheets
*Use baking sheets and
pans at least 2 inches
smaller than the oven
rack so heat can circulate
around the cookies for
even baking.*

Sift together flour, baking powder and baking soda; set aside.

Cream together shortening, brown sugar and sugar in bowl until light and fluffy, using electric mixer at medium speed. Add eggs, one at a time, beating well after each addition. Blend in vanilla and sour cream.

Gradually stir dry ingredients into creamed mixture, blending well. Stir in apples and pecans. Drop mixture by rounded teaspoonfuls, about 2 inches apart, on greased baking sheets.

Bake in 350° oven 12 minutes or until lightly browned. Remove from baking sheets; cool on racks. Sprinkle with sifted confectioners sugar. Makes 6 dozen.

FROSTED COCONUT-ORANGE COOKIES

"These are delicious with a frosty pitcher of lemonade on a hot summer day," a farm woman from Iowa told us.

1¾ c. sifted flour	½ tsp. grated lemon rind
¼ tsp. baking soda	3 tblsp. orange juice
¼ tsp. salt	1 tblsp. lemon juice
½ c. butter or	1 c. flaked coconut
regular margarine	Orange Frosting
⅔ c. sugar	(recipe follows)
1 egg	
½ tsp. grated orange	
rind	

Sift together flour, baking soda and salt; set aside.

Cream together butter and sugar in mixing bowl until light and fluffy, using electric mixer at medium speed. Add egg; beat well. Beat in orange rind and lemon rind.

Add dry ingredients alternately with orange juice and lemon juice to creamed mixture, beating well after each addition and using electric mixer at low speed. Stir in coconut. Drop mixture by rounded teaspoonfuls, about 3 inches apart, on greased baking sheets.

Bake in 350⁰ oven 12 minutes, or until edges are browned. Remove from baking sheets; cool on racks. Frost with Orange Frosting. Makes 3 dozen.

Orange Frosting: Combine 1⅓ c. sifted confectioners sugar, ½ tsp. grated orange rind, 1 drop yellow food coloring, ½ tsp. lemon juice and 1 tblsp. orange juice in bowl. Beat until smooth.

CRISP PEANUT BUTTER COOKIES

"My children like these better than the regular peanut butter cookies, if that's possible," a Vermont homemaker told us.

2 c. sifted flour	**¾ c. brown sugar,**
2 tsp. baking soda	**packed**
¼ tsp. salt	**2 eggs**
1 c. butter or	**1 tsp. vanilla**
regular margarine	**3 c. crushed Product 19**
1 c. peanut butter	**cereal**
¾ c. sugar	

Sift together flour, baking soda and salt; set aside.

Cream together butter, peanut butter, sugar and brown sugar in bowl until light and fluffy, using electric mixer at medium speed. Add eggs, one at a time, beating well after each addition. Blend in vanilla.

Gradually stir dry ingredients into creamed mixture, blending well. Stir in cereal. Drop mixture by rounded teaspoonfuls, about 3 inches apart, on ungreased baking sheets. Flatten each with floured fork, making crisscross pattern.

Bake in 350⁰ oven 8 to 10 minutes or until golden brown. Remove from baking sheets; cool on racks. Makes about 6 dozen.

AMISH OATMEAL COOKIES

Old-fashioned man-size cookies—3½ inches in diameter. Treat the field hands—they'll really enjoy these.

1½ c. raisins	3 c. sugar
1 c. salted peanuts	2 c. quick-cooking oats
6 c. sifted flour	3 tsp. baking soda
3 tsp. baking powder	1 c. buttermilk
1 tsp. salt	½ c. molasses
1 tsp. ground cinnamon	4 eggs
1 tsp. ground nutmeg	Flour
1½ c. lard or shortening	

To Grease Cookie Sheets
Grease cookie sheets lightly. Too much shortening on the baking sheet will cause cookies to spread and edges will be too thin and too brown. Do not use butter or margarine to grease sheets.

Grind raisins and peanuts in food grinder, using medium blade; set aside.

Sift together 6 c. flour, baking powder, salt, cinnamon and nutmeg into very large bowl or dishpan. Cut in lard until mixture forms fine crumbs, using pastry blender. Add ground raisin mixture, sugar and oats. Mix well, using hands if necessary.

Dissolve baking soda in buttermilk in small bowl. Add molasses and 3 of the eggs to buttermilk mixture. Beat with rotary beater until blended.

Add buttermilk mixture to flour mixture; mix well with spoon. Drop mixture by heaping teaspoonfuls or a small ice cream scoop, about 3 inches apart, on greased baking sheets. Flatten each with bottom of drinking glass dipped in flour to 2½-inch round.

Beat remaining egg in small bowl until blended. Brush tops of each round with egg.

Bake in 375° oven 8 to 10 minutes or until golden brown. Remove from baking sheets; cool on racks. Makes 4½ dozen.

JUMBO OATMEAL-PEANUT BUTTER COOKIES

Your hungry teenagers will like these extra-large cookies—so rich in protein and iron, too.

2 c. sifted flour	1 c. brown sugar, packed
1 tsp. baking soda	
1 tsp. salt	2 eggs
1 tsp. ground cinnamon	1 tsp. vanilla
¾ c. butter or regular margarine	¼ c. milk
	1½ c. quick-cooking oats
½ c. peanut butter	1 c. raisins
1 c. sugar	

Sift together flour, baking soda, salt and cinnamon; set aside.

Cream together butter, peanut butter, sugar and brown sugar in bowl until light and fluffy, using electric mixer at medium speed. Add eggs, one at a time, beating well after each addition. Blend in vanilla and milk.

Gradually stir dry ingredients into creamed mixture, blending well. Stir in oats and raisins. Drop mixture by tablespoonfuls, about 2 inches apart, on greased baking sheets.

Bake in 350° oven 15 minutes or until golden brown. Remove from baking sheets; cool on racks. Makes 3 dozen.

GRANDMOTHER'S GINGER COOKIES

One of our test kitchen home economists said that these reminded her of cookies her mother used to make.

4 c. sifted flour	1 egg
½ tsp. salt	1 c. molasses
2 tsp. ground ginger	2 tsp. baking soda
1 tsp. ground cinnamon	1 c. very hot water
1 tsp. ground nutmeg	Vanilla Frosting
½ c. shortening	(recipe follows)
1 c. sugar	

Sift together flour, salt, ginger, cinnamon and nutmeg; set aside.

Cream together shortening and sugar in bowl until light and fluffy, using electric mixer at medium speed. Add egg and molasses; beat until smooth.

Dissolve baking soda in very hot water in small bowl; mix well.

Add dry ingredients alternately with baking soda mixture to creamed mixture, beating well after each addition and using electric mixer at low speed. Cover and chill in refrigerator 1 hour.

Drop mixture by teaspoonfuls, about 3 inches apart, on greased baking sheets.

Bake in 375° oven 8 minutes, or until no imprint remains when cookies are lightly touched with finger. Remove from baking sheets; cool on racks. Makes 5½ dozen.

Vanilla Frosting: Combine 2 c. sifted confectioners sugar, 1 tsp. melted butter or regular margarine, 1 tsp. vanilla and 2 tblsp. milk in bowl. Beat until smooth.

WALNUT MERINGUE COOKIES

Chewy, soft meringue-based cookies filled with crispy rice cereal. Quick and easy—flavored with cinnamon.

1 egg white	1 c. toasted rice cereal
Dash of salt	½ c. finely chopped
¼ c. sugar	walnuts
½ tsp. ground cinnamon	

Beat egg white with salt in mixing bowl until foamy, using electric mixer at high speed. Gradually add sugar and cinnamon, beating until mixture is stiff and glossy. Fold in rice cereal and walnuts. Drop mixture by teaspoonfuls, about 3 inches apart, on well-greased baking sheets.

Bake in 350⁰ oven 10 minutes, or until very lightly browned. Remove from baking sheets; cool on racks. Makes 1½ dozen.

Note: Meringue cookies soften readily. It's best to store cookies in airtight container.

Colored Sugars
Buy colored sugar in small packages or jars or make your own. Stir 2 or 3 drops of food coloring into 2 tblsp. of granulated sugar. Make a bigger batch once you have found the shade you like.

RAISIN MERINGUE KISSES

This recipe takes basic meringue cookies one step further—contains cornflakes, raisins and coconut.

4 egg whites	2 c. cornflakes
¼ tsp. salt	1 c. chopped raisins
1 c. sugar	½ c. flaked coconut
1 tsp. vanilla	

Beat egg whites with salt in mixing bowl until soft peaks form, using electric mixer at high speed. Gradually add sugar, beating until very stiff peaks form. Beat in vanilla.

Stir in cornflakes, raisins and coconut. Drop mixture by heaping teaspoonfuls, about 2 inches apart, on greased baking sheets.

Bake in 350⁰ oven 20 minutes or until golden brown. Immediately remove from baking sheets; cool on racks. Makes 3½ dozen.

Note: Meringue cookies soften readily. It's best to store cookies in airtight container.

BAR COOKIES

All bar cookies are made by spreading dough in a pan. They are baked, cooled and cut into bars, squares, diamonds or the shape of your choice.

Bar cookies are the easiest of all the cookies to make. There's no rolling, dropping or shaping the dough. And you don't have to remove each cookie separately from the baking sheet.

Do avoid overmixing the dough or the cookie surface will be hard and the texture tough.

Spread the dough evenly in the pan so that all the cookie dough will bake evenly.

Use the pan size indicated in the recipe. If you use a larger pan, the dough will be too thin and will overbake. If you use a smaller pan, the dough will be too thick and will be undercooked and doughy.

Bake cookies only until they are done. Each one of our recipes has a test for doneness. In many recipes the cookies are done if they retain a slight imprint when they are pressed lightly with a finger. However, that rule does not apply to all bar cookies.

Family Cookies
Bar cookies are family favorites because they are quick and easy to make—also keep well.

CHOCOLATE-VANILLA LAYERED BARS

These cake-like bar cookies are made of two layers: yellow cake bottom and a brownie layer top.

1½ c. sifted flour	3 eggs
¼ tsp. salt	1 tsp. vanilla
¾ c. butter or regular margarine	1½ (1-oz.) squares unsweetened chocolate, melted and cooled
1½ c. sugar	

Sift together flour and salt; set aside.

Cream together butter and sugar in bowl until light and fluffy, using electric mixer at medium speed. Add eggs, one at a time, beating well after each addition. Beat in vanilla.

Gradually stir dry ingredients into creamed mixture, blending well. Spread two thirds of the batter in greased 9-inch square baking pan.

Stir melted chocolate into remaining batter. Spread chocolate batter evenly over vanilla batter in pan.

Bake in 350° oven 35 minutes, or until top springs back when touched lightly with finger. Cool in pan on rack. Cut into 3 × 1⅛-inch bars. Makes 24 bars.

CHERRY-WALNUT BARS

"I do a lot of baking for graduations, showers and brunches. This is the most requested recipe," a Minnesota woman said.

1½ c. sifted flour	2 c. sugar
⅓ c. brown sugar, packed	½ c. water
½ tsp. salt	1 tsp. almond extract
¾ c. butter or regular margarine	¼ tsp. salt
2 envs. unflavored gelatin	3 drops red food coloring
⅓ c. maraschino cherry juice	⅓ c. chopped red maraschino cherries
	⅓ c. chopped walnuts

Combine flour, brown sugar and ½ tsp. salt in bowl. Cut in butter until mixture resembles coarse meal, using pastry blender. Press mixture into bottom of greased 13 × 9 × 2-inch baking pan.

Bake in 325° oven 18 to 20 minutes or until golden brown.

Meanwhile, sprinkle gelatin over cherry juice in measuring cup; stir to soften.

Combine sugar and water in 2-qt. saucepan. Cover and bring to a boil over medium heat. Remove cover and boil 2 minutes.

Pour gelatin mixture into mixing bowl. Pour boiling sugar syrup over it. Beat until mixture becomes thick and begins to hold its shape, using electric mixer at high speed, 5 to 10 minutes. Beat in almond extract, ¼ tsp. salt and red food coloring. Fold in cherries and walnuts. Pour over warm baked crust. Let stand at room temperature overnight. Cut into 3¼ × 1⅛-inch bars. Makes 32 bars.

Baking Powder—Too Old?
If your baking powder is caked, moisture has gotten in and it has lost its leavening power. Don't take a chance on spoiling a recipe and wasting other ingredients. Throw out the old can and buy a fresh one.

SPICY RAISIN BARS

An Ohio woman wrote us, "I've been using this recipe since 1931. It's uncomplicated and I usually have the ingredients."

2 c. raisins	½ tsp. ground nutmeg
1 c. water	1 c. shortening
4 c. sifted flour	2 c. brown sugar, packed
1 tsp. baking powder	3 eggs
1 tsp. baking soda	1 tsp. vanilla
½ tsp. salt	Orange Glaze (recipe follows)
1½ tsp. ground cinnamon	
1½ tsp. ground allspice	

Combine raisins and water in 2-qt. saucepan. Bring to a boil, reduce heat and simmer, covered, 5 minutes. Remove from heat; cool completely.

Sift together flour, baking powder, baking soda, salt, cinnamon, allspice and nutmeg; set aside.

Cream together shortening and brown sugar in bowl until light and fluffy, using electric mixer at medium speed. Add eggs, one at a time, beating well after each addition. Blend in vanilla and cooled raisin mixture.

Gradually stir dry ingredients into creamed mixture, blending well. Divide dough in fourths. Spread each fourth on greased baking sheet, forming a 12 × 3-inch rectangle.

Bake in 350° oven 18 to 20 minutes or until golden brown. Cool on baking sheets on racks. Frost with Orange Glaze. Cut each rectangle into 12 bars, 1 inch wide. Makes 48 bars.

Orange Glaze: Combine 4 c. sifted confectioners sugar, 2 tblsp. melted butter or regular margarine and 4 tblsp. orange juice in bowl. Stir until smooth. Add 1 more tblsp. orange juice, if necessary, to make frosting of spreading consistency.

CHOCOLATE-ALMOND BARS

This unusual bar cookie combines chocolate and cream cheese. It was sent to us by a home economics teacher from New York.

1 (6-oz.) pkg. semisweet chocolate pieces	1½ c. sifted flour
1 (3-oz.) pkg. cream cheese	½ tsp. baking powder
	¼ tsp. salt
⅓ c. evaporated milk	½ c. butter or regular margarine
½ c. chopped walnuts	¾ c. sugar
2 tblsp. sesame seeds	1 egg
¼ tsp. almond extract	¼ tsp. almond extract

Combine chocolate pieces, cream cheese and evaporated milk in 2-qt. saucepan. Cook over medium heat, stirring constantly, until chocolate and cream cheese are melted and mixture is thick and smooth. Remove from heat. Stir in walnuts, sesame seeds and ¼ tsp. almond extract; set aside.

Sift together flour, baking powder and salt; set aside.

Cream together butter and sugar in bowl until light and fluffy, using electric mixer at medium speed. Blend in egg and ¼ tsp. almond extract.

Gradually stir dry ingredients into creamed mixture, blending well. Press one half of the dough in greased 12 × 8 × 2-inch glass baking dish (2-qt.). Top with chocolate mixture. Crumble remaining dough on top.

Bake in 375° oven 25 minutes, or until top is lightly browned. Cool in pan on rack. Cut into bars. Makes 24 bars.

CREAM CHEESE BARS

A very different kind of bar cookie featuring a crisp crust and a tart, creamy cheese filling that hints of lemon.

⅓ c. butter or regular margarine	¼ c. sugar
⅓ c. brown sugar, packed	1 egg
1 c. sifted flour	2 tblsp. milk
½ c. chopped walnuts	1 tblsp. lemon juice
1 (8-oz.) pkg. cream cheese, softened	½ tsp. vanilla

Cream together butter and brown sugar in bowl until light and fluffy, using electric mixer at medium speed. Stir in flour and walnuts, mixing until crumbly. Remove 1 c. crumb mixture and reserve for topping. Press remaining crumb mixture into bottom of greased 8-inch square baking pan.

Bake in 350⁰ oven 12 minutes or until golden brown.

Meanwhile, beat cream cheese in bowl until smooth, using electric mixer at medium speed. Gradually add sugar, egg, milk, lemon juice and vanilla, beating well. Spread cream cheese mixture over baked crust. Sprinkle with 1 c. reserved crumb mixture.

Bake in 350⁰ oven 25 minutes or until set. Cool in pan on rack. Cut into 2-inch squares. Store in refrigerator. Makes 16 squares.

CARAMEL-CHOCOLATE BARS

This easy-to-make brownie is made with a cake mix. The batter is layered into the pan with melted caramel mixture.

1 (14-oz.) bag caramels	¾ c. melted butter or
⅓ c. evaporated milk	regular margarine
1 (18½-oz.) box Swiss	1 (6-oz.) pkg. semisweet
chocolate cake mix	chocolate pieces
⅓ c. evaporated milk	1 c. chopped walnuts

Combine caramels and ⅓ c. evaporated milk in top of double boiler. Cover and place over boiling water until melted, stirring occasionaly. Keep warm.

Combine cake mix, ⅓ c. evaporated milk and butter in large bowl. Beat with electric mixer at medium speed 2 minutes, scraping bowl occasionaly. (Mixture is thick.) Spread one half of mixture in greased 13 × 9 × 2-inch baking pan.

Bake in 350⁰ oven 6 minutes. Remove from oven and cool on rack 2 minutes. Spread hot caramel mixture carefully over baked layer. Sprinkle with chocolate pieces.

Stir ½ c. of the walnuts into remaining cake batter. Drop batter by spoonfuls over all. Sprinkle with remaining ½ c. walnuts.

Bake in 350⁰ oven 18 minutes, or until top springs back when lightly touched with finger. Cool in pan on rack. Cut into 3¼ × 1⅛-inch bars. Makes 32.

COCONUT LEMON BARS

Tangy lemon-flavored filling with lots of chewy coconut spread over a golden brown butter crust.

1 c. sifted flour	1 tsp. baking powder
¼ c. sifted confectioners sugar	6 tblsp. lemon juice
	1½ c. sugar
½ c. butter or regular margarine	1 tsp. grated lemon rind
	3 c. flaked coconut
4 eggs	

Sift together flour and confectioners sugar into bowl. Cut in butter until mixture resembles coarse meal, using pastry blender. Press mixture into bottom of greased 13 × 9 × 2-inch baking pan.

Bake in 350° oven 15 to 18 minutes or until golden brown.

Meanwhile, combine eggs, baking powder, lemon juice, sugar and lemon rind in mixing bowl. Beat until smooth, using electric mixer at medium speed. Stir in coconut. Pour mixture over baked crust.

Bake in 350° oven 30 minutes more or until golden brown. Cool in pan on rack. Cut into 3¼ × 1⅛-inch bars. Makes 32.

RASPBERRY JAM SQUARES

"My family likes these all-purpose bars. Perfect for a snack with coffee or a dessert after dinner," wrote a Wisconsin woman.

1½ c. sifted flour	2 eggs, separated
½ tsp. salt	1 (10-oz.) jar red raspberry preserves (1 c.)
½ c. butter or regular margarine	
	½ c. sugar
¼ c. sugar	1 tsp. vanilla

Sift together flour and salt; set aside.

Cream together butter and ¼ c. sugar in mixing bowl until light and fluffy, using electric mixer at medium speed. Beat in egg yolks.

Stir dry ingredients into creamed mixture, mixing until crumbly. Press crumb mixture into ungreased 9-inch square baking pan.

Spread raspberry preserves over crumb layer.

Beat egg whites in another bowl until foamy, using electric mixer at high speed. Gradually beat in ½ c. sugar, beating until stiff, glossy peaks form. Blend in vanilla. Spread meringue carefully over preserves layer.

Bake in 350° oven 30 minutes or until golden brown. Cool in pan on rack. Cut into 2¼-inch squares. Makes 16 squares.

Cool Baking Sheets
Cool and clean off baking sheets before using again. Hot baking sheets melt the shortening and the cookies will spread.

To Grate Lemon or Orange Peel
Wash and dry the fruit. Rub it, using short strokes, across a small section of a fine grater. Grate only the colored part of the peel—the white part has a bitter taste. You will get about 1 tblsp. grated lemon rind from a medium lemon, and 2 tblsp. grated orange peel from a medium orange.

BUTTERMILK CINNAMON BARS

A three-layer bar featuring a crunchy nut-coconut crust, cinnamon-spiced cake layer and topped with a vanilla glaze.

2 c. sifted flour	1 tsp. baking soda
1¼ c. sugar	¾ tsp. salt
¾ c. brown sugar, packed	1 tsp. ground cinnamon
½ c. butter or	1 c. buttermilk
regular margarine	1 tsp. vanilla
½ c. chopped walnuts	Confectioners Sugar Icing
½ c. flaked coconut	(recipe follows)
1 egg	

Combine flour, sugar and brown sugar in bowl. Cut in butter until mixture forms coarse crumbs, using pastry blender. Combine 2 c. of the crumb mixture with walnuts and coconut. Press nut mixture into greased 13 × 9 × 2-inch baking pan.

Combine egg, baking soda, salt, cinnamon, buttermilk and vanilla in another bowl. Beat until smooth, using electric mixer at medium speed. Stir egg mixture into remaining crumb mixture, mixing just until moistened. Spread over crumb-nut layer.

Bake in 350° oven 35 minutes or until golden brown. Cool in pan on rack 10 minutes. Frost with Confectioners Sugar Icing. Cool completely. Cut into 3¼ × 1⅛-inch bars. Makes 32 bars.

Confectioners Sugar Icing: Combine ¾ c. sifted confectioners sugar, ½ tsp. vanilla and 4 tsp. milk in bowl; beat until smooth.

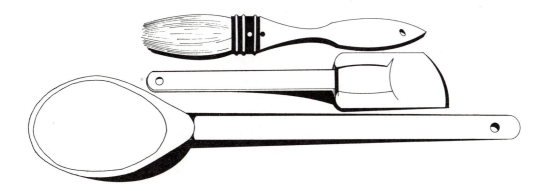

FUDGE-MARSHMALLOW BROWNIES

A rich brownie hidden under a blanket of chewy marshmallows and smooth, silky chocolate glaze. Sinfully rich, but so good.

1 c. butter or	2 c. sugar
regular margarine	1½ c. chopped pecans
⅓ c. baking cocoa	3 c. miniature
1½ c. sifted flour	marshmallows
Pinch of salt	Chocolate Glaze (recipe
4 eggs	follows)

Combine butter and cocoa in small saucepan. Cook over low heat, stirring constantly, until butter melts and mixture is smooth. Remove from heat and cool slightly.

Sift together flour and salt; set aside.

Combine eggs and sugar in bowl and beat until well blended, using electric mixer at medium speed.

Add dry ingredients alternately with cocoa mixture to egg mixture, beating well after each addition, using electric mixer at low speed. Stir in pecans. Spread mixture in greased 15½ × 10½ × 1-inch jelly roll pan.

Bake in 350° oven 20 minutes, or until no imprint remains when top is touched lightly with finger. Remove from oven; sprinkle with marshmallows. Return to oven 2 minutes more to soften marshmallows. Remove from oven. Press marshmallows to flatten. Cool in pan on rack. While still warm, pour on Chocolate Glaze. Cool completely. Cut into 2-inch squares. Makes 35 squares.

Chocolate Glaze: Combine 2 (1-oz.) squares unsweetened chocolate and ¼ c. butter or regular margarine in small saucepan. Cook over very low heat, stirring constantly, until melted. Remove from heat; cool slightly. Combine 2¼ c. sifted confectioners sugar, ¼ c. hot water, 1 tsp. vanilla and ⅛ tsp. salt in bowl. Stir in chocolate mixture. Beat until mixture becomes smooth and begins to thicken, using spoon.

GRANDMOM'S APRICOT SQUARES

You can use commercial apricot preserves or your own homemade version in this family heirloom recipe, which is very easy to prepare.

1½ c. sifted flour
1½ c. quick-cooking oats
1 c. brown sugar, packed
¾ c. soft butter or
    regular margarine

1 (10-oz.) jar apricot
    preserves (1 c.)

Combine flour, oats and brown sugar in bowl. Cut in butter until mixture is crumbly, using pastry blender. Press two thirds of crumb mixture into greased 8-inch square baking pan, building up sides to make ½-inch rim.

Spread apricot preserves over crumb layer. Sprinkle remaining crumbs on top; pat down gently.

Bake in 350° oven 35 minutes or until golden brown. Cool in pan on rack. Cut into 2-inch squares. Makes 16 squares.

APPLESAUCE FUDGIES

Applesauce and chocolate are combined in this unusual bar cookie. To make a bit more festive, dust with confectioners sugar.

½ c. butter or
    regular margarine
2 (1-oz.) squares
    unsweetened chocolate
1 c. sifted flour
½ tsp. baking powder
¼ tsp. baking soda

¼ tsp. salt
2 eggs
1 c. brown sugar, packed
1 tsp. vanilla
½ c. applesauce
½ c. chopped walnuts

Combine butter and chocolate in saucepan. Place over very low heat, stirring constantly, until melted. Remove from heat; cool slightly.

Sift together flour, baking powder, baking soda and salt; set aside.

Combine eggs, brown sugar and vanilla in bowl. Beat until well blended, using electric mixer at medium speed. Blend in chocolate mixture and applesauce.

Gradually stir dry ingredients into chocolate mixture, mixing well. Stir in walnuts. Pour mixture into greased 13 × 9 × 2-inch baking pan.

Bake in 350° oven 25 minutes, or until top springs back when touched lightly with finger. Cool in pan on rack. Cut into 2¼-inch squares. Makes 24 squares.

Gift Boxes For Cookies
All kinds of boxes, from candy containers to thin stationery boxes, may be used to package cookies for gifts.

TRI-LEVEL BROWNIES

"I make these for my family when they crave something rich and chocolaty," a South Carolina farm woman wrote us.

½ c. sifted flour	⅔ c. sifted flour
¼ tsp. baking soda	¼ tsp. baking powder
¼ tsp. salt	¼ tsp. salt
1 c. quick-cooking oats	¾ c. sugar
½ c. brown sugar, packed	1 egg
⅔ c. melted butter or regular margarine	½ tsp. vanilla
	¼ c. milk
1 (1-oz.) square unsweetened chocolate	½ c. chopped walnuts
	Chocolate Icing
¼ c. butter or regular margarine	(recipe follows)

Sift together ½ c. flour, baking soda and ¼ tsp. salt into mixing bowl. Add quick-cooking oats, brown sugar and ⅔ c. melted butter. Mix until crumbly, using fork. Press crumb mixture into greased 12 × 8 × 2-inch glass baking dish (2-qt.).

Bake in 350⁰ oven 10 minutes. Cool slightly.

Melt chocolate and ¼ c. butter in saucepan over very low heat, stirring constantly. Remove from heat and cool slightly.

Sift together ⅔ c. flour, baking powder and ¼ tsp. salt; set aside.

Combine chocolate mixture, sugar, egg and vanilla in bowl. Beat 1 minute or until well blended, using electric mixer at medium speed.

Add dry ingredients alternately with milk to chocolate mixture, beating well after each addition, using electric mixer at low speed. Stir in walnuts. Spread mixture over baked crust.

Bake in 350⁰ oven 25 minutes, or until no imprint remains when touched lightly with finger. Cool in baking dish on rack. Frost with Chocolate Icing. Cut into 2-inch squares. Makes 24 squares.

Chocolate Icing: Melt 2 tblsp. butter or regular margarine and 1 (1-oz.) square unsweetened chocolate over very low heat, stirring constantly. Remove from heat; cool slightly. Combine 1½ c. sifted confectioners sugar, 2 tblsp. hot water and 1 tsp. vanilla in bowl. Stir in chocolate mixture, beating until smooth and creamy.

TANGY LEMON SQUARES

Buttery-rich shortbread crust topped with a tangy lemon custard filling and sprinkled with confectioners sugar.

1 c. sifted flour	1 c. sugar
¼ c. sifted confectioners sugar	3 tblsp. lemon juice
	2 tblsp. flour
½ c. butter or regular margarine	½ tsp. baking powder
	¼ tsp. grated lemon rind
2 eggs	Sifted confectioners sugar

Combine 1 c. flour and ¼ c. confectioners sugar in bowl. Cut in butter until mixture forms fine crumbs, using pastry blender. Pat mixture into bottom of well-greased 9-inch square baking pan.

Bake in 350⁰ oven 15 to 18 minutes or until golden brown.

Meanwhile, combine eggs, sugar, lemon juice, 2 tblsp. flour, baking powder and lemon rind in mixing bowl. Beat until smooth, using electric mixer at high speed. Pour mixture over warm baked crust.

Bake in 350⁰ oven 25 minutes, or until no imprint remains when touched lightly with finger. Cool in pan on rack. When completely cooled, sprinkle with sifted confectioners sugar. Cut into 2¼-inch squares. Makes 16 squares.

DATE MERINGUE BARS

Very moist bars with a chewy date layer on the bottom and a tender meringue-like crust on top.

¾ c. sifted flour	1 tsp. vanilla
1 tsp. baking powder	2 c. chopped, pitted dates
½ tsp. salt	1 c. chopped walnuts
3 eggs	Sifted confectioners sugar
1 c. sugar	

Sift together flour, baking powder and salt; set aside.

Beat eggs in mixing bowl until thick and lemon-colored, using electric mixer at high speed. Gradually add sugar, beating well. Blend in vanilla.

Gradually stir dry ingredients into egg mixture, mixing well. Fold in dates and walnuts. Pour mixture into greased 13 × 9 × 2-inch baking pan.

Bake in 350⁰ oven 25 minutes or until golden brown. Cool in pan on rack. Sprinkle with sifted confectioners sugar. Cut into 3¼ × 1⅛-inch bars. Makes 32 bars.

Basket of Cookies
Give two gifts in one. Place homemade cookies in a pretty basket for a birthday or Christmas gift. Choose from fat cornucopias, flat trays, slender cracker holders, or even an old Easter basket sprayed a color of your choice. Line the basket with paper napkins having a birthday or Christmas motif. Fill with an assortment of your finest homemade cookies.

RAISIN SHORTBREAD BARS

Good and chewy raisin- and nut-studded bar cookie. Perfect to tuck into packed lunches or tote on picnics.

1 c. sifted flour	1 tsp. baking powder
¼ c. brown sugar, packed	1 tsp. vanilla
½ c. butter or	1 tsp. grated orange rind
regular margarine	½ tsp. salt
2 eggs	1½ c. chopped raisins
1 c. brown sugar, packed	1 c. chopped walnuts
2 tblsp. flour	Sifted confectioners sugar

Combine 1 c. flour and ¼ c. brown sugar in bowl. Cut in butter until mixture is crumbly, using pastry blender. Press crumb mixture into bottom of ungreased 13 × 9 × 2-inch baking pan.

Bake in 375⁰ oven 8 to 10 minutes or until golden brown. Cool in pan on rack.

Beat eggs until foamy, using electric mixer at high speed. Add brown sugar, 2 tblsp. flour, baking powder, vanilla, orange rind and salt; beat until thick and lemon-colored. Stir in raisins and walnuts. Spread mixture over cooled baked crust.

Bake in 375⁰ oven 20 minutes more, or until cake tester or wooden pick inserted in center comes out clean. Cool in pan on rack. While still slightly warm, cut into 3¼ × 1⅛-inch bars. Sprinkle with sifted confectioners sugar. Makes 32 bars.

EXTRA-RICH TWO-LAYER BARS

"I always pack these extra-rich bars for our camping trips. They are so good after a hike," a Wyoming woman wrote us.

1 c. butter or	2 tblsp. flour
regular margarine	¾ tsp. baking soda
2 c. sifted flour	1 tsp. vanilla
¼ c. sugar	1 c. chopped walnuts
1 tsp. salt	1 c. flaked coconut
2 eggs	Sifted confectioners sugar
1½ c. brown sugar, packed	

Beat butter in bowl until creamy, using electric mixer at medium speed. Stir in 2 c. flour, sugar and salt; mix well. Spread mixture in ungreased 13 × 9 × 2-inch baking pan.

Bake in 350⁰ oven 10 minutes.

Meanwhile, beat eggs slightly in another bowl, using rotary beater. Add brown sugar, 2 tblsp. flour, baking soda and vanilla; beat until blended. Stir in walnuts and coconut. Spread carefully over baked layer.

Bake in 350⁰ oven 20 minutes more or until set. Cool in pan on rack. Sprinkle with sifted confectioners sugar. Cut into 2¼ × 1-inch bars. Makes 52 bars.

STRAWBERRY MERINGUE BARS

"My family loves strawberries. I make my own strawberry jam to use in this recipe," says a Virginia farm woman.

⅔ c. shortening	1 c. finely chopped
⅓ c. sugar	walnuts
2 eggs, separated	1 (10-oz.) jar strawberry
1½ c. sifted flour	preserves (1 c.)
½ c. sugar	

Cream together shortening and ⅓ c. sugar in bowl until light and fluffy, using electric mixer at medium speed. Beat in egg yolks. Stir in flour, mixing well. Press mixture into bottom of ungreased 13 × 9 × 2-inch baking pan.

Bake in 350⁰ oven 15 minutes or until golden brown.

Meanwhile, beat egg whites in another bowl until frothy, using electric mixer at high speed. Gradually add ½ c. sugar, beating until stiff, glossy peaks form. Fold in walnuts.

Spread strawberry preserves over baked crust. Carefully spread walnut meringue mixture on top.

Bake in 350⁰ oven 25 minutes, or until meringue is golden brown. Cool in pan on rack. Cut into 3¼ × 1¼-inch bars. Makes 32 bars.

PEANUT BUTTER COOKIE BARS

Chewy oatmeal cookie layer spread with melted chocolate pieces and drizzled with a thin peanut butter glaze.

1 c. sifted flour	⅓ c. creamy peanut butter
¼ tsp. baking soda	½ tsp. vanilla
¼ tsp. salt	1 c. quick-cooking oats
½ c. butter or	1 (6-oz.) pkg. semisweet
regular margarine	chocolate pieces
½ c. sugar	Peanut Butter Icing
½ c. brown sugar, packed	(recipe follows)
1 egg	

Sift together flour, baking soda and salt; set aside.

Cream together butter, sugar and brown sugar in bowl until light and fluffy, using electric mixer at medium speed. Add egg, peanut butter and vanilla; beat well.

Gradually stir dry ingredients into creamed mixture, blending well. Stir in oats. Spread mixture in greased 13 × 9 × 2-inch baking pan.

Bake in 350⁰ oven 25 minutes, or until no imprint remains when touched lightly with finger. Remove from oven; sprinkle top with chocolate pieces. Let stand 5 minutes so chocolate can melt. Spread melted chocolate evenly over top. Cool in pan on rack.

When completely cooled, drizzle with Peanut Butter Icing. Cut into 2¼ × 1-inch bars. Makes 52 bars.

Peanut Butter Icing: Combine ½ c. sifted confectioners sugar, ¼ c. creamy peanut butter and 3 tblsp. milk in bowl; beat until smooth. Add 1 more tblsp. milk, if necessary, to make an icing that can be drizzled.

BUTTERSCOTCH BARS

Here is the perfect cookie for those of you who like extra-rich butterscotch-flavored sweets.

2 c. sifted flour	1 tsp. vanilla
1 tsp. baking soda	½ tsp. water
½ tsp. salt	1 c. chopped walnuts
1 c. butter or	1 (12-oz.) pkg.
regular margarine	butterscotch-flavored
⅔ c. brown sugar, packed	pieces
⅔ c. sugar	Butter Cream Frosting
2 eggs	(recipe follows)

Sift together flour, baking soda and salt; set aside.

Cream together butter, brown sugar and sugar in bowl until light and fluffy, using electric mixer at medium speed. Add eggs, one at a time, beating well after each addition. Blend in vanilla and water.

Gradually stir dry ingredients into creamed mixture, blending well. Stir in walnuts. Spread mixture in greased 15½ × 10½ × 1-inch jelly roll pan. Sprinkle butterscotch-flavored pieces over the top.

Bake in 375⁰ oven 2 minutes. Remove from oven; cut through batter with metal spatula to marbleize melted butterscotch and batter. Return to oven and bake 12 more minutes, or until top springs back when touched lightly with finger. Cool in pan on rack. While still warm, spread bars with Butter Cream Frosting. Cool completely. Cut into 2½ × 1½-inch bars. Makes 42 bars.

Butter Cream Frosting: Combine 2 c. sifted confectioners sugar, ¼ c. butter or regular margarine, 2 tblsp. milk and ½ tsp. vanilla in bowl; beat until smooth.

REFRIGERATOR COOKIES

Refrigerator cookies are made with a dough that is shaped into smooth firm rolls and must be refrigerated to harden the fat. Otherwise the dough will be too soft and spread too much during baking.

Use a knife with a long, sharp blade to slice the dough. The thinner the slices, the crisper the cookies will be. Be sure to slice them evenly so they will bake evenly.

Wrap unused dough and return it to the refrigerator. The dough will store well for a week or more. You can slice and bake as much as you need to fill up the empty cookie jar.

REFRIGERATOR CARAMEL NUT SLICES

"My mom has made these crunchy cookies for Christmas as long as I can remember," wrote a Missouri farm wife.

3½ c. sifted flour	½ c. shortening
1 tsp. baking soda	2 c. brown sugar, packed
½ tsp. salt	2 eggs
½ c. butter or regular margarine	1 c. chopped walnuts

Sift together flour, baking soda and salt; set aside.

Cream together butter, shortening and brown sugar in bowl until light and fluffy, using electric mixer at medium speed. Add eggs, one at a time, beating well after each addition.

Gradually stir dry ingredients into creamed mixture, blending well. Stir in walnuts. Divide dough in half and shape each half into 12-inch roll. Wrap in waxed paper and refrigerate overnight.

Cut each roll into 48 slices, about ¼-inch thick. Place slices, about 2 inches apart, on greased baking sheets.

Bake in 400⁰ oven 5 minutes or until golden brown. Remove from baking sheets; cool on racks. Makes 8 dozen.

REFRIGERATOR OATMEAL COOKIES

You get two kinds of oatmeal cookies when you make this recipe. Walnuts are stirred into one half and coconut into the other.

1½ c. sifted flour	1 c. sugar
1 tsp. baking soda	2 eggs
½ tsp. salt	1 tsp. vanilla
½ c. butter or	3 c. quick-cooking oats
regular margarine	½ c. chopped walnuts
½ c. shortening	½ c. flaked coconut
1 c. brown sugar, packed	

Sift together flour, baking soda and salt; set aside.

Cream together butter, shortening, brown sugar and sugar in bowl until light and fluffy, using electric mixer at medium speed. Add eggs, one at a time, beating well after each addition. Blend in vanilla.

Gradually stir dry ingredients into creamed mixture, blending well. Stir in oats. Divide dough in half. Stir walnuts into one half. Shape into 8-inch roll, about 1½ inches in diameter. Wrap in waxed paper.

Stir coconut into other half. Shape into 8-inch roll, about 1½ inches in diameter. Wrap in waxed paper. Chill wrapped rolls in refrigerator overnight.

Cut each roll into 24 slices, about ⅓-inch thick. Place slices about 2 inches apart, on greased baking sheets.

Bake in 375° oven 10 minutes or until golden brown. Remove from baking sheets; cool on racks. Makes 4 dozen.

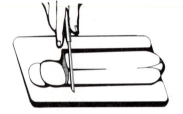

Quick Trick
For perfectly shaped round cookies, pack the dough for refrigerator cookies in empty frozen juice cans instead of shaping in rolls. Cover open end with aluminum foil or waxed paper; fasten with a rubber band. Chill. When ready to bake the cookies, cut the bottoms of the cans with a can opener that makes a smooth edge. Use the cutout lid to press against the bottom of the dough and push out just enough dough for one cookie at a time. Slice the dough, holding knife against can.

OLD-FASHIONED ICE BOX COOKIES

The Minnesota woman who sent in this recipe has won top honors two years in a row in a local newspaper cookie recipe contest.

1¾ c. sifted flour	⅔ c. sugar
¼ tsp. salt	1 egg
¾ c. butter or	1 tsp. vanilla
regular margarine	¾ c. finely chopped pecans

Sift together flour and salt; set aside.

Cream together butter and sugar in bowl until light and fluffy, using electric mixer at medium speed. Add egg and vanilla, beating well.

Gradually stir dry ingredients into creamed mixture, blending well. Stir in ¼ c. of the pecans. Divide dough in half. Shape each half into a 6-inch roll. Roll each in remaining ½ c. pecans. Wrap each in waxed paper. Chill in refrigerator overnight.

Cut each roll into 18 slices, about ⅓-inch thick. Place slices, about 2 inches apart, on greased baking sheets.

Bake in 350° oven 12 minutes or until golden brown. Remove from baking sheets; cool on racks. Makes 3 dozen.

REFRIGERATOR OATMEAL CHIPPERS

"These cookies keep well. I always had a jar of them in my room while I was in college," an Ohio woman told us.

1½ c. sifted flour	1 c. sugar
1 tsp. baking soda	2 eggs
½ tsp. salt	1 tsp. vanilla
1 c. butter or	3 c. quick-cooking oats
regular margarine	¼ c. semisweet chocolate
1 c. brown sugar, packed	pieces

Refrigerator Cookies
Refrigerator cookies can be made in an hour of spare time and chilled until needed. Then just slice and bake—a great convenience.

Sift together flour, baking soda and salt; set aside.

Cream together butter, brown sugar and sugar in bowl until light and fluffy, using electric mixer at medium speed. Add eggs, one at a time, beating well after each addition. Blend in vanilla.

Gradually stir dry ingredients into creamed mixture, blending well. Stir in oats. Divide dough in half. Shape each half into a 12-inch roll. Wrap each in waxed paper and refrigerate overnight.

Cut each roll into 36 slices, about ⅓-inch thick. Place slices, about 2 inches apart, on greased baking sheets. Place 6 chocolate pieces on top of each slice.

Bake in 350° oven 10 minutes or until golden brown. Remove from baking sheets; cool on racks. Makes 6 dozen.

REFRIGERATOR CINNAMON-ALMOND COOKIES

Keep these handy cookie rolls in your refrigerator for days when you have time to bake cookies, but not time to mix up a batch.

1 c. chopped, blanched almonds	1 c. butter or regular margarine
2 c. sifted flour	1 c. sugar
½ tsp. salt	1 egg
1 tsp. ground cinnamon	

To toast almonds, spread in 13 × 9 × 2-inch baking pan. Bake in 350° oven 15 minutes, stirring every 5 minutes. Remove from oven; cool completely.

Sift together flour, salt and cinnamon; set aside.

Cream together butter and sugar in bowl until light and fluffy, using electric mixer at medium speed. Beat in egg.

Gradually stir dry ingredients into creamed mixture, blending well. Stir in toasted almonds. Divide dough in half. Shape each half into 6-inch roll, about 1½ inches in diameter. Wrap each in waxed paper and refrigerate overnight.

Cut each roll into 24 slices, about ¼-inch thick. Place slices, about 2 inches apart, on greased baking sheets.

Bake in 350° oven 8 minutes or until golden brown. Remove from baking sheets; cool on racks. Makes 4 dozen.

REFRIGERATOR BUTTERSCOTCH WAFERS

To Freeze Cookies
Pack baked cookies in boxes, cans, or plastic containers. Cushion cookies with crushed plastic wrap or waxed paper. Thaw in original containers at room temperature about 15 minutes. Freeze up to 6 months.

"When I was 7 years old, I picked up the mail for a neighbor. She rewarded me with one of these cookies," wrote an Oregon woman.

1¼ c. sifted flour	1 c. brown sugar, packed
½ tsp. baking soda	1 egg
¼ tsp. cream of tartar	½ tsp. vanilla
¼ tsp. salt	½ c. chopped pecans
½ c. butter or regular margarine	

Sift together flour, baking soda, cream of tartar and salt; set aside.

Cream together butter and brown sugar in bowl until light and fluffy, using electric mixer at medium speed. Add egg and vanilla; blending well.

Gradually stir dry ingredients into creamed mixture, blending well. Stir in pecans. (Dough is soft.) Shape dough into 12-inch roll on waxed paper. Roll up in waxed paper. Refrigerate overnight.

Cut roll in 48 slices, about ¼-inch thick. Place slices, 2 inches apart, on greased baking sheets.

Bake in 375° oven 6 minutes or until golden brown. Remove from baking sheets; cool on racks. Makes 4 dozen.

REFRIGERATOR CHOCOLATE PINWHEELS

These crisp cookies are swirled with chocolate and vanilla dough. An attractive addition to any holiday cookie tray.

3 c. sifted flour	2 eggs
2 tsp. baking powder	2 tsp. vanilla
½ tsp. salt	2 (1-oz.) squares
1 c. butter or	unsweetened chocolate,
regular margarine	melted and cooled
1 c. sugar	

Sift together flour, baking powder and salt; set aside.

Cream together butter and sugar in bowl until light and fluffy, using electric mixer at medium speed. Add eggs, one at a time, beating well after each addition. Beat in vanilla.

Gradually stir dry ingredients into creamed mixture, blending well.

Divide dough in half. Blend chocolate into one half. Cover dough and refrigerate at least 1½ hours.

Divide chocolate dough and vanilla dough into halves. Return unused portions to refrigerator.

Roll out chocolate dough on waxed paper to 12x10-inch rectangle. Roll out vanilla dough on waxed paper to 12x10-inch rectangle. Place chocolate dough on top of vanilla dough, waxed paper side up. Peel off waxed paper. Roll up dough like a jelly roll, starting from wide edge and peeling off waxed paper from vanilla dough as you roll. Wrap roll in waxed paper and refrigerate until firm enough to slice, about 1½ hours. Repeat with remaining refrigerated chocolate and vanilla dough.

Cut each roll into 48 slices, about ¼-inch thick. Place slices, about 2 inches apart, on greased baking sheets.

Bake in 375° oven 7 minutes or until lightiy browned. Remove from baking sheets; cool on racks. Makes 8 dozen.

MOLDED COOKIES

Molded cookies are cookies that you form into desired shapes with your hands.

Some of these cookies retain their round ball shape during baking, while others flatten out. Some of the cookies are flattened out before you put them in the oven. You can use the bottom of a glass tumbler, greased lightly to press down the dough. Some recipes suggest that you dip the glass lightly in flour or sugar. And some cookies are flattened with the tines of a fork, pressing crosswise and then lengthwise to make a design.

SPICY ALMOND-CEREAL COOKIES

An unusual cookie flavored with cloves, ground almonds and rolled in crunchy cereal before baking.

2 c. sifted flour	1 egg yolk
¼ tsp. salt	2 tblsp. milk
1 tsp. ground cinnamon	2 c. ground, blanched
½ tsp. ground cloves	almonds
1 c. butter or	1½ c. Grape-Nuts
regular margarine	cereal
2 c. sifted confectioners	
sugar	

Sift together flour, salt, cinnamon and cloves; set aside.

Cream together butter and confectioners sugar in bowl until light and fluffy, using electric mixer at medium speed. Beat in egg yolk and milk.

Gradually stir dry ingredients into creamed mixture, blending well. Stir in almonds. Shape dough into 1-inch balls. Roll in cereal. Place balls, about 3 inches apart, on greased baking sheets. Flatten each with bottom of drinking glass.

Bake in 350° oven 10 minutes, or until no imprint remains when cookies are lightly touched with finger. Remove from baking sheets; cool on racks. Makes about 5 dozen.

Shaped Cookies
Shaped cookies are easy to handle. Dough may be molded into many shapes and sizes, such as balls, crescents or sticks. You can also flatten them with a glass dipped in sugar. Easy for children to make.

Double-Layer Lemon Pie
Light, delicate Lemon Velvet Pie (p. 302) is a two-layer combination of cloud-light lemon chiffon and tart, velvety lemon meringue filling. Serve topped with big puffs of whipped cream.

Main Dish Pie
Meatball-Vegetable Pie (p. 332) is a perfect supper to serve on a blustery winter night. Lots of rich gravy mingles with meat and assorted vegetables under a super flaky crust.

Frozen Dough
Special yeast recipes for doughs that can be shaped and frozen unbaked. Just thaw and bake on a day when you're too busy to make homemade bread. Clockwise from top: Apricot Braid (p. 52), Freezer Orange Buns (p. 53) and Freezer White Bread (p. 48).

Chocolate Desserts
Three extra rich and extra delicious treats to please any chocolate lover. Clockwise from top: Light Chocolate Brownie Cupcakes (p. 204), Chocolate Velvet Cake (p. 154) and Caramel-Chocolate Bars (p. 241).

HEIRLOOM BROWN SUGAR COOKIES

These easy, crisp cookies are a family favorite from Indiana. The recipe was originally called "fork cookies."

4¼ c. sifted flour	1 c. brown sugar, packed
2 tsp. baking soda	1 c. sugar
2 tsp. cream of tartar	3 eggs
½ tsp. salt	
1 c. butter or regular margarine	

Sift together flour, baking soda, cream of tartar and salt; set aside.

Cream together butter, brown sugar and sugar in bowl until light and fluffy, using electric mixer at medium speed. Add eggs, one at a time, beating well after each addition.

Gradually stir dry ingredients into creamed mixture, blending well. Shape mixture into 1¼-inch balls. Place balls, about 3 inches apart, on greased baking sheets. Flatten with floured fork in one direction.

Bake in 375° oven 10 minutes or until golden brown. Remove from baking sheets; cool on racks. Makes 6 dozen.

PEANUT BUTTER-APPLE COOKIES

This soft, moist cookie contains peanut butter and grated apple for an interesting flavor combination.

1½ c. sifted flour	½ c. brown sugar, packed
1 tsp. baking soda	½ c. sugar
½ tsp. ground cinnamon	1 egg
½ tsp. salt	½ tsp. vanilla
½ c. shortening	1 medium apple, pared, cored and grated
½ c. peanut butter	

Sift together flour, baking soda, cinnamon and salt; set aside.

Cream together shortening, peanut butter, brown sugar and sugar in bowl until light and fluffy, using electric mixer at medium speed. Add egg and vanilla, beating well.

Gradually stir dry ingredients into creamed mixture, blending well. Stir in apple. Shape dough into 1-inch balls. Place balls, about 3 inches apart, on greased baking sheets. Flatten with fork dipped in water, making a crisscross pattern.

Bake in 375° oven 10 minutes or until golden brown. Remove from baking sheets; cool on racks. Makes 3½ dozen.

Topping For Unbaked Cookies
Unbaked cookies can be simply decorated by pressing coconut lightly into the dough. Or use crushed hard candies such as peppermint sticks, lemon or orange drops.

PEANUT-RAISIN COOKIES

This old-fashioned recipe, flavored with ground raisins and peanuts, was found in a church cookbook printed 50 years ago.

1½ c. Spanish peanuts	½ c. butter or
1½ c. raisins	regular margarine
1 tsp. cooking oil	½ c. shortening
1½ c. sifted flour	1 c. brown sugar, packed
1½ tsp. baking powder	1 c. sugar
1½ tsp. baking soda	2 eggs

Combine peanuts and raisins. Pour cooking oil into food grinder to ease grinding. Grind peanuts and raisins, using fine blade; set aside.

Sift together flour, baking powder and baking soda; set aside.

Cream together butter, shortening, brown sugar and sugar in bowl until light and fluffy, using electric mixer at medium speed. Add eggs, one at a time, beating well after each addition.

Gradually stir dry ingredients into creamed mixture, blending well. Stir in ground peanut-raisin mixture. Shape dough into 1¼-inch balls. Place balls, about 3 inches apart, on greased baking sheets.

Bake in 375° oven 8 minutes or until golden brown. Cool on baking sheets 2 minutes. Remove from baking sheets; cool on racks. Makes 6 dozen.

COCONUT-CORNFLAKE CRISPS

Home-style cookie filled with chewy coconut and crunchy cornflakes. Great to dunk in hot coffee or milk.

1 c. sifted flour	1 egg
1 tsp. baking powder	1 tsp. vanilla
½ c. shortening	1 c. flaked coconut
½ c. sugar	1 c. cornflakes
½ c. brown sugar, packed	Sugar

Sift together flour and baking powder; set aside.

Cream together shortening, ½ c. sugar and brown sugar in bowl until light and fluffy, using electric mixer at medium speed. Blend in egg and vanilla.

Gradually stir dry ingredients into creamed mixture, blending well. Stir in coconut and cornflakes. Cover and chill dough in refrigerator 30 minutes.

Shape dough into 1-inch balls. Place balls, about 3 inches apart, on greased baking sheets. Flatten each with greased bottom of drinking glass dipped in sugar.

Bake in 350° oven 10 minutes or until golden brown. Remove from baking sheets; cool on racks. Makes 3½ dozen.

SPICY WALNUT-ALMOND COOKIES

"Here's a thin, rich cookie everyone likes. The recipe was brought here by a Dutch baker," a Washington farm woman wrote.

1 c. walnut pieces	½ tsp. ground nutmeg
1 c. blanched almonds	2 c. butter or
4½ c. sifted flour	regular margarine
¾ tsp. baking soda	1 c. sugar
½ tsp. salt	1 c. brown sugar, packed
3 tsp. ground cinnamon	⅔ c. dairy sour cream
½ tsp. ground cloves	Sugar

Grind walnut pieces and almonds in food grinder, using fine blade. Set aside.

Sift together flour, baking soda, salt, cinnamon, cloves and nutmeg; set aside.

Cream together butter, 1 c. sugar and brown sugar in bowl until light and fluffy, using electric mixer at medium speed.

Add dry ingredients alternately with sour cream to creamed mixture, beating well after each addition and using electric mixer at low speed. Stir in ground nuts. Cover and chill dough in refrigerator until firm enough to shape, about 2 hours.

Shape dough into 1¼-inch balls. Place balls, about 3 inches apart, on greased baking sheets. Flatten each with greased bottom of drinking glass dipped in sugar.

Bake in 375° oven 8 to 10 minutes or until golden brown. Remove from baking sheets; cool on racks. Makes 9 dozen.

SESAME COOKIE CRISPS

If you don't like sweets, here's the perfect cookie for you. It's rolled in sesame seeds and cornflakes.

2 c. sifted flour	1 c. sugar
½ tsp. baking soda	1 egg
¼ tsp. salt	1 tsp. vanilla
1 c. butter or	¾ c. cornflake crumbs
regular margarine	¼ c. sesame seeds

Sift together flour, baking soda and salt; set aside.

Cream together butter and sugar in bowl until light and fluffy, using electric mixer at medium speed. Add egg and vanilla; beat well.

Gradually stir dry ingredients into creamed mixture, blending well. Stir in ½ c. of the cornflake crumbs. Shape dough into 1-inch balls.

Combine remaining ¼ c. cornflake crumbs and sesame seeds. Roll balls in sesame seed mixture. Place balls, about 2 inches apart, on ungreased baking sheets.

Bake in 375° oven 12 to 14 minutes or until lightly browned. Remove from baking sheets; cool on racks. Makes 4 dozen.

CRISP SUGAR COOKIES

If your family likes extra-thin, crackle-topped sugar cookies, here's just the recipe.

2½ c. sifted flour	½ c. shortening
1 tsp. baking soda	½ c. brown sugar, packed
1 tsp. cream of tartar	½ c. sugar
½ tsp. salt	1 egg
½ c. butter or	1 tsp. vanilla
regular margarine	Sugar

Sift together flour, baking soda, cream of tartar and salt; set aside.

Cream together butter, shortening, brown sugar and ½ c. sugar in bowl until light and fluffy, using electric mixer at medium speed. Beat in egg and vanilla.

Gradually stir dry ingredients into creamed mixture, blending well. Shape dough into 1¼-inch balls. Roll in sugar. Place balls, about 2 inches apart, on greased baking sheets. Flatten each with greased bottom of drinking glass dipped in sugar.

Bake in 425° oven 6 minutes, or until lightly browned and crackled on top. Remove from baking sheets; cool on racks. Makes 4 dozen.

PEANUT BUTTER COOKIES

A Missouri woman won her first Blue Ribbon with this recipe. Her 10-year-old daughter won a Blue Ribbon with it, too.

2½ c. sifted flour	1 c. sugar
2 tsp. baking soda	1 c. brown sugar, packed
1 c. butter or	2 eggs
regular margarine	2 tsp. vanilla
1 c. peanut butter	Flour

Sift together 2½ c. flour and baking soda; set aside.

Cream together butter, peanut butter, sugar and brown sugar in bowl until light and fluffy, using electric mixer at medium speed. Add eggs, one at a time, beating well after each addition. Blend in vanilla.

Gradually stir dry ingredients into creamed mixture, blending well. Shape dough into 1-inch balls. Place balls, about 2 inches apart, on greased baking sheets. Flatten each with a floured fork, making a crisscross pattern.

Bake in 350° oven 10 to 12 minutes or until golden brown. Remove from baking sheets; cool on racks. Makes about 8½ dozen.

SPICY GINGER COOKIES

"My grandmother always made these for after-school snacks when I was a child," a Wisconsin farm woman told us.

4 c. sifted flour	1 c. shortening
2 tsp. baking soda	1 c. sugar
½ tsp. salt	1 egg
2 tsp. ground ginger	1 c. molasses
½ tsp. ground cinnamon	Sugar
½ tsp. ground cloves	

Sift together flour, baking soda, salt, ginger, cinnamon and cloves; set aside.

Cream together shortening and 1 c. sugar in bowl until light and fluffy, using electric mixer at medium speed. Add egg and molasses, beating well.

Gradually stir dry ingredients into creamed mixture, blending well. Cover and chill in refrigerator 2 hours.

Shape dough into 1-inch balls. Roll in sugar. Place balls, about 2 inches apart, on greased baking sheets.

Bake in 350° oven 12 minutes, or until no imprint remains when cookies are lightly touched with finger. Remove from baking sheets; cool on racks. Makes 7½ dozen.

JELLY-FILLED BUTTER COOKIES

For a change of pace, fill these buttery cookies with mint jelly or bright orange marmalade.

2 c. sifted flour	2 egg yolks
¼ tsp. salt	½ tsp. vanilla
1 c. butter or	1 c. finely chopped pecans
regular margarine	½ c. red currant jelly
½ c. brown sugar, packed	

Sift together flour and salt; set aside.

Cream together butter and brown sugar in bowl until light and fluffy, using electric mixer at medium speed. Add egg yolks and vanilla, beating well.

Gradually stir dry ingredients into creamed mixture, blending well. Shape dough into 1-inch balls. Roll in chopped pecans. Place balls, about 2 inches apart, on ungreased baking sheets.

Bake in 350⁰ oven 5 minutes. Remove from oven and make depression in center of each cookie, using a thimble or your finger. Return to oven and bake 8 minutes longer or until golden brown. Remove from baking sheets; cool on racks. When cookies are completely cooled, fill each with approximately ½ tsp. currant jelly. Makes 3½ dozen.

SNOW-CAPPED COCONUT COOKIES

These sugar-glazed butter cookies, featuring coconut and chopped pecans, have been a favorite in a Nebraska family for 25 years.

2 c. sifted flour	½ c. brown sugar, packed
1 tsp. baking soda	2 eggs
1 tsp. cream of tartar	1 tsp. vanilla
¼ tsp. salt	1 c. flaked coconut
¾ c. butter or	½ c. chopped pecans
regular margarine	Sugar
1 c. sugar	

Sift together flour, baking soda, cream of tartar and salt; set aside.

Cream together butter, 1 c. sugar and brown sugar in bowl until light and fluffy, using electric mixer at medium speed. Add eggs, one at a time, beating well after each addition. Blend in vanilla.

Gradually stir dry ingredients into creamed mixture, blending well. Stir in coconut and pecans. Cover and chill in refrigerator 3 hours or until firm enough to shape.

Shape dough into 1¼-inch balls. Dip tops into cold water and then in sugar. Place balls, sugared side up about 3 inches apart, on greased baking sheets.

Bake in 350⁰ oven 12 minutes or until golden brown. Remove from baking sheets; cool on racks. Makes 4 dozen.

CRISP GINGERSNAPS

These cookies have a strong, old-style ginger flavor and sport large cracks on top.

2 c. sifted flour	¾ c. shortening
2 tsp. baking soda	1 c. sugar
¼ tsp. salt	¼ c. molasses
1 tsp. ground cinnamon	1 egg
1 tsp. ground ginger	Sugar
¼ tsp. ground cloves	

Sift together flour, baking soda, salt, cinnamon, ginger and cloves; set aside.

Cream together shortening and 1 c. sugar in bowl until light and fluffy, using electric mixer at medium speed. Blend in molasses and egg.

Gradually stir dry ingredients into creamed mixture, blending well. Shape dough into 1¼-inch balls. Roll in sugar. Place balls, about 2 inches apart, on greased baking sheets.

Bake in 375⁰ oven 12 minutes, or until no imprint remains when cookies are lightly touched with finger. Remove from baking sheets; cool on racks. Makes 3½ dozen.

CRISPY THIN GINGERSNAPS

These thin, chewy ginger cookies with the traditional cracks on top are requested often in a North Dakota farm home.

2 c. sifted flour	1 c. sugar
2 tsp. baking soda	1 egg
1 tsp. ground cloves	¼ c. molasses
1 tsp. ground ginger	Sugar
1 tsp. ground cinnamon	
¾ c. butter or	
regular margarine	

Sift together flour, baking soda, cloves, ginger and cinnamon; set aside.

Cream together butter and 1 c. sugar in mixing bowl until light and fluffy, using electric mixer at medium speed. Add egg and molasses, beating well.

Gradually stir dry ingredients into creamed mixture, blending well. Cover and chill in refrigerator at least 4 hours, or until dough is firm enough to shape.

Shape dough into 1-inch balls. Roll in sugar. Place balls, about 2 inches apart, on greased baking sheets.

Bake in 350° oven 8 minutes, or until no imprint remains when cookies are lightly touched with finger. Remove from baking sheets; cool on racks. Makes 3 dozen.

PECAN-OATMEAL COOKIES

Farm-size, chewy cookies that are perfect for snacks in the field or for an after-school treat for children.

1½ c. sifted flour	1 c. sugar
1 tsp. baking powder	2 eggs
1 tsp. baking soda	1 tsp. vanilla
¼ tsp. salt	3 c. quick-cooking oats
1 c. butter or	Sifted confectioners sugar
regular margarine	48 small pecan halves
1 c. brown sugar, packed	

Sift together flour, baking powder, baking soda and salt; set aside.

Cream together butter, brown sugar and sugar in bowl until light and fluffy, using electric mixer at medium speed. Add eggs, one at a time, beating well after each addition. Blend in vanilla.

Gradually stir dry ingredients into creamed mixture, blending well. Stir in oats. Cover and chill in refrigerator 1 hour.

Shape dough into 1-inch balls. Place balls, about 3 inches apart, on greased baking sheets. Flatten each with greased bottom of drinking glass dipped in confectioners sugar. Place a pecan half on top of each.

Bake in 375⁰ oven 12 minutes or until golden brown. Remove from baking sheets; cool on racks. Makes 4 dozen.

ROLLED COOKIES

By their name, rolled cookies tell you just what they are. The dough for these cookies must be rolled out on a floured surface and cut into the shape of your choice with a lightly floured cookie cutter.

It's best to chill the cookie dough slightly before rolling. Then you will need less flour when you roll the dough out and won't run the risk of ending up with a dry cookie.

It's also best to roll a small amount of the dough at a time, from the center to the edge, keeping the rest of the dough in the refrigerator so that it will stay firm until you are ready to use it.

Do not overbake these cookies; just a few seconds can make the difference. Use a test for doneness in the specific recipe.

ROLLED BUTTER COOKIES

"When my grandmother made these, she baked a pecan half in the center of each for a treat," wrote a Texas farm woman.

3 c. sifted flour	2 c. sugar
1 tsp. baking soda	2 eggs
¼ tsp. salt	1 tsp. vanilla
1 c. butter or regular margarine	Colored decorating sugar

Sift together flour, baking soda and salt; set aside.

Cream together butter and sugar in bowl until light and fluffy, using electric mixer at medium speed. Add eggs, one at a time, beating well after each addition. Blend in vanilla.

Gradually stir dry ingredients into creamed mixture, mixing well. Divide dough into fourths. Roll out each fourth of dough on floured surface to ⅛-inch thickness. Cut with floured 2½-inch round cookie cutter. Place rounds, about 2 inches apart, on greased baking sheets. Sprinkle with colored decorating sugar.

Bake in 350⁰ oven 10 minutes or until lightly browned. Remove from baking sheets; cool on racks. Makes 5 dozen.

Rolled Cookies
Cut cookies close together with floured cookie cutter to get as many as possible from the first rolling. Too much rerolling will make your cookies tough.

NO-STICK ROLLED BUTTER COOKIES

A South Dakota woman has won several fair ribbons with these sugar-sprinkled cookies.

3 c. sifted flour	2 eggs
1 tsp. baking soda	1 c. sugar
2 tsp. cream of tartar	1 tsp. vanilla
1 c. butter or regular margarine	Sugar

Sift together flour, baking soda and cream of tartar into bowl. Cut in butter until mixture is crumbly, using pastry blender.

Beat eggs, 1 c. sugar and vanilla in another bowl until well blended, using rotary beater. Stir egg mixture into crumb mixture, mixing until blended. Cover and chill in refrigerator 15 minutes.

Divide dough into fourths. Roll each fourth of dough on floured surface to ⅛-inch thickness. Cut with floured 2-inch round cookie cutter. Place rounds, about 2 inches apart, on greased baking sheets. Sprinkle with sugar.

Bake in 350° oven 10 minutes or until golden brown. Remove from baking sheets; cool on racks. Makes 4 dozen.

OLD-FASHIONED ROLLED SUGAR COOKIES

To Decorate Cookies
With a clean, small paintbrush, cover the top or edges of rolled cookies with light corn syrup. Dip the cookies or just edges in colored sugar.

"We always enjoyed going to Grandma's for these. She used cream and eggs from the farm," wrote a Pennsylvania woman.

6 c. sifted flour	2 c. sugar
4 tsp. baking powder	3 eggs
1 tsp. baking soda	2 tsp. vanilla
1 tsp. salt	1 c. light cream
1 tsp. ground nutmeg	Sugar
1 c. shortening	

Sift together flour, baking powder, baking soda, salt and nutmeg; set aside.

Cream together shortening and 2 c. sugar in bowl until light and fluffy, using electric mixer at medium speed. Add eggs, one at a time, beating well after each addition. Beat in vanilla.

Add dry ingredients alternately with light cream to creamed mixture, beating well after each addition, using electric mixer at low speed.

Divide dough into fourths. Roll out each fourth of dough on floured surface to ¼-inch thickness. Cut into desired shapes, using floured 2-inch cookie cutters. Place cookies about 2 inches apart, on greased baking sheets. Sprinkle with sugar.

Bake in 400° oven 10 minutes or until golden brown. Remove from baking sheets; cool on racks. Makes 7 dozen.

GRANDMOTHER'S SUGAR COOKIES

"My son won a Blue Ribbon with these cookies—he was the only boy in 4-H Cooking Club," wrote a Wisconsin farm homemaker.

4 c. sifted flour	2 c. sugar
3 tsp. baking powder	3 eggs
1 tsp. baking soda	1 c. dairy sour cream
½ tsp. salt	Sugar
¼ tsp. ground nutmeg	
1 c. butter or regular margarine	

Sift together flour, baking powder, baking soda, salt and nutmeg; set aside.

Cream together butter and 2 c. sugar in mixing bowl until light and fluffy, using electric mixer at medium speed. Add eggs, one at a time, beating well after each addition.

Add dry ingredients alternately with sour cream to creamed mixture, beating well after each addition, using electric mixer at low speed. Cover and chill dough in refrigerator overnight.

Divide dough into fourths. Use one fourth of the dough at a time, keeping remaining dough in refrigerator. Roll out each fourth of dough on floured surface to ¼-inch thickness. Cut with 2½-inch round cookie cutter. Place rounds, about 2 inches apart, on greased baking sheets. Sprinkle with sugar.

Bake in 400⁰ oven 6 to 8 minutes or until lightly browned. Remove from baking sheets; cool on racks. Makes 6 dozen.

Painted Cookies
Tint small amount of undiluted evaporated milk with food coloring. Use a small, fine-tipped, clean brush to make designs on rolled cookies.

ROLLED MOLASSES CRINKLES

This dough can also be shaped into 1-inch balls and rolled in sugar. There's no change in baking temperature or time.

2¼ c. sifted flour	¾ c. shortening
2 tsp. baking soda	1 c. brown sugar, packed
¼ tsp. salt	1 egg
1 tsp. ground cinnamon	¼ c. molasses
½ tsp. ground ginger	Sugar

Sift together flour, baking soda, salt, cinnamon and ginger; set aside.

Cream together shortening and brown sugar in bowl until light and fluffy, using electric mixer at medium speed. Add egg and molasses, mix well.

Gradually stir dry ingredients into creamed mixture, mixing well. Cover and chill dough in refrigerator 4 hours.

Divide dough into fourths. Use one fourth of dough at a time, keeping remaining dough in refrigerator. Roll out each fourth of dough on floured surface to ⅛-inch thickness. Cut with floured 2½-inch round cookie cutter. Place rounds, about 2 inches apart, on greased baking sheets. Sprinkle with sugar.

Bake in 375° oven 8 minutes, or until no imprint remains when touched lightly with finger. Remove from baking sheets; cool on racks. Makes 3 dozen.

To Flour Cookie Cutter
Spoon a little flour into a small bowl. Dip the cookie cutter into the flour and tap it gently on the edge of the bowl to shake off the loose flour.

ROLLED SPICY FRUIT COOKIES

Man-size spice cookies flavored with molasses, brown sugar and lots of raisins and currants.

4 c. sifted flour	¼ tsp. ground cloves
1 tsp. baking powder	1 c. shortening
1 tsp. baking soda	1½ c. brown sugar, packed
½ tsp. salt	3 eggs
1 tsp. ground cinnamon	½ c. molasses
½ tsp. ground ginger	1 c. dried currants
¼ tsp. ground allspice	1 c. raisins

Sift together flour, baking powder, baking soda, salt, cinnamon, ginger, allspice and cloves; set aside.

Cream together shortening and brown sugar in bowl until light and fluffy, using electric mixer at medium speed. Add eggs, one at a time, beating well after each addition. Blend in molasses.

Gradually stir dry ingredients into creamed mixture, mixing well. Stir in currants and raisins. Cover and chill dough in refrigerator overnight.

Divide dough into fourths. Use one fourth of the dough at a time, keeping remaining dough in refrigerator. Roll out each fourth of dough on floured surface to ¼-inch thickness. Cut with floured 3-inch round cookie cutter. Place rounds, about 2 inches apart, on ungreased baking sheets.

Bake in 375° oven 10 minutes or until golden brown. Remove from baking sheets; cool on racks. Makes 4 dozen.

EXTRA-CRISP ROLLED COOKIES

"My grandmother used to wrap two of these in a napkin for me when I went to school," a Texas farm woman wrote to us.

2 c. sifted flour	1 c. sugar
½ tsp. baking powder	1 egg
½ tsp. baking soda	2 tblsp. milk
½ tsp. salt	1 tsp. vanilla
⅔ c. butter or	
regular margarine	

Sift together flour, baking powder, baking soda and salt; set aside.

Cream together butter and sugar in bowl until light and fluffy, using electric mixer at medium speed. Add egg, milk and vanilla; beat 2 more minutes.

Gradually stir dry ingredients into creamed mixture, blending well. Cover and chill dough in refrigerator 2 hours.

Divide dough in half. Use one half of dough first, keeping remaining dough in refrigerator. Roll out each half of dough on floured surface to ⅛-inch thickness. Cut with floured 2½-inch round cookie cutter. Place rounds, about 2 inches apart, on greased baking sheets.

Bake in 375° oven 5 to 7 minutes or until golden brown. Remove from baking sheets; cool on racks. Makes 3½ dozen.

ROLLED SUGAR COOKIES

A California farm woman said, "My sons call these 'the very best rolled cookies in the world'."

3¼ c. sifted flour
4 tsp. baking powder
1 tsp. salt
½ c. shortening
½ c. butter or
   regular margarine

1½ c. sugar
1½ tsp. vanilla
⅔ c. evaporated milk
Colored decorating sugar

Goldilocks Cookie
Spread a cookie with butter cream frosting. Use purple gumdrops for eyes, silver dragees for eyebrows and nose, yellow gumdrops for hair and cinnamon candies for mouth.

Sift together flour, baking powder and salt; set aside.

Cream together shortening, butter and sugar in bowl until light and fluffy, using electric mixer at medium speed. Blend in vanilla.

Add dry ingredients alternately with evaporated milk to creamed mixture, beating well after each addition, using electric mixer at low speed.

Divide dough into thirds. Roll out each third on floured surface to ¼ inch thickness. Cut with floured 2½-inch round cookie cutter. Place rounds, about 1½ inches apart, on greased baking sheets. Sprinkle with colored decorating sugar.

Bake in 375° oven 8 minutes or until very lightly browned. Remove from baking sheets; cool on racks. Makes 4½ dozen.

EXTRA-SPECIAL TEA COOKIES

Bite-size vanilla wafers topped with a pink cream cheese filling, then drizzled with a thin chocolate icing.

½ c. butter or
   regular margarine
½ c. sifted confectioners
   sugar
¼ tsp. salt
1 tsp. vanilla

1¼ c. sifted flour
Creamy Nut Filling
   (recipe follows)
Chocolate Icing
   (recipe follows)

Cream together butter, confectioners sugar, salt and vanilla in bowl until light and fluffy, using electric mixer at medium speed. Gradually stir in flour, mixing well.

Roll out dough on lightly floured surface to ¼ inch thickness. Cut in 1-inch rounds, using cookie cutter or doughnut hole cutter. Place rounds, about 1 inch apart, on ungreased baking sheets.

Bake in 350° oven 12 minutes or until lightly browned. Remove from baking sheets; cool on racks.

Top each cookie with ½ tsp. of Creamy Nut Filling. Then drizzle tops with Chocolate Icing. Makes 6½ dozen.

Creamy Nut Filling: Place 1 (3-oz.) pkg. cream cheese in bowl. Beat until creamy, using electric mixer at high speed. Add 1 c. sifted confectioners sugar, 2 tblsp. flour, 1 tsp. vanilla and 2 drops red food coloring; mix well. Stir in ½ c. chopped walnuts and ½ c. flaked coconut.

Chocolate Icing; Combine ½ c. semisweet chocolate pieces, 2 tblsp. butter or regular margarine and 2 tblsp. water in saucepan. Cook over low heat, stirring constantly, until chocolate melts. Stir in ½ c. sifted confectioners sugar, beating until smooth.

FILLED VANILLA WAFERS

Dainty, flaky wafers filled with a pink creamy filling—perfect for teas, weddings or women's luncheons.

1 c. soft butter or	Sugar
regular margarine	Butter Cream Filling
2 c. sifted flour	(recipe follows)
⅓ c. heavy cream	

Cream butter in bowl until soft and creamy, using electric mixer at medium speed.

Add flour alternately with heavy cream to butter, beating well after each addition, using electric mixer at low speed. Cover and chill dough in refrigerator 2 hours.

Divide dough into thirds. Use one third of the dough at a time, keeping remaining dough in refrigerator. Roll out each third on floured surface to ⅛ inch thickness. Cut with floured 1½-inch round cookie cutter with scalloped edge. Place rounds, about 1 inch apart, on ungreased baking sheets. Prick tops with fork; sprinkle with sugar.

Bake in 375° oven 7 minutes until set, but not browned. Cool on baking sheets on racks 3 minutes. Remove from baking sheets; cool on racks. When completely cooled, spread one cookie with Butter Cream Filling. Top with another cookie to form sandwich cookie. Makes 4 dozen sandwich cookies.

Butter Cream Filling: Combine ¾ c. sifted confectioners sugar, ¼ c. soft butter or regular margarine, 1 tsp. vanilla and 3 drops red food coloring in bowl. Beat until smooth, using electric mixer at low speed.

DATE-OATMEAL SANDWICH COOKIES

"My dad always made these cookies around Christmastime and stored them in a stone crock," a Wisconsin farm woman told us.

2 c. sifted flour	½ c. milk
1 tsp. baking soda	2 c. quick-cooking oats
½ tsp. salt	Date Filling
1 c. shortening	(recipe follows)
1 c. brown sugar, packed	Sifted confectioners sugar

Sift together flour, baking soda and salt; set aside.

Cream together shortening and brown sugar in bowl until light and fluffy, using electric mixer at medium speed. Add milk; blend well.

Gradually stir dry ingredients into creamed mixture, mixing well. Stir in oats. (Dough is soft.)

Divide dough in half. Roll out one half of dough on floured surface to ¼-inch thickness. Cut into 34 rounds, using floured 2½-inch round cookie cutter. Place rounds, about 2 inches apart, on greased baking sheets.

Roll out remaining dough. Cut into 34 rounds. Cut out center of each, using 1-inch cookie cutter or doughnut hole cutter. Place rounds, about 2 inches apart, on greased baking sheets.

Bake in 350⁰ oven 10 minutes or until lightly browned. Remove from baking sheets; cool on racks.

To make sandwich cookies: Spread Date Filling on whole rounds. Sprinkle sifted confectioners sugar on top of cutout rounds and place on top of other cookies, making sandwich cookies. Makes 34 sandwich cookies.

Date Filling: Combine 1 (8-oz.) pkg. pitted dates (chopped), ¾ c. sugar and ½ c. water in saucepan. Cook over medium heat, stirring constantly, until mixture comes to a boil and starts to thicken. Remove from heat. Mash dates with vegetable masher until smooth. Cool completely.

OLD-FASHIONED FILLED COOKIES

One of our home economists commented, "These remind me of the fruit-filled cookies my grandmother used to make."

2½ c. sifted flour	2 eggs
1 tsp. salt	1 tsp. vanilla
1 c. butter or	Prune, Fig or Apricot
regular margarine	Filling (recipes follow)
1 c. sugar	

Sift together flour and salt; set aside.

Cream together butter and sugar in bowl until light and fluffy, using electric mixer at medium speed. Add eggs, one at a time, beating well after each addition. Beat in vanilla.

Gradually stir dry ingredients into creamed mixture, mixing well. Cover and chill dough in refrigerator overnight, or until firm enough to roll out.

Divide dough in half. Use one half of the dough, keeping remaining dough in refrigerator. Roll out first half of dough on floured surface to ⅛ inch thickness. Cut 30 rounds, using floured 2-inch cookie cutter. Place rounds, about 2 inches apart, on ungreased baking sheets. Place 1 tsp. Prune Filling, Fig Filling or Apricot Filling in center of each round.

Roll out remaining dough. Cut 30 (2-inch) rounds. Cut out center of each, using ¾-inch cookie cutter. Place over filled rounds. Press edges of each cookie with floured fork.

Bake in 400° oven 8 minutes or until golden brown. Remove from baking sheets; cool on racks. Flavor of cookies improves if stored overnight in tightly covered container. Makes 2½ dozen.

Prune Filling: Combine 6 oz. prunes (1 c.) and ¾ c. water in small saucepan. Bring to boil over medium heat. Simmer 2 minutes. Cover and let stand until completely cooled. Drain off liquid. Purée prunes in blender until smooth. Combine puréed prunes, ¼ c. sugar, 2 tsp. grated orange rind, ¼ tsp. salt, ¼ tsp. vanilla and ½ c. chopped walnuts; mix well. Makes enough filling for 2½ dozen cookies.

Fig Filling: Grind 12 oz. dried figs (2 c.) in food grinder, using medium blade. (Makes 1 c. ground figs.) Combine ground figs, ⅓ c. orange juice, 2 tsp. grated orange rind, ¼ c. water, ⅛ tsp. salt and ¼ c. sugar in saucepan. Cook over medium heat, stirring constantly, 2 minutes or until thickened. Cool well. Stir in ¼ c. chopped walnuts. Makes enough filling for 2½ dozen cookies.

Apricot Filling: Combine 1 (6-oz.) pkg. dried apricots (1 c.) and 1 c. water in saucepan. Bring to a boil over medium heat. Simmer 5 minutes. Remove from heat. Purée apricots with cooking liquid in blender until smooth. Stir in ½ c. sugar and 2 tblsp. butter or regular margarine; cool completely. Makes enough filling for 2½ dozen cookies.

Shower Gift
Present the bride-to-be with your favorite recipe for rolled cookies and an assortment of cookie cutters. And if you really want to be lavish, give her a pastry cloth and a rolling pin with stockinet.

OLD-FASHIONED DATE-FILLED COOKIES

"My mother often baked these luscious filled cookies in a wood stove when I was a child," wrote a Washington farm wife.

2½ c. sifted flour	1 egg
3 tsp. baking powder	1 tsp. vanilla
¼ tsp. salt	½ c. milk
½ c. butter or	Date Filling
regular margarine	(recipe follows)
1 c. sugar	Sugar

Sift together flour, baking powder and salt; set aside.

Cream together butter and 1 c. sugar in mixing bowl until light and fluffy, using electric mixer at medium speed. Add egg and vanilla; beat well.

Add dry ingredients alternately with milk to creamed mixture, beating well after each addition, using electric mixer at low speed. Cover and chill dough in refrigerator at least 3 hours.

Meanwhile, prepare Date Filling.

Divide dough into fourths. Use one fourth of the dough at a time, keeping remaining dough in refrigerator. Roll out each fourth of the dough on floured surface to ⅛-inch thickness. With floured 2½-inch round cookie cutter, cut 18 rounds from each fourth of dough. Place 36 rounds, about 2 inches apart, on greased baking sheets. Place about 1 tsp. Date Filling in center of each round. Spread filling with back of spoon to flatten. Top each with another round. No need to seal edges because dough is soft and seals during baking. Sprinkle tops of each cookie with sugar.

Bake in 375° oven 10 to 12 minutes or until golden brown. Remove from baking sheets; cool on racks. Makes 3 dozen.

Date Filling: Combine ½ c. sugar and 2 tblsp. flour in saucepan; mix well. Add 1 c. chopped, pitted dates and 1 c. boiling water; mix well. Cook over medium heat, stirring constantly, until mixture comes to a boil. Simmer 2 minutes. Remove from heat and cool completely.

Cookie Cutters
For variety, cut rolled cookie dough with different sized cookie cutters. Or make your own patterns. Draw bells, hearts, cats, or anything you like on heavy cardboard. Cut out the drawing and grease one side. Place greased side down on the rolled dough, and cut around it with tip of a small knife.

DATE-FILLED POINSETTIAS

These attractive pinwheel-shaped refrigerator cookies, sprinkled with red sugar, are perfect for the holidays.

6 c. sifted flour	**2 tblsp. grated orange rind**
2 tsp. baking powder	**½ tsp. lemon extract**
1 tsp. baking soda	**¼ c. orange juice**
¼ tsp. salt	**1 c. dairy sour cream**
1 c. lard	**Date-Peanut Filling**
2 c. sugar	**(recipe follows)**
2 eggs	**Red decorating sugar**
1 tsp. vanilla	

Sift together flour, baking powder, baking soda and salt; set aside.

Cream together lard and sugar in bowl until light and fluffy, using electric mixer at medium speed. Add eggs, one at a time, beating well after each addition. Blend in vanilla, orange rind, lemon extract and orange juice.

Add dry ingredients alternately with sour cream to creamed mixture, beating well after each addition, using electric mixer at low speed. Cover and chill dough in refrigerator 3 hours.

Divide dough into fourths. Use one fourth of the dough at a time, keeping remaining dough in refrigerator. Roll out on floured surface to 12-inch square. Cut into 16 (3-inch) squares. To make poinsettias: Make diagonal cuts in each 3-inch square from corners to within ½-inch of center. Place about 1 tsp. Date-Peanut Filling in center of square. Fold right sides of each diagonal cut to center over filling, forming pinwheel. Place filled cookies, about 2 inches apart, on greased baking sheets. Sprinkle with red decorating sugar.

Bake in 350° oven 8 to 10 minutes or until golden brown. Remove from baking sheets; cool on racks. Makes 64 cookies.

Date-Peanut Filling: Combine 1 c. chopped, pitted dates, ⅔ c. water and 2 tblsp. lemon juice in 2-qt. saucepan. Cook over medium heat, stirring constantly, until mixture thickens. Remove from heat. Stir in ½ c. chopped, salted peanuts. Cool completely.

PRESSED COOKIES

Pressed cookies are cookies that are formed with a cookie press. The cookie dough, which is very stiff, is forced through a cookie press, a cylindrical instrument usually made of thin metal. The dough is packed into the hollow cylinder and forced by means of a plunger through a small opening to which attachments are fitted to form cookies of various shapes. Some presses have gauges to vary the thickness of the cookies—one gauge for thin crisp ones, another for the thicker type.

The dough for pressed cookies must be just right—that is pliable and soft, but not crumbly. If the dough becomes too soft, however, chill it slightly, but just slightly as dough that is too cold will crumble.

Put about one-fourth of the dough in the press at a time. Hold the press so it rests on the baking sheet, unless you are using a star or bar plate. Press the dough onto a baking sheet. Do not remove press until the dough forms a well-defined design. You may need to wait a few seconds to give the dough time to cling to the baking sheet.

If the cookie dough is the correct consistency, you will not need to exert much pressure on the press or the handle.

Pressed cookies are rich. Bake them on an ungreased baking sheet until they are set. Some pressed cookies are done when they are browned around the edges, while others do not brown at all. They are done when they are set.

SPRITZ PRESSED COOKIES

Almond-flavored cookies decorated with bits of red or green candied cherries. Perfect for holiday entertaining.

1 c. butter or regular margarine	1 egg yolk 1 tsp. almond extract
⅔ c. sifted confectioners sugar	2¾ c. sifted flour Quartered red and green
1 egg	candied cherries

Cream together butter and confectioners sugar in bowl until light and fluffy, using electric mixer at medium speed. Beat in egg, egg yolk and almond extract, blending well.

Gradually stir flour into creamed mixture, mixing well.

Fit flower or crown design into cookie press. Place one half of the dough in cookie press at a time. Force cookies through press, about 1 inch apart, on ungreased baking sheets. Place 1 quarter of red or green candied cherry in center of each.

Bake in 400° oven 7 to 10 minutes or until set, but not browned. Remove from baking sheets; cool on racks. Makes about 6 dozen.

Pressed Cookies
These dainty cookies become even more special by tinting dough with a few drops of food coloring.

PEANUT BUTTER PRESSED COOKIES

We topped each of these delicate peanut butter-flavored pressed cookies with a chocolate morsel. Doubly good.

1¾ c. sifted flour	½ c. sugar
¼ tsp. salt	1 egg yolk
¾ c. butter or regular margarine	½ tsp. vanilla

3 tblsp. creamy peanut
    butter
	⅓ c. semisweet chocolate
	    pieces

Sift together flour and salt; set aside.

Cream together butter, peanut butter and sugar in bowl until light and fluffy, using electric mixer at medium speed. Add egg yolk and vanilla, blending well.

Gradually stir dry ingredients into creamed mixture, mixing well.

Fit flower or crown design into cookie press. Place one half of the dough in cookie press at a time. Force cookies through press, about 1 inch apart, on ungreased baking sheets. Place one chocolate piece in center of each cookie.

Bake in 375° oven 6 to 8 minutes or until delicately browned. Remove from baking sheets; cool on racks. Makes about 5 dozen.

CHOCOLATE-PEPPERMINT COOKIE TREES

These tiny chocolate cookie trees are filled and then dipped into melted peppermint-flavored, green-tinted confection coating.

3½ c. sifted flour	1 tsp. vanilla
¼ tsp. salt	4 (1-oz.) squares
1½ c. butter or	unsweetened chocolate,
regular margarine	melted and cooled
1 c. sugar	Peppermint Filling
3 egg yolks	(recipe follows)

Sift together flour and salt; set aside.

Cream together butter and sugar in bowl until light and fluffy, using electric mixer at medium speed. Add egg yolks and vanilla; beat well. Blend in chocolate.

Gradually stir dry ingredients into creamed mixture, mixing well.

Fit tree design into cookie press. Place one half of the dough in cookie press at a time. Force cookies through press, about 1 inch apart, on ungreased baking sheets.

Bake in 375° oven 8 to 10 minutes or until set, but not browned. Cool cookies on baking sheet 2 minutes. Remove from baking sheets; cool on racks.

Spread the bottom of one cookie with Peppermint Filling. Top with another cookie to form a sandwich cookie. Fill all the cookies. Then dip each sandwich cookie into remaining Peppermint Filling so that filling coats half of cookie. Leave other half uncoated. Place on waxed paper until coating sets. Makes 5½ dozen.

Peppermint Filling: Melt 8 oz. cut-up white confection coating* in top of double boiler over hot water. When melted, stir in 2 drops green food coloring and ¼ tsp. peppermint extract. Keep mixture warm over hot water.

*Note: White confection coating is also called white chocolate or summer coating. It is sold by the pound in candy stores.

WHAT WENT WRONG WITH MY COOKIES?

My bar cookies were dry and crumbly—why?

You probably baked them too long.

My bar cookies were hard and crusty on top—why?

The dough was mixed too much.

My drop cookies were uneven in shape—why?

The dough might not have been measured and dropped carefully.

My drop cookies were dark and crusty around the edges—why?

They were probably baked too long. Or you used a baking sheet that was too large for the oven and the air could not circulate properly.

My molded cookies had odd, uneven shapes instead of nice round shapes—why?

Perhaps you didn't shape the dough firmly or evenly.

My molded cookies were too brown—why?

They were baked too long. Did you remove them from the cookie sheet with a spatula as soon as you took them from the oven?

My refrigerator cookies were very uneven in shape—why?

Did you chill the dough thoroughly? Refrigerator cookies contain lots of butter or margarine and the dough must be chilled long enough so the fat can get hard. Otherwise the dough will be too soft and spread in a hot oven.

My rolled cookies were tough—why?

You used too much flour when you rolled them out. Or you may have rolled them with a heavy hand instead of light, deft strokes.

My rolled cookies showed signs of flour on the surface—why?

You used too much flour when you rolled out the dough.

Chapter 6

Finest Country Pies

Pie is the great American dessert. It was the dessert most frequently served to families in Colonial times. In order to stretch their food supply, the early settlers used more crust than filling. Many of them brought their love of pie from England, where pies—especially main dish pies—were popular.

Everyone has his or her favorite pie. Some people prefer the all-American apple pie, running with juices and spicy with cinnamon and nutmeg. Others would insist that the best pie in the world is lemon meringue—tart and lemony under a blanket of golden meringue. Silky custard pie is a great New England favorite, especially on Saturday night when it tops off a baked-bean-and-hot-dog supper.

Farm women really responded when we asked them to send us their favorite pie recipes; we received a tremendous variety. There were many recipes for fruit pies, baked to use the bounty of country gardens; a wide variety of favorite apple pies; meringue pies that had won ribbons, and pumpkin and mincemeat for fall entertaining. Timesaving refrigerator pies were popular, too—it's so convenient to make a billowy chiffon pie today for toting to a church supper tomorrow.

On cold winter nights, farm and ranch women like to welcome their families home with main-dish pies, and we have their top favorites here—the ones that their families ask for over and over.

We have discovered, however, from visits with women and from their letters to us, that they feel making a good pastry crust is an art. And some women have said that they can make a terrific cake but when it comes to pie crust, they still haven't mastered the skill. They do make pies, but they are never truly pleased with the crusts. Some cooks feel that they will never be able to master making a pie crust.

To be of help, we have given a comprehensive, step-by-step lesson in making pie crust, and we explain in detail why all of the steps are important. It's often just one little step handled a bit carelessly that makes the difference between a mediocre crust and a perfect one.

Once you have become a perfect pie crust maker, or even before, you will want to try some of our country women's pies. They are spectacular.

A Minnesota woman sent us the recipe for White Christmas Pie. Her eight youngsters can't wait for it between holiday seasons. And they want it in July when it's over 100 degrees. They ask for it at Easter time, as well as for birthday celebrations.

For Thanksgiving you might want to try a Virginia family's favorite, Pumpkin Chiffon Pie, instead of the usual pumpkin. You'll like the airy lightness after the heavy holiday meal.

In the fall, make a Fresh Pear Pie to surprise your friends. It's different and delicious. The Wisconsin farm wife who sent us the recipe likes to smother the top with country-fresh whipped cream.

A beautiful pie, Easy Apple-Puff Pie, looks and tastes like baked apples laced with a creamy custard filling. It's a "once-a-week-pie" in a Michigan farm home, when the apples line the roadside stands. So easy but it looks just elegant.

After you've read this chapter and made some of these luscious pies, you just might end up with the reputation of the best pie-baker in your community.

PIE CRUST INGREDIENTS

Flour, salt, shortening and water are the basic ingredients of pastry. Other ingredients may be added in specific recipes. For example, spices, chopped nuts, or grated orange or lemon rind may be stirred into the pastry, or fruit juice might replace some of the water.

Flour. This is the backbone of pastry. We used all-purpose flour in all of our pastry recipes. The gluten in the flour gives the needed body to the flaky, tender pastry.

Salt. Adds flavor.

Shortening. This makes pastry tender and flaky. Some pastry is made with lard. In fact, many farm women insist that lard makes the very finest pastry. However, some people object to the slight flavor that lard adds to pastry.

Vegetable shortenings with their bland flavor and creamy texture are very suitable for pastry. Most of our pie crusts were made with shortening.

Butter tends to make a hard brittle crust if it is the main shortening used. Many cooks like to substitute a little butter for some of the shortening for a richer crust.

Too little shortening makes a crust that is thick and doughy. Too much shortening makes a crust that is just too delicate—it will crumble when you barely touch it.

Water. Binds and holds the fat and flour particles together. The amount of water is very important. If too little water is added, the dough will be crumbly and will not hold together when rolled out. If too much water is added, the dough will be sticky, hard to roll, and the baked pastry will be tough.

STEPS FOR MAKING PIE CRUST

Here are the basic steps for making perfect pastry:

Step 1—Mixing. Combine the flour and salt in a bowl. Cut in the shortening with a pastry blender until the mixture forms coarse crumbs. Be sure that the fat is distributed evenly through the flour. This is what will give you a flaky crust. Flakiness is caused by the many particles of fat, which are surrounded and separated by the flour. During the baking, the fat particles melt to form a delicate flake. If the dough is overhandled, the fat particles may melt during the mixing stage and blend with the flour to form a solid mass. The result will be a baked crust that is tough and hard.

Step 2—Adding water. Sprinkle iced water over the surface of the flour and fat mixture a tablespoon at a time, while tossing it quickly with a fork. Don't use a strong stirring or mixing motion as this would crush the fat particles and blend them too much with the flour. Iced water is important, because it helps to keep the fat cold. Push the moistened portions to one side before adding more water so that a dry portion can be sprinkled each time. Too much moisture will make the baked crust hard and brittle; too little will cause pastry to crack at the edges when you attempt to roll it out. It is difficult to give a specific amount of water, because the dryness of the flour will vary with the seasons and the humidity. Stop tossing while the mass still looks a bit crumbly and long before it is wet and slippery.

When the dough is moist enough to hold together under slight pressure, gather it gently into your hands and shape it into a ball.

If at this time you discover that you have added too much or too little water, it's too late to remedy the mistake. Just start over. Too much mixing or handling of the dough after the water has been added results in a tough crust with a very pale, smooth surface.

Step 3—Rolling. Roll out the pastry on a lightly floured board. A canvas cloth or coarse linen towel to cover the board is very helpful in keeping the dough from sticking and preventing too much flour from being incorporated into the dough. Rub flour into the cloth thoroughly, but try to use as little flour as possible. The more flour on the board, the tougher your pastry will be.

Flatten out the ball of dough slightly but quickly. Light deft strokes are the key to light, flaky pastry. Always roll from the center out until the dough is about an eighth of an inch thick. As the rolling pin approaches the edge of the dough on each stroke, lift it up, instead of rolling on over the edge. Rolling over the edge makes the edge too thin and it will split. Try to keep the dough in a circle as you roll out.

If the dough sticks to the board or pastry cloth (which it probably will, unless you are a very experienced pie-maker), lift it up with a spatula, and sprinkle a little flour on the spot. The dough should be lifted frequently during rolling, but it should never be turned over. If little bits of dough stick to the rolling pin, remove them immediately. Dough lumps have a way of gathering more lumps unto themselves and finally will tear a hole in the dough. Roll dough to size specified in your recipe.

Step 4—Fitting. Fitting pastry into the pie plate takes a little experience before you can do a perfect job. Run a spatula very carefully under the circle of dough to loosen any little spot of pastry that might be sticking to the board. Be very gentle so as not to break the pastry. A break, even when mended, it apt to split and let the good juices of the pie run through to the bottom of the pie plate. It will then bake onto the pie plate and make serving the pie a difficult job. If you do have a break in the dough, mend it by moistening the torn edges with cold water, patting a small piece of dough over the torn spot and pressing down the edges to make a neat patch.

Now fold the circle of dough in half and lift it carefully into the plate with the fold in the center. Unfold the dough and fit it loosely into the plate. Do not stretch or pull the dough or it will shrink when it bakes. Ease pastry into the plate so that it fits the shape of the plate. When the dough is fitted snugly to the plate, pat dough all over its surface to eliminate any air pockets underneath. Use your fingers or a little ball of dough for patting. For a 1-crust pie, trim the pastry with scissors ½ inch from the edge of the pie plate. Fold the edge under (it should be even with the edge of plate) and press pastry gently with fingers to form a high stand-up rim.

Flute the edge. Place index finger of one hand firmly on inside of rim and the thumb and index finger of other hand at the same point outside the rim. Pinch. Repeat all around the edge. If the pie shell is to be baked without a filling, prick the bottom and side of pastry with the tines of a fork. Prick closely and deeply into the pastry. This allows steam to escape, preventing the crust from puffing during baking. Do not prick pastry if the filling is going to bake along with the crust.

For a 2-crust pie, roll out about half of the pastry into a circle. The size is specified in each recipe that calls for a pie crust. Fit the circle into the pie plate; add the filling. Trim the lower crust even with the edge, using scissors. Roll the other half of the pastry to size specified in the recipe. Fold the dough in half. Cut several slashes in the dough near the center to allow steam to escape during baking.

Using finger tips, moisten edge of lower crust with water. Carefully center folded pastry on top of filling. Unfold pastry. Do not stretch. Pat top and bottom crust together on rim. Trim top crust with scissors so that it overhangs the lower crust by ½ inch. Tuck overhang under lower crust. Flute edge.

PASTRY FOR 9-INCH PIE SHELL

Carefully press out all the air beneath the crust when you place it in the pie plate or the crust will puff up when it's baked.

1 c. sifted flour	**2 to 3 tblsp. iced water**
½ tsp. salt	
⅓ c. plus 1 tblsp. shortening*	

Combine flour and salt in bowl. Cut in shortening until coarse crumbs form, using pastry blender. Sprinkle iced water over crumb mixture, a little at a time, tossing with fork until a dough forms.

Roll out dough on floured surface to 12-inch circle. Ease dough into 9-inch pie plate. Gently press out air pockets with finger tips. Fold under edge of crust and press into a rim. Flute edge. Prick entire surface of pie shell with fork. Refrigerate 30 minutes.

Bake in 450⁰ oven 10 to 15 minutes or until crust is golden brown. Cool on rack. Makes 1 (9-inch) pie shell.

*Note: You can substitute ⅓ c. lard for shortening. (You'll need slightly less lard than shortening.)

Evaporated Milk Glaze
For a lovely brown crust, brush top crust with evaporated milk before baking. For sparkle, sprinkle lightly with granulated sugar.

PASTRY FOR 2-CRUST 9-INCH PIE

Never stretch the dough while lining the pie plate or the pastry will lose its shape.

2 c. sifted flour	**¾ c. shortening***
1 tsp. salt	**4 to 5 tblsp. iced water**

Combine flour and salt in bowl. Cut in shortening until mixture forms coarse crumbs, using pastry blender. Sprinkle iced water over crumb mixture, a little at a time, tossing with fork until a dough forms.

Divide dough almost in half. Roll out larger half of dough on floured surface to 12-inch circle. Ease dough into 9-inch pie plate. Trim edge to 1 inch.

Fill as desired.

For top crust, roll out remaining dough to 11-inch circle. Place on top of filling. Trim edge of dough even with bottom crust. Fold bottom crust over top crust, forming a rim. Flute edge and cut vents. Bake as directed in pie recipe that you are using. Makes enough pastry for 2-crust 9-inch pie.

*Note: You can substitute ⅔ c. lard for the shortening. (You'll need slightly less lard than shortening.)

DOUBLE-CRUST FRUIT PIES

Here is a grand assortment of juicy, tender-crusted fruit pies to follow the seasons. Take your pick of apple, cherry, blueberry, strawberry, raspberry, rhubarb or cranberry.

Many of these pies have won Blue Ribbons as well as the praise of the man of the house, who says, "My wife makes the best fruit pies—even better than my Mother's." And that's about the highest praise you can get.

BASIC CHERRY PIE

To add a decorative touch to the top crust, punch out small cutouts with cookie cutters when dough is rolled out.

Pastry for 2-crust 9-inch pie	**½ tsp. salt**
2 (1-lb.) cans pitted sour cherries in water	**¼ tsp. almond extract**
¾ c. sugar	**1 tblsp. butter or regular margarine**
3 tblsp. cornstarch	**Sugar**

Divide pastry almost in half. Roll out larger half on floured surface to 12-inch circle. Line 9-inch pie plate with pastry. Trim edge to 1 inch.

Drain cherries, reserving ⅓ c. liquid.

Combine ¾ c. sugar, cornstarch and salt in bowl. Stir in cherries, ⅓ c. reserved liquid and almond extract; mix well. Pour into pastry-lined pie plate. Dot with butter.

Roll out remaining pastry to 11-inch circle. Adjust top crust; flute edge and cut vents. Sprinkle crust with sugar.

Bake in 425° oven 15 minutes. Reduce heat to 350° and bake 40 more minutes, or until crust is golden brown. Cool on rack. Makes 6 to 8 servings.

Monogrammed Tops
Farm women often cut initials with a knife for steam vents instead of slashing the pastry. A for apple, B for blueberry and C for cherry. These steam vents are very helpful at bake sales because they indicate at a glance the kind of pie that's under the golden crust.

Almond-flavored Pastry
Add ¼ tsp. almond extract to the water before you add it to the flour and shortening for a 2-crust pie. Especially good for cherry and peach pies.

BASIC APPLE PIE

Slightly warm apple pie with a piece of Cheddar cheese is a delightful dessert.

Pastry for 2-crust 9-inch pie	**1 tblsp. cornstarch**
6 c. thinly sliced, pared tart apples	**½ tsp. ground cinnamon**
	½ tsp. ground nutmeg
1 c. sugar	**Sugar**

Divide pastry almost in half. Roll out larger half on floured surface to 12-inch circle. Line 9-inch pie plate with pastry. Trim edge to 1 inch.

Combine apples, 1 c. sugar, cornstarch, cinnamon and nutmeg in bowl; mix well. Arrange apple mixture in pastry-lined pie plate.

Roll out remaining pastry to 11-inch circle. Adjust top crust; flute edge and cut vents. Sprinkle crust with sugar.

Bake in 400° oven 45 minutes, or until apples are tender. Cool on rack. Makes 6 to 8 servings.

Butter Balls
Combine 1½ c. sifted confectioners sugar with ½ c. butter, ¼ tsp. vanilla and ⅛ tsp. nutmeg. Thoroughly mix and chill. Spoon onto warm 2-crust apple pie or shape in balls and arrange on each serving.

Pastry Wheel
To cut perfect lattice strips for a pie, invest in a pastry wheel. It adds a crinkly edge to the pastry and makes it look very professional.

ORANGE-FLAVORED CRANBERRY PIE

"Even people who don't like cranberries enjoy my mother's original cranberry pie," wrote an elderly Wisconsin woman.

Orange Pastry (recipe follows)	**½ c. water**
1 c. sugar	**1 c. heavy cream**
1 tblsp. flour	**2 tblsp. sugar**
1 c. fresh or frozen cranberries, thawed	**1 tsp. vanilla**
	½ tsp. grated orange rind

Prepare Orange Pastry.

Divide almost in half. Roll out larger half on floured surface to 12-inch circle. Line 9-inch pie plate with pastry. Trim edge to 1 inch.

Combine 1 c. sugar and flour in bowl.

Cut cranberries in half. Add to sugar-flour mixture; toss to coat. Stir in water. Arrange cranberry mixture in pastry-lined pie plate.

Roll out remaining pastry. Cut into ½-inch strips. Lay half of strips over filling about 1 inch apart. Repeat with remaining strips, placing them in the opposite direction, forming a diamond or square pattern. Trim strips even with pie edge. Turn bottom crust up over ends of strips. Press firmly to seal edge. Press edge with floured fork.

Bake in 400° oven 15 minutes. Reduce heat to 350° and bake 30 more minutes, or until cranberries are tender and crust is golden brown. Cool on rack.

Whip heavy cream, 2 tblsp. sugar and vanilla in chilled bowl until soft peaks form, using electric mixer at high speed. Top pie with puffs of whipped cream sprinkled with orange rind before serving. Makes 6 to 8 servings.

Orange Pastry: Combine 2 c. sifted flour, ½ tsp. salt and ½ tsp. grated orange rind in bowl. Cut in ⅔ c. regular margarine until mixture resembles coarse meal, using pastry blender. Sprinkle 6 tblsp. iced water, a little at a time, tossing with fork until a dough forms.

CRANBERRY-RASPBERRY PIE

This special pie is festive enough for holiday entertaining. Tart cranberries and sweet raspberries are a great combination.

2 c. fresh or frozen cranberries, chopped	¼ tsp. salt
1 (10-oz.) pkg. frozen raspberries, thawed	¼ tsp. almond extract
1½ c. sugar	Almond Pastry (recipe follows)
2 tblsp. quick-cooking tapioca	1 tblsp. butter or regular margarine

Combine cranberries, raspberries, sugar, tapioca, salt and almond extract in bowl; mix well. Let stand while preparing Almond Pastry.

Divide Almond Pastry almost in half. Roll out larger portion on floured surface to 12-inch circle. Line 9-inch pie plate with pastry. Trim edge to 1 inch.

Pour the cranberry mixture into pastry-lined pie plate. Dot with butter.

Roll out remaining Almond Pastry. Cut into ½-inch strips. Lay half of strips over filling about 1 inch apart. Repeat with remaining strips, placing them in the opposite direction, forming a diamond or square pattern. Trim strips even with pie edge. Turn bottom crust up over ends of strips. Press firmly to seal edge. Flute edge.

Bake in 425° oven 10 minutes. Reduce temperature to 350° and bake 40 minutes more, or until crust is golden brown and filling is bubbly. Makes 6 to 8 servings.

Almond Pastry: Sift together 2¼ c. sifted flour, 1 tsp. salt and 1 tblsp. sugar into bowl. Cut in ¾ c. shortening until mixture forms fine crumbs, using pastry blender. Beat together 1 egg yolk, 2 tsp. almond extract and ¼ c. water. Sprinkle egg mixture over crumb mixture. Toss with fork until a soft dough forms.

FRESH BLUEBERRY PIE

The blueberries taste so fresh because the filling is not cooked before arranging in the pie crust.

Pastry for 2-crust	4 c. fresh blueberries
9-inch pie	1 tblsp. butter or
1 c. sugar	regular margarine
2½ tblsp. cornstarch	Sugar

Divide pastry almost in half. Roll out larger half on floured surface to 12-inch circle. Line 9-inch pie plate with pastry. Trim edge to 1 inch.

Combine 1 c. sugar and cornstarch in bowl. Add blueberries; toss to coat. Arrange blueberry mixture in pastry-lined pie plate. Dot with butter.

Roll out remaining pastry to 11-inch circle. Adjust top crust; flute edge and cut vents. Sprinkle crust with sugar.

Bake in 425° oven 40 minutes, or until crust is golden brown. Cool on rack. Makes 6 to 8 servings.

Sour Cream Topping
Combine 1 c. dairy sour cream, 2 tblsp. confectioners sugar and 1 tsp. grated orange rind. Mix and chill. Serve with any warm fruit pie.

Cinnamon-Ice Cream Topping
Blend ¼ tsp. cinnamon into 1 c. slightly softened vanilla ice cream. Spoon on warm apple or blueberry pie wedges.

BASIC RHUBARB PIE

A dash of grated orange rind lends a special flavor to this crusty, old-fashioned-tasting rhubarb pie.

Pastry for 2-crust	5 c. cut-up rhubarb, in
9-inch pie	1-inch lengths
1¼ c. sugar	1 tblsp. butter or
¼ c. cornstarch	regular margarine
2 tsp. grated orange rind	Sugar
¼ tsp. salt	

Divide pastry almost in half. Roll out larger half on floured surface to 12-inch circle. Line 9-inch pie plate with pastry. Trim edge to 1 inch.

Combine 1¼ c. sugar, cornstarch, orange rind and salt in bowl; mix well. Add rhubarb; toss to coat. Arrange rhubarb mixture in pastry-lined pie plate. Dot with butter.

Roll out remaining pastry to 11-inch circle. Adjust top crust; flute edge and cut vents. Sprinkle crust with sugar.

Bake in 425° oven 45 minutes, or until rhubarb is tender and crust is golden brown. Cool on rack. Makes 6 to 8 servings.

FRESH STRAWBERRY PIE

A colorful, bright red, fruit pie with just the right amount of sugar. A real treat topped with a spoon of whipped cream.

Pastry for 2-crust	**4 c. whole strawberries**
9-inch pie	**1 tblsp. butter or**
1 c. sugar	**regular margarine**
¼ c. cornstarch	**Sugar**

Divide pastry almost in half. Roll out larger half on floured surface to 12-inch circle. Line 9-inch pie plate with pastry. Trim edge to 1 inch.

Combine 1 c. sugar and cornstarch in bowl.

Hull strawberries and cut in half. Add to sugar-cornstarch mixture; toss until coated. Arrange strawberry mixture in pastry-lined pie plate. Dot with butter.

Roll out remaining pastry to 11-inch circle. Adjust top crust; flute edge and cut vents. Sprinkle crust with sugar.

Bake in 425° oven 40 minutes, or until crust is golden brown. Cool on rack. Makes 6 to 8 servings.

BLUSHING PEACH PIE

This delicacy got its name because the cinnamon candies or "red-hots" add a blush of red color to the peach filling.

Pastry for 2-crust	**3 tblsp. red cinnamon**
9-inch pie	**candies**
1 (29-oz.) can sliced	**1 tblsp. butter or**
peaches in syrup	**regular margarine**
½ c. sugar	**Sugar**
2 tblsp. cornstarch	

Hearts of Cheese
Buy packaged cheese slices and cut out hearts or any shape you wish. Arrange on 2-crust baked pie before or after cutting.

Divide pastry almost in half. Roll out larger half on floured surface to 12-inch circle. Line 9-inch pie plate with pastry. Trim edge to 1 inch.

Drain peaches, reserving ¼ c. syrup.

Combine ½ c. sugar and cornstarch in 1-qt. saucepan. Stir in reserved ¼ c. syrup. Cook over medium heat, stirring constantly, until mixture comes to a boil. Remove from heat.

Combine peaches, cooked syrup and cinnamon candies in bowl; mix lightly. Pour into pastry-lined pie plate. Dot with butter.

Roll out remaining pastry to 11-inch circle. Adjust top crust; flute edge and cut vents. Sprinkle with sugar.

Bake in 400° oven 25 to 30 minutes, or until crust is golden brown. Cool on rack. Makes 6 to 8 servings.

SHEET APPLE PIE

No need to pare the apples for this timesaving recipe. It serves 16 people—and the walnut topping is delicious.

Pastry for 2-crust	2 c. sifted flour
9-inch pie	1 c. brown sugar, packed
3 lbs. apples	1 c. butter or
¾ c. sugar	regular margarine
1 tblsp. lemon juice	½ c. chopped walnuts
1 tblsp. ground cinnamon	

Roll out pastry on floured surface to 18 × 13-inch rectangle. Fit into 15½ × 10½ × 1-inch jelly roll pan. Trim pastry 1 inch beyond edge of pan. Flute edge.

Quarter apples, but do not pare. Remove cores. Grate apples on medium grater, making 9 to 10 cups grated apples. Combine grated apples, sugar, lemon juice and cinnamon in bowl; mix well. Arrange apple mixture in pastry-lined jelly roll pan.

Combine flour and brown sugar in another bowl. Cut in butter until mixture is crumbly, using pastry blender. Stir in walnuts. Sprinkle walnut-crumb mixture over apples.

Bake in 400° oven 45 minutes, or until apples are tender. Cool in pan on rack. Makes 16 servings.

Water In Pastry
Too much water added to pastry dough can make the crust hard and brittle. Too little water makes pastry which cracks at edges when you roll it out.

APRICOT-RASPBERRY PASTRY BARS

A buttery cookie-like crust, spread with apricot and raspberry preserves. Looks so attractive and is so easy to prepare.

3 c. sifted flour	2 eggs, beaten
1 c. sugar	2 tsp. vanilla
1 tsp. baking powder	¾ c. apricot preserves
½ tsp. salt	¾ c. raspberry preserves
1 c. butter or	
regular margarine	

Sift together flour, sugar, baking powder and salt into bowl. Cut in butter until mixture forms fine crumbs, using pastry blender. Add eggs and vanilla, mixing well until dough forms, using a fork.

Roll out three fourths of the dough on floured surface to 16 × 12-inch rectangle. Transfer dough to baking sheet. Make ½-inch rim all around rectangle.

Spread apricot preserves on one half of the dough and raspberry preserves on the other half.

Roll out remaining pastry to 13 × 9-inch rectangle. Cut into 18 (13-inch) strips. Place 9 strips at an angle across filling on narrow side. Then place 9 remaining strips in the opposite direction, forming lattice top. Trim strips and seal to rim. Flute edges.

Bake in 325° oven 30 minutes, or until crust is golden brown. Cool on baking sheet on rack. Makes 32 servings.

OLD-TIME UPSIDE-DOWN APPLE PIE

"Grandmother used to make this when she had leftover pastry dough," a young Pennsylvania woman told us.

1 c. sifted flour	1 tblsp. butter or
¼ tsp. salt	regular margarine
⅓ c. regular margarine	⅓ c. sugar
3 tblsp. iced water	¹⁄₁₆ tsp. ground nutmeg
5 c. sliced, pared apples	Heavy cream

Combine flour and salt in bowl. Cut in margarine until mixture resembles coarse meal, using pastry blender. Sprinkle with iced water. Stir with fork until mixture holds together.

Roll out pastry on floured surface to 12-inch circle.

Place sliced apples in greased 9-inch pie plate. Cover with pastry. Trim pastry 1 inch beyond edge of pie plate; flute edges and cut vents.

Bake in 400° oven 30 minutes, or until apples are tender. Loosen crust around edges of pie plate. Invert onto serving plate. Carefully remove all the apples from the crust and place back into pie plate. Add butter, sugar and nutmeg to apples. Stir together with fork. Arrange apple mixture back on crust. Serve warm with a pitcher of heavy cream. Makes 6 servings.

Egg White Glaze
Brush slightly beaten egg white on top crust before baking for a pretty glaze.

ASSORTMENT OF SINGLE-CRUST PIES

When you're not in the mood to roll out two rounds of pie crust, try one of these delicious one-crust pies. There's a pie to suit every mood, every occasion and every schedule.

Start with pecan pie and then go on to lemon chess, buttermilk, tart and tangy lemon, chocolate, and coconut.

Pies that can be made ahead and refrigerated are included in this section. You'll find light-as-a-cloud chiffons, creamy custards, and the old-fashioned cream pies that are dear to a farm family's heart, full of country cream and eggs.

HERITAGE DUTCH APPLE PIE

Try serving a wedge of this pie, warm from the oven, with a large spoon of whipped cream flavored with sugar and vanilla.

6 c. sliced, pared tart red apples (6 medium)	1 c. sifted flour
½ c. sugar	¾ c. sugar
1 tsp. ground cinnamon	½ c. soft butter or regular margarine
1 (9-inch) unbaked pie shell with fluted edge	

Combine apples, ½ c. sugar and cinnamon in bowl; mix well. Arrange apple mixture in unbaked pie shell.

Combine flour and ¾ c. sugar in bowl. Cut in butter until mixture is crumbly, using pastry blender. Sprinkle crumbs over apples.

Bake in 400° oven 50 minutes, or until crust is golden brown and apples are tender. Makes 6 to 8 servings.

Beautiful Pastry
A perfect pastry is flaky, tender, delicious and evenly browned. It's not crumbly, but when broken, it shows layers of flat flakes, piled one above the other, with air spaces between.

CINNAMON APPLE TART

"My great-grandmother brought this recipe with her to Kansas from Pennsylvania," a Kansas farm wife told us.

⅔ c. sugar	6 large apples, pared*
3 tblsp. flour	2 tblsp. butter or regular margarine
¼ tsp. salt	⅓ c. water
1 tsp. ground cinnamon	Ground cinnamon
1 (9-inch) unbaked pie shell	

Combine sugar, flour, salt and cinnamon in bowl; mix well. Sprinkle one half of mixture in bottom of unbaked pie shell.

Cut apples in halves and remove cores. Arrange 7 apple halves, cut side down, in prepared pie shell. Cut each remaining apple half into four thick slices. Fill in spaces around apple halves with thick apple slices. Sprinkle with remaining sugar mixture. Dot with butter and pour water over all. Sprinkle with cinnamon.

Bake in 400° oven 15 minutes. Reduce heat to 350° and bake 30 more minutes, or until apples are tender. Cool on rack. Makes 6 to 8 servings.

*Note: We recommend using an all-purpose apple, such as McIntosh or winesap, in this recipe.

EASY APPLE-PUFF PIE

Such a simple-to-make pie. Sweetened condensed milk is poured over apple halves—makes a delightful custard filling.

6 medium apples, pared*	1 (14-oz can sweetened
1 (9-inch) unbaked pie	condensed milk
shell	Ground cinnamon

Cut apples in halves and remove cores. Prick surface of apples with fork. Place one apple half, cut side down, in center of unbaked pie shell. Arrange remaining apple halves in ring around center apple, overlapping adjacent apple halves. Pour sweetened condensed milk over apples. Sprinkle with cinnamon.

Bake in 425° oven 20 minutes. Reduce heat to 300° and bake 50 more minutes, or until apples are tender. Cool on rack. Makes 6 to 8 servings.

*Note: We recommend an all-purpose apple, such as McIntosh or winesap, for this recipe.

FRESH PEAR PIE

Here's just the recipe you need if you have an excess of pears from your tree. It's unusual and delicious!

3 c. thinly sliced, pared	3 eggs, beaten
pears	2 tsp. vanilla
½ c. light corn syrup	1 (9-inch) unbaked pie
¾ c. sugar	shell
2 tblsp. butter or	Sweetened whipped cream
regular margarine	Ground nutmeg

Combine pears, corn syrup and sugar in 3-qt. saucepan. Cook over medium heat until mixture comes to a boil. Reduce heat and simmer 5 minutes. Add butter; stir until melted. Stir a little of hot mixture into eggs; mix well. Then stir egg mixture into pear mixture, blending well. Stir in vanilla. Remove from heat.

Pour hot pear mixture into unbaked pie shell.

Bake in 350° oven 25 minutes, or until a knife inserted halfway between edge and center comes out clean. Cool on rack.

To serve, spread top of pie with sweetened whipped cream. Sprinkle with nutmeg. Refrigerate any leftover pie. Makes 6 to 8 servings.

BASIC RASPBERRY PIE

Good all year round because you use frozen raspberries. Delightful when spread with a thin layer of whipped cream.

Fruit Pastry
Substitute chilled, unsweetened pineapple or orange juice for the water in a basic pastry recipe. Add 1 tsp. grated orange rind. Good for cream, fruit and pumpkin pies.

2 (10-oz.) pkgs. frozen raspberries, thawed	¼ c. sugar
2½ tblsp. quick-cooking tapioca	1 (9-inch) unbaked pie shell
	Sweetened Cream (recipe follows)

Combine undrained raspberries, tapioca and sugar in bowl. Let stand 15 minutes.

Bake pie shell in 425° oven 5 minutes.

Pour prepared raspberries into partially baked pie shell. Reduce oven temperature to 375°. Bake 35 more minutes or until crust is golden brown. Cool on rack.

To serve, top pie with a thin layer of Sweetened Cream. Makes 6 to 8 servings.

Sweetened Cream: Combine ½ c. heavy cream, ½ tsp. vanilla and 1 tblsp. sugar in chilled bowl. Beat until soft peaks form, using electric mixer at high speed.

GRANDMOTHER'S SUPERB RHUBARB PIE

Unusual—a cinnamon-spiced rhubarb and custard filling is topped with a crusty brown hard meringue.

2 eggs	¾ c. sugar
1 (9-inch) unbaked pie shell with fluted edge	3 tblsp. flour
4 c. diced rhubarb	1 tsp. ground cinnamon

Break one of the eggs into unbaked pie shell. Roll egg around shell to seal crust. Remove egg; pour into mixing bowl. Add other egg to bowl.

Arrange rhubarb in prepared pie shell.

Add sugar, flour and cinnamon to eggs. Beat until thick and light colored, using electric mixer at high speed. Pour over rhubarb.

Bake in 400° oven 35 minutes, or until rhubarb is tender and top is golden brown. Cool on rack. Makes 6 to 8 servings.

PECAN PIE

Rich and flavorful—the dark corn syrup gives it a taste that's similar to molasses.

3 eggs	1 c. dark corn syrup
1 c. sugar	1 c. pecan halves
⅛ tsp. salt	1 (9-inch) unbaked pie
3 tblsp. butter or	shell
regular margarine,	
melted	

Combine eggs, sugar, salt, butter and corn syrup in bowl. Beat with electric mixer at medium speed until well blended. Stir in pecan halves. Pour mixture into unbaked pie shell.

Bake in 400° oven 10 minutes. Reduce temperature to 350° and bake 30 more minutes, or until knife inserted halfway between the center and edge comes out clean. Cool on rack. Makes 6 to 8 servings.

SPECIAL PECAN PIE

A North Carolina farm woman told us her friends and relatives think her pecan pie is "out of this world."

3 eggs	1 tblsp. vinegar
¾ c. sugar	1 tsp. vanilla
½ c. light corn syrup	1½ c. coarsely chopped
⅛ tsp. salt	pecans
1 tblsp. butter or	1 (9-inch) unbaked pie
regular margarine,	shell
melted	

Pastry Care
Don't stretch pastry dough and avoid tearing it. Handle pastry as you would a delicate flower. Then you will never have a shrunken or misshapen crust.

Combine eggs, sugar, corn syrup, salt, butter, vinegar and vanilla in bowl. Beat with electric mixer at medium speed until well blended, about 2 minutes. Stir in 1 c. of the pecans. Pour mixture into pie shell. Sprinkle with remaining ½ c. pecans.

Bake in 350° oven 45 minutes, or until knife inserted halfway between center and edge comes out clean. Cool on rack. Makes 6 to 8 servings.

PUMPKIN-PECAN PIE

A combination of two favorites—a creamy, spicy pumpkin layer covered with a chewy pecan mixture.

1 (1-lb.) can mashed pumpkin (2 c.)	⅔ c. evaporated milk
¼ c. sugar	1 (9-inch) unbaked pie shell with fluted edge
2 eggs	Molasses Topping
1 tsp. ground pumpkin pie spice	(recipe follows)
1 tsp. ground cinnamon	½ c. chopped pecans

Combine pumpkin, sugar, eggs, pumpkin pie spice, cinnamon and evaporated milk in bowl. Beat with electric mixer at low speed until smooth. Pour mixture into unbaked pie shell.

Bake in 425° oven 10 minutes. Reduce temperature to 350° and bake 15 more minutes.

Meanwhile, prepare Molasses Topping. Remove pie from oven. Pour Molasses Topping over all. Sprinkle with pecans. Return pie to oven and bake 35 more minutes, or until custard is set. Cool on rack. Makes 6 to 8 servings.

Molasses Topping: Beat 2 eggs in bowl until foamy, using electric mixer at medium speed. Add ½ c. dark corn syrup, 2 tblsp. brown sugar (packed), 2 tblsp. molasses, 1 tsp. vanilla, 1 tblsp. flour and ¼ tsp. salt. Beat until smooth, using electric mixer at low speed.

IMITATION PECAN PIE

Looks and tastes like a pecan pie, but it isn't. The cereal adds the crunchiness of pecans. Less expensive, too.

3 eggs	¼ tsp. salt
1 c. sugar	1½ c. toasted rice cereal
¾ c. light corn syrup	1 (9-inch) unbaked pie shell
¼ c. butter or regular margarine, melted	Sweetened whipped cream

Beat eggs in bowl until foamy, using electric mixer at high speed. Add sugar, corn syrup, butter and salt. Beat until smooth, using electric mixer at low speed. Stir in rice cereal. Pour mixture into unbaked pie shell.

Bake in 375° oven 40 minutes, or until knife inserted halfway between center and edge comes out clean. Cool on rack. Serve topped with puffs of sweetened whipped cream. Makes 6 to 8 servings.

TENNESSEE PEANUT PIE

Attractive, pecan-like pie made with chopped peanuts. Elegant, indeed, topped with a scoop of ice cream.

3 eggs	⅛ tsp. salt
1 c. dark corn syrup	1 tsp. vanilla
1 c. sugar	1 c. chopped peanuts
2 tblsp. butter or regular margarine, melted	1 (9-inch) unbaked pie shell

Combine eggs, corn syrup, sugar, butter, salt and vanilla in bowl. Beat with electric mixer at high speed until blended. Stir in peanuts. Pour mixture into unbaked pie shell.

Bake in 400⁰ oven 15 minutes. Reduce temperature to 350⁰ and bake 35 more minutes, or until filling is set around the edges and slightly soft in the center. Cool on rack. Makes 6 to 8 servings.

CRUSTY COCONUT PIE

"My mother used to make this pie for family gatherings. How we all looked forward to it," said a Louisiana woman.

½ c. milk	1 c. sugar
1 (3½-oz.) can flaked coconut	3 eggs
¼ c. butter or regular margarine	1 tsp. vanilla
	1 (9-inch) unbaked pie shell

Combine milk and coconut in bowl; set aside.

Cream together butter and sugar in another bowl until light and fluffy, using electric mixer at high speed. Add eggs, one at a time, beating well after each addition. Blend in vanilla. Stir in coconut-milk mixture. Pour mixture into unbaked pie shell.

Bake in 350⁰ oven 30 minutes, or until almost set in the center and crust is golden brown. Cool on rack. Makes 6 to 8 servings.

LEMON CHESS PIE

Old plantation favorite brought here originally from England. Its buttery-rich custard filling has a nut-brown topping.

4 eggs	1 tsp. cornmeal
2 c. sugar	1 tsp. flour
½ c. lemon juice	⅛ tsp. salt
½ c. butter or regular margarine, melted	1 (9-inch) unbaked pie shell

Pie Shell Slump
If your pie shell slumps, you may not have pressed the flutes firmly to the pie plate.

Beat eggs in bowl until well blended, using electric mixer at high speed. Gradually add sugar, beating well after each addition. Add lemon juice, butter, cornmeal, flour and salt. Beat well, using electric mixer at low speed. Pour mixture into unbaked pie shell.

Bake in 350° oven 40 minutes, or until top is browned. Do not overbake. Cool on rack. Makes 6 to 8 servings.

CREAMY BUTTERMILK PIE

A lemony custard pie with the texture of a cheesecake, topped with a sprinkle of ground nutmeg.

2 eggs	½ tsp. grated lemon rind
1 c. sugar	2 c. buttermilk
¼ c. flour	1 (9-inch) unbaked pie shell
2 tblsp. butter or regular margarine, melted	Ground nutmeg

Combine eggs, sugar, flour, butter, lemon rind and buttermilk in bowl. Beat with electric mixer at medium speed until blended. Pour mixture into unbaked pie shell. Sprinkle with nutmeg.

Bake in 425° oven 10 minutes. Reduce temperature to 325° and bake 25 more minutes, or until knife inserted halfway between the center and edge comes out clean. Cool on rack. Makes 6 to 8 servings.

FUNNY CAKE PIE

Yellow cake batter baked in a pie shell with a surprise fudge sauce under the cake. A real treat topped with ice cream.

1 c. sifted flour	2 (1-oz.) squares
1 tsp. baking powder	unsweetened chocolate
¼ tsp. salt	2 tblsp. butter or
¾ c. sugar	regular margarine
¼ c. cooking oil	½ c. sugar
1 egg	½ c. warm water
½ c. milk	½ tsp. vanilla
½ tsp. vanilla	1 (9-inch) unbaked pie
	shell

Sift together flour, baking powder and salt into bowl. Add ¾ c. sugar, oil, egg, milk and ½ tsp. vanilla. Beat with electric mixer at medium speed 2 minutes; set aside.

Melt together chocolate and butter in small saucepan over low heat. Remove from heat. Stir in ½ c. sugar, warm water and ½ tsp. vanilla. Cool well.

Pour chocolate mixture into unbaked pie shell. Spoon flour mixture (cake batter) on top. Spread evenly with metal spatula.

Bake in 350⁰ oven 50 minutes, or until cake tester or wooden pick inserted in center of pie comes out clean. Cool on rack. Makes 6 to 8 servings.

LEMON VELVET PIE

Light and airy and layered with two American favorites: lemon chiffon and lemon meringue.

1⅓ c. sugar	1 tsp. vanilla
6 tblsp. cornstarch	1 tblsp. unflavored gelatin
½ tsp. salt	¼ c. cold water
1½ c. cold water	1 c. light cream
2 egg yolks	2 egg whites, stiffly beaten
2 tblsp. butter or regular margarine	1 (9-inch) baked pie shell
⅓ c. lemon juice	1 c. heavy cream, whipped
1 tsp. grated lemon rind	

Combine sugar, cornstarch and salt in 2-qt. saucepan. Gradually stir in 1½ c. cold water. Cook over medium heat, stirring constantly, until mixture thickens and mounds when dropped from a spoon.

Slightly beat egg yolks, using a fork. Stir a small amount of hot mixture into egg yolks. Immediately pour back into remaining hot mixture, blending thoroughly. Cook over low heat 2 more minutes, stirring constantly. Remove from heat. Gently stir in butter, lemon juice, lemon rind and vanilla. Remove 1 c. of the filling; set aside to cool.

Soften gelatin in ¼ c. cold water 5 minutes. Add gelatin mixture to remaining hot filling and stir until dissolved. Gradually stir in light cream. Cool slightly.

When gelatin mixture begins to thicken, fold in beaten egg whites. Pour mixture into baked pie shell. Chill in refrigerator 15 minutes.

Carefully spread reserved 1 c. filling on top. Chill in refrigerator until set. Decorate top of pie with puffs of whipped cream. Makes 6 to 8 servings.

CHOCOLATE VELVET PIE

Rich, but oh, so good! A mild-flavored chocolate cream is buried under a blanket of whipped cream.

1¼ c. sugar	1½ tsp. vanilla
½ c. baking cocoa	1 (9-inch) baked pie shell
4 tblsp. cornstarch	1 c. heavy cream
¼ tsp. salt	2 tblsp. sugar
3 c. milk	1 tsp. vanilla
3 tblsp. butter or	1 (1-oz.) square
regular margarine	unsweetened chocolate

Sift together sugar, cocoa, cornstarch and salt; set aside.

Scald milk in top of double boiler. Gradually stir in sifted dry ingredients. Cook over boiling water, stirring constantly, until mixture begins to thicken. Cover and cook over simmering water 15 minutes. Remove from heat; add butter and 1½ tsp. vanilla. Stir until butter is melted. Cool 10 minutes.

Pour mixture into baked pie shell. Cover and refrigerate at least 2 hours or until set.

Just before serving, whip heavy cream until it begins to thicken, using electric mixer at high speed. Gradually add 2 tblsp. sugar and 1 tsp. vanilla, beating until soft peaks form. Spread over top of pie. Cut unsweetened chocolate into shavings, using vegetable peeler. Sprinkle over whipped cream. Makes 6 to 8 servings.

CANDY BAR PIE

This creamy dessert tastes like a milk chocolate candy bar in a pie shell. It's easy-to-fix, extra-rich and luscious.

1 (8-oz.) milk	1 c. heavy cream
chocolate bar	1 tsp. vanilla
21 large marshmallows	1 (9-inch) baked pie shell
½ c. milk	Sweetened whipped cream

Break chocolate bar into pieces. Combine chocolate, marshmallows and milk in top of double boiler. Place over simmering water until melted and mixture is smooth, stirring well. Remove from heat; cool completely.

Whip heavy cream and vanilla in bowl until stiff peaks form, using electric mixer at high speed. Fold cooled chocolate mixture into whipped cream. Pour into baked pie shell. Cover and chill in refrigerator at least 2 hours or until set. Serve decorated with sweetened whipped cream. Makes 6 to 8 servings.

CHOCOLATE MOUSSE PIE

Prepare this super-rich pie in the morning and serve in the evening. Truly elegant and a breeze to make.

1 (6-oz.) pkg. semisweet chocolate pieces	4 eggs, separated
3 tblsp. milk	1 tsp. vanilla
2 tblsp. sugar	1 (9-inch) baked pie shell
	Sweetened whipped cream

Combine chocolate pieces, milk and sugar in small saucepan. Cook over low heat until the chocolate melts. Remove from heat; cool well.

Add egg yolks to chocolate mixture, one at a time, beating well with spoon after each addition. Blend in vanilla.

Beat egg whites until stiff peaks form, using electric mixer at high speed. Fold egg whites into chocolate mixture. Pour mixture into baked pie shell. Cover and refrigerate several hours or until set.

Decorate with puffs of sweetened whipped cream before serving. Makes 6 to 8 servings.

ELEGANT FUDGE PIE

"Because this pie is so very rich, small pieces are usually satisfying after dinner," wrote an Iowa farm woman.

Vanilla Wafer Crust (recipe follows)	1 tsp. vanilla
¾ c. butter or regular margarine	3 eggs
	1 c. heavy cream
1 c. sugar	1 tblsp. sugar
2 (1-oz.) squares unsweetened chocolate, melted and cooled	½ tsp. vanilla

Prepare Vanilla Wafer Crust.

Press crumb mixture into 9-inch pie plate.

Bake in 300° oven 15 minutes or until very lightly browned. Cool on rack.

Meanwhile, cream together butter and 1 c. sugar in bowl until light and fluffy, using electric mixer at medium speed. Beat in melted chocolate and 1 tsp. vanilla. Add eggs, one at a time, beating 4 minutes after each addition. Pour mixture into cooled Vanilla Wafer Crust. Chill in refrigerator 2 hours before serving.

Whip heavy cream, 1 tblsp. sugar and ½ tsp. vanilla in chilled bowl until soft peaks form, using electric mixer at high speed. Spread whipped cream evenly over the top of the pie before serving. Makes 10 servings.

Vanilla Wafer Crust: Combine 1 c. vanilla wafer crumbs (25 wafers), ½ c. finely chopped pecans and ¼ c. melted butter or regular margarine in bowl; mix well.

CHOCOLATE CANDY PIE

A handed-down heirloom recipe from Minnesota. If you like a gentle chocolate flavor, this creamy pie is for you.

25 large marshmallows	**1 (8-oz.) milk chocolate**
½ c. milk	**almond bar**
1 c. heavy cream,	**1 (9-inch) baked pie**
whipped	**shell**

Combine marshmallows and milk in top of double boiler. Place over simmering water until marshmallows are melted, stirring well. Remove from heat. Cool completely.

Fold cooled marshmallow mixture into whipped cream. Coarsely grate chocolate bar, using medium blade. Fold chocolate into cream mixture. Turn into baked pie shell. Cover and refrigerate 2 hours or until set. Makes 6 to 8 servings.

RANCHER'S DELIGHT PIE

An Idaho ranch wife sent us this recipe. She calls it her "instant"
pie because it's made with instant pudding mixes.

Oatmeal Crust	3½ c. milk
(recipe follows)	1 tsp. vanilla
1 (4½-oz.) pkg. instant	1 (2-oz.) env. whipped
chocolate pudding mix	topping mix
1 (3¾-oz.) pkg. instant	½ c. milk
pistachio pudding mix	½ tsp. vanilla

Prepare Oatmeal Crust.

Divide dough in half. Roll each half into 11-inch circle. Line 2 (8-inch) pie plates with pastry. Flute edges. Prick with fork. Bake in 375° oven 10 to 15 minutes or until golden brown. Cool on racks.

Combine chocolate pudding mix, pistachio pudding mix, 3½ c. milk and 1 tsp. vanilla in bowl. Beat slowly 2 minutes, using rotary beater. Refrigerate 5 minutes. Scoop filling into shells. Cover and refrigerate until set.

Prepare whipped topping mix with ½ c. milk and ½ tsp. vanilla according to package directions. Decorate each pie with puffs of whipped topping before serving. Makes 2 pies, 6 servings each.

Oatmeal Crust: Combine 2 c. sifted flour, ½ c. quick-cooking oats, 1 tblsp. sugar, ½ tsp. salt and ¼ tsp. baking powder in mixing bowl. Cut in 1 c. butter or regular margarine until crumbs form, using pastry blender. Stir in 1 egg. Add enough iced water so dough holds together, about 1 to 2 tblsp.

ORANGE BLOSSOM PIE

Here's a pie with a tropical theme—orange-flavored tapioca cream
filling sprinkled with toasted coconut.

2 c. milk	2 eggs, separated
½ c. quick-cooking tapioca	1 c. heavy cream, whipped
½ c. sugar	1 (9-inch) baked pie shell
⅛ tsp. salt	½ c. toasted, flaked
1 tsp. grated orange rind	coconut*

Heat milk in top of double boiler.

Combine tapioca, sugar and salt in small bowl. Stir tapioca mixture into hot milk. Cook over boiling water, stirring constantly, until mixture begins to thicken, about 4 minutes. Stir in orange rind. Cook 15 more minutes, stirring occasionally. Mixture is very thick.

Beat egg yolks slightly, using a fork. Stir a small amount of hot mixture into egg yolks. Immediately pour yolk mixture back into remaining hot mixture, blending thoroughly. Cook 1 more minute.

Remove from heat. Let mixture cool while preparing egg whites.

Beat egg whites in bowl until stiff but not dry peaks form. Fold egg whites into slightly cooled pudding mixture. Fold in whipped cream. Pour filling into baked pie shell. Sprinkle with toasted coconut. Chill in refrigerator until set. Makes 6 to 8 servings.

*Note: To toast coconut, place coconut in 8-inch square baking pan. Bake in 350⁰ oven 7 to 10 minutes, stirring once, or until coconut is toasted.

ORANGE-MARSHMALLOW PIE

With its orange-and-almond crust and its orange-and-lemon filling, this citrus pie is doubly tasty and nutritious.

Orange Pastry (recipe follows)	**6 tblsp. orange juice**
1 (10½-oz.) bag miniature marshmallows	**2 tblsp. lemon juice**
	1 tblsp. grated orange rind
	2 c. heavy cream, whipped

Prepare Orange Pastry.

Roll out Orange Pastry on floured surface to 13-inch circle. Line 9-inch pie plate with Orange Pastry. Trim edge to 1½ inches. Flute edge. Prick bottom and sides of crust with fork.

Bake in 400⁰ oven 12 minutes or until golden brown. Cool on rack.

Combine marshmallows, orange juice and lemon juice in top of double boiler. Cook over boiling water, stirring occasionally, until marshmallows are melted and mixture is smooth. Remove from heat. Stir in orange rind. Cool to lukewarm.

Fold whipped cream into cooled filling. Pour into Orange Pastry pie shell. Chill in refrigerator until set. Makes 6 to 8 servings.

Orange Pastry: Combine 1½ c. sifted flour, 1 tblsp. sugar, ½ tsp. salt, 1 tsp. grated orange rind and ⅓ c. ground almonds in bowl. Cut in ½ c. shortening until mixture forms coarse crumbs, using pastry blender. Sprinkle crumb mixture with 4 to 5 tblsp. orange juice, a little at a time, mixing with fork until flour mixture is moistened and a dough forms.

Refrigerate Cream Pies
Refrigerate cream pies, custard pies or any pies that contain gelatin and whipped cream. Pies that sit at room temperature could spoil and cause food poisoning. After serving the pie, put it back in the refrigerator.

PRUNE-MARSHMALLOW PIE

Mocha-flavored and fluffy-flecked with bits of cooked prunes. This is a different kind of pie.

20 large marshmallows	1 c. heavy cream, whipped
¾ c. milk	1 c. finely chopped,
2 tsp. instant coffee	cooked prunes
powder	1 (8-inch) baked pie shell
⅛ tsp. salt	with fluted edge
½ tsp. chocolate extract	

Combine marshmallows, milk, coffee powder and salt in 2-qt. saucepan. Cook over low heat, stirring constantly, until marshmallows are melted. Remove from heat. Stir in chocolate extract. Chill in refrigerator until mixture thickens slightly.

Fold in whipped cream and prunes. Pour mixture into baked pie shell. Chill in refrigerator until set, 4 to 6 hours. Makes 6 servings.

Shiny Pans For Pies
Use pans that are not shiny for pies, such as glass or dull aluminum. They do not reflect the heat away from the pie.

FLUFFY FRUIT PIE

So refreshing! The orange-pineapple-cherry combination gives this a delightful fruity taste.

1 (8½-oz.) can crushed	1 c. evaporated milk,
pineapple	chilled
¼ c. red maraschino	1½ tsp. lemon juice
cherry juice	¼ c. sliced red maraschino
1 (3-oz.) pkg. orange-	cherries
flavored gelatin	1 (9-inch) baked pie shell
½ c. sugar	

Combine undrained pineapple and maraschino cherry juice in 2-qt. saucepan. Cook over medium heat, stirring constantly, until mixture comes to a boil. Add orange gelatin, stirring until gelatin is dissolved. Remove from heat. Stir in sugar and pour mixture into a large bowl. Chill in refrigerator until mixture mounds slightly when dropped from a spoon, about 30 minutes.

Meanwhile, chill bowl and beaters in refrigerator.

Combine chilled evaporated milk and lemon juice in chilled bowl. Beat until stiff peaks form, using electric mixer at high speed. Fold whipped evaporated milk mixture into chilled gelatin mixture. Fold in maraschino cherries. Pour mixture into baked pie shell. Chill in refrigerator until set. Makes 6 to 8 servings.

STRAWBERRY CREAM PIE

The baked pie shell is first lined with sweetened whipped cream. Then the thickened strawberries are arranged in the center.

1 (10-oz.) bag frozen whole strawberries, thawed	1 c. heavy cream
	1 tsp. sugar
	1 tsp. vanilla
¾ c. sugar	1 (9-inch) baked pie shell
2½ tblsp. cornstarch	
4 drops red food coloring	

Drain strawberries, reserving juice. Add enough water to juice to make 1 c.

Combine ¾ c. sugar and cornstarch in 2-qt. saucepan. Stir in reserved 1 c. juice and red food coloring. Cook over medium heat, stirring constantly, until mixture boils. Cook 1 minute. Remove from heat and cool to lukewarm.

Stir in drained strawberries. Chill in refrigerator until mixture begins to thicken.

Whip heavy cream, 1 tsp. sugar and vanilla in chilled bowl until soft peaks form, using electric mixer at high speed. Spread whipped cream on bottom and sides of baked pie shell. Pour chilled strawberry mixture into center. Chill in refrigerator until set, 2 to 3 hours. Makes 6 to 8 servings.

LEMON CHIFFON PIE

This makes an extra-high chiffon pie. The filling is heaped into a 10-inch pie shell. Light and delicate.

6 eggs, separated	⅔ c. boiling water
⅔ c. sugar	½ tsp. cream of tartar
½ tsp. salt	⅔ c. sugar
6 tblsp. lemon juice	1 (10-inch) baked pie shell
2 tsp. grated lemon rind	
1 (3-oz.) pkg. lemon-flavored gleatin	

Combine egg yolks, ⅔ c. sugar and salt in top of double boiler; mix well. Stir in lemon juice and lemon rind. Cook over simmering water, stirring occasionally, until mixture coats a metal spoon, 7 to 10 minutes.

Dissolve lemon gelatin in boiling water in bowl. Stir hot cooked custard into dissolved gelatin. Place bowl of gelatin mixture in a bowl filled with iced water. Stir gently until mixture mounds slightly when dropped from spoon. Remove bowl from water; set aside.

Beat egg whites and cream of tartar in another bowl until foamy, using electric mixer at high speed. Gradually add ⅔ c. sugar, beating until stiff peaks form. Fold custard mixture into egg white mixture. Pour into baked pie shell. Chill in refrigerator 2 hours or until set. Makes 10 servings.

SUNNY LEMON PIE

This pretty pie is a top favorite in the homes of many California citrus growers. So light and lemony.

4 eggs, separated	3 tblsp. water
¼ c. lemon juice	1 c. sugar
1 tsp. grated lemon rind	1 (9-inch) baked pie shell

Beat egg yolks until thick in top of double boiler, using electric mixer at medium speed. Gradually stir in lemon juice, lemon rind, water and ½ c. of the sugar. Cook over simmering water, stirring constantly, until thickened. Remove from heat.

Beat egg whites in a bowl until stiff peaks form when beaters are slowly lifted, using electric mixer at high speed. Gradually add remaining ½ c. sugar, 1 tblsp. at a time, beating well after each addition. Continue beating until egg whites form stiff, glossy peaks.

Fold one half of egg white mixture into warm egg yolk mixture, folding until no egg whites show. Pour mixture into baked pie shell.

Spoon remaining egg white mixture around edge of pie. Spread mixture until it touches inner edge of crust all around, using back of a spoon.

Bake in 350⁰ oven 15 minutes, or until meringue is just lightly browned. Cool on rack. Makes 6 to 8 servings.

PUMPKIN CHIFFON PIE

Airy pumpkin-flavored chiffon filling blanketed with sweetened whipped cream and dusted with ground nutmeg.

1 env. unflavored gelatin	¾ c. canned mashed
⅓ c. brown sugar, packed	pumpkin
¼ tsp. salt	¼ c. sugar
1 tsp. ground cinnamon	1 (9-inch) baked pie shell
¼ tsp. ground allspice	1 c. heavy cream
2 eggs, separated	2 tblsp. sugar
¾ c. evaporated milk	1 tsp. vanilla
¼ c. water	

Carmelized Almonds
Place ¼ c. blanched almonds and 2 tblsp. sugar in skillet. Cook, stirring constantly, until golden brown. Pour on greased baking sheet at once. Cool and break apart. Sprinkle over chiffon pies at serving time.

Combine gelatin, brown sugar, salt, cinnamon, allspice, egg yolks, evaporated milk, water and pumpkin in top of double boiler. Beat until smooth, using rotary beater. Cook, stirring constantly, over simmering water until mixture thickens, 5 to 7 minutes. Remove from heat.

Place double boiler top in bowl of iced water. Stir until mixture is room temperature. Remove from iced water; set aside.

Beat egg whites in bowl until foamy, using electric mixer at high speed. Gradually add ¼ c. sugar, beating until stiff, glossy peaks form. Fold pumpkin mixture into egg white mixture. Pour into baked pie shell. Chill in refrigerator until set.

Whip heavy cream, 2 tblsp. sugar and vanilla in chilled bowl until soft peaks form, using electric mixer at high speed. Spoon puffs of whipped cream on top of pie. Makes 6 to 8 servings.

PURPLE PLUM PIE

Cool, light and refreshing chiffon-like pie. Just right for dessert on a hot summer day.

1 (3-oz.) pkg. raspberry-flavored gelatin	2 (2-oz.) envs. whipped topping mix
1 c. boiling water	1 c. milk
1 (1-lb.) can pitted purple plums, drained	1 tsp. vanilla
½ c. cold water	1 (9-inch) baked pie shell

Dissolve raspberry gelatin in boiling water in bowl.

Place drained plums and ½ c. cold water in blender jar.

Blend until mixture is in small chunks (do not blend until smooth). Stir plum mixture into gelatin. Refrigerate until mixture mounds slightly when dropped from a spoon.

Prepare 2 envs. whipped topping mix with milk and vanilla according to package directions. Divide prepared topping in half. Fold one half into gelatin mixture. Pour gelatin mixture into baked pie shell. Chill pie in refrigerator until set. Chill remaining prepared topping.

To serve, top pie with puffs of remaining prepared topping. Makes 6 to 8 servings.

WHITE CHRISTMAS PIE

Snowy white, delicate chiffon pie with mild almond flavor decorated with coconut and red maraschino cherries.

1 env. unflavored gelatin	½ c. heavy cream, whipped
¼ c. cold water	3 egg whites
½ c. sugar	¼ tsp. cream of tartar
4 tblsp. flour	½ c. sugar
½ tsp. salt	1½ c. flaked coconut
1½ c. milk	1 (9-inch) baked pie shell
¾ tsp. vanilla	Sweetened whipped cream
¼ tsp. almond extract	Red maraschino cherries

Soften gelatin in cold water.

Combine ½ c. sugar, flour and salt in 2-qt. saucepan. Gradually stir in milk. Cook over medium heat, stirring constantly, until mixture comes to a boil. Cook 1 minute. Remove from heat. Stir in softened gelatin. Cool at room temperature until partially set.

Blend in vanilla and almond extract. Fold in whipped cream.

Beat egg whites with cream of tartar in bowl until foamy, using electric mixer at high speed. Gradually add ½ c. sugar, beating until stiff, glossy peaks form. Fold gelatin mixture into egg white mixture. Fold in 1 c. of the coconut. Pour mixture into baked pie shell. Sprinkle with remaining ½ c. coconut. Chill in refrigerator until set.

Serve decorated with puffs of sweetened whipped cream and red maraschino cherries. Makes 6 to 8 servings.

CHERRY CREAM PIE

Keep these ingredients handy for a lovely, last-minute cherry-topped dessert.

1 (3¼-oz.) pkg. vanilla pudding and pie filling mix	¼ tsp. vanilla
	1 (9-inch) baked pie shell
	1 (21-oz.) jar cherry pie filling
2 c. milk	
2 egg yolks	
1 tblsp. butter or regular margarine	¼ tsp. almond extract

Combine pudding mix and milk in 2-qt. saucepan. Cook over medium heat, stirring constantly, until mixture comes to a boil. Cook 1 minute. Remove from heat.

Beat egg yolks slightly, using a fork. Stir a small amount of hot mixture into egg yolks. Immediately pour back into remaining hot mixture, blending thoroughly. Cook 2 more minutes over low heat, stirring constantly. Remove from heat. Gently stir in butter and vanilla. Cool 5 minutes.

Pour slightly cooled filling into baked pie shell. Chill in refrigerator until set.

Before serving, combine cherry pie filling with almond extract; mix well. Spread cherry mixture over top of filling. Makes 6 to 8 servings.

BANANA CREAM PIE

An outstanding pie featuring the traditional layer of sliced bananas spread with creamy custard and topped with whipped cream.

¾ c. sugar	1 tsp. vanilla
2 tblsp. flour	2 large bananas, sliced
2 tblsp. cornstarch	1 (9-inch) baked pie shell
¼ tsp. salt	1 c. heavy cream
2 c. milk	2 tblsp. sugar
3 egg yolks	½ tsp. vanilla
2 tblsp. butter or	
regular margarine	

Combine ¾ c. sugar, flour, cornstarch and salt in 3-qt. saucepan. Gradually stir in milk. Cook over medium heat, stirring constantly until mixture comes to a boil. Cook 2 minutes. Remove from heat.

Beat egg yolks slightly, using a fork. Stir a small amount of hot mixture into egg yolks. Immediately pour yolk mixture back into remaining hot mixture, blending thoroughly. Cook 2 more minutes, stirring constantly. Remove from heat. Gently stir in butter and 1 tsp. vanilla. Cool 5 minutes.

Place sliced bananas in bottom of baked pie shell. Pour slightly cooled pudding over bananas. Chill in refrigerator until set, about 3 hours.

To serve, whip heavy cream with 2 tblsp. sugar and ½ tsp. vanilla in chilled bowl until soft peaks form, using electric mixer at high speed. Spread whipped cream over top of pie. Makes 8 servings.

COCONUT CREAM PIE

Whipped cream is folded into the coconut custard filling to make it light and delicate.

⅔ c. sugar	2 tsp. vanilla
¼ c. cornstarch	1 c. heavy cream, whipped
¼ tsp. salt	1⅓ c. flaked coconut
2½ c. milk	1 (9-inch) baked pie shell
3 egg yolks	
1 tblsp. butter or	
regular margarine	

Combine sugar, cornstarch and salt in 3-qt. saucepan. Gradually stir in milk. Cook over medium heat, stirring constantly, until mixture comes to a boil. Cook 2 minutes. Remove from heat.

Beat egg yolks slightly, using a fork. Stir a small amount of hot mixture into egg yolks. Immediately pour yolk mixture back into remaining hot mixture, blending thoroughly. Cook 2 more minutes over low heat, stirring constantly. Remove from heat. Gently stir in butter and vanilla. Cool completely.

Fold whipped cream into cooled filling. Then fold in 1 c. of the coconut. Pour mixture into baked pie shell. Chill in refrigerator until set, about 2 hours. Sprinkle top of pie with the remaining ⅓ c. coconut before serving. Makes 6 to 8 servings.

MERINGUE PIES

Light-as-air meringue makes a tempting topping on many different pies. It bakes high and fluffy with golden brown peaks and makes your pies picture-pretty.

Here are the basic steps for making a meringue for pies:

Step 1—Separating Eggs. Separate the eggs as soon as you have removed them from the refrigerator. They separate more easily when cold. Let them stand until they are room temperature, because then they will beat to a much higher volume.

Step 2—Beating. Place the egg whites in small bowl of electric mixer. Add cream of tartar. Beat at high speed until mixture is frothy. Do not beat them until they are stiff!

Step 3—Adding Sugar. Gradually add the sugar, about a tablespoon at a time, beating well after each addition, about 30 seconds. The sugar sweetens the foam and keeps the tiny bubbles of egg white pliant so that the meringue can stretch to its maximum volume. Adding the sugar at the proper time is a very important step. Adding the sugar at the frothy stage helps to prevent beading of the baked meringue, which is caused by sugar that is not thoroughly dissolved.

Step 4—Testing for Stiffness. Continue to beat until stiff, glossy peaks are formed. To test for stiff peaks, slowly withdraw the egg beater and hold up. The meringue should form pointed peaks so stiff they stand upright and don't curl over.

Step 5—Topping the Pie. With a tablespoon, place mounds of meringue around the edge of the filling. To prevent shrinking, spread the meringue so that it touches the inner edge of the crust all around. Heap remaining meringue in center of pie and push very gently out to the border. With back of spoon, pull up points of meringue or make deep swirls.

Step 6—Baking. Bake according to recipe directions. When baked, the meringue should be a very delicate brown. Cool on a rack away from drafts.

PEANUT BUTTER MERINGUE PIE

The unusual peanut butter-flavored crumbs lining the pie shell and decorating the top make this special.

¾ c. sifted confectioners sugar	3 eggs, separated
⅓ c. creamy peanut butter	2 tblsp. butter or regular margarine
1 (9-inch) baked pie shell	1 tsp. vanilla
3 tblsp. cornstarch	¼ tsp. cream of tartar
¾ c. sugar	1 tsp. cornstarch
⅛ tsp. salt	2 tblsp. sifted confectioners sugar
2 c. milk	

Place ¾ c. confectioners sugar in bowl. Cut in peanut butter until mixture resembles coarse meal, using pastry blender. Sprinkle one half of crumb mixture in baked pie shell, reserving remaining crumb mixture.

Combine 3 tblsp. cornstarch, sugar, and salt in top of double boiler. Gradually stir in milk. Cook over boiling water, stirring constantly, until mixture thickens. Cover and cook 10 minutes, stirring occasionally.

Beat egg yolks slightly, using a fork. Stir a small amount of hot mixture into egg yolks. Immediately pour yolk mixture back into remaining hot mixture, blending thoroughly. Cook 2 more minutes, stirring constantly. Remove from heat. Gently stir in butter and vanilla. Let mixture cool while preparing meringue.

To make meringue, beat egg whites, cream of tartar and 1 tsp. cornstarch in bowl until foamy, using electric mixer at high speed. Gradually add 2 tblsp. confectioners sugar, beating well after each addition. Continue beating until stiff, glossy peaks form when beaters are slowly lifted.

Pour slightly cooled filling into baked pie shell. Spoon some of the meringue around edge of filling. Spread meringue so it touches inner edge of crust all around, using back of spoon. Heap remaining meringue in center. Push out gently to meet meringue border. Sprinkle with remaining crumb mixture.

Bake in 350° oven 12 to 15 minutes or until meringue is lightly browned. Cool on rack. Makes 6 to 8 servings.

BUTTERSCOTCH MERINGUE PIE

We recommend using dark brown sugar in this recipe because it adds more butterscotch flavor and color to the filling.

Nut Pastry
Add ⅔ c. ground pecans or walnuts to the dry ingredients in a basic pastry recipe. Good for butterscotch, chocolate and custard pies.

¾ c. dark brown sugar, packed	2 tsp. vanilla
3 tblsp. cornstarch	6 tblsp. sugar
2 c. milk	½ tsp. vanilla
3 eggs, separated	1 (9-inch) baked pie shell
3 tblsp. butter or regular margarine	

Combine brown sugar and cornstarch in 2-qt. saucepan. Gradually stir in milk. Cook over medium heat, stirring constantly, until mixture comes to a boil. Cook 1 minute. Remove from heat.

Beat egg yolks slightly, using a fork. Stir a small amount of hot mixture into egg yolks. Immediately pour yolk mixture back into remaining hot mixture, blending thoroughly. Cook 2 more minutes over low heat, stirring constantly. Remove from heat. Gently stir in butter and 2 tsp. vanilla. Let mixture cool. Prepare meringue.

To make meringue, beat egg whites in bowl until foamy, using electric mixer at high speed. Gradually add 6 tblsp. sugar, 1 tblsp. at a time, beating well after each addition. Add ½ tsp. vanilla. Continue beating until stiff, glossy peaks form when beaters are slowly lifted.

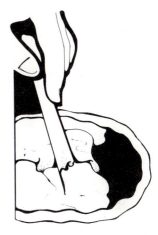

Pour slightly cooled filling into baked pie shell. Spoon some of the meringue around edge of filling. Spread meringue so it touches inner edge of crust all around, using back of spoon. Heap remaining meringue in center. Push out gently to meet meringue border.

Bake in 350⁰ oven 12 to 15 minutes or until meringue is lightly browned. Cool on rack. Makes 6 to 8 servings,

COTTAGE CHEESE MERINGUE PIE

A cheesecake-like filling with a hint of lemon is topped with a delicate and lovely meringue.

1 c. small curd cottage cheese	2 tblsp. butter or regular margarine
½ c. sugar	3 tblsp. lemon juice
¼ c. flour	1½ tsp. grated lemon rind
⅔ c. milk	¼ c. sugar
2 eggs, separated	1 (8-inch) baked pie shell

Place cottage cheese in blender jar. Blend until smooth; set aside.

Combine ½ c. sugar and flour in 2-qt. saucepan. Gradually stir in milk. Cook over medium heat, stirring constantly, until mixture thickens. Remove from heat.

Beat egg yolks slightly, using a fork. Stir a small amount of hot mixture into egg yolks. Immediately pour yolk mixture back into remaining hot mixture, blending thoroughly. Cook 2 more minutes over low heat, stirring constantly. Remove from heat. Gently stir in cottage cheese, butter, lemon juice and lemon rind. Let mixture cool while preparing meringue.

To make meringue, beat egg whites in bowl until foamy, using electric mixer at high speed. Gradually add ¼ c. sugar, 1 tblsp. at a time, beating until stiff, glossy peaks form when beaters are slowly lifted.

Pour slightly cooled filling into baked pie shell. Spoon some of the meringue around edge of filling. Spread meringue so it touches inner edge of crust all around, using back of spoon. Heap remaining meringue in center. Push out gently to meet meringue border.

Bake in 325° oven 15 minutes or until meringue is lightly browned. Cool on rack. Makes 6 servings.

Buckling Pie Shell
If your pie shell buckles, you've added too few fork pricks on sides and bottom of the unbaked pastry.

LIME MERINGUE PIE

We added a bit of food coloring to give this filling an especially inviting lime green color. Tart and light.

1 c. sugar	5 tblsp. lime juice
4 tblsp. cornstarch	1 tsp. grated lime rind
¼ tsp. salt	6 tblsp. sugar
1½ c. cold water	2 drops green food coloring
3 eggs, separated	
2 tblsp. butter or regular margarine	1 (9-inch) baked pie shell

Combine ½ c. of the sugar, cornstarch and salt in top of double boiler; mix well. Gradually add cold water, stirring well. Cook over boiling water, stirring constantly, until mixture thickens and mounds when dropped from a spoon. Cover and cook 10 more minutes, stirring occasionally.

Combine egg yolks and remaining ½ c. sugar; mix well. Stir a small amount of hot mixture into egg yolk-sugar mixture. Immediately pour yolk mixture back into remaining hot mixture, blending thoroughly. Cook 2 more minutes, stirring constantly. Remove from heat. Add butter, lime juice and lime rind. Do not stir. Let mixture cool while preparing meringue.

To make meringue, beat egg whites in bowl until foamy, using electric mixer at high speed. Gradually add 6 tblsp. sugar, 1 tblsp. at a time, beating well after each addition. Continue beating until stiff, glossy peaks form when beaters are slowly lifted.

Gently stir slightly cooled filling until blended. Then stir in green food coloring. Pour slightly cooled lime filling into baked pie shell. Spoon some of the meringue around edge of filling. Spread the meringue so it touches inner edge of crust all around, using back of spoon. Heap remaining meringue in center. Push out gently to meet meringue border.

Bake in 325⁰ oven 12 to 15 minutes or until meringue is lightly browned. Cool on racks. Makes 6 to 8 servings.

LEMON-ORANGE MERINGUE PIE

*A double citrus-flavored pie blending the gentle flavor of oranges
with the tangy taste of lemons. So refreshing.*

1 c. sugar	2 tblsp. lemon juice
4 tblsp. cornstarch	3 tblsp. orange juice
¼ tsp. salt	1 tsp. grated lemon rind
1½ c. cold water	1½ tsp. grated orange rind
3 eggs, separated	6 tblsp. sugar
2 tblsp. butter or	1 (9-inch) baked pie shell
regular margarine	

Combine ½ c. of the sugar, cornstarch and salt in top of double
boiler; mix well. Gradually add cold water, stirring well. Cook over
boiling water, stirring constantly, until mixture thickens and
mounds when dropped from a spoon. Cover and cook 10 more
minutes, stirring occasionally.

Combine egg yolks and remaining ½ c. sugar; mix well. Stir a
small amount of hot mixture into egg yolk-sugar mixture. Immediately pour yolk mixture back into remaining hot mixture, blending
thoroughly. Cook 2 more minutes, stirring constantly. Remove
from heat. Add butter, lemon juice, orange juice, lemon rind and
orange rind. Do not stir. Let mixture cool. Prepare meringue.

To make meringue, beat egg whites in bowl until foamy, using
electric mixer at high speed. Gradually add 6 tblsp. sugar, 1 tblsp. at
a time, beating well after each addition. Continue beating until stiff,
glossy peaks form when beaters are slowly lifted.

Gently stir slightly cooled filling until blended. Pour filling into
baked pie shell. Spoon some of the meringue around edge of filling.
Spread meringue so it touches inner edge of crust all around, using
back of spoon. Heap remaining meringue in center. Push out gently
to meet meringue border.

Bake in 325° oven 15 minutes or until meringue is lightly browned.
Cool on rack. Makes 6 to 8 servings.

BANANA MERINGUE PIE

Lovely, smooth vanilla-flavored custard layered with sliced bananas and swirled with a golden brown meringue.

⅔ c. sugar	1 tsp. vanilla
¼ c. cornstarch	6 tblsp. sugar
½ tsp. salt	1 (9-inch) baked pie shell
2½ c. milk	2 medium bananas, sliced
3 eggs, separated	

Combine ⅔ c. sugar, cornstarch and salt in top of double boiler. Gradually stir in milk. Cook over boiling water, stirring constantly, until mixture thickens and mounds when dropped from a spoon. Cover and cook 10 more minutes, stirring occasionally.

Beat egg yolks slightly, using a fork. Stir a small amount of hot mixture into egg yolks. Immediately pour yolk mixture back into remaining hot mixture, blending thoroughly. Cook 2 more minutes, stirring constantly. Remove from heat. Gently stir in vanilla. Let mixture cool while preparing meringue.

To make meringue, beat egg whites in bowl until foamy, using electric mixer at high speed. Gradually add 6 tblsp. sugar, 1 tblsp. at a time, beating well after each addition. Continue beating until stiff, glossy peaks form when beaters are slowly lifted.

Pour a little slightly cooled filling into baked pie shell. Arrange sliced bananas over filling. Top with remaining filling. Spoon some of the meringue around edge of filling. Spread meringue so it touches inner edge of crust all around, using back of spoon. Heap remaining meringue in center. Push out gently to meet meringue border.

Bake in 325° oven 12 to 15 minutes or until meringue is lightly browned. Cool on rack. Makes 6 to 8 servings.

LEMON MERINGUE PIE

An all-American favorite. This pie features a tangy smooth custard topped with a delicately browned meringue.

1 c. sugar	5 tblsp. lemon juice
4 tblsp. cornstarch	1½ tsp. grated lemon rind
¼ tsp. salt	6 tblsp. sugar
1½ c. cold water	1 (9-inch) baked pie shell
3 eggs, separated	
2 tblsp. butter or	
regular margarine	

Tough Pastry
If your pastry is tough, perhaps you mixed it too long, handled it too much or used too much water. Good pastry takes speed, a light hand and deft rolling.

Combine ½ c. of the sugar, cornstarch and salt in top of double boiler; mix well. Gradually add cold water, stirring well. Cook over boiling water, stirring constantly, until mixture thickens and mounds when dropped from a spoon. Cover and cook 10 more minutes, stirring occasionally.

Combine egg yolks and remaining ½ c. sugar; mix well. Stir a small amount of hot mixture into egg yolk-sugar mixture. Immediately pour yolk mixture back into remaining hot mixture, blending thoroughly. Cook 2 more minutes, stirring constantly. Remove from heat. Add butter, lemon juice and lemon rind. Do not stir. Let mixture cool while preparing meringue.

To make meringue, beat egg whites in bowl until foamy, using electric mixer at high speed. Gradually add 6 tblsp. sugar, 1 tblsp. at a time, beating well after each addition. Continue beating until stiff, glossy peaks form when beaters are slowly lifted.

Gently stir lemon filling until blended. Pour slightly cooled lemon filling into baked pie shell. Spoon some of the meringue around edge of filling. Spread meringue so it touches inner edge of crust all around, using back of spoon. Heap remaining meringue in center. Push out gently to meet meringue border.

Bake in 325° oven 12 to 15 minutes or until meringue is lightly browned. Cool on rack. Makes 6 to 8 servings.

CHOCOLATE CINNAMON PIE

A spicy, buttery cocoa mixture is swirled into a crisp meringue shell in this refrigerated pie. So easy to make.

Meringue Crust
  (recipe follows)
½ c. butter or
  regular margarine
¾ c. sugar
½ c. plus 2 tblsp.
  baking cocoa
1 tsp. ground cinnamon

2 eggs
1 (2-oz.) env. whipped
  topping mix
½ c. milk
½ tsp. vanilla
1 (1-oz.) square semi-
  sweet chocolate

Prepare Meringue Crust.

Cream together butter and sugar in bowl until light and fluffy, using electric mixer at high speed. Add cocoa and cinnamon. Add eggs, one at a time, beating well after each addition (about 5 minutes).

Prepare whipped topping mix with milk and vanilla according to package directions. Fold prepared whipped topping into chocolate mixture. Turn into Meringue Crust. Cover and refrigerate 2 hours or until set.

Cut semisweet chocolate into shavings, using vegetable peeler. Use chocolate shavings to decorate pie before serving. Makes 6 to 8 servings.

Meringue Crust: Beat together 2 egg whites, dash of salt and ½ tsp. vinegar in bowl until foamy, using electric mixer at high speed. Gradually add ⅔ c. sugar, beating until very stiff glossy peaks form. Beat in ¼ tsp. vanilla. Spread meringue on bottom and sides of well-greased 9-inch pie plate. Bake in 275° oven 1 hour, or until light brown and crisp to touch. Cool on rack.

SNOW-CAPPED CHOCOLATE PIE

Thick and deliciously chewy pecan-chocolate meringue crust filled with whipped cream and decorated with grated chocolate.

3 egg whites	1 c. buttery cracker
1 tsp. vanilla	crumbs
¾ c. sugar	½ c. chopped pecans
1 tsp. baking powder	1 c. heavy cream
1 (4-oz.) bar German	2 tblsp. sugar
sweet chocolate,	1 tsp. vanilla
grated	

Beat egg whites and 1 tsp. vanilla in bowl until foamy, using electric mixer at high speed. Gradually add ¾ c. sugar and baking powder, beating until stiff peaks are formed.

Reserve 2 tblsp. grated chocolate for topping. Fold remaining grated chocolate, cracker crumbs and pecans into egg white mixture. Spread on bottom and sides of greased 9-inch pie plate.

Bake in 325° oven 25 minutes or until lightly browned. Cool on rack.

Whip cream in bowl until it begins to thicken, using electric mixer at high speed. Gradually add 2 tblsp. sugar and 1 tsp. vanilla, beating until soft peaks form. Turn into meringue shell. Sprinkle with reserved 2 tblsp. grated chocolate. Cover and refrigerate 6 to 8 hours or overnight. Makes 6 to 8 servings.

Meringue Shells
Choose a cool, dry day to make meringue shells, if possible. Humidity often softens meringues.

CREAM-FILLED MERINGUE PIE

A meringue crust with ground pecans and cracker crumbs is the unique feature of this pie. Top with whipped cream and pecans.

3 egg whites	1 c. ground pecans
½ tsp. cream of tartar	1½ c. heavy cream
1 c. sugar	3 tblsp. sugar
2 tsp. vanilla	1 tsp. vanilla
½ c. unsalted soda	¼ c. chopped pecans
cracker crumbs	

Beat egg whites with cream of tartar in bowl until foamy, using electric mixer at high speed. Gradually add 1 c. sugar, beating until very stiff peaks form. Beat in 2 tsp. vanilla. Fold in cracker crumbs and 1 c. ground pecans. Spread meringue mixture on bottom and sides of well-greased 9-inch pie plate.

Bake in 350° oven 40 minutes, or until very delicately browned. Cool on rack.

Whip heavy cream, 3 tblsp. sugar and 1 tsp. vanilla in chilled bowl until soft peaks form, using electric mixer at high speed. Spread cream mixture over baked meringue layer. Sprinkle with ¼ c. chopped pecans. Chill until serving time. Makes 6 to 8 servings.

FRUIT AND CREAM TART

A festive "pizza" made with pie crust, cream cheese filling and a decorative topping of glazed fruit.

Pastry for 2-crust 9-inch pie	**¼ c. water**
1 (3-oz.) pkg. cream cheese, softened	**½ c. orange juice**
	¼ c. lemon juice
¾ c. sugar	**1 pt. fresh strawberries**
1 tblsp. milk	**1 (11-oz.) can mandarin orange segments drained**
1 tblsp. grated orange rind	
⅔ c. heavy cream	
2 tblsp. cornstarch	**2 medium bananas, sliced**

Prepare pastry.

Roll out pastry on floured surface to 15-inch circle. Line 14-inch pizza pan or baking sheet with pastry. Form ½-inch rim; flute edge.

Bake in 425° oven 12 to 15 minutes or until golden brown. Cool on rack.

Combine cream cheese, ¼ c. of the sugar, milk and orange rind in bowl. Beat with electric mixer at medium speed until smooth. Gradually add heavy cream, beating until thick and creamy. Spread mixture over cooled pizza crust. Refrigerate.

Combine remaining ½ c. sugar and cornstarch in 2-qt. saucepan. Stir in water, orange juice and lemon juice. Cook over medium heat, stirring constantly, until mixture comes to a boil and is thick and clear. Cook 1 minute. Remove from heat. Let mixture cool while preparing fruit.

Reserve 3 large strawberries with leaves; set aside. Hull remaining strawberries and cut in slices. Arrange sliced strawberries around inner edge of crust. Then form a ring of sliced bananas. Continue making concentric circles with mandarin oranges and remaining bananas. Place any remaining sliced strawberries in last ring with whole strawberries in center. Spoon cooled sauce evenly over all fruit. Chill in refrigerator at least 2 hours before serving. Makes 12 to 16 servings.

MAIN-DISH PIES

On a bitter cold winter night, farm women like to warm their families up with a complete meal in a pie piping hot from the oven.

Fork-tender meat combined with vegetables and a rich, savory gravy nestled between a light, flaky pie crust is a much-requested meal, especially by the men in the family.

Here is an inviting assortment of homemade pies that have been great favorites in farm homes for years. Besides the double-crust pies, we have one-crust pies filled with delicious combinations of hearty, healthful ingredients. And you'll find some intriguing crusts here, too. A puffy mashed potato crust or a spicy golden brown stuffing crust are a delicious change from the conventional pie pastry.

Busy farm women love this meal, too, because all they need to round it out are a crisp tossed salad, and ice cream or fruit for dessert.

HAMBURGER PIE

A hot Vegetable Sauce containing peas, carrots and parsley in a thickened beef base is the highlight of this pie.

1 tblsp. cooking oil	1 tsp. chili powder
1½ lbs. ground beef	Dash of Tabasco sauce
½ c. chopped celery	Pastry for 2-crust
¼ c. chopped green pepper	9-inch pie
1 clove garlic, minced	Sesame seeds
1 (8-oz.) can tomato sauce	Vegetable Sauce
1 tblsp. Worcestershire	(recipe follows)
sauce	

Heat cooking oil in 10-inch skillet over medium heat. Add ground beef and cook until meat begins to change color. Add celery, green pepper and garlic. Saute until mixture is well browned. Add tomato sauce, Worcestershire sauce, chili powder and Tabasco sauce. Simmer, uncovered, 15 minutes. Remove from heat; cool completely.

Meanwhile, divide pastry almost in half. Roll out larger half on floured surface to 12-inch circle. Line 9-inch pie plate with pastry. Trim edge to 1 inch.

Pour cooled meat mixture into pastry-lined pie plate.

Roll out remaining pastry. Cut into ½-inch strips. Lay half of strips over filling about 1 inch apart. Repeat with remaining strips, placing them in the opposite direction, forming a diamond or square pattern. Trim strips even with pie edge. Turn bottom crust up over ends of strips. Press firmly to seal edge. Flute edge. Sprinkle pastry strips with sesame seeds.

Bake in 400° oven 25 minutes or until golden brown. Let stand 10 minutes before serving. Pass Vegetable Sauce to ladle over wedges. Makes 6 to 8 servings.

Vegetable Sauce: Melt 3 tblsp. butter or regular margarine in 2-qt. saucepan. Stir in ¼ c. flour. Gradually stir in 2 c. beef bouillon. Cook over medium heat, stirring constantly, until thickened. Add 1 c. cooked peas, 1 c. diced, cooked carrots and 1 tblsp. chopped fresh parsley. Heat thoroughly.

GROUND BEEF-CHEESE PIE

This main-dish pie is so simple-to-fix because its custard has a mayonnaise base. No top crust is needed.

¾ lb. ground beef	¾ c. mayonnaise
½ c. finely chopped onion	¾ c. milk
	4 tsp. cornstarch
2 c. shredded Cheddar cheese	3 eggs
	½ tsp. salt
1 (9-inch) unbaked pie shell with fluted edge	⅛ tsp. pepper

Cook ground beef and onion in 10-inch skillet over medium heat until well browned. Remove from heat.

Arrange hot beef mixture and Cheddar cheese in unbaked pie shell.

Combine mayonnaise, milk, cornstarch, eggs, salt and pepper in bowl. Beat until smooth, using rotary beater. Pour egg mixture over beef mixture in pie shell.

Bake in 350° oven 35 minutes, or until golden brown and puffy. Let stand 10 minutes before serving. Makes 6 to 8 servings.

SAVORY SAUSAGE AND POTATO PIE

This easy-to-make pie crust is made with mashed potatoes, corn-flake crumbs and egg. It's flecked with parsley.

Potato Crust
  (recipe follows)
1 lb. bulk pork sausage
½ c. green pepper strips
2 tsp. cornstarch
1 (10½-oz.) can mushroom
  gravy

1 (12-oz.) can Mexican-
  style corn, drained
1 c. shredded Cheddar
  cheese

Prepare Potato Crust.

Spread Potato Crust mixture evenly in greased 10-inch pie plate.

Brown pork sausage in 10-inch skillet, breaking up into chunks with spoon. Remove and drain on paper towels. Pour off all fat except 1 tblsp. Add green pepper to fat in skillet; saute 5 minutes or until tender-crisp. Stir in drained sausage and cornstarch. Add gravy and corn; mix well. Heat thoroughly. Pour hot filling into Potato Crust. Sprinkle with Cheddar cheese.

Bake in 400° oven 25 minutes or until golden brown. Let stand 10 minutes before serving. Makes 6 to 8 servings.

Potato Crust: Pare 1½ lbs. all-purpose potatoes (5 medium). Quarter potatoes and cook in boiling, salted water in saucepan over medium heat 25 minutes or until tender. Drain well and mash until smooth, using potato masher. Stir in 1 egg (beaten), ½ c. chopped onion, ½ c. cornflake crumbs and 2 tsp. dried parsley flakes; mix well.

CHICKEN AND STUFFING PIE

Leftover turkey works equally well in this recipe. The thyme and pimientos flavor the gravy.

Stuffing Crust
  (recipe follows)
1 (4-oz.) can sliced
  mushrooms
2 tsp. flour
1 tblsp. butter or
  regular margarine
½ c. chopped onion
1 (10½-oz.) can chicken
  giblet gravy

3 c. cubed, cooked chicken
1 c. frozen peas
2 tblsp. diced pimientos
1 tblsp. dried parsley
  flakes
1 tsp. Worcestershire sauce
½ tsp. dried thyme leaves
4 slices processed
  American cheese

Prepare Stuffing Crust.

Press Stuffing Crust mixture into greased 10-inch pie plate.

Drain mushrooms, reserving liquid. Stir flour into reserved mushroom liquid; set aside.

Melt butter in 10-inch skillet over medium heat. Add mushrooms and onion; saute until onion is tender. Add mushroom liquid mixture, gravy, chicken, peas, pimientos, parsley flakes, Worcestershire sauce and thyme. Heat thoroughly. Remove from heat.

Pour hot filling into Stuffing Crust.

Bake in 375° oven 20 minutes.

Meanwhile, cut each slice of American cheese into 4 strips. Place cheese strips on top of pie in a lattice design. Bake 5 more minutes. Let stand 10 minutes before serving. Makes 6 to 8 servings.

Stuffing Crust: Combine 1 (8-oz.) pkg. herb-seasoned stuffing mix, ¾ c. chicken broth, ½ c. melted butter or regular margarine and 1 egg (beaten) in bowl. Mix until moistened.

TUNA-CHEESE PIE

Most of these ingredients are in the average kitchen. Great recipe to keep handy for last-minute supper guests.

Pastry for 2-crust	**¼ tsp. salt**
9-inch pie	**⅛ tsp. pepper**
1 c. sliced, pared carrots	**1½ c. milk**
¼ tsp. salt	**1 tsp. Worcestershire sauce**
1 c. frozen peas	**1 c. shredded Cheddar**
3 tblsp. butter or	**cheese**
regular margarine	**2 (6½-oz.) cans tuna,**
¼ c. finely chopped onion	**drained and broken in**
3 tblsp. flour	**chunks**
½ tsp. dry mustard	

Divide pastry almost in half. Roll out larger half on floured surface to 12-inch circle. Line 9-inch pie plate with pastry. Trim edge to 1 inch.

Cook sliced carrots with ¼ tsp. salt in boiling water in saucepan 8 minutes. Add peas; cook 5 more minutes. Drain well. Rinse vegetables with cold water; drain well. Set aside.

Melt butter in 2-qt. saucepan. Add onion; sauté until tender. Stir in flour, mustard, ¼ tsp. salt and pepper. Cook 1 minute, stirring constantly. Gradually stir in milk and Worcestershire sauce. Cook, stirring constantly, until mixture comes to a boil. Add cheese, stirring until melted. Add tuna and cooked vegetables; mix well. Turn hot mixture into pastry-lined pie plate.

Roll out remaining pastry to 11-inch circle. Adjust top crust; flute edge and cut vents.

Bake in 400° oven 30 to 35 minutes or until crust is golden brown. Let stand 10 minutes before serving. Makes 6 to 8 servings.

CHICKEN-MUSHROOM QUICHE

Creamy custard filling, chock-full of sautéed mushrooms and onions, is poured over cubed chicken and grated Romano cheese.

Quiche Pastry
(recipe follows)

3 tblsp. butter or
regular margarine

¼ c. chopped onion

6 oz. fresh mushrooms,
sliced

⅓ c. grated Romano
cheese

1¼ c. cubed, cooked
chicken

½ c. shredded Swiss
cheese

2 eggs

1 c. light cream

3 drops Tabasco sauce

¼ tsp. salt

⅛ tsp. pepper

Prepare Quiche Pastry.

Roll out Quiche Pastry on floured surface to 15-inch circle. Line 10-inch quiche pan or 10-inch pie plate with pastry. Trim edge even with edge of quiche pan.

Melt butter in 10-inch skillet over medium heat. Add onion; sauté until tender. Add mushrooms; sauté until tender. Remove from heat.

Sprinkle Romano cheese in bottom of pastry-lined quiche pan. Layer chicken in pan; sprinkle with mushroom-onion mixture. Top with Swiss cheese.

Beat eggs in bowl until blended, using rotary beater. Add light cream, Tabasco sauce, salt and pepper; beat until blended. Pour over mixture in quiche pan.

Bake in 425° oven 10 minutes. Reduce temperature to 325° and bake 15 more minutes, or until knife inserted near center comes out clean. Let stand 5 minutes before serving. Makes 6 to 8 servings.

Quiche Pastry: Sift together 1½ c. sifted flour and ½ tsp. salt in bowl. Cut in ½ c. regular margarine until coarse crumbs form, using pastry blender. Sprinkle 4 to 5 tblsp. iced water over crumb mixture, a little at a time, stirring with fork until all the flour is moistened and a dough forms.

PORK-VEGETABLE PIE

Perfectly seasoned pork pie with carrots and green beans. Enhanced by an unusual herb-flavored flaky pastry.

Thyme-Seasoned Pastry (recipe follows)	$\frac{1}{16}$ tsp. pepper
3 tblsp. butter or regular margarine	1¼ c. chicken broth
1 c. chopped green pepper	¼ tsp. gravy browning
¼ c. chopped onion	2½ c. cubed, cooked pork
3 tblsp. flour	1 c. sliced, cooked carrots
1 tsp. salt	1½ c. cooked cut green beans
¼ tsp. ground ginger	1 egg yolk, beaten
⅛ tsp. dry mustard	2 tsp. water

Prepare Thyme-Seasoned Pastry.

Divide Thyme-Seasoned Pastry almost in half. Roll out larger half on floured surface to 12-inch circle. Line 9-inch pie plate with pastry. Trim edge to 1 inch.

Melt butter in 10-inch skillet over medium heat. Add green pepper and onion; saute until tender. Stir in flour, salt, ginger, mustard and pepper. Cook 1 minute, stirring constantly. Gradually stir in chicken broth. Cook, stirring constantly, until mixture comes to a boil. Remove from heat.

Stir in gravy browning, pork, carrots and green beans. Pour into pastry-lined pie plate.

Roll out remaining pastry to 11-inch circle. Adjust top crust; flute edge and cut vents. Combine egg yolk and water. Brush over top crust.

Bake in 400° oven 30 to 35 minutes, or until crust is golden brown. Let stand 10 minutes before serving. Makes 6 to 8 servings.

Thyme-Seasoned Pastry: Combine 2⅓ c. sifted flour, ¾ tsp. salt and ⅛ tsp. dried thyme leaves in bowl. Cut in ¾ c. regular margarine until coarse crumbs form, using pastry blender. Add 6 to 8 tblsp. iced water, a little at a time, tossing with fork until a dough forms.

MEATBALL-VEGETABLE PIE

Tiny meatballs tucked into a tomato sauce with carrots and peas. Colorful as well as tasty combination.

Flaky Pastry
  (recipe follows)
1 lb. ground beef
¾ c. soft bread crumbs
¼ c. minced onion
2 tblsp. chopped fresh
  parsley
1 tsp. salt
½ tsp. dried marjoram
  leaves
⅛ tsp. pepper
1 egg, slightly beaten
2 tblsp. milk
2 tblsp. cooking oil
1 (1-lb.) can stewed
  tomatoes
1 tblsp. cornstarch
2 beef bouillon cubes
1 c. frozen peas, thawed
1 c. sliced, cooked carrots

Prepare Flaky Pastry.

Divide Flaky Pastry almost in half. Roll out larger half on floured surface to 15-inch circle. Line 10-inch pie plate with pastry. Trim edge to 1 inch.

Combine ground beef, bread crumbs, onion, parsley, salt, marjoram, pepper, egg and milk in bowl. Mix lightly, but well. Divide mixture into fourths. Shape each fourth into 12 tiny meatballs.

Heat cooking oil in 10-inch skillet over medium heat. Brown meatballs in hot oil. Remove meatballs from skillet as they brown. Drain on paper towels. Pour off drippings from skillet.

Combine some of liquid from stewed tomatoes with cornstarch. Add cornstarch mixture, stewed tomatoes and bouillon cubes to skillet. Cook over medium heat, stirring constantly, until mixture comes to a boil. Stir in peas and carrots. Remove from heat.

Arrange meatballs in pastry-lined pie plate. Pour hot mixture over all. Roll out remaining pastry in 12-inch circle. Adjust top crust; flute edge and cut vents.

Bake in 400° oven 15 minutes. Reduce temperature to 350° and bake 25 more minutes, or until crust is golden brown. Let stand 10 minutes before serving. Makes 8 servings.

Flaky Pastry: Sift together 2⅔ c. sifted flour and ¾ tsp. salt into bowl. Cut in 1 c. regular margarine until mixture is crumbly, using pastry blender. Sprinkle crumb mixture with 7 to 8 tblsp. iced water, a little at a time, mixing well with a fork until flour is moistened and a dough forms.

STEAK AND POTATO PIE

Cubes of tender steak and potatoes in brown gravy encased in flaky pie crust. Add a green salad for a complete meal.

3 tblsp. flour	2 c. chopped onion
½ tsp. paprika	1¾ c. beef broth
⅛ tsp. pepper	2 c. diced, pared potatoes
⅛ tsp. ground ginger	Golden Pastry
⅛ tsp. ground allspice	(recipe follows)
1 lb. beef round steak,	1 egg yolk, beaten
cut in ½-inch cubes	1 tblsp. water
⅓ c. cooking oil	

Combine flour, paprika, pepper, ginger and allspice. Dredge steak cubes with flour mixture. Heat oil in 4-qt. Dutch oven. Brown steak cubes in hot oil, stirring frequently. When cubes begin to brown, stir in onion and cook mixture until well browned. Add beef broth. Bring to a boil; reduce heat and cover. Simmer 1 hour or until meat is tender. Add potatoes and cook 20 more minutes or until potatoes are tender. Remove from heat. Let mixture cool while preparing Golden Pastry.

Roll out two thirds of Golden Pastry on floured surface to 15-inch circle. Line 10-inch pie plate with pastry. Trim edge to ½ inch. Pour slightly cooled meat mixture into pastry-lined pie plate. Roll out remaining Golden Pastry to 12-inch circle. Adjust top crust; flute edge and cut vents. Combine egg yolk and water. Brush over top crust.

Bake in 400° oven 30 minutes, or until crust is golden brown. Let stand 10 minutes before serving. Makes 8 servings.

Golden Pastry: Sift together 2⅔ c. sifted flour and 1 tsp. salt into bowl. Cut in 1 c. shortening until coarse crumbs form, using pastry blender. Sprinkle 7 to 8 tblsp. iced water over crumb mixture, a little at a time, stirring with fork until all the flour is moistened and a dough forms.

Pie Crust Trimmings
Never reroll pie crust trimmings. Rerolling toughens crust. Instead, cut the trimmings into strips. Sprinkle with grated cheese or cinnamon and sugar. Bake and serve with coffee.

WHAT WENT WRONG WITH MY PIE?

My crust was very pale and dull looking—why?

It was either underbaked or you handled the pastry too much when you mixed it together and rolled it out. Handle pastry as little as possible.

My crust was smooth instead of blistery—why?

You may have added too much flour. That is easy to do when you roll it out on a floured surface. Use a pastry cloth, and rub the flour into the meshes until it almost disappears. A stockinet on the rolling pin, rubbed with flour, helps too.

My pie edge was uneven—why?

You may not have been careful when you shaped the pastry in the pie pan. Ease it in gently but be sure it's pressed firmly against the dish with no air bubbles.

My pie was shrunken—why?

This is a sure sign that you stretched the pastry when you fitted it into the pan.

My crust was very tough—why?

You probably added too much water to the flour and shortening. Or you could have added too much flour when rolling out the crust.

My crust was doughy and compact—why?

You might have added too much water. Add as little water as possible, but enough to be able to form the dough into a ball. The water should be added very gradually to the shortening-flour mixture.

My crust was dry and mealy—why?

The trouble could be that you didn't add enough water, but more likely you cut the shortening into the flour too finely.

Index

All-Purpose Baking Mix, 112
Almond(s)
    Bars, Chocolate-, 240
    Blanching of, 147
    Brunch Coffee Cake, 132
    -Cereal Cookies, Spicy, 256
    Cookies
        Refrigerator Cinnamon-, 254
        Spicy Walnut-, 259
    Filling, 74
    -Flavored
        Angel Food Cake, 191
        Pastry, 287
    Pastry, 289
    Toasting of, 166
Amish
    Oatmeal Cookies, 234
    Sugar Cookies, 220
Anadama Bread, 38
Angel Food Cake(s)
    Almond-Flavored, 191
    Party, 189
    Peppermint, 190
Apple
    Cakes
        Crumb-Topped, 160
        Sliced, 161
        Coffee Cake, 135
        Cookies, Peanut Butter-, 257
        Crumb Kuchen, 44
        Crunch Muffins, 119
        Honey Buns, 109
        -Pecan Drop Cookies, 232
    Pies
        Basic, 288
        Heritage Dutch, 294
        Old-Time Upside-down, 293
        -Puff, Easy, 295
        Sheet, 292
    Tart, Cinnamon, 294
Applesauce
    Bread, Spicy, 126
    Cake(s)
        Chocolate-, 168
        Spicy, 160
    Drop Cookies, Spicy, 224
    Fudgies, 245
    Layer Cake, 149
    Oatmeal Cookies, 230
Apricot
    Braid, 52
    Filling, 88, 273
    -Raspberry Pastry Bars, 292
    Squares, Grandmom's, 245

Bacon
    and Onion Muffins, 116
    -Onion Rolls, 64
Baking
    Basics of, The, 9-14
    Choose the right pans, 11
    Ingredients
        how to measure, 14
        Types of Wheat Flours, 12
    Powder, 141
    Soda, 141
    Tips
        Chopping sticky fruits, 165
        Eggs
            Don't wash, 161
            Fresh, 161
        Greasing pans, 88
        how to
            beat eggs, 153
            beat eggs slightly, 152
            grate lemon or orange peel, 242
            measure nuts, 204
        Measuring Liquids, 85
        on baking powder, 238
    Your oven, 12
Banana
    -Carrot Tea Loaf, 124
    Cream Pie, 314
    Custard Chiffon Cake, 202
    Meringue Pie, 321
    Nut Muffins, 118
    Walnut
        Bars, 156
        Bread, 125
Bar Cookies, 237-251, *see also* Cookies
Basic
    Apple Pie, 288
    Cake Frosting, 210
    Cherry Pie, 287
    Dinner Rolls, 58
    Raspberry Pie, 296
    Rhubarb Pie, 290
    Spicy Gingerbread, 176
    White
        Bread, 25
        Layer Cake, 144
Batter Breads, *see* Breads
Biscuit(s), *see* Breads
    Cutter, 107
Black Bottom Cupcakes, 204
Blue Ribbon Peppermint Chiffon, 203
Blueberry Pie, Fresh, 290
Blushing Peach Pie, 291
Bohemian Kolaches, 88

Boston Cream Pie, 147
Braided German Sweet Bread, 79
Bran
    Bread, Perfect, 32
    Muffins
        Country, 120
        Date Nut, 121
        Old-Fashioned, 121
Bread(s), 15-136
    Avoid excess flour, 67
    Croutons, 40
    Flour storage, 80
    how to measure flour, 62
    Quick, 105-136
        Baking Mix, All-Purpose, 112
        Biscuit(s), 106-111
            and Honey, 110
            Apple Honey Buns, 109
            Cheddar Cheese, 112
            Coarse-Textured, 108
            Curry, 112
            Extra-Good, Basic, 107
            Flaky Baking Powder, 108
            how to make flaky, 107
            Lopsided, how to avoid, 107
            Measure liquid carefully, 108
            Mile-High, 107
            Mix, Make-Ahead, 111
            Parmesan Cheese Crescents, 110
            Perfect, 108
            Pinwheels, Old-Fashioned, 108
            Sage, 112
            Steps for making, 106
            Swirls, Butterscotch, 110
        Coffee Cake(s), 112, 131-135
            Almond Brunch, 132
            Apple, 135
            Brown Sugar, 133
            Butter-Rich, 131
            Crumb, 131
            Peach Kuchen, 134
            Poppy Seed, 134
            Sour Cream-Pear, 135
        Corn Bread(s)
            Honey, 128
            Skillet, 128
        Easy Cinnamon, 132
        Irish Soda, 130
        Muffins, 113-121
            Apple Crunch, 119
            Bacon and Onion, 116
            Banana Nut, 118
            Basic Sweet, 113
            Bran

            Country, 120
            Old-Fashioned, 121
        Cheese, 115
        Chive, 120
        Coconut, 119
        Cornmeal, Golden, 116
        Cranberry, 114
        Date Nut Bran, 121
        Golden, 112
        Heirloom Raisin, 119
        High-Protein, 115
        in a basket, 114
        Molasses Refrigerator, 120
        Oatmeal, 118
        Pecan Cinnamon, 114
        Pumpkin, 117
            Oat, 117
        Spicy Apricot Oat, 115
        Steps for making, 113
        Surprise, 116
    Swiss Cheese-Whole Wheat, 129
    Tea, 122-127
        Banana
            -Carrot, 124
            Walnut, 125
        Candied Orange Rind, 126
        Carrot-Walnut, 125
        Cranberry Loaf, Festive, 127
        Lemon, 123
        Pineapple Nut, 124
        Prune, Purple Ribbon, 122
        Pumpkin, Grand Champion, 123
        Spicy Applesauce, 126
        Walnut Brown, 130
        What went wrong with my, 136
        Whole Wheat Raisin, 129
Salt, Watch that, 71
Yeast, 11-101
    Cheese Bread Sticks, 50
    Cinnamon Toast, 27
    Coffee Cake(s), 71-85
        Apricot Braid, 52
        Batter
            Apple Crumb Kuchen, 44
            Polish Babka, 46
            Quick Caramel Crunch, 44
            Regal Savarin Ring, 45
            Sally Lunn, 46
        Braided German Sweet, 79
        Christmas
            Coffee Ring, 81
            Eve Saffron Ring, 80
        Coconut Crown, 72
        Danish Kringle, 74

338

Extra-Large Honey-Maple, 82
Grandma's Cinnamon Bubble Ring, 82
Greek Orange Braid, 76
Italian Panettone, 85
Lemon Custard-Filled Crescent, 73
Maple Butter Twist, 71
Raisin Spice Tea Ring, 78
Russian Kulich, 84
Swedish Tea Ring, 77
Whole Wheat Maple Ring, 75
Expiration Date on, 100
Freezing, 29
Frozen Dough(s), 47-53
   Apricot Braid, 52
   Freezer
      Cinnamon Loaves, 49
      Orange Buns, 53
      White, 48
   Honey-Wheat Germ, 50
   Round Pumpernickel Loaves, 51
Fruits 'n' Nuts, 77
how to
   knead, 20
   make a chewy crust, 36
   make a tender crust, 36
Ingredients, Basic, 18
Individual Toast Cups, 26
Loaf(ves), 24-43, 48-52, 55
   Anadama, 38
   Batter, see also Coffee Cakes
      Herbed Sour Cream, 41
      Raisin-Cinnamon, 43
      Rich Egg, 42
   Caraway, 31
   Cinnamon
      Freezer, 49
      -Raisin, 37
   Frozen Doughs, 47-53
      Apricot Braid, 52
      Freezer White, 48
      Honey-Wheat Germ, 50
      Round Pumpernickel, 51
   Herbed Sour Cream, 41
   Honey-Wheat Germ, 50
   Pumpernickel
      Hearty, 30
      Round, 51
   Raisin
      Cinnamon-, 37
         Batter, 43
      Date-, 38
      Golden, 36
      Outstanding, 35
   Rich Egg Batter, 42

Rye Sandwich, 30
Sourdough, 55
Swiss Cheese-Mustard, 39
Three-Flavored Braid, 34
Welsh Rarebit, 40
White
   Basic, 25
   Cinnamon
      Glazed, 28
      Golden, 27
   Country-Style, 24
   Freezer, 48
   No-Knead French, 24
   Orange-Cinnamon Swirl, 26
   Sourdough, 55
   Southern, 26
White
   Whole Wheat
      Country-Style, 28
      -Potato, 32
Made with milk, 74
Overhang, 24
Pan selection, 39
Pizza, Homemade, 70
Rolls, 64-67, see also Sweet Rolls
   Bacon-Onion, 64
   Basic Dinner, 58
   Christmas Morning Brioche, 62
   Clover Leaf, 59
   Crescents, 59
   Frankfurter, Favorite, 65
   Golden Parmesan, 42
   Hamburger Buns
      Favorite, 65
      Mini, 66
   Melt-in-your-Mouth, 60
   Pan, 58
   Parker House, 58
      Easy, 61
   Potato, 60
   Refrigerated, 63
   Soft Dinner, 57
   Twin Roll-Ups, 58
   Whole Wheat Sandwich Buns, 66
Rounds, 48
Soft Pretzels, 68
Sourdough
   Biscuits, Golden, 56
   Bread, 55
   Modern Starter, 54
Shell-Top, 43
Stale flour, 96
Steps for making, 19
Streaky Bread, 35
Sweet Rolls, 86-100

Bohemian Kolaches, 88
Butterscotch Crescent, 89
Cinnamon Coffee, 95
Country-Style Sticky Buns, 93
Cream Cheese-Filled, 90
Danish-Style
  Helen's, 98
  Pastries, Mock, 99
Extra-Special Cinnamon, 97
Four-in-One, 86
Hot Cross Buns, 100
No-Knead Sticky Buns, 94
Orange
  Buns, Freezer, 53
  Butterfly, 87
Pennsylvania Dutch Cinnamon
Buns, 96
Pineapple
  Cinnamon Buns, 92
  Coconut Rolls, 86
Prune-Filled, 86
Raspberry/Almond, 86
Squash Buns, 87
Sticky Bun Variation, 91
Versatile Potato, 91
Toast Shells, 26
What went wrong with my, 101
Zweiback Toast, Homemade, 69
Brioche, Christmas Morning, 62
Broiled
  Icing, 163
  Peanut Butter Frosting, 156
  Praline Topping, 195
Brown
  Bread, Walnut, 130
  -Rim Butter Cookies, 221
  Sugar
  Coffee Cake, 133
  Cookies, Heirloom, 257
  Glaze, 89
  Syrup, 72
  Topping, 94
Browned Butter Frosting, 158
Brownie(s)
  Fudge-Marshmallow, 244
  Tri-Level, 146
Butter
  Balls, 288
  Cakes, 139, *See* Cakes
  Cookies
    Brown-Rim, 221
    Frosted Christmas, 221
    Jelly-Filled, 262
    No-Stick Rolled, 266

Cream
  Filling, 149, 271
  Frosting, 251
Frosting, 207
-Rich Coffee Cake, 131
Buttermilk
  Cinnamon Bars, 243
  Pie, Creamy, 300
Butterscotch
  Bars, 250
  Biscuit Swirls, 110
  Crescent Rolls, 89
  Meringue Pie, 317
  -Oatmeal Cookies, 222
  Wafers, Refrigerator, 254

Cake(s), 137-213
  Beating by hand, 177
  Butter, 143-187, 204-208
    Cupcakes, 204-208
      Black Bottom, 205
      Chunky Chocolate, 204
      Cocoa-Raisin, 207
      Lemon Crunch, 206
      Light Chocolate Brownie, 204
      Milk Chocolate, 206
      Orange, 208
      Spicy Raisin, 208
    Danish Prune, 158
    Fruitcake(s), 179-182
      Best-Ever, 179
      Loaves, Golden, 181
      Miniature, 180
      Rich, 182
    Layer
      Applesauce, 149
      Basic White, 144
      Boston Cream Pie, 147
      Chocolate Velvet, 154
      Coconut-Pecan, 148
      Date-Walnut, 153
      Lemon-Filled, 152
      Old-Fashioned Coconut, 150
      Strawberries and Cream Spectacular,
        151
      with Cherry Frosting, Yellow, 146
      with Orange Frosting, White, 145
    Oblong
      Apple, Sliced, 161
      Banana-Walnut Bars, 156
      Carrot-Pecan, 158
      Choco-Date, 164
      Chocolate

-Applesauce, 168
Foolproof, 163
Preacher, 166
-Raisin, 169
Spice, 164
Crumb-Topped Apple, 160
Frosted Coffee Bars, 172
Gingerbread
Crumb-Topped, 175
Heirloom, 175
Orange-Raisin, 159
Peanut Butter-Chocolate Chip, 167
Pineapple
-Carrot, 157
-Topped Cocoa, 166
Upside-Down, 177
Raisin
Old-Fashioned, 162
Surprise, 162
Spice, Heirloom, 172
Spicy Applesauce, 160
Squares
Marble Molasses, 174
Peanut Butter, 156
Sunday, 155
Pineapple Upside-Down, Skillet, 178
Pound Cake(s), 183-187
Confectioners Sugar, 184
Grandma's Chocolate, 185
Mary's Sugar, 187
Old-Fashioned, 183
Pumpkin, 186
Walnut, 184
Square
Gingerbread
Basic Spicy, 176
Old-Fashioned, 176
Marble Squares A la Mode, 168
with Lemon Sauce, Nutmeg, 173
Steps for making a, 143
Checkerboard, 169
Cherry-Chocolate, 170
Chocolate, Quick-Fix, 142
Cutting the, 142
Decorating
Basic Cake Frosting, 210
Floral Basket Cake, 211
Flowered Cupcakes, 212
how to
frost a cake for, 210
make a shell border, 210
make a stand-up leaf, 212
make drop flowers. 211
Make-Ahead Decorations, 210

Pink-Flowered Sheet, 212
Decoration(s)
Chopped Walnut, 185
Easy, 144
Foam
Angel Food, 189-191
Almond-Flavored, 191
don't grease pans, 189
Party, 189
Peppermint, 190
Steps for making an, 188
Chiffon, 199-203
Banana Custard, 202
Blue Ribbon Peppermint, 203
Cocoa, 199
Layer, Chocolate, 200
Orange, 201
Spicy, 200
Luscious Dessert, 190
Sponge, 192-198
Cake Roll, Strawberry-Filled, 196
Five-Egg, 194
Jelly Roll, My Favorite, 197
Lazy Daisy, 194
Lemon, 198
Pineapple Cream Roll, 196
Squares, Praline-Topped, 195
Strawberry, Special, 192
Flour, 140
Frosting(s), see Frostings
how to
beat egg whites until stiff, 195
beat eggs until thick and lemon-colored,
193
crack whole walnuts, 181
flour pans, 171
fold egg whites, 197
frost, 142
line cake pans, 151
Ingredients, Basic, 140
Polka Dot Decorations, 149
Pretty borders, 148
Simple design, 147
Star, 198
Strawberry-Filled Roll, 196
Toasted, 202
What went wrong with my, 213
Whipped Cream Frosted, 174
Candied Orange Rind Bread, 126
Candy Bar Pie, 303
Caramel
-Chocolate Bars, 241
Nut Slices, Refrigerator, 251
Caraway Loaves, 31

Carrot
  -Pecan Cake, 158
  -Pineapple, 157
  Tea Loaf, Banana-, 124
  -Walnut Bread, 125
Cheese
  Muffins, 115
  Pie, Ground Beef-, 327
  Pie, Tuna-, 329
Cherry
  -Chocolate Cake, 170
  Cream Pie, 313
  Pie, Basic, 287
  -Walnut Bars, 238
Chewy Coconut Macaroons, 225
Chicken
  and Stuffing Pie, 328
  -Mushroom Quiche, 330
Chiffon Cakes, *see* Cakes
  Pies,
    Lemon, 310
    Pumpkin, 311
Chive Muffins, 120
Choco-Date Cake, 164
Chocolate
  -Almond Bars, 240
  -Applesauce Cake, 168
  Bars, Caramel-, 241
  Cake(s)
    Cherry-, 170
    Foolproof, 163
    Preacher, 166
    Quick-Fix, 171
  Candy Pie, 305
  Chiffon Layer Cake, 200
  Chip Cake, Peanut Butter, 167
  Chip-Oatmeal Cookies, 224
  Cinnamon Pie, 323
  Cookies, Orange-, 231
  Cupcakes, Chunky, 204
  Date Cake, 170
  Drizzle, 199
  Drop Cookies, 229
  Glaze, 147, 244
  Icing, 246, 271
  Mousse Pie, 304
  -Peppermint Cookie trees, 278
  Pie, Snow-Capped, 324
  Pinwheels, Refrigerator, 255
  Raisin
    Cake, 169
    Oat Cookies, 226
  Spice Cake, 164
  -Vanilla Layered Bars, 237

Velvet
  Cake, 154
  Pie, 303
Christmas
  Coffee Ring, 81
  Eve Saffron Braid, 80
  Morning Brioche, 62
Chunky Chocolate Cupcakes, 204
Cinnamon
  Apple Tart, 294
  Bars, Buttermilk, 243
  Batter Loaf, Raisin-, 43
  Coffee
    Cake, Easy, 132
    Rolls, 95
  Crumb Topping, 161
  -Ice Cream Topping, 290
  -Pecan Topping, 161
  Pie, Chocolate, 323
  -Raisin
    Bread, 37
    Filling, 78
  Swirl Bread, Orange-, 26
Clover Leaf Rolls, 59
Cocoa
  Chiffon Cake, 199
  -Coffee Frosting, 206
  Cream Frosting, 200
  Creme Frosting, 166
  Icing, 167
  -Raisin Cupcakes, 207
Coconut
  Cookies, Snow-Capped, 262
  -Cornflake Crisps, 258
  Cream Pie, 314
  Crown Coffee Cake, 72
  Filling, 89
  how to tint, 158
  Lemon Bars, 242
  Muffins, 119
  -Oatmeal Cookies, 226
  -Pecan
    Layer Cake, 148
    Topping, 195
  Pie, Crusty, 299
Coffee Bars, Frosted, 172
Coffee Cake(s)
  Quick, 131-135
    Almond Brunch, 132
    Apple, 135
    Brown Sugar, 133
    Butter-Rich, 131
    Crumb, 131
    Easy Cinnamon, 132

Peach Kuchen, 134
Poppy Seed, 134
Sour Cream, 133
  -Pear, 135
Yeast
  Batter
    Apple Crumb Kuchen, 44
    Polish Babka, 46
    Quick Caramel Crunch, 44
    Regal Savarin Ring, 45
    Sally Lunn, 46
  Braided German Sweet, 79
  Christmas
    Coffee Ring, 81
    Eve Saffron Braid, 80
  Coconut Crown, 72
  Danish Kringle, 74
  Extra-Large Honey-Maple, 82
  Greek Orange Braid, 76
  Italian Panettone, 85
  Lemon Custard-Filled Crescent, 73
  Maple Butter Twist, 71
  Raisin Spice Tea Ring, 78
  Russian Kulich, 84
  Swedish Tea Ring, 77
  Whole Wheat Maple Ring, 75
Coffee Frosting, Cocoa-, 206
Confectioners Sugar
  Icing, 79, 84, 87, 96, 99, 243
  Pound Cake, 184
Cookie(s), 215-279
  Baking Sheets, 232
  Basket of, 247
  Bars
    Applesauce Fudgies, 245
    Buttermilk Cinnamon, 243
    Butterscotch, 250
    Caramel-Chocolate, 241
    Cherry-Walnut, 238
    Chocolate
      -Almond, 240
      -Vanilla Layered, 237
    Coconut Lemon, 242
    Cream Cheese, 240
    Date Meringue, 247
    Extra-Rich Two-Layer, 249
    Fudge-Marshmallow Brownies, 244
    Grandmom's Apricot Squares, 245
    Peanut Butter, 250
    Raisin Shortbread, 248
    Raspberry Jam Squares, 242
    Spicy Raisin, 230
    Strawberry Meringue, 249
    Tangy Lemon Squares, 247

Tri-Level Brownies, 246
Basic Tips, 218
Colored Sugars, 236
Cooling of, 226
Drop, 219-236
  Amish
    Oatmeal, 234
    Sugar, 220
  Apple-Pecan, 232
  Applesauce Oatmeal, 230
  Brown-Rim Butter, 221
  Butterscotch-Oatmeal, 222
  Chewy Coconut Meringue, 225
  Chocolate, 229
    Chip-Oatmeal, 224
    -Raisin Oat, 226
  Coconut-Oatmeal, 226
  Crisp
    Oatmeal, 228
    Peanut Butter, 233
  Farmhouse Walnut, 223
  Frosted
    Christmas Butter, 221
    Coconut-Orange, 232
  Grandmother's Ginger, 235
  Jumbo Oatmeal-Peanut Butter, 234
  Old-Fashioned Raisin, 228
  Orange-Chocolate, 231
  Raisin, 226
    Meringue Kisses, 236
    -Molasses, 223
  Sour Cream, 219
  Spicy Applesauce, 224
  Sugar, 222
  Texas Ranger, 230
  Walnut Meringue, 236
Gift boxes for, 245
how to
  drop, 230
  freeze, 254
  grease cookie sheets, 234
  store crisp, 225
  store soft, 223
Mixing and shaping, 218
Molded, 256-265
  Coconut-Cornflake Crisps, 258
  Crisp(s)
    Gingersnaps, 263
    Sesame, 260
    Sugar, 260
  Crispy Thin Gingersnaps, 264
  Heirloom Brown Sugar, 257
  Jelly-Filled Butter, 262

Peanut
    Butter, 261
      -Apple, 257
    Raisin, 258
Pecan-Oatmeal, 264
Snow-Capped Coconut, 262
Spicy
    Almond-Cereal, 256
    Ginger, 261
Walnut-Almond, Spicy, 259
Oven spacing, 230
Pressed, 276-278
    Chocolate-Peppermint, 278
    Peanut Butter, 277
    Spritz, 277
Refrigerator, 251-255
    Butterscotch Wafers, 254
    Caramel Nut Slices, 251
    Chocolate Pinwheels, 255
    Cinnamon-Almond, 254
    Oatmeal, 252
      Chippers, 253
    Old-Fashioned Ice Box, 253
    Quick Trick, 252
Rolled, 265-275
    Butter, 265
      No-stick, 266
    Cutters, 274
    Date
      -Filled Poinsettias, 275
      -Oatmeal Sandwich, 272
    Extra
      -Crisp, 269
      -Special Tea, 270
    Filled Vanilla Wafers, 271
    Goldilocks, 270
    Grandmother's Sugar, 267
    how to
      decorate, 266
      flour cookie cutter, 268
      paint, 267
    Molasses Crinkles, 268
    Old-Fashioned
      Date-Filled, 274
      Filled, 273
    Spicy Fruit, 268
    Shower Gift, 273
    Sugar, 270
      Old-Fashioned, 266
Shaped, 256
to cheer a sick boy, 220
Topping for unbaked, 257
Tree, 219
use cool baking sheets, 242

What went wrong with my, 279
Corn Bread
    Honey, 128
    Skillet, 128
Cornmeal Muffins, Golden, 116
Cottage Cheese
    Filling, 88
    Meringue Pie, 318
Country
    Bran Muffins, 120
    -Style
      Sticky Buns, 93
      White Bread, 24
      Whole Wheat Bread, 28
Cranberry
    Loaf, 127
    Muffins, 114
    Pie, Orange-Flavored, 288
    -Raspberry Pie, 289
Cream
    -Filled Meringue Pie, 324
    Sweetened, 296
Cream Cheese
    Bars, 240
    -Filled Rolls, 90
    Filling, 90
    Frosting, 165
Creamy
    Buttermilk Pie, 300
    Cherry Frosting, 146
    Coffee Frosting, 154
    Custard Filling, 147
    Lemon Filling, 73
    Nut Filling, 270
    Orange Frosting, 204
    Pecan Frosting, 148
Crescents, 59
Crisp(s)
    Coconut-Cornflake, 258
    Gingersnaps, 263
    Oatmeal Cookies, 228
    Peanut Butter Cookies, 233
    Sugar Cookies, 260
Crispy Thin Gingersnaps, 264
Crumb
    -Topped
      Apple Cake, 160
      Gingerbread, 175
    Topping, 117
Crust(s)
    Meringue, 323
    Oatmeal, 306
    Potato, 328
    Stuffing, 329

Vanilla Wafer, 305
Crusty Coconut Pie, 299
Cupcakes, *see* Cakes
Curry Biscuits, 112

Danish
   Kringle, 74
   Prune Cake, 158
   -Style Rolls, Helen's, 98
Date
   Cake(s)
      Choco-, 164
      Chocolate, 170
   -Filled Poinsettias, 275
   Filling, 272, 274
   Meringue Bars, 247
   Nut Bran Muffins, 121
   -Oatmeal Sandwich Cookies, 272
   -Peanut Filling, 275
   -Raisin Bread, 38
   -Walnut Cake, 153
Deep Chocolate Frosting, 170
Dinner Rolls, 57-64
   Bacon-Onion, 64
   Basic, 58
   Christmas Morning Brioche, 62
   Clover Leaf, 59
   Crescents, 59
   Melt-in-Your-Mouth, 60
   Pan, 58
   Parker House, 58
     Easy, 61
   Potato Yeast, 60
   Refrigerated Yeast, 63
   Soft, 57
   Twin Roll-Ups, 58
Double-Crust Fruit Pies, *see* Pies
Drop Sugar Cookies, 222

Easy
   Apple-Puff Pie, 295
   Cinnamon Coffee Cake, 132
   Parker House Rolls, 61
Egg White Glaze, 293
Elegant Fudge Pie, 304
Evaporated Milk Glaze, 286
Extra
   -Crisp Rolled Cookies, 269
   -Good Basic Biscuits, 107
   -Large Honey-Maple Coffee Cake, 82
   -Rich Two-Layer Bars, 249
   -Special

Cinnamon Rolls, 97
Tea Cookies, 270

Farmhouse Walnut Cookies, 223
Favorite Hamburger or Frankfurter Buns, 65
Festive Cranberry Loaf, 127
Fig Filling, 273
Filled Vanilla Wafers, 271
Filling(s)
   Almond, 74
   Apricot, 88, 273
   Butter Cream, 149, 271
   Cinnamon-Raisin, 78
   Coconut, 89
   Cottage Cheese, 88
   Cream Cheese, 90
   Creamy
      Custard, 147
      Nut, 270
   Date, 272, 274
      -Peanut, 275
   Fig, 273
   Honey, 81
   Lemon, 152
      Creamy, 73
   Maple-Cinnamon, 83
   Pecan, 75, 77
   Peppermint, 278
   Pineapple Cream, 197
   Prune, 273
Five-Egg Sponge Cake, 194
Flaky
   Baking Powder Biscuits, 108
   Biscuits, 107
   Pastry, 332
Floral Basket Cake, 211
Flour
   All-Purpose, 13
   Cake, 13
   Changes, 55
   Stone-Ground Whole Wheat, 13
   Whole Wheat, 13
Fluffy
   Frosting, 152
   Fruit Pie, 308
Foam Cake(s) 139, 188-203, *see also* Cakes
Foolproof Chocolate Cake, 163
Four-in-One Yeast Rolls, 86
Frankfurter Buns, Favorite, 65
Freezer
   Cinnamon Loaves, 49
   Orange Buns, 53
   White Bread, 48

Freezing Bread, 29
French Bread, No-Knead, 24
Fresh
   Blueberry Pie, 290
   Pear Pie, 295
   Strawberry Pie, 291
Frosted
   Christmas Butter Cookies, 221
   Coconut-Orange Cookies, 232
   Coffee Bars, 172
Frosting(s)
   Basic Cake, 210
   Broiled Peanut Butter, 156
   Browned Butter, 158
   Butter, 207
     Cream, 251
   Chocolate, Deep, 170
   Cocoa
     Cream, 200
     Creme, 166
   Coffee, 206
   Cream Cheese, 165
   Creamy
     Cherry, 146
     Coffee, 154
     Orange, 204
     Pecan, 148
   Fluffy, 152
   Orange, 233
     Butter, 145
   Penuche, Rich, 163
   Seafoam, 162
   7-Minute, 150
     Penuche, 145
   Two-Toned Swirl, 190
   Vanilla, 95, 221, 235
Frozen Yeast Dough(s), 47-53
   Apricot Braid, 52
   Cinnamon Loaves, 49
   Honey-Wheat Germ Bread, 50
   Orange Buns, Freezer, 53
   Pumpernickel Loaves, Round, 51
   White Bread, Freezer, 48
Fruit
   and Cream Tart, 325
   Cookies, Rolled Spicy, 268
   Pie, Fluffy, 308
Fruitcake(s), 139, 178-182
   Best-Ever, 179
   Loaves, Golden, 181
   Miniature, 180
Fudge
   -Marshmallow Brownies, 244
   Pie, Elegant, 304

   Sauce, 168
Funny Cake Pie, 301

Ginger Cookies
   Grandmother's, 235
   Spicy, 261
Gingerbread(s)
   Basic Spicy, 176
   Crumb-Topped, 175
   Heirloom, 175
   Old-Fashioned, 176
Gingersnaps
   Crisp, 263
   Crispy Thin, 264
Glazed Cinnamon Bread, 28
Glaze(s), 28, 173
   Brown Sugar, 89
   Chocolate, 147, 244
   Confectioners Sugar, 87
   Egg White, 293
   Evaporated Milk, 286
   Honey, 83
   Orange, 239
   Vanilla, 72, 74, 75, 77, 81, 97, 157
Golden
   Cinnamon Loaves, 27
   Fruitcake Loaves, 181
   Parmesan Rolls, 42
   Pastry, 333
   Raisin Loaves, 36
   Sourdough Biscuits, 56
Grand Champion Pumpkin Bread, 123
Grandma's
   Chocolate Pound Cake, 185
   Cinnamon Bubble Ring, 82
Grandmom's Apricot Squares, 245
Grandmother's
   Ginger Cookies, 235
   Sugar Cookies, 267
   Superb Rhubarb Pie, 296
Greek Orange Braid, 76
Ground Beef-Cheese Pie, 327

Hamburger Buns
   Favorite, 65
   Mini, 66
   Pie, 326
Hearty Pumpernickel Loaves, 30
Heirloom
   Brown Sugar Cookies, 257
   Gingerbread, 175
   Raisin Muffins, 119

Spice Cake, 172
Helen's Danish-Style Rolls, 98
Herbed Sour Cream Batter Bread, 41
Heritage Dutch Apple Pie, 294
High-Protein Muffins, 115
Homemade
    Pizza, 70
    Zweiback Toast, 69
Honey
    Corn Bread, 128
    Filling, 81
    Glaze, 83
    Topping, 109
    -Wheat Germ Bread, 50
Hot Cross Buns, 100

Ice Cream Topping, Cinnamon-, 290
Icing(s), 80, 98, 100
    Broiled, 163
    Chocolate, 246, 271
    Cocoa, 167
    Confectioners Sugar, 79, 84, 96, 99, 243
    Orange, 76
    Peanut Butter, 250
    Vanilla, 78, 87, 91
Imitation Pecan Pie, 298
Introduction, 7
Irish Soda Bread, 130
Italian Panettone, 85

Jelly-Filled Butter Cookies, 262
Jelly Roll, My Favorite, 197
Jumbo Oatmeal-Peanut Butter Cookies, 234

Kuchen, Apple Crumb, 44
Kitchen, Quick Peach, 134

Layer Cakes, see also Cakes
Lazy Daisy Cake, 194
Lemon
    Chess Pie, 300
    Chiffon Pie, 310
    Coconut Lemon Bars, 242
    Crunch Cupcakes, 206
    Custard-Filled Crescents, 73
    -Filled Layer Cake, 152
    Filling, 152
        Creamy, 73
    Glaze, 159
    Meringue Pie, 322
    -Orange Meringue Pie, 320

Sauce, Tangy, 173
Sponge Cake, 198
Squares, Tangy, 247
Tea Bread, 123
Velvet Pie, 302
Light Chocolate Brownie Cupcakes, 204
Lime Meringue Pie, 318

Macaroons, Chewy Coconut, 225
Main-Dish Pies, 326-334, see Pies
Make-Ahead
    Biscuit Mix, 111
    Cake Decorations, 209-212
Maple
    Butter Twist, 71
    -Cinnamon Filling, 83
Marble
    Molasses Cake Squares, 174
    Squares A la Mode, 168
Marshmallow
    Brownies, Fudge-, 244
    Pie(s)
        Orange-, 307
        Prune-, 308
Mary's Sugar Pound Cake, 187
Meatball-Vegetable Pie, 332
Melt-in-Your-Mouth Rolls, 60
Meringue
    Crust, 323
    Pie(s), 315-322
        Banana, 321
        Butterscotch, 317
        Cottage Cheese, 318
        Lemon, 322
            -Orange, 320
        Lime, 318
        Peanut Butter, 316
    Shells, 324
    Steps for making, 315
Mile-High Biscuits, 107
Milk Chocolate Cupcakes, 206
Mini Hamburger Buns, 66
Miniature Fruitcakes, 180
Mock Danish-Style Pastries, 99
Modern Sourdough Starter, 54
Molasses
    Cake Squares, Marble, 174
    Cookies, Raisin-, 223
    Crinkles, Rolled, 268
    Refrigerator Muffins, 120
    Topping, 298
Molded Cookies, 256-465, see Cookies
Monogrammed Tops, 287

Muffins, *see* Breads
Mushroom Quiche, Chicken-, 330
Mustard Bread, Swiss Cheese-, 39
My Favorite Jelly Roll, 197

No-Knead
  French Bread, 24
  Sticky Buns, 94
No-Stick Rolled Butter Cookies, 266
Nut
  Bran Muffins, Date, 121
  Bread, Pineapple, 124
  Crunch Topping, 119
  Muffins, Banana, 118
Nutmeg Cake with Lemon Sauce, 173

Oat
  Cookies, Chocolate-Raisin, 226
  Muffins, Spicy Apricot, 115
Oatmeal
  Cookies
    Amish, 234
    Applesauce, 230
    Butterscotch-, 222
    Chocolate Chip-, 224
    Coconut-, 226
    Crisp, 228
    Pecan-, 264
    Refrigerator, 252
  Crust, 306
  Muffins, 118
  -Peanut Butter Cookies, Jumbo, 234
Old-Fashioned
  Biscuit Pinwheels, 108
  Bran Muffins, 121
  Coconut Layer Cake, 150
  Date-Filled Cookies, 274
  Filled Cookies, 273
  Gingerbread, 176
  Ice Box Cookies, 253
  Pound Cake, 183
  Raisin
    Cake, 162
    Drop Cookies, 228
  Rolled Sugar Cookies, 266
Old-Time Upside-Down Apple Pie, 293
Orange
  Blossom Pie, 306
  Butter Frosting, 145
  Butterfly Rolls, 87
  Chiffon Cake, 201
  -Chocolate Cookies, 231

-Cinnamon Swirl Bread, 26
Cookies, Frosted Coconut-, 232
Cupcakes, 208
-Flavored Cranberry Pie, 288
Frosting, 233
Glaze, 239
Icing, 76
-Marshmallow Pie, 307
Pastry, 289
-Raisin Cake, 159
Rind Bread, Candied, 126
Outstanding Raisin Bread, 35

Pan Rolls, 58
Parker House Rolls, 58
Parmesan Cheese Crescents, 110
Party Angel Food Cake, 189
Pastry, *see* Pies
  Flaky, 332
  Golden, 333
  for 9-inch Pie Shell, 286
  Quiche, 330
  Thyme-Seasoned, 331
  for 2-Crust 9-inch Pie, 286
Peach
  Kuchen, Quick, 134
  Pie, Blushing, 291
Peanut
  Butter
    -Apple Cookies, 257
    Cake Squares, 156
    -Chocolate Chip Cake, 167
    Cookies, 261
      Crisp, 233
      Bars, 250
      Jumbo Oatmeal-, 234
      Pressed, 277
    Frosting, Broiled, 156
    Icing, 250
    Meringue Pie, 316
  Pie, Tennessee, 299
  -Raisin Cookies, 258
Pear Pie, Fresh, 295
Pecan
  Bread, Whole Wheat-, 33
  Cake, Carrot-, 158
  Cinnamon Muffins, 114
  Drop Cookies, Apple-, 232
  Filling, 75, 77
  -Oatmeal Cookies, 264
  Pie, 297
    Imitation, 298
    Pumpkin, 298

Special, 297
   Topping, Cinnamon-, 161
Pennsylvania Dutch Cinnamon Buns, 96
Penuche Frosting, Rich, 163
Peppermint
   Angel Food Cake, 190
   Chiffon Blue Ribbon, 203
   Cookie Trees, Chocolate, 278
   Filling, 278
Perfect Bran Bread, 32
Pie(s), 281-334
   Apple, Old-Time Upside-Down, 293
   Butter Balls, 288
   Carmelized Almonds, 311
   Crust
      Ingredients, 284
      Monogrammed Top, 287
      Steps for making, 284
      Trimmings, 333
   Double-Crust
      Apple
         Basic, 288
         Sheet, 292
      Apricot-Raspberry Pastry Bars, 292
      Blueberry, Fresh, 290
      Cherry, Basic, 287
      Orange-Flavored Cranberry, 288
      Peach, Blushing, 291
      Rhubarb, Basic, 290
      Strawberry, Fresh, 291
   Hearts of Cheese, 291
   Main-Dish, 326-333
      Chicken
         and Stuffing, 328
         -Mushroom Quiche, 330
      Hamburger, 326
      Ground Beef-Cheese, 327
      Meatball-Vegetable, 332
      Pork-Vegetable, 331
      Sausage and Potato, Savory, 328
      Steak and Potato, 333
      Tuna-Cheese, 329
   Pastry
      Almond, 289
        -Flavored, 287
      Beautiful, 294
      Care, 297
      Evaporated Milk Glaze, 286
      Fruit, 296
      for 9-Inch Pie Shell, 286
      Nut, 317
      Orange, 289
      Shiny Pans for, 308
      Tough, 322

      for 2-Crust 9-Inch Pie, 286
      Water in, 292
      Wheel, 288
   Shell
      Slump, 300
      Buckling, 318
   Single-Crust, 293-325
      Baked
         Apple
            Heritage Dutch, 294
            -Puff, Easy, 295
            Tart, Cinnamon, 294
         Buttermilk, Creamy, 300
         Coconut, Crusty, 299
         Funny Cake, 301
         Lemon Chess, 300
         Pear, Fresh, 295
         Pecan, 297
            Imitation, 298
            Pumpkin, 298
            Special, 297
         Rhubarb, Grandmother's Superb, 296
         Raspberry, Basic, 296
         Tennessee Peanut, 299
      Cream
         Banana, 314
         Cherry, 313
         Coconut, 314
         Refrigerate, 307
      Lemon, Sunny, 310
      Meringue
         Banana, 321
         Butterscotch, 317
         Cottage Cheese, 318
         Cream-Filled, 324
         Lemon, 322
           -Orange, 320
         Lime, 318
         Peanut Butter, 316
         Steps for making, 315
      Refrigerated
         Candy Bar, 303
         Chocolate
            Candy, 305
            Cinnamon, 323
            Mousse, 304
            Snow-Capped, 324
            Velvet, 303
         Fluffy Fruit, 308
         Fruit and Cream Tart, 325
         Fudge, Elegant, 304
         Lemon
            Chiffon, 310
            Velvet, 302

Orange
    Blossom, 306
    -Marshmallow, 307
    Prune-Marshmallow, 308
    Pumpkin Chiffon, 311
    Purple Plum, 312
    Rancher's Delight, 306
    Strawberry Cream, 309
    White Christmas, 312
  What went wrong with my, 334
Pineapple
  -Carrot Cake, 157
  Cinnamon Buns, 92
  Coconut Rolls, 86
  Cream
    Filling, 197
    Roll, 196
  Nut Bread, 124
  -Topped Cocoa Cake, 166
  Topping, 167
  Upside-Down Cake, 177
    Skillet, 178
Pizza, Homemade, 70
Plum Pie, Purple, 312
Polish Babka, 46
Poppy Seed Coffee Cake, 134
Potato
  Bread, Whole Wheat, 32
  Crust, 328
  Pie, Steak and, 333
  Yeast Rolls, 60
Pork-Vegetable Pie, 331
Pound Cakes, 139, 183-187
  Confectioners Sugar, 184
  Chocolate, Grandma's, 185
  Mary's Sugar, 187
  Old-Fashioned, 183
  Pumpkin, 186
  Walnut, 184
Praline
  -Topped Sponge Squares, 195
  Topping, Broiled, 195
Preacher Chocolate Cake, 166
Pressed Cookies, 276-278
  Chocolate-Peppermint Trees, 278
  Peanut Butter, 277
  Spritz, 277
Pretzels, Soft, 68
Prune
  Bread, Purple Ribbon, 122
  Cake, Danish, 158
  -Filled Rolls, 86
  Filling, 273
  -Marshmallow Pie, 308

Pumpernickel
  Loaves
    Hearty, 30
    Round, 51
Pumpkin
  Bread, Grand Champion, 123
  Chiffon Cake, 311
  Muffins, 117
    Oat, 117
  -Pecan Pie, 298
  Pound Cake, 186
Purple
  Plum Pie, 312
  Ribbon Prune Bread, 122

Quiche, Chicken-Mushroom, 330
  Pastry, 330
Quick Caramel Crunch Coffee Cake, 44
  Crumb Coffee Cake, 131
  -Fix Chocolate Glaze, 171
  Peach Kuchen, 134

Raisin
  Bars, Spicy, 238
  Bread(s)
    Cinnamon-, 37
    Date-, 38
    Outstanding, 35
    Whole Wheat, 129
  Cake(s)
    Chocolate-, 169
    Old-Fashioned, 162
    Orange-, 159
    Surprise, 162
  -Cinnamon Batter Loaf, 43
  Cookies, Peanut-, 258
  Cupcakes, Cocoa-, 207
  Drop
    Cookies, 226
      Old-Fashioned, 228
  Loaves, Golden, 36
  Meringue Kisses, 236
  -Molasses Cookies, 223
  Oat Cookies, Chocolate, 226
  Shortbread Bars, 248
  Spice Tea Ring, 78
Rancher's Delight Pie, 306
Raspberry
  Almond Rolls, 86
  Jam Squares, 242
  Pastry Bars, Apricot-, 292
  Pie(s)

Basic, 296
  Cranberry-, 289
Refrigerated Yeast Rolls, 63
Refrigerator Cookies, 253
  Butterscotch Wafers, 254
  Caramel Nut Slices, 251
  Chocolate Pinwheels, 255
  Cinnamon-Almond, 254
  Oatmeal, 252
    Chippers, 253
Regal Savarin Ring, 45
Rhubarb Pie(s)
  Basic, 290
  Grandmother's Superb, 296
Rich
  Egg Batter Bread, 42
  Fruitcake, 182
  Penuche Frosting, 163
Rolls, *see* Breads
Rolled Cookies, 265-275, *see* Cookies
  Molasses Crinkles, 268
  Spicy Fruit Cookies, 268
  Sugar Cookies, 270
Round Pumpernickel Loaves, 51
Russian Kulich, 84
Rye Sandwich Bread, 30

Sage Biscuits, 112
Sally Lunn, 46
Sandwich Cookies
  Date-Oatmeal, 272
  Filled Vanilla Wafers, 271
Sauce(s)
  Fudge, 168
  Vegetable, 327
Sausage and Potato Pie, Savory, 328
Seafoam Frosting, 162
Sesame Cookie Crisps, 260
7-Minute Frosting, 150
  Penuche, 145
Sheet Apple Pie, 292
Shortening Cakes, 139, *see* Cakes, Butter
  One-Bowl Method, 139
Skillet
  Corn Bread, 128
  Pineapple Upside-Down Cake, 178
Sliced Apple Cake, 161
Snow-Capped
  Chocolate Pie, 324
  Coconut Cookies, 262
Soft
  Dinner Rolls, 57
  Pretzels, 68

Sour Cream
  Coffee Cake, 133
  Drop Cookies, 219
  -Pear Coffee cake, 135
  Topping, 290
Sourdough
  Biscuits, Golden, 56
  Bread, 55
  Modern Starter, 54
Southern White Bread, 26
Special
  Pecan Pie, 297
  Strawberry Sponge Cake, 192
Spice
  Cake(s)
    Chocolate, 164
    Heirloom, 172
Spicy
  Almond-Cereal Cookies, 256
  Applesauce
    Bread, 126
    Cake, 160
    Drop Cookies, 224
  Apricot Oat Muffins, 115
  Chiffon Cakes, 200
  Fruit Cookies, Rolled, 268
  Ginger Cookies, 261
  Raisin
    Bars, 238
    Cupcakes, 208
  Walnut-Almond Cookies, 259
Sponge Cakes, *see* Cakes
Spritz Pressed Cookies, 277
Steak and Potato Pie, 333
Sticky Bun Variation, 91
Strawberry(ies)
  and Cream Spectacular, 151
  Cream Pie, 309
  -Filled Cake Roll, 196
  Meringue Bars, 249
  Pie, Fresh, 291
  Sponge Cake, Special, 192
Stuffing
  Crust, 329
  Pie, Chicken and, 328
Sugar Cookies
  Amish, 220
  Crisp, 260
  Drop, 222
  Grandmother's, 267
  Old-Fashioned Rolled, 266
  Rolled, 270
Sunday Cake Squares, 155
Sunny Lemon Pie, 310

Surprise Raisin Cake, 162
Swedish Tea Ring, 77
Sweet Rolls, *see* Breads
  Squash Buns, 87
Sweetened
  Cream, 296
  Vanilla Cream, 153
Swiss Cheese
  -Mustard Bread, 39
  -Whole Wheat, 129

Tangy
  Lemon
    Sauce, 173
    Squares, 247
Tart, Fruit and Cream, 325
Tea Breads, 105, *see also* Breads
Tennessee Peanut Pie, 299
Texas Ranger Cookies, 230
Three-Flavored Braid, 34
Thyme-Seasoned Pastry, 331
Topping(s)
  Brown Sugar, 94
  Cinnamon
    Crumb, 161
    -Ice Cream, 290
  Coconut-Pecan, 195
  Crumb, 117
  Honey, 109
  Molasses, 298
  Nut Crunch, 119
  Pecan-Cinnamon, 161
  Pineapple, 167
  Sour Cream, 290
Tri-Level Brownies, 246
Tuna-Cheese Pie, 329
Twin Roll-Ups, 58
Two-Toned Swirl Frosting, 190

Vanilla
  Frosting(s), 95, 221, 235
  Glaze(s), 72, 74, 75, 77, 78, 81, 97, 157
  Icing(s), 87, 91
  Layered Bars, Chocolate-, 237
  Wafer(s), 305
    Crust, 305
    Filled, 271
  Whipped Cream, 193
Vegetable
  Pie(s)
    Meatball-, 332
    Pork-, 331

Sauce, 327
Versatile Potato Rolls, 91

Wafer Crust, Vanilla, 305
Walnut
  -Almond Cookies, Spicy, 259
  Bars, Banana, 156
  Bread
    Banana, 125
    Carrot-, 125
  Brown Bread, 130
  Cake, Date-, 153
  Cookies, Farmhouse, 223
  Meringue Cookies, 236
  Pound Cake, 184
Welsh Rarebit Bread, 40
Wheat
  Germ Bread, Honey-, 50
  Kernel of, 23
    Bran, 23
    Endosperm, 23
    Germ, 23
Whipped
  Cream, 151
    Vanilla, 193
White
  Bread, *see* Breads
  Christmas Pie, 312
  Layer Cake with Orange Frosting, 145
Whole
  -Grain Flours, Refrigerate, 32
  Wheat
    Breads, *see* Breads
    Loaf, Swiss Cheese-, 129
    Maple Ring, 75
    -Pecan Bread, 33
    -Potato Bread, 32
    Raisin Bread, 129
    Sandwich Buns, 66

Yeast Breads, *see* Breads
  how to make light, tender breads, 31
Yellow Layer Cake with Cherry Frosting, 146

Zweiback Toast, Homemade, 69